Adolescent Identity

Routledge Studies in Anthropology

Adolescent Identity

Evolutionary, Cultural and
Developmental Perspectives

Edited by
Bonnie L. Hewlett

 Routledge
Taylor & Francis Group
NEW YORK   LONDON

First published 2013
by Routledge
711 Third Avenue, New York, NY 10017

Simultaneously published in the UK
by Routledge
2 Park Square, Milton Park, Abingdon, Oxon OX14 4RN

*Routledge is an imprint of the Taylor & Francis Group,
an informa business*

Library of Congress Cataloging-in-Publication Data
   Adolescent identity : evolutionary, cultural and developmental
perspectives / edited by Bonnie L. Hewlett.
      p. cm. — (Routledge studies in anthropology ; 7)
   Includes bibliographical references and index.
   1.   Adolescent psychology. 2.   Adolescence. 3.   Teenagers.
   4.   Identity (Psychology)   I. Hewlett, Bonnie L. (Bonnie Lynn), 1961–
   BF724.A2757 2012
   155.5—dc23
   2012008502

ISBN: 978-0-415-89012-0 (hbk)
ISBN: 978-0-203-10238-1 (ebk)

Typeset in Sabon
by IBT Global.

Printed and bound in the United States of America on sustainably sourced
paper by IBT Global.

To our children who bring such joy into our lives.
To Alice Schlegel who understands the importance of research highlighting the lives and experiences of our world's adolescents.

Contents

Figures

Tables

Acknowledgments

There are many people who have been involved in the writing of this book and the time and research it represents. I am forever indebted to our children, Forrest, Jessica, David, Jordan, Allison, Erika and Lindsey, who are one of the main reasons I started on this journey of adolescent research, and to the adolescents of the Central African Republic, all of whom shared so generously their stories, friendship, trust, and many long moments of their lives with me. I would like to thank the contributors to this volume for their hard work and enthusiasm. I am deeply indebted to Max Novick, the talented and patient editor at Taylor and Francis Press who has been key in guiding me through this process. To the reviewers who provided detailed comments, I extend my appreciation for their careful reading and insight provided. I would like to thank Aimee Stout for her help and interest in adolescents. I am grateful (in many ways) for the editing suggestions and positive comments of Jordan Bentz, our son. I want to express my gratitude to Alice Schlegel, whose friendship and guidance I highly value and appreciate. I am grateful to my husband, Barry, whom I cannot thank enough for his encouragement through the years.

1 Introduction
Adolescent Identity, Risk, and Change

Bonnie L. Hewlett

Nearly half of the people inhabiting the world today are under the age of twenty-five—the largest generation of young people in human history. Of those, 85 percent are coming of age in developing countries, experiencing disproportionate economic, social, and political representation in relation to powerful forces operating at global, national, and local levels. In addition to facing inadequate access to healthcare and education, gender inequality, widespread unemployment, political conflict, and the proliferation of HIV/AIDS, over 500 million are surviving on less than two dollars per day (UNFPA 2005, 4, 45). Deprivation, poor health, powerlessness, and poverty are however, not the lived experiences of adolescents everywhere. Our world's adolescents encounter and respond to challenges of physiological development, identity formation, risk, culture change, and globalization in unique and diverse ways. With varying degrees of agency, and opportunity, dependent upon factors such as rural or urban living, economic circumstances, gender, religion, family, and social support, this young generation navigates the complex process of adolescent identity development within a changing and challenging world (ibid.).

This book presents a holistic transdisciplinary view of the thoughts and experiences of adolescents from around the world, including small-scale and complex societies. Developmental psychology has provided important insights into adolescence, but these studies are usually conducted in Western or highly stratified cultures. Adolescent research from a diversity of cultures is needed to evaluate existing characterizations about adolescence and adolescent identity development. The richest and most exciting research often emerges from cross-cultural, transdisciplinary approaches that integrate a range of perspectives on key issues. The chapters in this volume bring together anthropological, evolutionary, and developmental methods and theories that educate, provoke, and help us to think more holistically about the adolescents of our world.

Adolescence became part of human life history when, according to some, a longer period of dependence conferred significant reproductive advantages, allowing young people to "learn and practice" economic, social, and sexual behaviors of adults before they themselves began reproducing (the "brain-growth model" [Bogin 2009; Bogin this volume] and "embodied capital" [Kaplan 1996 in Bock 2005]). Others proposed that the juvenile period was extended so that they could avoid risk by growing more slowly (Janson and van Schaik 1993). As evolutionary life history researchers note, there is a "constant relationship" between the length of the juvenile period and the length of the adult span of life ("adult mortality model" [Charnov 1993 in Blurton Jones 2005, 105]). When adult mortality is high, it "pays" to begin reproduction earlier, whereas conversely when adult mortality is low, it is beneficial to grow larger and delay reproduction (ibid.). However the world's first teenagers came to be, one could speculate that these youth already possessed the social-cognitive abilities that enabled them to understand self and others (Bogin 2009; Meltzoff 2002; Premack and Woodruff 1978). *Homo sapiens* adolescents, and perhaps other intelligent hominids, such as Neanderthals, had a concept of self and self in relation to others, as identity development would have begun with the appearance of empathy, attachment, and a theory of mind. But within an increasingly complex social world, it is more than likely early *Homo sapiens* teenagers who first developed complex individual and social identities (Schlegel, personal communication).

Undergoing a surge of biological, cognitive, and evolutionary changes, the brains of the first adolescents would have been capable of abstract and innovative thought, able to use concepts skillfully, successively relating them to each other in more complex ways (Bogin 2009; Gogtay et al. 2004). Gathering information about the "social aspects of reproductive maturity"—cooperation, competition, risk taking, and reputation building—these adolescents would have been capable of learning about economic, social, political, and sexual skills necessary for reproductive success and survival (Ellis, this volume; Schlegel, personal communication; Bogin 2009). Although adapting and adjusting to diverse ecological settings and conditions, adolescents within early hunting-gathering societies would have formed identities within an intimate, supportive, and familiar social world which may have contributed to limited or reduced frequencies of identity conflict, depression, psychological distress, and suicide, often associated with modern adolescent development. But adolescence was no doubt for these first teenagers, as it is for today's young people, an intense and challenging time of risk and change, of learning and growth, of biological and social development.

Structuring their own adaptations to the harsh and delightful realities of their lives, young people of today increasingly participate in a broad social, economic, and political world. The research presented in this volume positions their lives within this wider social, cultural, and temporal context in order to understand the impact of risk, change, adversity, and globalization on personal and social identity development. The following chapters by international scholars on adolescents from around the world, increase our awareness of, and respect for, their individual biologically and culturally influenced lives and experiences as they develop a sense of self as a certain kind of person, a personal identity, and a sense of self in association with a group, role, or another person, a social identity (Schlegel this volume; Markstrom this volume).

Several chapters in the volume question the cross-cultural applicability of Erikson's (1968) classic acute adolescent identity crisis. Often times upholding and reinforcing cultural practices beneficial to themselves, their families, and the larger society, adolescents in many places in the world navigate their way quite well through childhood, adolescence and into adulthood. While these adolescents possess coping strategies buffering adversities they face as they develop a sense of oneself in the movement from identity immaturity to identity maturity, others find the development of personal and social identities challenging (Marcia 1966; Schlegel this volume). Facing the loss of supportive and changing kinship structures, and/or struggling with the push and pull of an increasingly interconnected world, where "new needs are born of new desires," these adolescents call into question long held beliefs and practices, unsure how to reconcile a sense of "self as" and a "self with" in a rapidly changing environment (Schlegel this volume; Bauchet and Guillaume 1982, 208; Gebru 2009; Bucholtz 2002).

The contributors to this volume bring together cultural, developmental, and evolutionary approaches, addressing such questions as: When did the period of adolescence emerge in human evolutionary history? When is risky behavior an adaptive feature of adolescence? Why do great variations in the experiences of adolescent identity development exist? Why is identity formation problematic for some adolescents and not for others? How do globalization, adverse environments, and cultural change challenge our world's young people? The international scholars in this volume powerfully make the case for culturally sensitive research, illuminating the diverse experiences of our world's youth and bridging critical gaps in our understanding of adolescent identity formation, risk, and change. Cultural context is predictive of biological, social, and developmental uniqueness; comparisons from the U.S., Central Africa, Kuwait, Dominica, Haiti, Canada, China, Polynesia, and Micronesia provide insights into how evolutionary, historical, social, and cultural structures and relationships influence the manifestation of individual variations during this important time in the human life span.

HOW WE HAVE COME TO UNDERSTAND ADOLESCENCE

For decades the work of Erik Erikson (1963), J. Marcia (1966), and Margaret Mead ([1928] 1961) framed anthropologists' understanding of adolescent identity formation. In the ensuing decades few anthropologists carried on Mead's pioneering work, challenging Western-centric beliefs about adolescent rebellion, mood swings, and conflict—irrespective of Freeman's critique

(Bucholtz 2002; Condon 1987; Mead [1928] 1961; Freeman 1983)—and the study of adolescence all but disappeared from scholarly debate. Anthropological studies undertaken since Mead's classic work echoed the traditions of past theorists, focusing upon event specific research (e.g., initiation, courtship, marriage, or rites of passage), portraying the adolescent as an incomplete member of culture, in the process of becoming complete, as an adult, or concentrating upon biologically driven developmental aspects of adolescent life and experience. Anthropology's study of adolescence was limited by a concern with understanding how adolescent behavior could lead to a better understanding of adults; interesting in passing only, a "stage" on the way to the destination of adulthood (Bucholtz 2002). Child-focused research, and, especially, research specific to adolescents, remained marginalized and under-theorized (Hirschfeld 2002; Bird-David 1992). Adolescents' knowledge, behaviors, identity development, and activities were not viewed as theoretically or ethnographically interesting (Hewlett and Lamb 2005, 2). Children, as Ingold (1994, 745) noted, and it could be said adolescents even more so, were "conspicuous by their very absence."

Not until the Whitings' (1975) Harvard Adolescence Project (Davis and Davis 1989; Condon 1987; Hollos and Leis 1986; Burbank 1988; Marquez 1999) and the now classic cross-cultural work by Schlegel and Barry (1991) did anthropologists respond to the need for systematic research with adolescents and begin to challenge the universality of the life *stage*, nature, and experience of adolescence (Condon 1987). Thus, in the late 1980s and 1990s a small group of theorists sought to understand the adolescent life experiences, as related by the adolescents themselves (for a more current example, see Jeffrey and Dyson 2008). More recently, an "anthropology of youth" has emerged, as cultural context was demonstrated to be predictive of developmental and biological uniqueness; adolescents are active producers, rejuvenators, contesters, and conservators of culture and, within these contexts, create their own unique "youth culture" (Caudill 1988; James and Prout 1990; Gaskins and Corsaro 1992; Toren 1993; Talai-Amit and Wulff 1995; Caputo 1995; Sharp 1995, 2002; Wulff 1995; Prout and James 1997; Marquez 1999; Hirschfeld 2002; Bucholtz 2002; Arnett 2004). Anthropologists, and others using anthropological methodologies, thus began reaching across many cultures and disciplines, laying the foundation linking interdisciplinary, cross-cultural theoretical and empirical analyses. The contributors to this volume expand and build upon this rich tradition by integrating biology and culture and utilizing diverse theoretical and methodological approaches in their insightful and culturally sensitive research.

Developmental psychologists, educators, and sociologists continue to contribute the majority of adolescent studies, with their research guided by a variety of theoretical orientations: attachment theory (Bowlby 1958, 1969; Ainsworth and Witting 1969; Lamb et al. 1985); socialization theory (Ochs and Schieffelin 1979; Salzmann 1998); social-cognitive theories (Piaget 1954; Vygotsky 1978; Kegan 1982); and identity development theories (Erikson 1963; Marcia 1966; Gardner 1998). Psychological, sociological, and education studies of adolescence were and continue to be an important focus of research because local, national, and international policy makers were concerned with what was perceived as an increase in adjustment problems occurring among Euro-American middle-class adolescents evidenced in delinquent behavior, violence, alcohol and drug abuse, and teenage pregnancy (Condon 1987). Research conducted covered topics including: poor self-image (but see Nichter 2000); obesity (see Spruijt-Metz 2011); identity issues (for an overview, see Meeus 2011); deviant behavior (Loeber and Burke 2011); child–parent conflict; and alienation and displacement of familial relations by those of peer relations (Gardner 1998; but see also Brown and Bakken 2011). The results of these studies often do not reflect the experiences of adolescents everywhere, a point that emerges in chapters by Markstrom (Chapter 6), Hewlett and Hewlett (Chapter 4), Takeuchi (Chapter 7), Quinlan and Hansen (Chapter 11), and Ahmed and Gibbons (Chapter 10). As Henrich et al. (2010, 3) suggest, the foundation of data in the behavioral sciences is "drawn from an extremely narrow slice of human diversity" with the implicit assumption that "findings from this narrow slice generalize to the species".

Reviews of leading psychology journals found that 96 percent of research subjects come from Western industrialized countries, including North America, Europe, Australia, and Israel (Henrich et al. 2010, 3; Arnett 2008). This means that 96 percent of psychological research subjects come from countries inhabited by 12 percent of the world's population (Henrich et al. 2010, 3). Other research studies based upon Euro-American youths generalize results to include youths across many cultures, while presuming to be "culture free" with a "one experiment fits all" paradigm (ibid.). The large and largely non-representative data sampling is derived mainly from Western undergraduates with the Euro-American teen and young adult (or as Henrich suggests, the "WEIRD"; his acronym for Western, Educated, Industrialized, Rich, Democratic) taken as the template for adolescents and young adults everywhere. "Acultural" research, experiments, and studies not only raise important methodological questions, but provide results that speak to the bias of the research questions explored, the "culturally bound university based researcher," and the "culturally framed data analysis" (ibid.). Importantly, the studies that follow in this book raise the awareness of the danger of over-generalizing results to the broader worldwide community of adolescents.

A Western middle-class model, for example, often taken as a template for adolescents everywhere, tends to idealize childhood as a "golden age" and sees adolescence as a period of learning, identity development, "school, friends, and family" or "dances, fads, and peer groups," largely devoid of the responsibilities of adult life; this is not characteristic of the experiences of the world's children or adolescents, particularly among the world's poor (Korbin 2003, 431; Panter-Brick and Smith 2000, 161). Globally, many adolescents struggle with personal and social identity in the face of risk, poverty, rapid culture change, depression, the push/pull of tradition and modernity, and the threat of physical, political, and social violence, as illustrated by Chandler and Dunlop (Chapter 5), van Meijl (Chapter 9), Kovats-Bernat (Chapter 8), and Jankowiak and Moore (Chapter 12). Whereas the majority of adolescent-centered studies have been based in the U.S. or other industrialized societies, research by the contributors to this book demonstrate the importance of outward-looking scholarship (Jeffrey and Dyson 2008, 3). Anthropologists studying adolescent identity formation have long understood the importance of cultural context, and developmental psychologists increasingly consider identity formation within socio-cultural, national, and global contexts (Markstrom 2011, 1–2; see also van Meijl, Chandler, this volume). Such scholarship furthers an understanding of adolescent development and offers new direction for future research.

WHAT IS ADOLESCENCE AND WHO ARE ADOLESCENTS?

Throughout history, adolescence and adolescents have had many diverse accounts and classifications. The riddle of the Sphinx, "what walks on four legs in the morning, two at noon and three in the evening," gives three stages to life (Cobbs 2001, 27). Homer divided life into three stages, infancy, youth, and old age, and Shakespeare noted six (or seven, depending on interpretation). In his play *As You Like It* he wrote, "the infant mewling and puking . . . the whining schoolboy . . . the lover, sighing like a furnace . . . a soldier, full of strange oaths . . . the justice, fair round belly . . . the sixth age shifts . . . with spectacles on nose . . . turning again toward . . . second childishness" (Act II Scene VII Line 9). Aristotle described youth as "heated by Nature as drunken men by wine," whereas Socrates stated that youths were "inclined" to "contradict their parents and tyrannize their teachers" (in Arnett 1999, 317). A century or so before Stanley Hall, pioneer of the scientific study of adolescence, applied the phrase *sturm und drang* to describe adolescence, Rousseau, advising parents of this "stormy" period of development had this to say: "As the roaring of waves precedes the tempest, so the murmur of rising passions announces the tumultuous change . . . Keep your hand upon the helm, or all is lost" ([1762] 1962, 172–173, in Arnett 1999, 317). Characterizations of human life "stages," "transitions," "phases," or "bridges" one traverses from one age to the next have varied over the centuries. As cultures change over time, so do terms, theories, and conceptualizations about adolescents. And, as Michael Cole cautions, "The concepts/theories (we use) act as lenses that filter our different aspects of experience, leading us to overlook some, forget some, over-estimate other observable features of the living process of development . . . creating a 'synoptic illusion' of similarity that misleads about what is happening; folk theories rush in to make the illusion work" (personal communication).

This brings us to several hotly debated questions: Is adolescence simply a historical-cultural phenomenon? What parameters—biological, cultural, or both—should be used to determine this life phase? How is adolescence cross-culturally and inter-disciplinarily defined? Looking beyond American majority society, Schlegel and Barry (1991) found that the use of a term for adolescence is found in fourteen out of thirty-nine societies for boys and seventeen out of forty-one societies for girls. Of the 186 preindustrial societies found within the standard cross-cultural sample, information on adolescence as a socially defined stage exists in 173 societies for males and in 175 for females (Schlegel and Barry 1991; see also Bucholtz 2002, 525–552). Are the terms translatable and useful? What "adolescence" means to the researchers and to the society being studied is of importance, particularly as contemporary research has largely been influenced by Euro-Western definitions and characterizations of adolescence—the "teenage stage" framed around chronological age, signaled by a "biologically expressed" beginning, generally thirteen years of age, and a "socially determined" completion, generally nineteen years of age (Condon 1987, xvii; Schlegel and Barry 1991). In the Whiting's comprehensive study of adolescence, the researchers found it difficult to find a suitable and comprehensive definition of adolescence and noted that it was not "feasible to develop precise definitions that had any degree of cross-cultural comparability" (Condon 1987, xvii). The Harvard group relied upon a broad interpretation of adolescence as being that time between the end of childhood and the "attainment of adult social status", a state "culturally defined and culturally variable" and often determined by marriage and subsequent parenthood, but "other social criteria are recognized also, such as economic independence and employment" (Condon 1987, xvi- 9; Gibbons 2000, 404).

The beginning and end of adolescence, if culturally recognized, varies by society, and even within a single culture there can be different ages at which an individual is respected as and considered an adult and allowed the responsibilities, tasks, and roles of adulthood. This makes multidisciplinary and cross-cultural approaches challenging. In their comparative look at adolescence, Schlegel and Barry (1991) found that there are societies, such as the Copper Eskimo of Alaska and the Yanomamo of Venezuela, where childhood ends and social adolescence begins before puberty. Among the Aka hunter-gatherers of central Africa, it is the adolescents themselves who often determine when to call oneself an adolescent (see Hewlett and Hewlett and Takeuchi, this volume). Is it useful then to frame the beginning and ending of adolescence around biological markers? The Harvard researchers utilized measures of physical maturation as a guideline and researched the effect that physical maturation had upon socio-emotional development. However, using physical or hormonal change and growth as definitive measures can be problematic, as the Whiting researchers found; because although physiological measurements taken around the beginning of the growth spurt to the achievement of full skeletal maturity or hormonal changes accompanying the move from sexual immaturity to sexual maturity can be measured objectively, these data can also be difficult and problematic to gather, due to "social constraints and logistical problems" (Condon 1987, xvii; see also Dorn and Biro 2011 and Worthman 1993). While a "non-correspondence" between "different markers of biological change and social adolescence" often exists (Cole, personal communication), it is as Schlegel notes, "important to distinguish between social adolescence, with its cultural meanings and expectations, and biological adolescence, on which cultural treatment of adolescence builds" (personal communication). Further compounding this dilemma, as Schlegel and Barry also found, often the time frame for social and biological adolescence varies not only cross-culturally, but also between the genders in that males experience a period of development that is typically longer than that of girls. Males generally marry and become fathers later than females, and the attainment of full adult status is thus longer in coming (1991).

This leads to other vigorous debates among social scientists and addressed by the authors of this book; is adolescence a "stage," a "transitioning period," a "phase," or a "process" framed by, as noted in the preceding, cognitive development, physical or social maturity? Currently there is a plethora of literature calling for an expanded definition of adolescence, encompassing a "new emergent stage of youth" and an end to the insistence of a "stage-like nature of adolescence" as there is no "clear cut bio-social-behavioral" shift to the onset of adulthood (Cole, personal communication; Arnett 2001; Jankowiak and Moore, this volume).

Herein lies the difficulty—how to make use of a comprehensive socio-cultural definition of adolescence, and talk about identity development as well, when indigenous definitions of adolescence and social scientists from various disciplines, interpret this stage differently (Schlegel and Barry 1991). Definitions of adolescence in this book reflect this dilemma: some authors recognize the physiological changes as defining the beginning of adolescence (e.g., the beginning of the adolescent growth spurt, the beginning of puberty and/or menarche)—see Ellis (Chapter 3), Bogin (Chapter 2), and Markstrom (Chapter 6). Others recognize it as culturally defined and recognized—see Hewlett and Hewlett (Chapter 4), Takeuchi (Chapter 7), van Meijl (Chapter 9), Ahmed and Gibbons (Chapter 10), Quinlan and Hansen (Chapter 11), and Jankowiak and Moore (Chapter 12). The very definitions, parameters, duration, and timing of adolescence vary across genders, cross-disciplinarily and cross-culturally. But what is equally important, and often missing in the debate, is that "how we define and name things matters" (Cole, personal communication). Basing policies, intervention strategies, and social services upon universal and broadly framed definitions and categorizations misses the unique and diverse vulnerabilities and experiences of adolescents, and as such, overlooks or underestimates the structural factors affecting our world's young people (see, for example, Panter-Brick and Smith 2000; Hetch 1998; Coulton et al. 2006; Boyden and de Berry 2005; Frankenberg et al. 2000). Words, after all, have been used to dispossess and to malign. But words have also been used to empower and to humanize

(Adichie 2010). There is a responsibility in scholarship, as Cole suggests, to acknowledge and understand the impact our created categories, our words, may have upon those we study.

THE STUDY OF ADOLESCENCE: ORGANIZATION, THEORETICAL INTEGRATION, AND NEW CONTRIBUTIONS

The chapters in this volume enrich our understanding of adolescence both ethnographically and theoretically, providing insights into the lives, identity development, and experiences of adolescents around the world. Whereas major works on adolescents generally fall into different evolutionary, developmental, and cultural approaches, few texts use an integrated approach to illustrate the interactions between biology (e.g., onset of puberty, risk-taking behaviors), ecology (e.g., settlement size, political-economic setting), development (e.g., cognitive and physical changes with age), and culture (e.g., ideas, cultural models about adolescence) (Hewlett and Lamb 2002). For this reason, this book advocates an integrated biosocial and multidisciplinary approach. Throughout the life course individual choices and interests within different social and natural environments may vary (Hewlett and Lamb 2002; Hewlett and Hewlett 2008). Human biology and culture both have their own properties and need to be understood in detail, as they interact to pattern adolescent behaviors. Adolescent development can only be understood as an interaction among biology, ecology, development, and culture.

The book is divided into three parts, with identity development thematically interwoven throughout. Part I includes three chapters with evolutionary and biocultural views of adolescence. Part II raises issues concerned with development, identity, and risky environments as well as the rituals that situate and define adolescents within their socio-cultural environment. Part III addresses identity formation in a globalized world, the push and pull of tradition and modernity. Several chapters integrate developmental and cultural approaches or cultural and biological approaches to understand and explain aspects of adolescence. The integrated theoretical approach this book promotes is formulated as a heuristic tool for thinking about these interactions, in the hope that this will lead to greater understanding of adolescent identity development and experience (Hewlett and Lamb 2002).

PART I

Evolution: History and Hunter-Gatherers

We, as humans, share a phylogenetic history with non-human primates. Several features of human adolescence are impacted by this phylogenetic history and contribute to cross-cultural universals and a biologically based human nature (Hewlett and Lamb 2002; Hewlett and Hewlett 2008).

Although many scholars are familiar with the biological (genetic) aspects of evolutionary theory, few are familiar with evolutionary approaches to culture, which examines interactions between biology, culture, and the environment (Hewlett and Lamb 2002). Recent contributions by the anthropological study of adolescence have been with evolutionary approaches emphasizing this interaction between biology and culture. Evolutionary theory is useful for several reasons. First, it focuses on individuals because the unit of natural selection is the reproductive fitness of individuals, not groups. Individuals are active agents in their cultural and natural environments. Cultural beliefs and practices can be manipulated, added to, or discarded by individuals given their particular political, economic, or natural environment. Second, as noted, contemporary evolutionary theory is bio-cultural, emphasizing the interactions between biology and culture (Hewlett and Lamb 2002; Hewlett and Hewlett 2008).

New insights have been gained in the anthropological study of adolescent behavior through the lens of evolutionary or bio-cultural approaches, emphasizing the ways in which individuals try to enhance their reproductive fitness (i.e., adaptation) in particular social, ecological, and demographic settings (see Hawley 2011). For example, Bogin suggests that during human evolution, selection "operated to first shorten the infancy stage, then prolong the growth period," finally resulting in greater longevity. An adolescence stage of development evolved as the growth period expanded. In Chapter 2, Bogin presents the Reserve Capacity Hypothesis (RCH) and combines the RCH with a multilevel selection model for human biological evolution. He takes into account "the impact of the evolution of human childhood and adolescence," in which adolescents contribute subsistence and labor to the pool of resources available to rear infants and children successfully, allowing the mother to then "accumulate new reserve capacity . . . such as fat stores and bone mass" (2009, 567–577). The "new" life-history stages of childhood, adolescence, and grandmotherhood help to explain the greater longevity and reproductive success of humans versus nonhuman primates, as the building of reserve capacity led to greater health, fitness, and longer life spans (ibid.).

More than at any other time in life, adolescents are inclined to engage in risky behaviors, potentially harmful to themselves, others around them, or society as a whole (Ellis, this volume). Behaviors, those working with adolescents see as a problem needing fixing. In Chapter 3, Ellis challenges the dominant developmental psychopathology model of risky adolescent behavior by systematically applying contemporary evolutionary perspectives on adolescent behavior and identity development. Human adolescence is a time for reproductive maturity in both the biological and social sense. As risky behavior, competition, and *cooperation*, signal phenotypic quality while adolescents build reputations and social identities, is it misleading to pathologize risky behaviors as maladaptive? (Schlegel and Barry 1991; Ellis, this volume; see also Casey et al. 2011). And what, Ellis asks, is "in it for the adolescent"? Can risk-taking behavior be adaptive? As his chapter demonstrates, much can be gained by studying the "adaptive logic and motivation" prompting so many risky adolescent behaviors (Ellis et al. 2012).

Whereas cultural anthropologists try and explain human behavior, and ethnographic descriptions are significant and interesting contributions, it is also important to try to understand *why* humans behave the way they do, especially in terms of mental health, depression, psychological distress, and self-harming behavior, and how best to address these critical problems facing some of today's adolescents. Using an evolutionary model to study risky behavior, Ellis' integrated approach provides an important means of analysis, prediction of developmental responses within high-risk environments, and the potential for the development of prevention and intervention strategies targeting high-risk adolescents (Ellis, this volume).

Finally, some evolutionary theorists incorporate culture into their research (see, for example, Boyd and Richerson 2002; Richerson and Boyd 1998; Wiesfeld 2003). Culture is both dynamic and conservative; some elements can change based on the acquisition of new knowledge or different personal experiences, but some elements can also be remarkably resistant to change. Culture is acquired early in life, is often based on several lived experiences, is shared with many others in the community, and often has a strong emotional component (Cavalli-Sforza and Feldman 1981; Hewlett and Hewlett 2008). Many anthropologists have turned to studies of hunter-gatherers to understand human nature, stemming from the realization that for 99 percent of hominid evolutionary history, a hunting-gathering way of life prevailed, the longest and most critical stage in the emergence of our human species (Bird-David 2005). In Chapter 4, Hewlett and Hewlett describe common features of hunting-gathering adolescence based upon their work with Aka "pygmies," hunter-gatherers of the Congo Basin. Building upon the earlier work of Konner (2005) and the hunting-gathering model of infancy and early childhood patterns of care, this chapter identifies generalizations about hunter-gatherer adolescents and how they might be distinct from adolescents in cultures with differing modes of production. It considers cultural and evolutionary influences on developmental outcomes that can provide insights into adaptive responses of adolescents to their environments.

In their chapter, Hewlett and Hewlett report that Aka adolescent life includes a high degree of freedom, a cultural emphasis placed upon trust and sharing, predictability of social relations, close personal relations with parents, peers, and siblings, and a sense of belonging. Aka adolescents come and go as they please; begin sexual relations and select a mate without parental influence. Aka adolescent identity, sexual exploration, and autonomy formation is based upon the development of the sense of self, nurtured within the intimate community of family, siblings, and friends. The Aka provide another non-Western example of a cultural system where adolescence is not a time of turmoil, that interdependence does not need to be gained at the expense of parental relations, and that peer relations do not supplant parental–familial relations. The differences between adolescence as experienced within the U.S. versus the rainforest of Central African Republic are profound. For example, as Aka adolescence is characterized by a high degree of autonomy, lack of parental interference, and the knowledge of each person as a unique individual, rebellion is not necessary. In contrast, U.S. parents are often unwilling to relinquish control over children, who are encouraged, often pressured, to do well in school and excel in athletics. U.S. adolescents often do not have money/resources and remain dependent for quite some time upon their parents (Arnett 2004). They are often characterized as exhibiting extreme mood variability and "acting out" in order to assert their individual identity and distinguish themselves from adults. It is, perhaps, time to reconsider how we think about adolescence and adolescent development.

In this section, Bogin (Chapter 2) and Ellis (Chapter 3) lay the biological and socio-psychological foundation for discussions of identity: it was the selection for a long period of adolescence associated with *Homo sapiens* coupled with an emergent cognitive capacity that gave time for the first teenagers to develop complex identities (Bogin, this volume; Schlegel, personal communication). In Chapter 4, the Hewletts underscore how that by looking at modern hunting-gathering populations, it may be possible to gain an understanding of how adolescence unfolds in contexts that characterized most of human history.

PART II

Culture and Development: Ritual, Risk, and Identity

How does culture inform the social development of the adolescent? How can we come to understand, for example, the way in which Aka, Apache, Chinese, Haitian, or Pacific Island adolescents develop culturally specific identities, ideologies, and schemas? The cultural approach emphasizes the concept of culture, minimally defined as shared knowledge, beliefs, and practices, socially transmitted from generation to generation, to explain what happens during adolescence and adolescent development (Hewlett and Hewlett 2008). Culture is shared, historic, and integrated (Hewlett and Lamb 2002; Hewlett 2004). Fieldwork involving participant observations leads to a fuller understanding of the socio-cultural realities and contexts of individuals. The contributors to this section incorporate qualitative and quantitative ethnographic methods. A socio-cultural perspective is essential because culture dramatically impacts how individuals think and feel, patterning how they understand and categorize the world as well as define their physical, symbolic, and emotional realities.

Culture develops within the political, social, economic structures, institutions, technology, and artifacts that are a part of the ecologies in which individuals live and make decisions. Ethnographic accounts contribute to the study of adolescents by investigating the culture(s) within which adolescents constitute their personal and social identities, revealing concepts existing in particular contexts and at particular times (Hewlett 2005; Cole 2011; Cole and Cole 2000). Several contributors in this section also apply a developmental approach, which includes a range of theories linked by the assumption that age and developmental stage are key factors in explaining variability of experience in the development of sense of self and social identity (Cole 2011).

In Chapter 7, Takeuchi reports on the food taboos of Aka adolescents of the Congo Basin, and how by choosing which foods to avoid, Aka males are expressing and confirming individual social identity. In this egalitarian society, where sharp divisions of labor and deferential treatment or status based upon gender or age are absent, Aka adolescents assess their own positions in various stages of life and make independent decisions regarding which foods to avoid and which personal identity to express (Takeuchi, this volume). Food taboos associated with hunting speak of the weakness, the childlikeness, of a developing youth in comparison to the strength of an adult male hunter. By adhering to taboos, the adolescent manages this socially meaningful task in the process of becoming a complete grown man. These crucial foundational schemas are, particularly for the Aka, transmitted and framed around biological development, i.e., knowledge of food taboos associated with varying with life stages, in which both the family and individual have restrictions on what they can eat.

Chandler and Dunlop (Chapter 5), Markstrom (Chapter 6), and Kovats-Bernat (Chapter 8) provide accounts of adolescents within a changed and challenging world, exemplifying the integration of diverse perspectives with their developmental, anthropological, and historically based studies. Chandler and Dunlop's chapter on the First Nations adolescents of Canada begins by detailing the history of adolescent identity research and then proceeds from this foundation to examine the problems confronting many Indigenous youth, speaking to the roles culture and history play in the course of their development of identity. The authors' study points to the importance of cultural continuity as a protective factor against suicide via lateral transfers of Indigenous knowledge.

Markstrom, Chapter 6, researching North American Indian adolescents, provides an exploration of processes of socialization where, within the "ebb and flow of cultural traditions," young girls find affirmation, empowerment, and place as they take on new roles, statuses, identities, and spiritualities in the broader society. For North American Indian adolescents, the coming-of-age ceremonies ascribe a "socially valued and endorsed identity" in a sociocultural environment that influences how the adolescent comes to understand the self (Markstrom 2008, 59; 2011; Markstrom, Chapter 6). At the heart of Markstrom's chapter is her description, analysis, and interpretation of the coming-of-age rituals for adolescent girls, linking the continuation of tradition through time and space and the development of identity.

How do social categories, labels such as Indigenous, a street child, an adolescent, relate to other categories, to research and analysis, to participatory approaches, humanitarian interventions, policy-relevant research, and the social appraisal of the adolescent (Boyden and de Berry 2005)? Understanding the importance of framing research within the social, structural, historical, and cultural aspects of adolescents' subjective experiences takes into account their personal narratives of tragedy and joy, resiliency, and strength (2005, 48). Kovats-Bernat's work (Chapter 8) with Haitian street youths speaks to the variety of responses and ways in which adolescents use social and emotional resources to survive and deal with horrific circumstances (de Smedt 1998; Frankenberg et al. 2000 in Boyden and de Berry 2005). Assessing the causes, effects, and social consequences of the armament of Haitian society, and focusing special attention to Port-au-Prince street children and adolescents, Kovats-Bernat demonstrates how vital an understanding of the individual lived experience is. Contrary to the perceived notions by many humanitarian agencies, he found there can be complex and far more salient factors in understanding young people's experiences, needs, and vulnerabilities (Kovats-Bernat, this volume; Boyden and de Berry 2005, 47–48). By considering what adolescents understand as their problems, how they experience and explain their place in the world, how they interpret, adapt to, and transform their reality, important and effective policy, program, and intervention strategies can be developed (Hetch 1998, 24–25; Coulton et al. 2006).

PART III

Globalization: Tradition, Modernity, and Identity

As a result of globalization—the increasing interconnectedness of economic, political, and ecological forces—the sense of self, and identity of adolescents are often affected in profound ways (Hall 2002). However, not all adolescents have a negative response to globalization. Some instead respond positively to the challenges of rapid socio-cultural change. Adolescents, as we will see in the following chapters, are actively experimenting with, protesting, interpreting, and selecting which cultural changes they decide to incorporate into their lives, both reshaping and conserving their cultures (Anderson-Fye 2003). In this section, van Meijl (Chapter 9), Ahmed and Gibbons (Chapter 10), Quinlan and Hansen (Chapter 11), and Jankowiak and Moore (Chapter 12) integrate developmental and cultural perspectives, and illuminate how globalization evokes new, and often opposing, demands. The distinct experiences, for example, of the Tongan and Maori adolescents encountering historic forces, an older generations enduring traditional beliefs and values, coupled with changing times and desires, often makes identity formation more difficult for the Pacific Island adolescents. Forming competing and plural identities, these young people express at times, ethnic confusion and disaffection, but as well some are able to negotiate an ethnic and self-identity that functions well for them in their day-to-day lives (van Meijl this volume; Schlegel this volume).

Ahmed and Gibbons, Chapter Ten, illustrate through drawings of ideal men and women, the identity quandary faced by Kuwaiti adolescents who feel as well the push and pull of commitment to tradition while encountering modernity and innovation. Drawings of traditional attire are associated with traditional values, religious piety, and gendered roles in terms of childcare and family. Images of the ideal man or woman in modern Western clothing suggest values found in paid work, leisure activities, consumerism, and attractiveness. The authors report that some Kuwaiti adolescents seem able to integrate the two perspectives.

In the first longitudinal study on television viewing of Dominican rural youth, Quinlan and Hansen (Chapter 11) found that television viewing is a shared social activity, fostering liberalized gender views, especially among teens and young adults. Interviews with parents suggest other positive benefits of television viewing, including improvement in school, better spoken English, an increasing awareness of the global world, but the mothers and fathers also list negatives such as provocative dressing, aggression, and increased rudeness by youth, as being some of the biggest changes since television was introduced. This study demonstrates how relatively little television changes peoples' lives when social and economic relations remain the same. Local cultures will use and interpret new technologies and ideas in ways that suit them best (Schlegel, personal communication).

Structuring their own adaptations to the difficult and delightful realities of their lives, Chinese young adults, as Jankowiak and Moore illustrate in Chapter 12, are more amenable to personal development, more concerned with self-expression, and yearn for an emotional connection with their romantic partners and spouses. Like so many of the adolescents and young adults portrayed in the following chapters, the Chinese youth increasingly seek to act meaningfully, forming distinct identities, within a cultural, social, and economic world so different from that of their parent's generation.

CONCLUSION

As our geopolitical boundaries become increasingly permeable, as human populations are rapidly becoming interconnected, it is vital that we listen to and better understand our world's adolescents. It is our hope that these chapters encourage others to seek answers to questions generated in this volume. By developing and applying models of bio-cultural processes we can better appreciate both the diversity and universality of the adolescent experience, and the interactions between culture, ecology, development, and biology. Analytical perspectives from collaborative studies such as these, enable us to critique existing structural socio-cultural conditions and more fully address social issues of uncertainty, risk, inequity, and distress as the adolescent develops a sense of self in diverse global contexts. In looking at and listening to adolescents beyond Euro-American borders, it may be possible to develop more insightful and inclusive public policies and intervention strategies for our world's adolescents (Coulton et al. 2006).

REFERENCES

Adichie, Chimamanda. 2010. "The Danger of a Single Story." Video on TED.com. http://www.ted.com/talks/chimamanda_adichie_the_danger_of_a_single_story.html (accessed December 17, 2010).

Ainsworth, M.D. and Wittig, B.A. "Attachment and Exploratory Behavior of One-Year-Olds in a Strange Situation," Determinants of Infant Behavior 4 (1969): 129–173.

Anderson-Fye, E. A "Coca-Cola" Shape: Cultural Change, Body Image, and Eating Disorders in San Andres, Belize," Culture, Medicine and Psychiatry 28, 4 (2004): 561–595.

Arnett, J. "Adolescent Storm and Stress Reconsidered," American Psychologist 54, no. 5 (1999): 317–326.

———. 2001. Adolescence and Emerging Adulthood: A Cultural Approach. Upper Saddle River, NJ: Prentice Hall.

———. "The Neglected 95 Percent: Why American Psychology Needs to Become Less American," American Psychologist 63 (2008): 602–614.

Bahuchet, Serge and Henri Guillaume. 1982. Aka-Farmer Relations in the Northwest Congo Basin, in Politics and History in Band Societies, edited by E. Leacock and R. B. Lee. Cambridge: Cambridge University Press, pp. 189–211.

Belsky, J. "Attachment, Mating, and Parenting: An Evolutionary Interpretation," Human Nature 8, no. 4 (1997): 361–381.

Bird-David, N. "Beyond 'The Original Affluent Society': A Culturalist Reformation," Current Anthropology 33 (1992): 25–46.

———.2005. Studying children in hunter-gatherer societies: Reflections from a Nayaka perspective, in Hunter-Gatherer Childhoods: Evolutionary, Developmental and Cultural Perspectives, edited by Hewlett, B.S. and M.E. Lamb. New Brunswick: Aldine, pp. 92–101.

Blurton Jones, N. 2005. Introduction. Section 2 Why does childhood exist? in Culture and Ecology of Hunter-Gatherer Children, edited by B.S. Hewlett and M.E. Lamb. New York: Aldine, pp. 129–146.

Bock, J. 2005. What makes a competent adult forager? in Culture and Ecology of Hunter-Gatherer Children, edited by B.S. Hewlett and M.E. Lamb. New York: Aldine, pp. 109–128.

Bogin, B. "Childhood, adolescence, and longevity: A multilevel model of the evolution of reserve capacity in human life history," American Journal of Human Biology 21 (2009): 567–577.

Bowlby, J. "The nature of the child's tie to his mother," International Journal of Psycho- Analysis XXXIX (1958): 1–23.

———. 1969. Attachment. New York: Basic Books.

Boyd, R. and Richerson, P.J. "Group Beneficial Norms Can Spread Rapidly in a Structured Population," Journal of Theoretical Biology 215 (2002): 287–296.

Boyden, J. and de Berry, J. 2005. Children and Youth on the Front Line. New York: Berghan Books.

Brown, B.B. and Bakken, J.P. "Parenting and Peer Relationships: Reinvigorating Research on Family-Peer Linkages in Adolescence," Journal of Research on Adolescence 21, no. 1 (2011): 153–165.

Burbank, V.K. "Aboriginal Adolescence: Maidenhood in an Australian Aboriginal Community," Ethos 15 no. 2 (1988): 226–234.

Bucholtz, M. "Youth and Culture Practice," Annual Review Anthropology 31 (2002): 525–552.

Caputo, V. 1995. Anthropology's Silent 'Others' A Consideration of Some Conceptual and Methodological Issues for the Study of Youth and Children's Cultures, in *Youth Cultures: A Cross Cultural Perspective*, edited by V.A. Talai and H. Wulff. New York: Routledge, pp.19–42.

Casey, B.J., Jones, R.M., and Somerville, L.H. "Braking and Accelerating of the Adolescent Brain," Journal of Research on Adolescence 21 no. 1 (2011): 21–33.

Caudill, W. 1972. "Tiny Dramas: Vocal Communication between Mother and Infant in Japanese and American Families," in Childhood Socialization, edited by G. Handel. New York: Aldine De Gruyter, pp. 49–72.

Cavalli-Sforza, L. L., and M. W. Feldman. 1981. Cultural Transmission and Evolution. Princeton NJ: Princeton University Press.

Charnov, E.L. 1993. Life History Invariants: Some Explorations of Symmetry in Evolutionary Ecology. New York: Oxford University Press.

Cobbs, N.J. 2001. Adolescence Continuity, Change and Diversity. Mountain View, CA: Mayfield Publishing Company.

Cole, M. and Packer, M. 2011. Culture in Development, in *Cognitive Development: An Advanced Textbook*, edited by Bornstein, M. and Lamb, M. New York: Psychology Press, pp. 51–107.

Cole, M. and Cole, S. 2000. The Development of Children. New York: Worth Publishers.

Condon, R.G. 1987. Inuit Youth. New Brunswick, New Jersey: Rutgers University Press.

Coulton, C.J., Crampton, D., Irwin, M., Spilsbury, J., and Korbin, J.E. "How neighborhoods influence child maltreatment: A review of the literature and alternative pathways," Child Abuse and Neglect 31 (2007): 1117–1142.

Davis, S.S. and Davis, D.A. 1989. Adolescence in a Moroccan Town. London: Rutgers University Press.

de Smedt, J. "Child Marriages in Rwandan Refugee Camps," Africa 68 no. 2 (1998): 211–237.

Dorn, L.D. and Biro, F.M. "Puberty and Its Measurement: A Decade in Review," Journal of Research on Adolescence 21, no. 1 (2011): 180–195.

Ellis, B.J., Del Giudice, Dishion, T.J., M., Figueredo, A.J., Gray, P., Griskevicius, V., Hawley, P.H., Jacobs, W.J., James, J., Volk, A.A., and Wilson, D.S. "The evolutionary basis of risky adolescent behavior: Implications for science, policy, and practice," Developmental Psychology 48 (2012): 598–623.

Erikson, E.H. 1968. Identity: Youth and Crisis. New York: Norton.

———. 1963. Childhood and Society. 2nd ed. New York: Norton.

Frankenberg, R., Robinson, I., and Delahooke, A. 2000. Encountering Essentialism in Behavioral Science: The Example of the 'Vulnerable Child' Ethnographically Examined. London: Centre for the Study of Health, Sickness and Disablement, Brunel University.

Freeman, D. 1983. Margaret Mead and Samoa: The Making and Unmaking of an Anthropological Myth. Cambridge, MA: Harvard University Press.

Gardner, H.W. and Mutter, J.D. 1998. Lives across Cultures. Boston: Allyn and Bacon.

Gaskins, S., Miller, P. J. and Corsaro, W. A. "Theoretical and methodological perspectives in the interpretive study of children," New Directions for Child and Adolescent Development (1992): 5–23.

Gebru, B. T. 2009. "Looking Beyond Poverty: Poor Children's Perspectives and Experiences of Risk, Coping and Resilience in Addis Ababa." PhD diss. University of Bath.

Gibbons, J. L., and Gielen, U. P. "Special issue: Adolescence in international and cross-cultural perspective," International Journal of Group Tensions 29 1–2 (2000): 1–218.

Gogtay, N., Giedd, J.N., Lusk, L., Hayashi, K.M., Greenstein, D., Vaituzis, A.C., Nugent, T.F., Herman, D.H., Clasen, L.S., Toga, A.W., Rapoport, J.L., and Thompson, P.M. "Dynamic Mapping of Human Cortical Development during Childhood through Early Adulthood," Proceedings of the National Academy of Sciences 101 no. 21 (2004): 8174–8179.

Hall, K.D. 2002. Lives in Translation: Sikh Youth as British Citizens. Philadelphia: University of Pennsylvania Press.

Hawkes, K. "Grandmothering, Menopause and the Evolution of Human Life Histories," Proceedings of the National Academy of Sciences 95 (1998): 1336–1339.

Hawley, P.H. "The Evolution of Adolescence and the Adolescence of Evolution: The Coming of Age of Humans and the Theory about the Forces that Made Them," Journal of Research on Adolescence 21 no. 1 (2011): 307–316.

Heinrich, H., Heine, S.J., and Norenzayan, A. "The weirdest people in the world?" Behavioral and Brain Sciences 33 (2010): pp 61–83.

Hetch, T. 1998. At Home in the Street: Street Children of Northeast Brazil. New York: Cambridge University Press.

Hewlett, B.S. 1992. Intimate Fathers: The Nature and Context of Aka Pygmy Paternal Infant Care. Ann Arbor: University of Michigan Press.

———. 2005. Emerging Issues in the Study of Hunter-Gatherer Children, in *Culture and Ecology of Hunter-Gatherer Children*, edited by B.S. Hewlett and M.E. Lamb. New York: Aldine, pp. 3–19.

Hewlett, B.S. and Hewlett, B.L. 2008. Ebola, Culture, Politics: The Anthropology of an Emerging Disease. Case Studies on Contemporary Social Issues. Belmont: Wadsworth Publishing.

Hewlett, B. S., Lamb, M., Leyendecker, B. and Scholmerick, A. "Internal Working Models, Trust, and Sharing among Foragers," Current Anthropology 41 (2000a): 287–297.

———. 2000b. Parental investment strategies among Aka foragers, Ngandu Farmers and Euro-American urban industrialists, in *Adaptation and Human Behavior*, edited by L. Cronk, N. Chagnon, and W. Irons. New York: Aldine de Gruyter, pp. 155–177.

Hewlett, B. S. and M. Lamb. 2002. "Integrating evolution, culture and developmental psychology: Explaining caregiver-infant proximity and responsiveness in central Africa and the USA," in *Between culture and biology: Perspectives on ontogenetic development*, edited by H. Keller, Y. H. Poortinga, and A. Schölmerich. Cambridge: Cambridge University Press, pp. 241–269.

Hirschfeld, L. A. "Why don't anthropologists like children?" American Anthropologist New Series 104 no. 2 (Jun. 2002): pp. 611–627.

Hollos, M. and Leis, P.E. "Descent and Permissive Adolescent Sexuality in Two Ijo Communities," Ethos 14 no. 4 (1986): 395–408.

Ingold, T. 1994. "Introduction to social life: Companion encyclopedia of anthropology," in *Humanity, Culture and Social Life*, edited by T. Ingold. London: Routledge, pp. 329–349.

Janson, C.H. and van Schaik, C.P. 1993. "Ecological risk aversion in juvenile primates: Slow and steady wins the race," in *Juvenile Primates*, edited by M.E. Pereira and L.A. Fairbanks. New York: Oxford University Press, pp. 57–74.

James, Allison and Prout, Alan. 1990. Constructing and Reconstructing Childhood: Contemporary Issues in the Sociological Study of Childhood. New York: Falmer Press.

Jeffrey, C. and J. Dyson. 2008. Telling Young Lives. Portraits of Global Youth. Philadelphia, PA: Temple University Press.

Kaplan, H. "A Theory of Fertility and Parental Investment in Traditional and Modern Societies," Yearbook of Physical Anthropology 39 (1996): 91–135.

Kegan, R. The Evolving Self. Cambridge, MA: Harvard University Press, 1982.

Konner, M. 2005. "Hunter gatherer infancy and childhood: The !Kung and others," in *Culture and Ecology of Hunter-Gatherer Children*, edited by B.S. Hewlett and M.E. Lamb. New York: Aldine, pp. 19–64.

Korbin, J. "Children, Childhoods and Violence," Annual Review of Anthropology 32 (2003): 431–446.

Lamb, M., Thompson, R., Gardner, W., and Charnov, E. 1985. Infant–Mother Attachment: The Origins and Developmental Significance of Individual Differences in Strange Situation Behavior. Hillsdale, NJ: Lawrence Erlbaum.

Marcia, J.E. "Development and Validation of Ego-Identity Status," Journal of Personality and Social Psychology 3 (1966): 551–558.

Markstrom, C. A. "Identity Formation of American Indian Adolescents: Local, National, and Global Considerations," Journal of Research on Adolescence 21 (2011): 519–535.

————2008. Empowerment of North American Indian Girls: Ritual Expressions at Puberty. Lincoln, University of Nebraska Press.

Marquez, Patricia C. 1999. The Street Is My Home. Stanford, CA: Stanford University Press.

Mead, Margaret. [1928] 1961. Coming of Age in Samoa: A Psychological Study of Primitive Youth for Western Civilization. New York: Morrow.

Meeus, W. "The Study of Adolescent Identity Formation 2000–2010: A Review of Longitudinal Research," Journal of Research on Adolescence 21 no. 1 (2011): 75–94.

Meltzoff, A.N. 2002. "Imitation as a mechanism of social cognition: Origins of empathy, theory of mind, and the representation of action," in *Handbook of Childhood Cognitive Development*, edited by U. Goswami. Oxford: Blackwell Publishers, pp. 6–25.

Nichter, M. 2000. Fat Talk: What Girls and Their Parents Say about Dieting. Cambridge, MA: Harvard Univ. Press.

Ochs, E. and Schieffelin, B. 1979. Developmental Pragmatics. New York: Academic Press.

Panter-Brick, C. and Smith, M. 2000. Abandoned Children. New York: Cambridge University Press.

Piaget, J. 1954. The Construction of Reality of the Child. New York: Academic Press.

Premack, D.G. and Woodruff, G. "Does the Chimpanzee Have a Theory of Mind?" Behavioral and Brain Sciences 1 (1978): 515–526.

Prout, A. and James, A. 1997. "A new paradigm for the sociology of childhood? Provenance, promise, and problems," in *Constructing and Reconstructing Childhood: Contemporary Issues in the Sociological Study of Childhood*, edited by A. James and A. Prout. London: Falmer Press, pp. 7–33.

Richerson, P.J. and Boyd, R. 1998. "The evolution of human ultra-sociality," in *Indocrinability, Ideology and Warfare*, edited by I. Eibl-Eibesfeldt and F.K. Salter. New York: Berghan, pp. 238–262.

Rousseau, J.J. [1792] 1962. The Emile of Jean Jacque Rousseau, edited and translated by W. Boyd. New York: Teachers College Press, Columbia University.

Salzmann, Z. 1998. Language, Culture and Society. Boulder, CO: Westview Press.

Schlegel, A. 1977. "Male and Female in Hopi Thought and Action," in *Sexual Stratification*, edited by Schlegel, A. New York: Columbia, pp. 245–269.

Schlegel, A. and Barry, H. 1991. Adolescence: An Anthropological Inquiry. New York: Free Press.

Shakespeare, W. 2008. "As You Like It," in *The Norton Anthology* 2nd edition., edited by Greenblatt, S., W. Cohen, J. E. Howard, and K. Eisaman Maus. New York: W.W Norton, pp. 20–30.

Sharp L.A. "Playboy princely spirits of Madagascar: possession as youthful commentary and social critique," Anthropology Quarterly 68 2 (1995): 75–88.

————2002. The Sacrificed Generation: Youth, History and the Colonized Mind in Madagascar. Berkeley: University of California Press.

Spruijt-Metz, D. "Etiology, Treatment, and Prevention of Obesity in childhood and Adolescence: A Decade in Review," Journal of Research on Adolescence 21 no. 1 (2011): 129–152.

Super, C.M. and Harkness, S.A. 1992. The infant's niche in rural Kenya and metropolitan America, in *Cross-Cultural Research at Issue*, edited by. L.L. Adler. New York: Academic Press, pp. 247–255.

Talai-Amit, V. and Wulff, H. 1995. Youth Cultures, A Cross-Cultural Perspective. London: Routledge.

Toren, C. "Making History. The Significance of Childhood Cognition for a Comparative Anthropology of the Mind," Man 28 (1993): 461–478.

United Nations Population Fund, (UNFPA) (2005). State of World Population 2005. The Promise of Equality: Gender Equity, Reproductive Health and the Millennium Development Goals, Technical Report. United Nations Population Fund: New York.

Vygotsky, L.S. 1978. Mind in Society: The Development of Higher Psychological Processes. Cambridge, MA: Harvard University Press.

Weisfeld, G. 2003. Adolescence, in *The Encyclopedia of Sex and Gender Vol. 2.*, edited by Carol Ember and Melvin Ember. New Haven, CT: Human Relations Area Files Press, pp. 42–56.

Whiting, B.B. and Whiting, J.W.M. 1975. Children of Six Cultures: A Psycho-Cultural Analysis. Cambridge, MA: Harvard University Press.

Worthman, C.M. 1993. Biocultural interactions in human development, in *Juvenile Primates: Life History, Development and Behavior*, edited by M. Pereira and L. Fairbanks. Oxford: Oxford University Press, pp. 339–358.

Wulff, H. 1995. Introducing youth culture in its own right: The state of the art and new possibilities, in *Youth Cultures: A Cross-Cultural Perspective*, edited by Amit-Talai, V. and Wulff, H. London: Routledge, pp. 1–18.

Part I
Evolution
History and Hunter-Gatherers

2 Childhood, Adolescence, and Longevity

A Chapter on Human Evolutionary Life History

Barry Bogin

Compared with other primates, human life history is slow: people grow slowly, reproduce at a late age, and live to an old age. A list of human life history stages and their defining characteristics is given in Table 2.1. Part of the reason for slow human life history is that human beings have more stages of life history. Between birth and death the nonhuman primates, including the great apes (chimpanzee, bonobo, gorilla, orangutan), have three stages of life history. These are the infant, juvenile, and adult stages. Human life history evolution is characterized by the addition of childhood, adolescence, and a female post-reproductive period as biologically, behaviorally, and mathematically definable stages of the life cycle (Bogin and Smith 1996; Hawkes et al. 1998; Hawkes 2006; Bogin 1999).

Human life history differs in several other ways from our closest living relatives—chimpanzees and bonobos. In addition to a slower rate of growth and maturation and a later age at first birth, humans have a shorter interval between births, greater survival of offspring to adulthood, greater longevity, the capacity to adopt and care for the offspring of other people, and to provide care for grandchildren. These human–chimpanzee differences may be seen by comparing Emma Darwin, the wife of Charles Darwin, with Fifi, a chimpanzee studied in the wild by Jane Goodall. Fifi gave birth to nine infants and eight survived to adulthood. Mrs. Darwin gave birth to ten offspring and seven survived to adulthood. At first blush, it seems that Fifi has the advantage in offspring surviving to adulthood. However, the pattern of fertility of these two female primates was quite different (Figure 2.1). Fifi's first birth was at age thirteen years, her last birth was at age forty-four years, and she died at age forty-six years. Mrs. Darwin's first birth was at age thirty-one years, her last birth at age forty-eight years, and she died at age eighty-eight years.

Table 2.1   Stages in the Human Life Cycle

Stage	Growth Events/Duration (approximate or average)
Prenatal Life	
Fertilization	
First trimester	Fertilization to twelfth week: embryogenesis
Second trimester	Fourth through sixth lunar month: rapid growth in length
Third trimester	Seventh lunar month to birth: rapid growth in weight and organ maturation
Birth	
Postnatal Life	
Neonatal period	Birth to twenty-eight days: extrauterine adaptation, most rapid rate of postnatal growth and maturation
Infancy	Second month to end of lactation, usually by thirty-six months: rapid growth velocity, but with steep deceleration in growth rate, feeding by lactation, deciduous tooth eruption, many developmental milestones in physiology, behavior, and cognition
Childhood	Years three to seven: Moderate growth rate, dependency on older people for care and feeding, midgrowth spurt, eruption of first permanent molar and incisor, cessation of brain growth by end of stage
Juvenile	Years seven to ten for girls, seven to twelve for boys: slower growth rate, capable of self-feeding, cognitive transition leading to learning of economic and social skills
Puberty	Occurs at end of juvenile stage and is an event of short duration (days or a few weeks): reactivation of central nervous system of sexual development, dramatic increase in secretion of sex hormones
Adolescence	The stage of development that lasts for five to ten years after the onset of puberty: growth spurt in height and weight, permanent tooth eruption almost complete, development of secondary sexual characteristics, sociosexual maturation, intensification of interest in and practice of adult social, economic, and sexual activities
Adulthood	
Prime and transition	From twenty years old to end of childbearing years: homeostasis in physiology, behavior, and cognition; menopause for women by age fifty
Old age and senescence	From end of childbearing years to death: decline in the function of many body tissues or systems

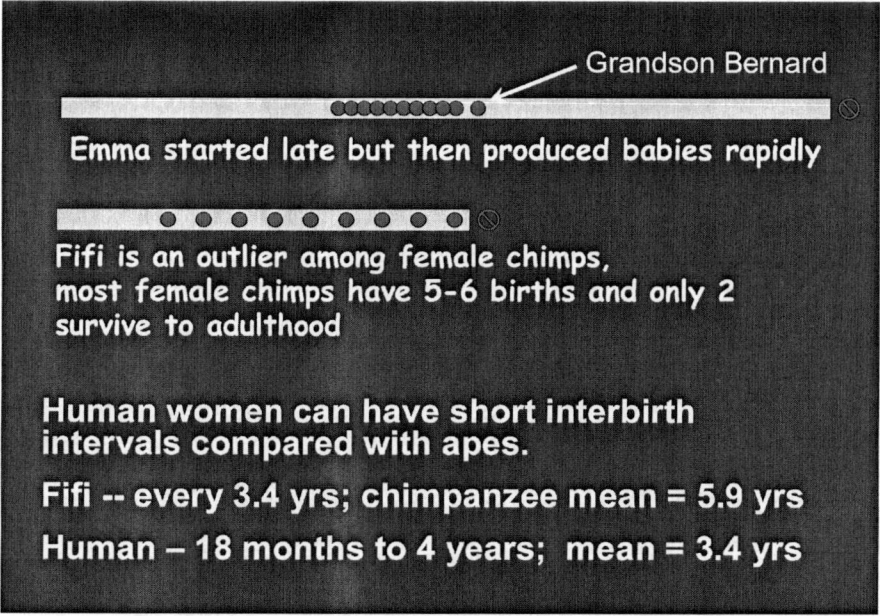

Figure 2.1 The reproductive histories of Fifi and Emma Darwin. With thanks to Prof. David Haig, Department of Organismic and Evolutionary Biology, Harvard University for the illustration of the reproductive lifelines of Emma Darwin and Fifi.

Fifi is an exceptional female chimpanzee in terms of number of births and surviving offspring, as chimpanzees in the wild average five to six births, of which only two survive to adulthood. Emma Darwin's fertility is high for humans, but not unusual. Some human societies, such as the Hutterites of North America, have average fertilities of nearly ten offspring per woman (Bogin 2001). Mrs. Darwin also had the advantage of short intervals between births. This human advantage is permitted by the addition of the childhood life history stage and the human style of bio-cultural reproduction.

Both childhood and bio-cultural reproduction are described in greater detail later in this chapter. Before doing so, a few words are needed about post-reproductive women. Most human societies have a special social role for women who have passed the age of reproduction. Some of these social roles are positive, what may be called the "valuable grandmother." Other social roles are negative, for instance, when older women are confined to care homes or left alone in their own homes.

MODELS OF HUMAN HISTORY EVOLUTION

Attempts have been made to accommodate human life history into a universal model that applies to all primates, possibly all animals. One example of these attempts is the invariant-symmetry model of Eric Charnov (Charnov 1993; Charnov and Berrigan 1993). The Grandmother Hypothesis (GH) for the evolution of human longevity developed by Kristen Hawkes and colleagues (1998; Hawkes 2006) is based on Charnov's model of symmetry between rates of adult mortality and rates of growth and development to age at first birth. The GH finds that selection for lower adult mortality and greater longevity allowed for the evolution of the prolonged growth in human beings compared with the great apes. The Charnov model and the GH refer to the extended period of growth for humans as the juvenile stage. By "juvenile" they mean the time from the end of infancy to the age at first birth. The Charnov model and the GH do not recognize the human stages of childhood and adolescence.

In contrast to universal models of life history evolution, other researchers propose that human evolution entailed selection for unique biological and behavioral characteristics of human beings, including novel features of human life history. The proponents of non-universal models of human life history evolution focus on human brain size relative to body size, brain structure, language, and social organization as examples of the unique characteristics (Lieberman 1991; Hauser, Chomsky, and Fitch 2002; DeFelipe 2011). Taking this perspective, Douglas Crews (2003) and Barry Bogin (2009) offer an alternative to the GH of Hawkes and colleagues called the Reserve Capacity Hypothesis (RCH). The RCH posits that the evolution of the human childhood and adolescent stages of life history prolonged the period of growth and development. Under favorable conditions for physical and social development, prolonged human growth results in greater health and biological resilience at adulthood, which leads to enhanced fertility and greater longevity compared with apes. In essence, the GH proposes that selection operated to first lower adult mortality and then allow for greater longevity and finally a longer period of human growth. The RCH proposes that selection first operated to add the childhood and the adolescence stages to human life history, then lower adult mortality, and finally greater longevity was possible. Both hypotheses contain similar elements, but in a very different order.

In this chapter, the GH model is reanalyzed using new values for some of its key variables (see Bogin [2009] for a more formal presentation of the analysis presented in this chapter). The original values of the GH are given in Table 2.2. The GH compares the values for several life history events of the great apes and human beings. The human life history variables of the GH are based on data from the Dobe !Kung of Botswana and the Ache of Paraguay, two well-studied societies of living hunter-gatherers. Based on these forager societies, the estimate of average age at first birth is set at about eighteen years. Average adult longevity for those girls who live to their age at first birth is set at 32.9 years, which totals to an average expected human life span of 50.9 years.

Table 2.2 Original Values of Life History Parameter Estimates as Published by Hawkes et al. (1998) and New Values of the Parameters as Used in the Present Analysis (See Text for Details)

Species	Average adult life span[a]	Age at maturity[b]	Age at weaning/independence	α^c	αM	Ratio of weaning/independence weight to adult weight	Daughters per year, b	ab
Original values								
Orangutan	17.9	14.3	6.0	8.3	0.46	0.28	0.063	0.52
Gorilla	13.9	9.3	3.0	6.3	0.45	0.21	0.126	0.79
Chimpanzee	17.9	13.0	4.8	8.2	0.46	0.27	0.087	0.70
Humans	32.9	17.3	2.8	14.5	0.44	0.21	0.142	2.05
New Values								
Humans—weaning	48.9	18.3	2.8	15.5	0.32	0.23	0.155	2.40
Humans—juvenile	48.9	18.3	7.0	11.3	0.23	0.39	0.155	1.75
Humans—energy balance	48.9	18.3	12.0	6.3	0.13	0.73	0.155	0.98

[a]Defined as the age at first birth to death; estimated as 1/M for all values, w:th = the adult instantaneous mortality rate, which is defined as the probability of survival during the reproductive stage of life.
[b]Defined as age at first birth minus gestation.
[c]Defined as the period of independent growth from weaning (end of lactation) to reproduction (adult stage).

The GH also assumes equivalence between some behavioral events for great ape and human. One of these is age at feeding independence, which in the GH is assumed to be the age at weaning, defined as the termination of maternal lactation. Based on average age at weaning for the !Kung and Ache forager societies, the GH sets the age at human feeding independence at 2.8 years of age. The GH places much emphasis on the value of two important life history parameters derived from Charnov's model. The first is αM, defined as the length of the period of independent growth multiplied by the adult instantaneous mortality rate. The value of αM is approximately equal for the apes and humans ($\alpha M \approx 0.45$). The symmetry for αM between species shows the positive correlation between adult mortality and length of the growth period in these primate species. This correlation provides circumstantial support for the GH.

The second life history emphasized by the GH is αb, defined as the length of the period of independent growth multiplied by the number of daughters produced per year. This parameter measures, essentially, the fertility rate adjusted for the time is takes to grow up and begin reproduction. For many animal species, there is a trade-off between growing and reproducing—the longer it takes to grow to maturity the lower the total number of offspring produced. The phrase "independent growth" is defined as the period between weaning (the end of lactation) and the onset of reproduction for females (that is, adulthood). The GH analysis estimates a value for αb = 2.05, which gives humans a fertility rate that is more than double the rate for any of the great apes (Table 2.2). This is unexpected because it takes human beings longer to grow to maturity than it takes the apes to do so. The GH accounts for this unexpected and nonsymmetrical human fertility advantage by proposing that humans do have something unique compared with the apes. To wit, post-menopausal grandmothers provide assistance to their daughters and grandchildren. This assistance takes the form of physical, economic, and emotional support, which helps to decrease the daughters' interval between births and to increase infant and juvenile survival.

As explained in the preceding, the GH is silent about the impact of the evolution of human childhood and adolescence (Bogin 1993, 1997, 1999). The GH considers the period from weaning to first birth as equivalent in both the great apes and humans and calls this period of time the "juvenile" stage of life. The juvenile stage as defined by the GH is shown in Table 2.2 under the parameter α—the period of independent growth. In this view, human juvenility is just prolonged compared with the apes, stretched out over 14.5 years versus the six to eight years of the apes.

A CLOSER LOOK AT HUMAN LIFE HISTORY

The reanalysis of the GH presented here takes into account the impact of the evolution of human childhood and adolescence. Life history stages may be defined in several ways and one of the most fruitful is to do so in terms of feeding behavior and rates of body growth. In the traditional human societies, such as hunter-gatherers, the infancy stage lasts from birth to age thirty to thirty-six months and is characterized by feeding via lactation, with complimentary foods added by the end of the first year (Sellen 2006, 2007). The transition to childhood is characterized by the termination of maternal lactation and the completion of deciduous tooth eruption. The limitations of a deciduous dentition and small digestive system require that children eat easy-to-chew and nutrient-dense foods. Older members of the social group acquire, prepare, and provision these foods to children. This style of cooperative care frees the child's mother from lactation and much care and feeding of the child. The mother may then accumulate new reserve capacity (RC), such as fat stores and bone mass lost during pregnancy and lactation, and in time, devote her resources to a new pregnancy and lactation of a new infant. The childhood stage ends at about age 6.9 years.

The juvenile stage spans age 7.0 years to onset of the adolescent growth spurt (approximately age ten for girls and age twelve for boys in healthy, well-nourished populations). Juvenile mammals are sexually immature, but physically and mentally capable of providing for much of their own care (Pereira and Fairbanks 1993). Human juveniles have the physical capabilities to eat the adult-type diet, as the first permanent molars and the central incisors have erupted by age 7.0 years. Human juveniles may perform important work, including food production. Juveniles may produce some of their own food intake and also help gather, hunt, or produce food that is consumed by other members of the social group. In addition, juveniles may help to care for children via various forms of "babysitting" (Weisner 1987). There are detailed ethnographic descriptions for this type of work by juvenile humans for many forager societies, such as the Ache, Hiwi, !Kung (Kaplan et al. 2000); traditional farming societies such as the Maya of the Yucatan, Mexico (Kramer 2005); and both historical and contemporary urban-industrial societies (Bogin 1999, 2001).

It is important to understand that even though juveniles make contributions to the dietary and social welfare of the group, as well as to themselves, these juveniles still cannot achieve positive energy balance. This means that the juveniles consume more food than they produce. Older members of the social group must provision the juveniles so that they may achieve energy balance, otherwise they will starve and die. This has been documented by meticulous collections of energy expenditure and energy production for the Dobe !Kung (Lee 1979, pp. 250–280), for the Yucatan Maya (Kramer 2005), for Bangladeshi villagers (Cain 1977; Robinson, Lee, and Kramer 2008), and a few other groups. A recent example is an analysis of Yucatan Maya energy allocation published by Kramer and Ellison (2010). The research is based on a one-year study observing boys, girls, men, and women of various ages and collecting physical activity, food production, food consumption, and other time allocation information. The Yucatan Maya are subsistence farmers, meaning that they grow most of the food that they eat. The authors calculate the percentage of physical activity devoted to subsistence activities, such as fieldwork to grow food, "food processing and preparation, tending animals, collecting firewood, hauling water, hunting, beekeeping, resource procurement and manufacture" (2010, 138). The results are reproduced in Figure 2.2 and show that juveniles (age seven to ten years) expend less than 25 percent of their energy on subsistence. It is not until age fifteen years that girls are working as hard as adult women, and for boys it is not until twenty to twenty-five years that they reach adult male levels of subsistence production. A study of Bangladeshi village farmers finds similar results, with girls and boys not able to produce enough food to feed themselves until age ten and eleven, respectively, and neither sex able to "pay" for their total energy and material requirements until their early twenties (Robinson, Lee, and Kramer 2008).

The next step on the developmental path to energy independence is the life stage of adolescence. The adolescence stage includes the years of post-pubertal growth, approximately ages ten to eighteen years for girls and ages twelve to twenty-five years for boys. Human adolescence is a stage of sexual

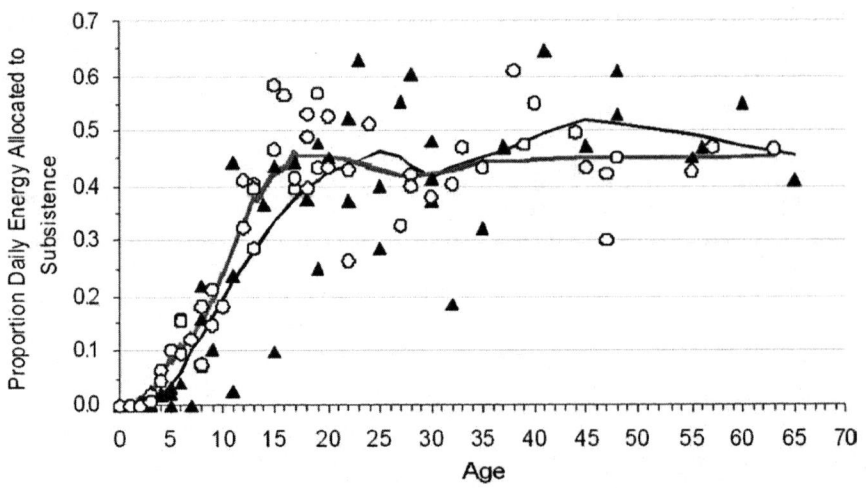

Figure 2.2 Proportion of an individual's total daily energetic expenditure allocated to subsistence activity.

Notes: Calculated for Maya males (n = 47; triangles and black line) and females (n = 63; open circles, grey line). An individual expends a fixed amount of daily energy on basal metabolic rate based on his or her sex, age, and weight. The additional amount of daily energy is spent performing basic subsistence activities (fieldwork, food processing and preparation, tending animals, collecting firewood, hauling water, hunting, beekeeping, resource procurement, and manufacture). Individual activity budgets are proportion of time spent in different tasks weighted by their corresponding PAL or relative energy expenditure. Individual data points smoothed using a LOWESS procedure with an interpolation value of 0.3.

and socioeconomic maturation and includes the adolescent growth spurt in height and weight. Human skeletal growth velocity in body length stands in contrast to all other mammals, even the African apes. Human amounts and rates of growth are illustrated in Figure 2.3. Chimpanzee amounts and rates of growth are illustrated in Figure 2.4 note the lack of an adolescent growth spurt for the chimpanzee. Life history stages are labeled in both figures, and it may be seen how these stages relate to changes in the rate of growth.

Human female reproductive maturity takes place during the latter part of the adolescent stage, and this differs from the apes as well. Healthy, well-nourished girls achieve physiologically defined fecundity (i.e., 80 percent of menstrual cycles release an ovum) at a median age of eighteen years. The worldwide median age of human first birth is age nineteen years. This is up to six years later than in the other apes. Human boys may produce fertile spermatozoa by 13.5 years, but are not likely to become fathers until after age twenty years. Even though sexually mature and capable of producing sufficient quantities of food to exceed their own energy requirements, teenage boys and girls remain immature in terms of sociocultural knowledge and experience. To gain sufficient experience for successful adulthood and

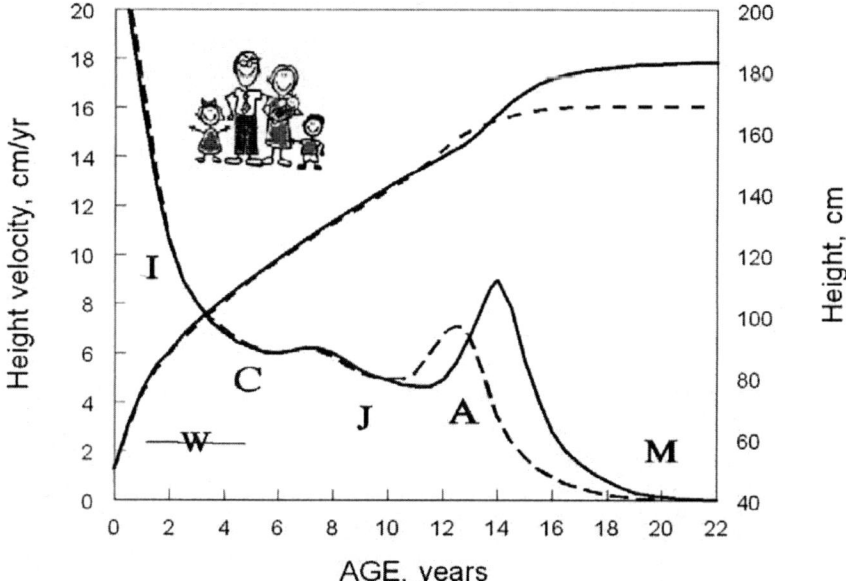

Figure 2.3 Distance and velocity curves of growth for healthy, well-nourished human beings.

Notes: These are modal curves based on height data for the Western Europe and North America populations. The stages of postnatal growth are abbreviated as follows: I = infancy, C = childhood, J = juvenile, A = adolescence, M= mature adult. W= range of weaning age, centered on mean age of 3.0 years. Modified from Bogin (1999).

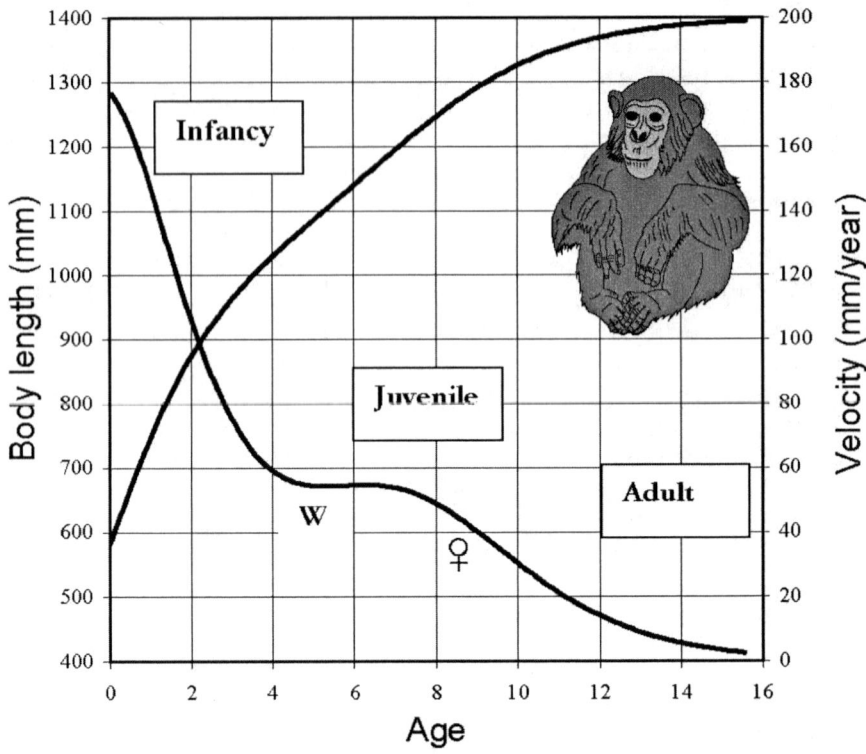

Figure 2.4   A model of distance and velocity curves for chimpanzee growth in body length (growth of the summed length of crown to rump, thigh, and leg).
Notes: This is based on the longitudinal study of captive chimpanzee growth conducted by Hamada and Udono (2002). In the wild, weaning (W) usually takes place between forty-eight and sixty months of age (Pusey 1983). Original figure from Bogin (2006a).

marriage—a uniquely human social, economic, and political system—adolescent boys and girls in all societies engage in many types of economic, social, sexual, and ideological apprenticeships, or rites of passage as they are called by anthropologists. These informal and formal settings for learning lead to greater adult reproductive and sociocultural success (Bogin [2011a] provides more detail on adolescent apprenticeships and sexual selection for the adolescent stage of human life history).

REANALYSIS OF THE GH MODEL

According to these human life history parameters, the end of the childhood stage at 6.9 years of age is, theoretically, the minimum age for human feeding independence. A seven-year-old juvenile could survive without help from older people, but in reality there is no human society in which seven-year-olds do so. Indeed, the research reviewed in the preceding indicates that feeding independence is not achieved until age ten to twelve years, and usually later. Accordingly, for the reanalysis of the GH model presented in Table 2.2 new parameter estimates of age 7.0 and 12.0 for the age at independence are employed. The reanalysis also uses growth and fertility data from healthier human populations than the foragers used in the original GH. Human forager groups show evidence of nutritional deprivation in terms of low height-for-age, low weight-for-age, and low body fat stores (Bogin, 2011b).

Contemporary foragers have relatively high infant mortality, which lowers expectation of life at birth. High levels of infant mortality are also widely used as a measure of adversity in overall health (details of forager health and the new growth and fertility data, which come from several industrial and agricultural societies, may be found in Bogin [2009]).

Using the new demographic, growth, and fertility data, the estimate of average adult life span after first birth is 48.9 years for the human species, that is, a total life span of 67.9 years. This value accords better with actuarial data for healthy human populations than does the forager value. At age twenty years, women in Japan have a life expectancy of 65.79 more years, Australian women have an expectancy of 64.1 more years of life, and Portuguese women have an expectancy of 62.81 more years of life (data from publicly available life tables for 2004–2007). Criticism that these contemporary societies have artificially prolonged life span must be tempered by the fact that in the year 1900, twenty-year-old women in the U.S. had a life expectancy of 43.5 more years (Haines 1998), even with relatively high female adult mortality from complications of childbirth and infectious disease. The new value for average adult life span shown in Table 2.2 of 48.9 years falls well within the range of these actuarial data.

Age at maturity rises one year, to 18.3 years, and this places the age at first birth for humans at about nineteen years of age, which is the empirically derived demographic average (Bogin 2001). The addition of the childhood and adolescence stages of human life history changes the value for the key variables in the GH model. With independence set at age 7.0 or 12.0 years, the new values of αM (the period of independent growth times the adult instantaneous mortality rate) are lower than those for the apes. The new values for αb (the length of the period of independent growth multiplied by the number of daughters produced per year) are smaller than the value in the original GH model, but still larger than any of the apes. In the new model human symmetry with the apes is lost for all parameters. This change points to human-specific (unique) life history characteristics to account for the human condition. One possibility is that natural selection in human evolution operated to first shorten the infancy stage (wean early compared with apes), then prolong the independent period of growth, at least the period of growth that is independent from lactation by the mother. These changes eventually result in the new human life history stages of childhood and adolescence. These two new life history stages may lead to greater longevity, and eventually, the existence of post-menopausal women who may act as valuable grandmothers toward their daughters and grand-offspring. The next two sections of this chapter explain how all of this may come about.

RESERVE CAPACITY

The validity of this reanalysis of the GH may be tested by the RCH. Physiological systems of the mammalian body must grow, develop, mature, and perform at some minimal level for post-natal life of the individual to be possible. These systems (nervous, pulmonary, cardiovascular, kidney, etc.) usually, "*overshoot their physiologically necessary capacity*" during the pre-adult and early adult years (Crews 2003, 76; italics original.) By overshooting the necessary capacity (NC) an individual has RC that may be channeled into trade-offs between greater growth, immune function, mating behavior, and/or reproduction and parental investment.

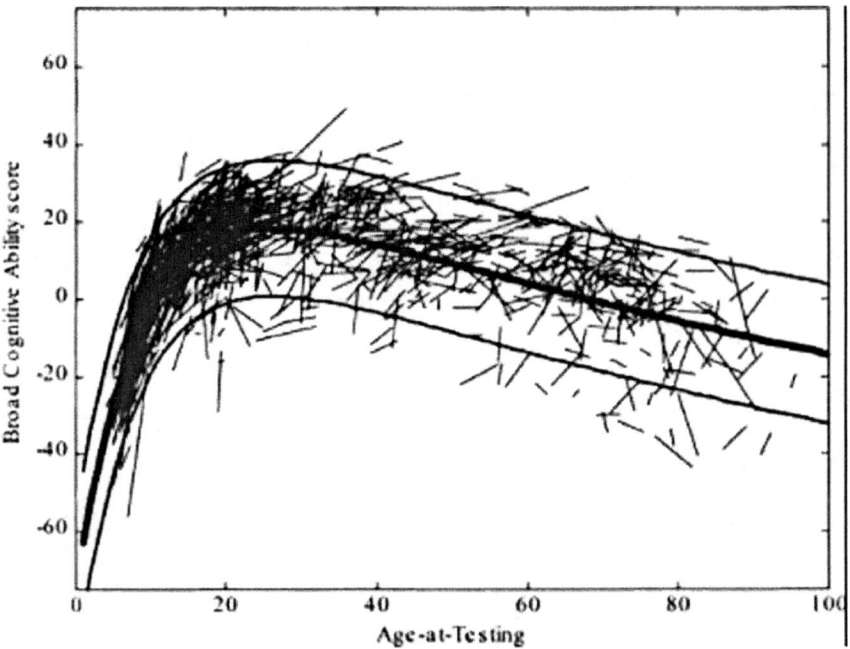

Figure 2.5 Age changes in broad cognitive ability (BCA).

Notes: The smoothed curves estimate the mean and 95 percent confidence boundaries around the scores for latent variance components in BCA, which peaks at age 26.2 years. Also shown are the individual line plots of the longitudinal data to illustrate the goodness of fit of the fitted smoothed curves. Reproduced with permission from McArdle et al. (2002).

An example of overshooting NC is given in Figure 2.5. Jack McArdle and colleagues (2002) analyze a sample of 1,193 individuals, each of whom was tested on two occasions with the Woodcock–Johnson Psycho-Educational Battery, Revised, "a wide-range comprehensive set of individually administered tests of intellectual ability, scholastic aptitude, and achievement" (2002, 119). The participants were aged two to ninety-five years old at the time of testing. Longitudinal structural equation modeling was used to estimate age changes in test scores. The findings for broad cognitive ability (BCA, the average of seven composite scores of intellectual functioning) are shown in Figure 2.5. The age trends estimate that cognitive capacity reaches its zenith at age twenty-six years and then declines. Equally important to note is the variance among individuals as estimated by the 95 percent confidence interval. This interval shows an approximate forty-point range by age twenty years. Those individuals at the higher boundary, that is, those with who accumulated greater RC before age twenty years, may still have positive BCA scores up to age one hundred years. Those with average BCA development will deplete positive RC for BCA by age sixty years. This is a striking range of difference and has important implications for cognitive performance, human capital formation, adult economic and social abilities, parental and grandparental investment in offspring, and healthy aging.

The amount of RC a person has may be expressed conceptually as:

Reserve capacity (RC) = Total achieved capacity (TAC) – Necessary capacity (NC)   (1)

Crews (2003) proposes that human RC is greater than that found in other primate species, and many other mammalian species, due to an increase in TAC, a decrease in NC, or both. With the development of greater RC during the years of growth, human beings are able to live longer than any other primate species. Expressed in terms of the life history stages of RC building, the Crews model may be expressed conceptually as follows for nonhuman primates:

RC_t = *gestation ± infancy ± juvenile adult*   (2)

For the human species the formula is:

RC_t = *gestation ± infancy ± childhood ± juvenile ± adolescence ± early adult later adult* (3),

where RC_t is RC at age = t, and the life history stage of gestation, infancy, etc., are developmental periods when RC may be gained or lost. Equations (2) and (3) assume that maternal investment and RC accumulation during gestation is positive only. Dire situations in which embryonic or fetal reserves are depleted prior to birth are likely to preclude survival. Life stages after birth may have positive or negative investment into RC building, but the investments cannot be less than NC at any stage. The nonhuman primates, including the great apes, have three life history stages prior to adulthood. Humans have five stages prior to adulthood. Compared with great apes, the additional human stages of childhood and adolescence, combined with slower rates of growth, development, and maturation between birth and adulthood, result in more time for creating and losing RC. For humans, RC building may continue into early adulthood, ending by age twenty-five to thirty-five years when the initial indications of senescent declines are noted in many body systems (Crews 2003). Women in traditional societies, and female primates in general, are likely to experience declines in RC with their first pregnancy. The demands of reproduction mean that RC is lost via pregnancies, lactations, and other maternal investments in offspring. Because of the loss of RC with pregnancy and birth, the age at first reproduction for women is equivalent to the age at onset of aging. The evolution of the human adolescent life stage, and the delay in age at first reproduction, is one reason for the greater longevity of human women compared with the apes.

MULTILEVEL SELECTION

The RCH may be combined with a multilevel selection model for human bio-cultural evolution. Multilevel selection is part of a maturing view of biological evolution in terms of a nested set of selective processes (Wilson and Wilson 2007). The RCH and the multilevel model provide a complex, but comprehensive, perspective on some aspects of the evolution of human life history.

The multilevel evolutionary hypothesis presented here begins with a fundamental Darwinian-type selection for decreased birth intervals via the evolution of early weaning and childhood. At Level 1, the childhood stage of life history frees to mother to reproduce again more quickly and with lower mortality risk than any other primate. However, the evolution of childhood prolongs offspring dependency to age 7.0 years or beyond. This leads to Level 2, which is an evolutionary trade-off between prolonged offspring dependency and the evolution of bio-cultural reproduction (also called cooperative breeding). Human bio-cultural reproduction is based on social systems that recognize kinship, marriage, religion, economic, and political bases for social roles and behavior. This includes roles and behaviors related to the care of pregnant women and their offspring by both biological and socially defined family members. A case of human bio-cultural reproduction is shown in Figure 2.6.

Level 3 includes interrelated selection processes, such as expansion of brain size and elaboration of cognitive capacities in terms of technology

Figure 2.6 Cooperative care of children by women and juvenile girls. Notes: The example is from the Kaqchikel-speaking Maya region of Guatemala. The women perform household and food preparation duties, and the juvenile girls play with and care for the children. Photograph by Barry Bogin.

and language, in addition to the social organization of families and larger social groups and the formation of social groups that practice cooperative childcare (Locke and Bogin 2006).

Level 4 is the evolution of slower rates of growth, development, and maturation leading to the potential to build greater RC during the human childhood, juvenile, and adolescent stages. Combined with bio-cultural reproduction the investment of food, care, and education by many members of the social group into the dependent infants and children Levels 3 and 4 explain in large part why a greater percentage of human young survive to adulthood than the young of any other primate species.

Level 5 is the emergence of a significant post-reproductive stage of life for women. In the combined RCH and multilevel model presented here, the human female post-reproductive life stage did not evolve only as a new feature of the genome. Rather, greater life span emerges epigenetically, that, above the level of the genome. This greater life span is derived from the selection for RC building during a longer pre-reproductive life span. A post-reproductive stage of life is a consequence of the limitations of mammalian biology in terms of the senescent decline of the reproductive system after age forty years (Crews 2003) combined with human bio-cultural strategies to take greatest advantage of this situation. Once life expectancy passed the age of forty-five to fifty years, "a post-reproductive life stage of significant duration and menopause became commonplace" (Bogin and Smith 1996, 714). Age fifty years is the approximate upper limit for fertility for most female mammals, including human women, because the number of ova remaining in the ovaries is insufficient to maintain reproductive cycles (Crews 2003). An evolutionary trade-off resulting from this new post-reproductive life stage for women is the creation of bio-cultural roles for "grandmothers." Investments of time and energy by older women toward their daughters and grandchildren will feed back to the bio-cultural reproductive system and enhance the RC of the younger generations. Over evolutionary time, this feedback has the potential to have impact on the genome and epigenome of human species. The available fossil evidence has been interpreted to indicate that the evolution of the present-day pattern of human life history, with a significant life span past age fifty years, is no older than fifty thousand years before present (Caspari and Lee 2004, 2006).

The new human life history stages of childhood, adolescence, and grandmotherhood help to account for the greater reproductive success and greater longevity of human adults over other primates. The building of a better, healthier body and the developing of greater biological, behavioral, and cultural resilience prior to sexual maturity lead to greater adult health, fitness, and longevity.

REFERENCES

Bogin, B. "Why Must I Be a Teenager at All?" New Scientist 137 (1993): 34–38.
———. "Evolutionary Hypotheses for Human Childhood," Teabook of Physical Anthropology 40 (1997): 63–89.
———. 1999. Patterns of Human Growth. 2nd ed. Cambridge: Cambridge University Press.
———. 2001. The Growth of Humanity. New York: Wiley.
Bogin, B. 2006. Modern human life history: the evolution of human childhood and adult fertility, in *The Evolution of Human Life History*, edited by K. Hawkes and R. Paine. Santa Fe, New Mexico, School of American Research Press, pp. 197–230
———. "Childhood, Adolescence, and Longevity: A Multi-level Model of the Evolution of Reserve Capacity in Human Life History," American Journal of Human Biology 21 (2009): 567–577.
———. 2011a. Puberty and adolescence: An evolutionary perspective, in *Encyclopedia of Adolescence*, edited by B.B. Brown and M. Prinstein. Oxford: Elsevier, pp. 275–286.
———. !Kung nutritional status and the original "affluent society"—a new analysis. Anthropologischer Anzeiger: Journal of Biological and Clinical Anthropology, 68 2011b): 349–366.
Bogin, B. and Smith, B.H. "Evolution of the Human Life Cycle," American Journal of Human Biology 8 (1996): 703–716.
Cain, M.T. "The Economic Activities of Children in a Village in Bangladesh," Population and Development Review 3 (1977): 201–227.
Caspari, R. and Lee, S.H. "Older Age Becomes Common Late in Human Evolution," Proceedings of the National Academy of Sciences USA 101 (2004): 10895–10900.
———. "Is Human Longevity a Consequence of Cultural Change or Modern Biology?" American Journal of Physical Anthropology 129 (2006): 512–517.

Charnov, E.L. 1993. Life History Invariants. Oxford: Oxford University Press.

Charnov, E.L. and Berrigan, D. "Why Do Primates Have Such Long Lifespans and So Few Babies?" Evolutionary Anthropology 1 (1993): 191–194.

Crews, D. 2003. Human Senescence: Evolutionary and Biocultural Perspectives. Cambridge: Cambridge University Press.

DeFelipe, J. "The Evolution of the Brain, the Human Nature of Cortical Circuits, and Intellectual Creativity," Frontiers of Neuroanatomy 5 (2011): 1–17.

Haines, M.R. "Estimated Life Table for the United States, 1850–1910," Historical Methods 31 (1998): 149–169.

Hamada, Y. and Udono, T. "Longitudinal Analysis of Length Growth in the Chimpanzee (Pan troglodytes)," American Journal of Physical Anthropology 118 (2002): 268–284.

Hauser, M.D., Chomsky, N., and Fitch, W.T. "The Faculty of Language: What Is It, Who Has It, and How Did It Evolve?" Science 298 (2002): 1569–1579.

Hawkes, K. 2006. Slow life histories and human evolution, in *The Evolution of Human Life History*, edited by K. Hawkes and R. Paine. Santa Fe, NM: School of American Research Press, pp. 95–126.

Hawkes, K., OíConnell, J.F., Blurton-Jones, N.G., Alvarez, H., and Charnov, E.L. "Grandmothering, Menopause, and the Evolution of Human Life Histories," Proceedings of the National Academy of Sciences USA 95 (1998): 1336–1339.

Kaplan, H., Hill, K., Lancaster, J. and Hurtado, A.M. A theory of human life history evolution: diet, intelligence, and longevity. Evolutionary Anthropology, 9 (2000): 156–185.

Kramer, K.L. 2005. Maya Children: Helpers at the Farm. Cambridge, MA: Harvard University Press.

Kramer, K.L. and Ellison, P.T. "Pooled Energy Budgets: Resituating Human Energy Allocation Trade-Offs," Evolutionary Anthropology 19 (2010): 136–147.

Lee, R.B. 1979. *The !Kung San: Men, Women, and Work in a Foraging Society.* Cambridge: Cambridge University Press.

Leiberman, P. 1991. Uniquely Human. Cambridge, MA: Harvard University Press.

Locke, J.L. and Bogin, B. "Language and Life History: A New Perspective on the Development and Evolution of Human Language," Behaviour and Brain Sciences 29 (2006): 259–325.

McArdle, J.J., Ferrer-Caja, E., Hamagami, F., and Woodcock, R.W. "Comparative Longitudinal Structural Analyses of the Growth and Decline of Multiple Intellectual Abilities over the Life Span," Developmental Psychology 38 (2002): 115–142.

Pereira, M.E. and Fairbanks, L.A. 1993. Juvenile Primates: Life History, Development, and Behavior. New York: Oxford University Press.

Pusey, A. "Mother–Offspring Relationships in Chimpanzees after Weaning," Animal Behavior 31 (1983): 363–377.

Robinson, R.S., Lee, R.D., and Kramer, K.L. "Counting Women's Labour: A Reanalysis of Children's Net Production Using Cain's Data from a Bangladeshi Village," Population Studies (Cambridge) 62 (2008): 25–38.

Sellen, D.W. 2006. Lactation, complementary feeding and human life history, in *The Evolution of Human Life History*, edited by R.L. Paine and K. Hawkes. Santa Fe, NM: School of American Research, pp. 155–196.

———. "Evolution of Infant and Young Child Feeding: Implications for Contemporary Public Health," Annual Review of Nutrition 27 (2007): 123–148.

Weisner, T.S. 1987. Socialization for parenthood in sibling caretaking societies, in *Parenting Across the Life Span: Biosocial Dimensions*, edited by J.B. Lancaster, J. Altmann, A.S. Rossi and L.R. Sherrod. New York: Aldine de Gruyter, pp. 237–270.

Wilson, D.S. and Wilson, E.O. "Rethinking the Theoretical Foundation of Sociobiology," Quarterly Review of Biology 82 (2007): 327–348.

3 Risky Adolescent Behavior
An Evolutionary Perspective

Bruce J. Ellis

Behaviors such as aggression, crime, promiscuity, reckless driving, and drug use are often called risky because they are likely to harm the individuals who engage in them, others around them, or society as a whole. Adolescents are more likely to engage in these behaviors than people at any other stage of the life cycle (Institute of Medicine [IOM] and National Research Council [NRC] 2011; Steinberg 2008). Thus, the legal system, policy makers, and scientists have focused an enormous amount of attention on risky adolescent behavior as a problem in need of a solution.

Given the problems caused by risky adolescent behaviors, it is tempting to regard them as maladaptive. Indeed, the prevailing conceptual framework for thinking about these behaviors considers them to be negative or disturbed developmental outcomes arising from stressful life experiences (together with personal or biological vulnerabilities). According to this framework, children raised in supportive and well-resourced environments (e.g., who live in communities with social networks and resources for young people; who have strong ties to schools and teachers; who benefit from nurturing and supportive parenting that includes clear and consistent discipline; who are exposed to prosocial peers) tend to develop normally and exhibit healthy behavior and values. In contrast, children raised in high-stress environments (e.g., who experience poverty, discrimination, low neighborhood attachment, and community disorganization; who feel disconnected from teachers and schools; who experience high levels of family conflict and negative relationships with parents; who are exposed to delinquent peers) often develop abnormally and exhibit problem behaviors that are destructive to themselves and others. Different developmental outcomes are regarded as "adaptive versus maladaptive" depending on the extent to which they promote versus threaten young people's health, development, and safety. I refer to this set of guiding assumptions as the *developmental psychopathology model* of risky adolescent behavior (Ellis et al. 2012).

Although the validity of developmental psychopathology model seems self-evident, one purpose of this chapter is to show that it is at once inadequate and incomplete. To understand why, consider the basic definition of risk as "the possibility of suffering harm or loss" (YourDictionary.com).

This definition—the backbone of the "risk factor" approach to psychiatric and biomedical disorder—only captures the downside of risk without considering why people take risks. Risky behaviors are not maladaptive if the expected benefits outweigh the expected costs. People take *calculated* risks all the time, at all stages of the life cycle. We cannot legitimately regard risky behaviors as maladaptive based only on their costs. Yet, a balanced cost-benefit analysis is seldom performed in the developmental psychopathology literature, which is dominated by pathologizing views of risk.

Then there is the question of who benefits and in what metric. As much as we might endorse the principle of "do unto others as you would have others do unto you," people often act for the benefit of themselves or a circumscribed group at the expense of, or at least without considering the welfare of, other individuals and groups. Further, risky adolescent behaviors can result in net harm in terms of a person's own phenomenology and well-being (e.g., producing miserable feelings or a shortened life), the welfare of others around them, or the society as a whole, but still be *adaptive* in an evolutionary sense. Consider, for example, high-risk behaviors that expose adolescents to danger and/or inflict harm on others but increase dominance in social hierarchies and leverage access to mates (e.g., Gallup, O'Brien, and Wilson 2011; Palmer and Tilley 1995; Sylwester and Pawłowski 2011).

These examples should make it clear that "risky" is not the same as "maladaptive." The problems associated with risky adolescent behaviors are real, and there is a strong need to reduce them, but regarding them as dysfunctional is merely a label, not a solution. Rather, from an evolutionary perspective, viable solutions involve understanding the functions of risk taking in the contexts of adolescents' lives.

Although taking into account both costs and benefits of risky behavior is a crucial first step, it is important to go beyond economic cost-benefit models and understand the concept of adaptive behavior from an *evolutionary* perspective. Traditional economic models make assumptions about utility maximization that are false for people of all ages and especially for adolescents (Beinhocker 2006; Hodgson and Knudsen 2010). We are a biological species, albeit one with remarkable capacities for psychological and cultural change. We have a long evolutionary history, and many other primates, mammals, and vertebrates share our adaptations. Adolescence, that developmental period when organisms sexually mature and attempt to break into the breeding pool, is a period of heightened risk in *many* species (Weisfeld 1999), and it behooves us to understand why in terms of understanding the causes and consequences of risk taking. It is not an accident that risky adolescent behaviors are all about the standard metrics of evolutionary success—survival and sex—and attaining the resources, relationships, and social status that ensure these outcomes.

I will call the study of risky adolescent behavior from an evolutionary perspective the *evolutionary model*, in contrast to the developmental psychopathology model. The two models are not mutually exclusive, and they both share the same practical goal of reducing problem behaviors for the long-term benefit of individuals and society (regardless of the evolutionary adaptiveness of the behavior). The evolutionary model, however, can help us achieve that goal through increased understanding of the adaptive logic and motivation that underlies so many risky adolescent behaviors (Ellis et al. 2012). As discussed in the following sections, even when risky behavior *is* genuinely pathological (i.e., harmful from both an evolutionary and developmental psychopathology perspective), a detailed understanding of adaptations in the context of past and present environments is often needed to understand the nature of the pathology.

Both the developmental psychopathology model and the evolutionary model have a compelling internal logic that makes them appear self-evident. It seems obvious that high-risk behaviors must be dysfunctional. It seems equally obvious that there must be something in it for the kids who engage in these behaviors. The developmental psychopathology model has strongly influenced thinking about adolescent development over the past half century; it is truly the dominant model. The evolutionary model has roots that extend into the past, but has only started to mature during the last two decades and is still relatively unknown by developmental psychologists. Although pieces of the current evolutionary model have been presented elsewhere (e.g., Belsky, Steinberg, and Draper 1991; Ellis et al. 2011; Ellis et al. 2009; Figueredo and Jacobs 2010; Hawley 2011; Weisfeld 1999), this chapter attempts to pull those pieces together and systematically apply them to risky adolescent behavior.

The evolutionary model contrasts with the developmental psychopathology model, which emphasizes that exposure to environmental adversity places children and adolescents at elevated risk for developing cognitive, social, emotional, and health problems (e.g., Luthar 1999; McLoyd 1998; Shonkoff, Boyce, and McEwen 2009). Although evolutionary models also recognize the strong effects of environmental stress, the developmental psychopathology and evolutionary models conceptualize environmental stress and adversity, as well as environmental resources and support, in a different manner. According to the developmental psychopathology model, positive or supportive environments, by definition, promote "good" developmental outcomes (as defined by dominant Western values; e.g., health, happiness, secure attachment, high self-esteem, emotion regulation, educational and professional success, stable marriage), whereas negative or stressful environments, by definition, induce "bad" developmental outcomes (as defined by that same value system; e.g., poor health, insecure attachment, substance abuse, conduct problems, depression, school failure, teenage pregnancy).

In contrast, from an evolutionary perspective, environments that are positive in character disproportionately afford resources and support that enhance fitness, whereas environments that are negative in character disproportionately embody stressors and adversities that undermine fitness. The evolutionary model posits that natural selection shaped our neurobiological mechanisms to detect and respond to the different ratios of costs and benefits afforded by positive versus negative environments. Most important, these responses are not arbitrary but instead function to adaptively calibrate developmental and behavioral strategies to match those environments (e.g., Belsky, Steinberg, and Draper 1991; Chisholm 1999; Ellis 2004). This view of development challenges the prevailing psycho-pathology analysis of dysfunctional outcomes within settings of adversity. In particular, an evolutionary perspective contends that both stressful and supportive environments have been part of human experience throughout our history, and that developmental systems shaped by natural selection respond adaptively to both kinds of contexts (Ellis et al. 2011, 2012). Thus, stressful environments do not so much *disturb* development as *direct or regulate* it toward strategies that are *adaptive* under stressful conditions (or at least were adaptive during our evolutionary history).[1]

It is important to note that optimal adaptation (in the evolutionary sense) to challenging environments is not without real consequences and costs. Harsh environments often harm or kill people, and the fact that children and adolescents developmentally adapt to such rearing conditions (reviewed in Ellis et al. 2009; Pollak 2008) does not imply that such conditions either promote child well-being or should be accepted as unmodifiable facts of life (i.e., David Hume's "naturalistic fallacy"). Developmental adaptations to high-stress environments enable individuals to make the best of a bad situation (i.e., to mitigate the inevitable fitness costs), even though "the best" may still constitute a high-risk strategy that jeopardizes the person's health and survival (e.g., Mulvihill 2005; Shonkoff, Boyce, and McEwan 2009) and is harmful to the long-term welfare of the society as a whole. Further, there are genuinely novel environments, such as Romanian or Ukrainian orphanages (Dobrova-Krol et al. 2010; Nelson et al. 2007), that are beyond the normative range of conditions encountered over human evolution. Selection simply could not have shaped children's brains and bodies to respond adaptively to collective rearing by paid, custodial, non-kin caregivers (Hrdy 1999). Exposures to such challenging yet (evolutionarily) unprecedented conditions can be expected to induce pathological development, not evolutionarily adaptive strategies (as discussed in the following).

The developmental psychopathology model has led researchers to focus on the deleterious effects of adverse environments, such as the impact of familial and ecological stressors on mental health outcomes (e.g., adolescent onset of psychopathology). Dysfunctional behavior in adolescence is seen as the natural consequence of exposure to harsh, unpredictable, or uncontrollable socio-ecological contexts. As such, the developmental psychopathology model places undue emphasis on expected *costs* and largely ignores expected *benefits* of risk taking, making it difficult to explain adolescent motives for risky behavior. As discussed by Ellis et al. (2012), this bias has led the field to neglect a critically important question: What's in it for the adolescent?

44   *Bruce J. Ellis*

Because different risk-taking strategies are potentially adaptive or mal-adaptive, depending on context, we can expect natural selection to favor risk-taking strategies that are contingent upon reliable and valid environmental cues. Central to this perspective is the concept of conditional adaptations: "evolved mechanisms that detect and respond to specific features of childhood environments, features that have proven reliable over evolutionary time in predicting the nature of the social and physical world into which children will mature, and entrain developmental pathways that reliably matched those features during a species' natural selective history" (Boyce and Ellis 2005, 290). For a comprehensive treatment of conditional adaptation, see West-Eberhard (2003). Conditional adaptations underpin development of contingent survival and reproductive strategies and thus enable individuals to function competently in a variety of different environments. Viewed from within this framework, the adolescent who responds to a dangerous environment by developing insecure attachments, adopting an opportunistic interpersonal orientation, engaging in a range of externalizing behaviors, and sustaining an early sexual debut is no less functional than the adolescent who responds to a well-resourced and supportive social environment by developing the opposing characteristics and orientations (see Belsky, Steinberg, and Draper 1991; Ellis et al. 2011).

In summary, the developmental psychopathology model is limited in its ability to explain patterns of risky adolescent behavior because it does not explicitly model evolutionary constraints—how natural selection shaped the adolescent brain to respond to environmental opportunities and challenges—and does not adequately address why adolescents engage in risk-taking behaviors in the first place. Explaining high-risk behaviors as adaptive in an evolutionary sense does not justify high-risk behavior in a normative sense; however, by providing a unique vantage point on the functions of risky adolescent behavior, the evolutionary model can lead to practical solutions that have not been forthcoming from the developmental psychopathology perspective (Ellis et al. 2012).

RISKY ADOLESCENT BEHAVIOR: FOUR KEY INSIGHTS FROM AN EVOLUTIONARY PERSPECTIVE

The Adolescent Transition Is an Inflection Point in Development of Socio-Competitive Competencies and Determination of Social and Reproductive Trajectories

Spanning the years from the onset of puberty until the onset of adulthood, adolescence is fundamentally a transition from the pre-reproductive to the reproductive phase of the life span. The developing person reallocates energy and resources toward transforming into a reproductively competent individual. From an evolutionary perspective, a major function of adolescence is to attain reproductive status—to develop the physical and social competencies needed to gain access to a new and highly contested biological resource: sex and, ultimately, reproduction. Both sexual promiscuity and the intensity of sexual competition peak during adolescence and early adulthood (Weisfeld 1999; Weisfeld and Coleman 2005), when most people have not yet found a stable partner and the mating market is maximally open. This time of heightened promiscuity and competition may help young people determine their own status and attractiveness, refine their mate preferences, and practice mate attraction strategies (Weisfeld and Coleman 2005). These processes are central to establishment of identity in adolescence. Most critically, as outlined in the following, the adolescent transition is an inflection point (i.e., a sensitive period for change) in developmental trajectories of status, resource control, mating success, and other fitness-relevant outcomes (Ellis et al., 2012).

To achieve success at the critical adolescent transition, natural selection has favored a coordinated suite of rapid, punctuated changes—puberty—across multiple developmental domains. Driven by maturational changes in secretion of growth hormones, adrenal androgens, and gonadal steroids, pubertal development includes maturation of primary and secondary sexual characteristics, rapid changes in metabolism and physical growth, activation of new drives and motivations, and a wide array of social, behavioral, and affective changes (Table 3.1). These puberty-specific processes function to build reproductive capacity and increase socio-competitive competencies in boys and girls. Thus, increases in height, weight, and muscularity, more prominent jaws and cheekbones, emergence of body and facial hair, greater cardiovascular capacity and upper-body and grip strength, and broader shoulders make the male body more hardy, formidable, and sexually attractive to females; breast development, fuller lips, widening of the hips, fat accumulation, and attainment of adult height and weight signal fertility and make the female body more sexually attractive to males. Changes in metabolic rates, food consumption, and sleep patterns support this physical metamorphosis. The adolescent phase shift also increases nighttime activity (when most sexual and romantic behavior occurs). Heightened sexual desire increases motivation to pursue, attract, and maintain mating relationships. Increased sensation-seeking and emotional responsivity promote novelty-seeking and exploration and may increase pursuit of socially mediated rewards. Higher levels of aggression and social dominance both facilitate and reflect the higher-stakes competition that is occurring in adolescence over sex, status, and social alliances. Delinquent and risky behaviors (e.g., crime, rule-breaking, fighting, risky driving, drinking games) often have signaling functions that enhance reputations for bravery and toughness and can leverage position in dominance hierarchies, especially for males. Distancing of parent–child relationships increases autonomy and reorients the adolescent toward peer relationships and the mating arena. Increasing levels of anxiety and depression in girls may reflect heightened sensitivity to

Table 3.1   Puberty-Specific Morphological and Biobehavioral Changes (Independent of Age). Adopted from Ellis et al. (2012)

Puberty-Specific Change	Empirical Research
1. *Sexual development.* Maturation of primary and secondary sexual characteristics. Growth spurt in height and weight. Each stage of pubertal development moves the adolescent toward greater physical reproductive capacity.	
2. *Sleep.* Circadian shift in sleep timing preference, with later onset of sleep and morning rise times, occurs in mid-puberty. Increased sleepiness, which may indicate increased need for sleep, is linked to more advanced pubertal development.	Carskadon et al. 1980; Crowley, Acebo, and Carskadon 2007; Holm et al. 2009; Sadeh et al. 2009; Wolfson and Carskadon 1998
3. *Appetite and eating.* Total caloric intake increases over the stages of pubertal development, with approximately a 50 percent increase from pre-puberty to late-puberty. Sharpest increases occur from pre- to mid-puberty in girls and mid- to late-puberty in boys, corresponding to the periods of most rapid growth in females and males, respectively.	Shomaker et al. 2010
4. *Sexual motivation.* Each stage of pubertal development increases the probability of being romantically involved (e.g., dating), being sexually active, sexually harassing members of the other sex, and being "in love." Effects generally apply to both boys and girls.	McMaster et al. 2002; Richards and Larson 1993; Richards et al. 1998; Smolak, Levine, and Gralen 1993; Udry 1987
5. *Sensation-seeking* (wanting or liking high-sensation, high-arousal experiences). Boys and girls with more advanced pubertal development display higher levels of sensation-seeking and greater drug use.	Martin et al. 2002; Quevedo et al. 2009; Steinberg 2008
6. *Emotional reactivity.* Boys and girls with more advanced pubertal development (pre to early vs. mid to late) display greater reactivity of neurobehavioral systems involved in emotional information processing.	Quevedo et al. 2009; Silk et al. 2009; see also Graber, Brooks-Gunn, and Warren 2006
7. *Aggression/delinquency.* Progression through each Tanner stage is associated with increasing levels of aggression and delinquency in both boys and girls.	Najman et al. 2009; Ge et al. 2002
8. *Social dominance.* During pubertal maturation, higher levels of testosterone are associated with greater social dominance or potency in boys. This relation appears to be strongest in boys who affiliate with nondeviant peers.	Reynolds et al. 2007; Rowe et al. 2004; Schaal et al. 1996; Tremblay et al. 1998
9. *Parent–child conflict.* Parent–child conflict/distance increases and parent–child warmth decreases over the course of pubertal maturation. Some research suggests a curvilinear relation, with conflict/distance peaking at mid-puberty. Effects generally apply to both boys and girls.	Laursen, Coy, and Collins 1998; Paikoff and Brooks-Gunn 1991; Sagrestano et al. 1999; Steinberg 1987, 1988
10. *Depression and anxiety.* More advanced pubertal maturation, as well as underlying changes in pubertal hormone levels, are associated with more symptoms of depression and anxiety and greater stress perception in girls.	Angold, Costello, and Worthman, 1998; Angold et al. 1999; Ge et al. 2003; Hayward et al. 1992; Huerta and Brizuela-Gamino 2002; Patton et al. 1996; Warren and Brooks-Gunn 1989

negative social evaluations (discussed in the following). Although any given puberty-specific change listed in Table 3.1 may be modest in size, taken together the pubertal transformation is dramatic.

Puberty-specific neuromaturational changes, together with age- and experience-dependent changes in the adolescent brain, make human adolescence a period of major and dynamic synaptic reorganization, ranging from neurogenesis to programmed cell death, elaboration and pruning of dendrites and synapses, myelination, and sexual differentiation (Blakemore and Choudhury 2006; Sato et al. 2008). It has been hypothesized that this remodeling and refinement of behavioral circuits opens the brain to environmental input and thus creates a sensitive period for learning and developmental change (Blakemore and Choudhury 2006; Sato et al. 2008). Adolescence may thus constitute a window of vulnerability and opportunity—an inflection point where experiences can disproportionately influence developmental trajectories.

Consistent with the sensitive period hypothesis, there is a dramatic increase during adolescence in death and disability (e.g., U.S. morbidity and mortality rates) related to depression, eating disorders, alcohol and other substance use, accidents, suicide, homicide, reckless behavior, violence, and risky sexual behavior (IOM and NRC 2011; Steinberg 2008). Further, in addition to directly measureable morbidity and mortality, adolescence is also a key time in the development of many health behaviors and habits (e.g. smoking cigarettes, exercise and eating habits) that will have an enormous impact on long-term health across the life span. At the same time, however, adolescence is a key period of opportunity to impact developmental trajectories in positive directions. It is a time when youth develop healthy habits, interests, skills and inclinations, and align their motivations and inspirations toward positive goals. At a psychological level, these changes and reorganization that occur in adolescence are often consolidated through identity formation.

From an evolutionary perspective, the adolescent inflection and associated identity formation processes are critical because they regulate development of alternative reproductive strategies (see Ellis et al. 2012). Maturational experiences in adolescence interact with social context to shape long-term social and reproductive trajectories. Among males, early maturing boys tend to be taller and stronger than their same-age peers and often attain high status within the peer group (reviewed in Weisfeld 1999). Jones (1957) found that early maturing boys were more socially poised and less anxious in adolescence. In longitudinal analyses, these boys, although only achieving about the same final height as their later-maturing peers, remained more self-assured in adulthood, scored higher on personality characteristics associated with dominance, and were more likely to attain executive positions in their careers. In a more recent longitudinal study, height attained in adolescence, rather than final adult height, positively predicted income in adult males (Persico, Postlewaite, and Silverman 2004), again suggesting long-term consequences of "stature" in adolescence. Finally, early maturing boys (but not early maturing girls) display a more unrestricted sociosexual orientation (i.e., greater willingness to engage in casual sex) and have a higher number of lifetime sexual partners in young adulthood than do later maturing boys (Ostovich and Sabini 2005; see also Ellis 2004). Interestingly, pubertal status is clearly linked to levels of aggressive/delinquent behavior in pubescent boys, but timing of puberty does not feed forward to predict aggressive/delinquent behavior in young men (Najman et al. 2009). It may be that status obtained in adolescence is long lasting and obviates the need for elevated externalizing behaviors in adulthood.

Extant research has also documented the long-term sequelae of early pubertal development in girls. Women who experienced early pubertal development, compared with their later maturing peers, tend to have higher levels of serum estradiol and lower sex hormone binding globulin concentrations that persist through twenty to thirty years of age; have shorter periods of adolescent subfertility (the time between menarche and attainment of fertile menstrual cycles); experience earlier ages at first sexual intercourse, first pregnancy, and first childbirth; display more negative implicit evaluations of men in early adulthood; attain lower educational outcomes and occupational status and engage in more aggressive/delinquent behavior as young adults; and are heavier, carry more body fat, and display higher allostatic loads (cumulative biological "wear and tear") in adolescence and early adulthood (Allsworth, Weitzen, and Boardman 2005; Belles, Kunde, and Neumann 2010; Emaus et al. 2008; Najman et al. 2009; van Lenthe, Kemper, and van Mechelen 1996; reviewed in Ellis 2004; Weichold, Silbereisen, and Schmitt-Rodermund 2003). These effects can be conceptualized as part of a developmental continuum in which early environmental conditions (e.g., scarcity or unpredictability or resources, conflictual family relationships, lack of parental warmth and support) predict earlier pubertal maturation in girls (Belsky, Steinberg, and Draper 1991; Ellis 2004; Ellis et al. 1999; Ellis and Essex 2007), which in turn regulates important dimensions of social and reproductive development (see especially Belsky et al. 2010; James, Ellis, Schlomer and Garber 2012).

Whether measured in terms of developmental psychopathology or reproductive fitness, much is at stake at the adolescent transition. For this reason, I hypothesize that natural selection favored especially strong emotional and behavioral responses to social successes and failures at this juncture. This hypothesis concurs with (a) animal data showing heightened vulnerability to stress in adolescence, particularly among females, as a result of increased glucocorticoid receptor expression in the cortex and stronger and more prolonged corticosterone responses following acute stress (Andersen and Teicher 2008); and (b) human data demonstrating increasing reactivity of stress-sensitive neuroendocrine systems over the transition to adolescence (Gunnar et al. 2009; Stroud et al. 2009).

Among individuals whose current condition or circumstances are predictive of future reproductive failure (e.g., unemployed, unmarried,

marginalized young men with few resources or prospects), low-risk strategies that minimize variance in outcomes have limited utility. In contrast,
high-risk activities (e.g., confrontational and dangerous competition with
other males, gang membership, criminal activities), which by definition
increase variance in outcomes, become more tolerable—even appealing—
because success at these activities can yield otherwise unobtainable fitness
benefits for disenfranchised individuals (Wilson and Daly 1985). In this
sense, risky behavior may strategically increase access to status, resources,
and mating—the pillars of reproductive success. Extensive data supports
this theorizing, uniformly demonstrating markedly elevated rates of violence among young, poor, marginalized males (e.g., Archer 2009)—a group
that may largely account for the dramatic rise in serious violence and delin-
quency in adolescence. Further, peer aggression and risk-taking behaviors
among adolescents are reliably associated with greater mating opportunities (Gallup, O'Brien, and Wilson 2011; Palmer and Tilley 1995; Pellegrini
and Long 2003; Sylwester and Pawłowski 2011).

The other side of the coin is sharply elevated rates of depression and
anxiety in adolescent girls. A critically important resource at stake for adolescent girls is social support. Humans are a cooperatively breeding species
(Hrdy 2009), and women in traditional societies depend on an extended
social network, including both mates and female allies, to help raise very
energetically expensive offspring, obtain and share resources, and provide
protection. Over evolutionary history, adolescence may have been a critical
time for girls to develop their social base and relationship skills. For this
reason, I hypothesize that selection favored heightened sensitivity to threats
and opportunities regarding formation of social relationships in adolescent
girls. Consistent with this hypothesis, adolescent girls are more concerned
than adolescent boys about being negatively evaluated, have a greater need
for social approval, are more empathic, and are more reactive to interpersonal conflict and peer stress (reviewed in Andrews and Thomson 2009;
Rose and Rudolph 2006). This heightened sensitivity to social evaluation
and conflict may interact with perceived threats to social relationships to
produce elevated levels of anxiety and depression in pubescent girls. Social
inclusion and acceptance are critical in this context, as early pubertal
development only predicts increasing levels of depressive symptoms among
adolescent girls who are low in popularity or have problematic peer relationships (Conley and Rudolph 2009; Teunissen et al. 2011). This finding
converges with evolutionary models that conceptualize depression as an
adaptation to social exclusion or other complex social problems and whose
function is to minimize social risk under the circumstances (Allen and Badcock 2003) and promote sustained analysis of the contexts that triggered
the depressive episode, including generating and evaluating potential solutions (Andrews and Thomson 2009).

Finally, the adolescent transition can be put in a broader context by
considering the developmental changes that take place several years earlier,

in the passage from early to middle childhood (the *juvenile transition*; Del Giudice, Angeleri, and Manera 2009). The juvenile transition is marked by the endocrine event of adrenarche (the start of androgen secretion by the adrenal gland) and the emergence or intensification of important sex differences in behavior and cognition. Moreover, some processes that culminate in adolescence (e.g., developmental changes in aggression levels) actually begin at this stage. In an evolutionary perspective, middle childhood may promote social competition before reproductive maturity, as the status and social resources acquired during this stage can increase the chances of succeeding at later stages. Further, the social feedback received during middle childhood can allow for adaptive recalibration of competitive strategies before navigating the more consequential social arena of adolescence (Del Giudice, Angeleri, and Manera 2009).

Evolutionary Models Provide a Foundation for Delineating Basic Dimensions of Environmental Stress and Their Different Effects on Risky Adolescent Behavior

The adolescent transition is a sensitive period for change in developmental *pathways*—pathways that have already been influenced by earlier life experiences. As articulated earlier, an evolutionary perspective ineluctably implies that natural selection shaped child and adolescent development to be responsive to rearing conditions. A key issue, therefore, involves identifying the experiences and environmental conditions that guide this process. Following Bronfenbrenner's (1979) multilayered ecology of human development, many social developmentalists (e.g., Belsky 1984; Conger et al. 2002; McLoyd 1998) have called attention to the extent to which rearing environments are generally stressful or supportive, thus highlighting such factors as parental sensitivity and harshness, marital quality, parental mental health, and socioeconomic status. Although research based on such thinking has uncovered a variety of developmentally significant environmental influences, it has not been explicitly informed by evolutionary theory and, consequently, has not focused on or delineated *basic dimensions* of environmental stress and support that guide conditional adaptation. Indeed, without a model of the *content* of environmental factors, a common practice has been to aggregate multiple sources of stress in family environments, or to examine the additive effects of multiple stressors, to test a key hypothesis from the developmental psychopathology model: that the more stressors children are exposed to, the more their developmental competencies will be compromised (e.g., Evans and English 2002; Fergusson and Woodward 2000; Scaramella et al. 1998; Gutman, Sameroff, and Eccles 2002). Although these methods for assessing cumulative contextual risk are empirically productive—accounting for substantial variance in adolescent behavior—they do not address why different types of childhood experiences matter (Belsky, Schlomer, & Ellis, 2012).

Recently, Ellis and associates (2009) identified, via a within- and between-species analysis, distinct contextual dimensions that account for much of the variation in patterns of development both across *and* within species. Life history theory, a branch of evolutionary biology addressing how organisms allocate time and energy to various activities over their life cycle, guided this analysis (e.g., Ellis et al. 2009; Stearns 1992; Roff 2002). Due to structural and resource limitations, organisms cannot simultaneously maximize the major life functions of bodily maintenance (e.g., immune function, predator defenses); growth (acquisition of physical, social, and cognitive competencies); and reproduction (mating and parenting). Instead, individuals make trade-offs that prioritize resource and energy expenditures, so that greater investment in one domain occurs at the expense of investment in other domains. Thus, there is a trade-off between somatic growth and current reproduction because both require substantial energetic investment; for example, some primate species (e.g., prosimians) and individuals within species have relatively short periods of growth and begin to reproduce relatively early in life, whereas some other primate species (e.g., all great apes) and individuals within species defer reproduction to devote more time and energy to growing before reproducing. Likewise, there is a trade-off between quality and quantity of offspring, so that some species and individuals within species bear many offspring, but provide relatively little parental care, whereas others invest heavily in the bearing and rearing of fewer offspring. According to life history theory, natural selection favors individuals that "schedule" development and activities (i.e., allocate energy and resources) in a manner that optimizes trade-offs over the life course and across varying ecological conditions. Life history strategies are adaptive solutions to a number of simultaneous fitness trade-offs.[2]

Both within and across species, developmental patterns that arise from different trade-offs vary on a slow–fast continuum. Humans, of course, are not immune to these processes. Thus, some people adopt slower strategies characterized by later reproductive development and behavior, a preference toward relatively stable pair-bonds, an orientation toward longer-term investments and outcomes, and allocation of resources toward enhancing the growth and long-term survival of both oneself and offspring, whereas others display faster strategies characterized by the opposite pattern (Ellis et al. 2009; Figueredo et al. 2006; Kaplan and Gangestad 2005). Slow life history strategies, therefore, are inherently low risk (i.e., low variance), focusing on producing relatively few high-quality offspring that are likely to survive and reproduce. In contrast, fast life history strategies are comparatively high risk (i.e., high variance), focusing on mating opportunities and producing a greater number of offspring with more variable outcomes. In total, the fast life history strategist is a short-term planner, taking benefits opportunistically with little regard for long-term consequences, whereas the slow life history strategist is a long-term planner, delaying immediate gratification in the service of future eventualities.

Because the costs and benefits of different life history trade-offs vary as a function of individual characteristics and local circumstances (e.g., resource availability, local mortality rates), the optimal life history strategy—in fitness terms—for one individual may not be the same for another. According to recent advances in life history theory, *energetic conditions, extrinsic morbidity-mortality,* and *unpredictability,* as signaled by observable cues, are the key dimensions of the environment that regulate development toward slower versus faster life history strategies (Ellis et al. 2009). Energetic stress (i.e., malnutrition, low energy intake, negative energy balance, and associated internal stressors such as disease) causes the developing person to shift toward a slower life history strategy (Ellison 2001). This translates into development of a more energy-sparing phenotype: slower growth, delayed sexual maturation, low gonadal steroid production, small adult body size, and low fecundity. Along these lines, monogamous marriage and father-present social systems are more likely to occur among hunter-gatherers inhabiting harsh physical environments where biparental care (male provisioning) is substantial and important for offspring survival and reproductive success (Draper and Harpending 1988; Geary 2000; Kaplan and Lancaster 2003, table 7.1; Marlowe 2003).

Development of fast life history strategies depends on adequate bioenergetic resources to support growth and development. Once this energetic threshold is crossed, other environmental conditions (i.e., extrinsic morbidity-mortality, unpredictability) become salient determinants of life history strategy (Ellis et al. 2009). Extrinsic morbidity-mortality constitutes external sources of disability and death that are relatively insensitive to the adaptive decisions of the organism. When environmental factors cause high levels of extrinsic morbidity-mortality, even prime-age adults suffer relatively high levels of disability and death. According to life history theory, environmental cues indicating high levels of extrinsic morbidity-mortality cause individuals to develop faster life history strategies (Belsky et al. 1991; Chisholm 1993, 1999; Ellis et al. 2009; Quinlan 2007). Faster strategies in this context—a context that devalues future reproduction—function to reduce the risk of disability or death prior to reproduction. Accordingly, exposure to environmental cues indicating extrinsic morbidity-mortality (such as exposures to violence, dangerous ecological conditions, or harsh child-rearing practices) should shift life history strategies toward current reproduction by maturing and starting mating early (Belsky et al. 1991), even at a cost for one's future reproductive potential. Moreover, high extrinsic morbidity-mortality means that investing in parental care has quickly diminishing returns (by definition, parental effort beyond a basic level cannot shield offspring against extrinsic morbidity-mortality). Thus, high extrinsic morbidity-mortality favors quantity versus quality of offspring.

In addition to the effects of levels of extrinsic morbidity-mortality, variation in extrinsic morbidity-mortality over time and space—environmental unpredictability—also regulates development of life history strategies (Ellis et al. 2009). In environments that fluctuate unpredictably (e.g., changing randomly between Conditions A and B, so that exposure by parents or their young offspring to Condition A does not reliably forecast whether offspring will mature into Condition A or B), long-term investment in a development of a slow life history strategy does not optimize fitness; all of the energy invested in the future is wasted if the individual matures into an environment where life expectancy is short. Instead, people should detect and respond to signals of environmental unpredictability (e.g., stochastic changes in ecological context, geography, economic conditions, family composition, parental behavior) by adopting faster life history strategies. Because levels of and variability in extrinsic morbidity-mortality are distinct, developmental exposures to each of these environmental factors should uniquely contribute to variation in life history strategy (Ellis et al. 2009). Recent longitudinal analyses of the National Longitudinal Study of Adolescent Health, the Minnesota Longitudinal Study of Risk and Adaptation, and the NICHD Study of Early Child Care and Youth Development support this prediction (Brumbach, Figueredo, and Ellis 2009; Belsky, Schlomer, and Ellis 2012; Simpson et al. 2012).

This evolutionary analysis of key environmental influences on life history development differs in basic ways from the developmental psychopathology perspective, which emphasizes the harmful effects of cumulative stress. Whereas the developmental psychopathology model advances the hypothesis that the more stressors children are exposed to, the more their developmental competencies will be compromised, resulting in emotionally and behaviorally dysregulated functioning in adolescence, the evolutionary model clearly implies that biobehavioral development adjusts in different ways to different kinds of environmental stress. First, cross-cultural analyses indicate that exposure to chronically harsh ecological conditions, such as resource scarcity, tends to shift parents and children toward slower life history strategies, including later sexual maturation and onset of reproduction, more stable marital relationships, lower fertility, and relatively high parental investment per child. Second, developmental exposures to morbidity and mortality cues (e.g., attending the funerals of several high school friends during adolescence) should have different effects on risky adolescent behavior depending on the extent to which contextual factors indicate that the causes of disability and death are extrinsic. Barak Obama's autobiography, *Dreams from my Father*, where he compares life in Djarkarta (Indonesia) with life in a Chicago housing project (Altgeld Gardens) nicely illustrates this distinction:

> I saw those Djarkarta markets for what they were: fragile, precious things. The people who sold their goods there might have been poor, poorer even than the folks in Altgeld. They hauled 50 pounds of firewood on their back every day, they ate little, they died young. And yet for all that poverty, there remained in their lives a discernable order, a

tapestry of trading routes and middle men, bribes to pay, and customs to observe, the habits of a generation played out every day. It was the absence of such coherence that made a place like Altgeld so desperate, I thought to myself; it was the loss of order. (183)

Although levels of disability and death may have been even higher in Djarkarta than Altgeld, only in Djarkarta was there a "discernable order" that made it possible to meaningfully manage and control morbidity and mortality hazards. Such control is a necessary precondition to pursuing slower life history strategies, which by definition entail more delayed pay-offs. Environmental contexts like Djarkarta may promote harsh parenting, not because such contexts undermine parental effort, but because it is important for parents to control their children's behavior firmly in environments marked by high levels of threat from preventable sources. In contrast, the context around Altgeld Gardens, such as the highly publicized murder (captured on videotape) of sixteen-year-old Derrion Albert in 2009, who got caught up in a large gang fight while walking home from school and was brutally stomped and beaten to death, presents unmanageable and unpreventable hazards to the developing person. This kind of extrinsic morbidity-mortality strongly shifts adolescents toward risky and dangerous behavior (Ellis et al. 2009). Finally, separate from the effects of extrinsic morbidity-mortality, unpredictable environments—wherein factors such as economic conditions, parental caregivers, school and peer contexts, and residential patterns substantially fluctuate over time—also shift adolescents toward fast life history strategies (Belsky, Schlomer, and Ellis 2012; Ellis et al. 2009; Simpson et al. 2012).

Environmental Mismatches Can Dysregulate Adolescent Development and Behavior

Because evolutionary processes have no foresight and can only adapt organisms to their current environments, natural selection shaped our brains and bodies to solve recurrent problems faced by our ancestors. Hence, people develop in a species-typical manner (i.e., normal, adaptive development) when they experience species-typical conditions over ontogeny. That is, consistent with Brunswik's (1955) theory of probabilistic functionalism, the developing person makes use of and depends on systematic information and relations in the ecological contexts in which development regularly and predictably occurs.

Problems may occur, however, when the developing person experiences environments outside of the species-typical range. Such changed environments can cause adolescents to become maladapted to their new circumstances (e.g., depressed, overweight, dangerously impulsive, hyperaggressive, addicted to drugs). This kind of *mismatch* takes two basic forms. First, the *elimination* of something important from the environment that was reliably present in the past and necessary for normal development and functioning can cause a mismatch. Second, the *introduction* of something new into the environment (or a change in the amount, rate, or ratio of an environmental factor) that derails normal development and functioning can cause a mismatch. This occurs when the new environmental condition falls outside of the parameters encountered over evolutionary history and the organism's response to it is neither prepared nor functional. Either way, the result can be pathological—bad for self and others in the short and long term. A sophisticated knowledge of evolution aids our understanding of the nature of the pathology and is critical to devising successful policy solutions.

A straightforward example of mismatch is the diminution in breast-feeding. Mother's milk was the exclusive food for infants throughout our evolutionary history. The idea that cow's milk or formula could substitute for breast milk reflected profound ignorance of the physiological, psychological, and social adaptations associated with breastfeeding. The resulting mismatch has affected cognitive development. In the largest randomized control trial conducted on breastfeeding to date, Kramer et al. (2008) studied over seventeen thousand mothers and their infants in maternity hospitals in Belarus. The experimental group received a breast-feeding intervention modeled after an initiative by the World Health Organization and UNICEF. The outcome variable was cognitive and academic performance at age 6.5 years. The experimental intervention led to a large increase in exclusive breast-feeding at age three months (43.3 percent for the experimental group vs. 6.4 percent for the control group) and a significantly higher percentage of breast-feeding at all months, up to and including twelve months. At 6.5 years, children from the experimental group had higher means on all of the Wechsler Abbreviated Scales of Intelligence measures, with cluster-adjusted mean differences of 7.5 for verbal IQ, 2.9 for performance IQ, and 5.9 for full-scale IQ. Teachers' academic ratings were significantly higher in the experimental group for both reading and writing.

A pervasive form of mismatch is generated by consumer products that manipulate our neurobiological mechanisms into feeling as if they are attaining fitness-relevant rewards when in fact they are not. For example, the dopamine-mediated reward mechanisms found in the mesolimbic system in the brain evolved to provide a pleasurable reward in the presence of adaptively relevant stimuli like food or sex. In contemporary environments, however, these same mechanisms are subverted by the use of psychoactive drugs such as cocaine and amphetamines, which deliver huge dollops of pleasurable reward in the absence of the adaptively relevant stimuli—often to the users' detriment (Durrant et al. 2009; Nesse and Berridge 1997). Other common adolescent addictions, such as video games and pornography, may operate via the same mechanisms.

The obesity epidemic evident in the West may also be rooted in environmental mismatch. Obesity is a major development problem affecting tens of millions of teenagers worldwide (e.g., Hill 2006). Other than the obvious physical health problems, overweight adolescents suffer stigmatization, social exclusion, bullying, and diminished opportunities for social and mating relationships (Brownell et al. 2005). Profound changes in diet and exercise that separate modern lifestyles from those of our ancestors—a divergence that has accelerated since the 1980s (Hill 2006)—contribute to escalating obesity rates. Before the domestication of draft animals and the development of wind- or water-powered mills, human activities were entirely dependent on human exertion; our biochemistry and physiology are designed to function optimally under such high physical-activity conditions (Eaton and Eaton 2003). Moreover, studies of hunter-gatherers and the archeological and paleontological record suggest that ancestral human diets were characterized by markedly lower levels of refined carbohydrates, sodium, and saturated fats and markedly higher levels of fiber, protein, and unsaturated fats than modern Western diets (Eaton and Konner 1985; Konner and Eaton 2010). Although various human populations have undergone some evolutionary changes in response to agricultural diets (e.g., lactose and gluten tolerance; see Cochran and Harpending 2009), for the most part we remain physiologically adapted to our ancestral dietary patterns. According to the mismatch hypothesis, our current "departures from the nutrition and activity patterns of our hunter-gatherer ancestors have contributed greatly and in specifically definable ways to the endemic chronic diseases of modern civilization" (Konner and Eaton 2010, 594), including the adolescent obesity epidemic.

Although we have yet to pinpoint specific nutrients that support healthy social and cognitive development but are lacking in the modern diet, one candidate is a deficiency of omega-3 polyunsaturated fatty acids (PUFA), as well as a high ratio of omega-6 to omega-3 PUFA, which negatively impact central nervous system development and function (Heinrichs 2010), particularly in childhood (Schuchardt et al. 2010). The estimated ratio of omega-6 to omega-3 PUFA intake in ancestral hunter-gatherers was about 1:1, whereas the ratio in modern Western diets ranges from 15:1 to 17:1 (Simopoulos 2002). This ratio dramatically increased over the last one hundred years, when mechanized vegetable oil production and the emphasis on grain feeds for domestic livestock caused a large upsurge in consumption of omega-6 fatty acids. Before the Agricultural Revolution, all the major food groups that people consumed contained omega-3 fatty acids: meat, wild plants, eggs, fish, nuts, and berries. Modern agricultural practices, however, sharply reduced the omega-3 content in these kinds of foods (Simopoulos 2002).

From the mismatch point of view, omega-3 deficiency relative to excessive levels of omega-6 upset a PUFA balance that we are physiologically adapted to, and this imbalance has affected child, adolescent, and adult health. Epidemiological and randomized control studies across many domains of prevention, intervention, and treatment suggest that increasing omega-3 and decreasing omega-6 intake improves physical health throughout life (Lavie et al. 2009; Riediger et al. 2009), such as by protecting against cardiovascular diseases and cancer. An emerging body of research also suggests that

PUFA play a role in regulating adolescent mood and behavior. Although there is considerable heterogeneity in study methodologies and results, increasing evidence implicates a lack of omega-3 PUFA, or an imbalance between omega-3 and omega-6 PUFA, in unipolar and bipolar depression, stress-induced aggression and hostility, and inattention, hyperactivity, and impulsivity (e.g., Embry and Biglan 2008; Lavialle et al. 2010; Schuchardt et al. 2010). In total, the altered levels and ratios of PUFA in modern diets may be analogous to feeding formula to infants—a subtle change in the environment that happens to alter something that our brains "rely" upon, based on its reliable presence during our genetic evolution.

As a final example, consider the increasingly high rates of adolescent depression (Hankin et al. 1998; Kessler, Avenevoli, and Merikangas 2001). Adolescence is one of the peak risk periods for development of depression, with a mean onset of 14.7 years of age in females and 15.4 years of age in males (Lewinsohn, Joiner, and Rohde 2001). Because an important cause of depression may be environmental mismatches, one focus of evolutionarily guided treatment programs is on restoring ancient patterns of diet, sleep, exercise, natural light exposure, and social connectedness (Ilardi 2009). In addition, prevention and treatment of depression in modern industrialized societies may benefit from restoring measured exposure to a variety of microorganisms or their antigens that were abundant throughout mammalian evolution. Commonly referred to as "old friends," these microorganisms train our immune system to tolerate many benign but potentially pro-inflammatory stimuli. "Loss of exposure to the old friends may promote major depressive disorder by increasing background levels of depressogenic cytokines and may predispose vulnerable individuals in industrialized societies to mount inappropriately aggressive inflammatory responses to psychosocial stressors, again leading to increased rates of depression" (Raison, Lowry, and Rook 2010, 1211). The analogy with breast-feeding, exercise, and fatty acids is clear. A factor reliably present during the genetic evolution of the immune system (certain microorganisms) became incorporated into the way the immune system develops in individuals. When the environment changes in a way that was not experienced in the past (with the depletion of these microorganisms), the immune system can malfunction. It does not matter that the immune system adaptively responds to some kinds of environmental change. Environments that were not experienced during the genetic evolution of the system can still dumbfound it.

Differences between Adolescents in Susceptibility to Environmental Influences—Both Stressful and Supportive—Should Be Considered When Designing Interventions for High-Risk Youth

A core premise of the developmental psychopathology model is that supportive rearing environments promote healthy development and positive behavioral adjustment, whereas stressful rearing environments undermine healthy development and induce problem behaviors destructive to self and others. Although much empirical research concurs with these hypothesized pathways of social development, the main effects of rearing conditions on adolescent development are typically modest in size (e.g., Gerard and Buehler 1999; Sentse et al. 2009). These modest main effects may reflect that fact that not all children are equally susceptible to rearing and other contextual experiences, as indicated by a long history of research on parenting x temperament interactions and burgeoning research on gene x environment interactions. Nevertheless, much work still focuses on contextual effects that apply equally to all children and adolescents; such an approach fails to consider the possibility that whether, how, and to what degree early experiences influence child and adolescent development may critically depend upon individual characteristics.

A set of evolutionary-developmental models, which converge on differential susceptibility to environmental influence as a fundamental factor underlying variation in human personality and development, support this logic (Belsky 1997, 2005; Boyce and Ellis 2005; Ellis, Jackson, and Boyce 2006; Ellis et al. 2011). In recent years, researchers have made significant progress in understanding how environmental exposures interact with genotypes and phenotypes to differentially shape human development. It has become increasingly clear that individuals with different characteristics vary not only in whether and how much environmental stressors and adversity negatively affect them (in terms of conventionally defined mental health outcomes; e.g., Caspi et al. 2002, 2003), but also in the extent to which environmental resources and supports positively influence them (Bakermans-Kranenburg and van IJzendoorn 2011; Blair 2002; Kochanska et al., in press; Quas, Bauer, and Boyce 2004). Most notable, however, is the recurrent finding that the very characteristics of individuals that make them disproportionately vulnerable to adversity sometimes also make them disproportionately likely to benefit from contextual support (reviewed in Belsky and Pluess 2009; Ellis et al. 2011). Evolutionary models suggest that fluctuating selection pressures that generated different fitness payoffs across different social, physical, and historical contexts maintains this differential susceptibility to environmental influence (or at least did so during the course of human evolution) (Belsky 1997, 2005; Boyce and Ellis 2005; Ellis, Jackson, and Boyce 2006; Ellis et al. 2011; Wolf, van Doorn, and Weissing 2008).

Like an orchid whose survival and flourishing is intimately tied to the nurturing or neglectful qualities of the environment (Boyce and Ellis 2005), individuals characterized by heightened susceptibility to the environment display enhanced sensitivity to *both* negative and positive environments, i.e., to both risk-promoting and development-enhancing environmental conditions. This enhanced sensitivity increases *developmental* receptivity to the rearing experiences. That is, more susceptible individuals are more likely to experience sustained developmental change, not just transient fluctuations in functioning, in response to environmental exposures. As reviewed by Belsky and Pluess (2009) and Ellis et al. (2011), variation in susceptibility to the environment constitutes a central mechanism in the regulation of alternative patterns of human development; specifically, differential susceptibility moderates the effects of environmental exposures on a broad array of developmental and life outcomes. Ultimately, this means that experiences and environments influence the development of some adolescents more than others, even if these experiences and environments are exactly the same.

Neurobiological variation at multiple levels of analysis, ranging from behavioral indicators to peripheral neuroendocrine pathways, brain circuitry, and both genetic and epigenetic variation ground and subserve individual differences in openness to environmental influence. A biobehavioral process involving heightened susceptibility to both risk-promoting and development-enhancing environmental contexts is common to each level of analysis. Research on differential susceptibility among adolescents has used *genetic* markers (e.g., variation in the serotonin-transporter gene [*5–HTTPLR*] or the dopamine D4 receptor [*DRD4*], *neurobiological* markers (e.g., variation in the neuroendocrine stress response systems, volumetric differences in the hippocampus), and *behavioral* markers (e.g., negative emotionality/difficult temperament) of sensitivity to the environment. At all three of these levels, the effects of rearing conditions and experiences on physical and social development commonly differ depending on measured susceptibility factors (reviewed in Belsky and Pluess 2009; Ellis et al. 2011).

Such differential susceptibility has far-reaching implications for understanding whether and how much a range of rearing conditions affects adolescent risk taking, for better and for worse. Consider just two well-studied phenomena: depressive symptomatology and externalizing behavioral problems in adolescence. Although the fact that stressful rearing conditions and life events predict depression is well established, a growing literature has begun to address the question, *for whom* do these effects occur? The answer often depends on established genotypic and phenotypic markers of context sensitivity. Eley and colleagues (2004) observed that adolescent girls growing up in more and less risky family environments manifested higher and lower levels of depression, respectively, although this mainly proved true in the case of those homozygous for short alleles on the serotonin-transporter gene (*5–HTTPLR*). These results proved strikingly similar to the depression-related findings subsequently reported by Taylor and associates (2006), who documented interactions between *5–HTTPLR* and the effects of both early adversity (i.e., problematic child-rearing history) and recent life events in young adulthood. Likewise, Whittle et al. (2011) prospectively examined the effects of aggressive maternal behavior on change in depressive symptoms from early to middle adolescence. Among girls with larger bilateral hippocampal volumes, exposure to higher versus lower levels of maternal aggression was associated, respectively, with exacerbation of depressive symptoms over time versus lower severity of depressive symptoms at follow-up; no such effects occurred among girls with other hippocampal volumetric characteristics (or among boys). Finally, Aron, Aron, and Davies (2005, studies 2 and 3) observed that a problematic child-rearing history predicted high levels of self-reported shyness and negative affectivity among older adolescents, whereas its absence predicted low levels of these same dependent constructs; this relation obtained principally in the case of students scoring high on sensory-processing sensitivity.

A comparable body of research has emerged in relation to externalizing behaviors. Lengua's (2008) investigation of a temperament x parenting interactions during early adolescence showed that children who were highly prone to negative emotion in the form of frustration increased in externalizing problems over time when mothers were rejecting, but decreased when mothers manifested little rejection; no such parenting effects were evident for same-age peers scoring low on frustration. Similar results emerged when Pluess and Belsky (2010) investigated whether differential susceptibility to childcare quality in the first 4.5 years of life affected teacher-reported externalizing behavior problems and teacher–child conflicts when children were ten to eleven years of age. They found heightened susceptibility among infants with difficult temperaments to both the developmental benefits of good-quality childcare and the developmental costs of poor-quality childcare. These types of "for better and for worse" effects have been further documented in studies of the effects of both childhood adversities (e.g., interparental violence, experiences of violent victimization, parental neglect, inconsistent discipline) and provision of environmental supports (i.e., interventions that increase family cohesion, communication, and authoritative parenting) on adolescent conduct problems, criminal behavior, and drug and alcohol use (Brody et al. 2009; Foley et al. 2004; Nilsson et al. 2006). Across these diverse studies, both the negative effects of childhood adversity and the positive effects of environmental supports were significantly stronger in adolescents who carried susceptibility alleles (i.e., the low-*MAOA*-activity allele or one or two short alleles on *5–HTTLPR*).

SUMMARY AND CONCLUSION

Central to an evolutionary analysis of adolescence are adaptationist hypotheses about function—why some features of adolescence have been maintained by natural selection instead of others. A guiding assumption of the current paper is that understanding the functions of adolescence is essential to explaining why adolescents engage in risky behavior, and that successful prevention-intervention depends on working with instead of against adolescent goals and motivations (Ellis et al., 2012). Like the theory of stage-environment fit

(Eccles et al. 1993), the evolutionary model emphasizes the importance of match between adolescents' needs and opportunities.

From an evolutionary perspective, a major function of adolescence is to attain reproductive status—to develop the physical and social competencies needed to gain access to a new and highly contested biological resource: sex and, ultimately, reproduction. Puberty-specific developmental changes function to build reproductive capacity and increase socio-competitive competencies at this critical juncture. Much is at stake at the adolescent transition; it is an inflection point (i.e., a sensitive period for change) in development of status, resource control, mating success, and other fitness-relevant outcomes. Consistent with the sensitive period hypothesis, there is a dramatic increase during adolescence in death and disability related to depression, eating disorders, alcohol and other substance use, accidents, suicide, homicide, reckless behavior, violence, and risky sexual behavior. I hypothesize that natural selection favored especially strong emotional and behavioral responses to social successes and failures during the adolescent transition—an important window of vulnerability and opportunity for setting long-term social and reproductive trajectories. Identity formation is central to the reorganization and change that occurs in adolescence as individuals discover and move into new social and reproductive niches.

Given the high stakes, adolescence may be a phase of the life span that historically had great influence on fitness and thus was under intense selection pressures. The legendary self-absorption of adolescents may reflect an evolved motivation to "look out for number one" at that time of life that, evolutionarily speaking, matters the most. The strong sculpting of adolescence by natural selection may have favored high-risk behavioral strategies in contexts that could potentially boost fitness—even at a cost to personal safety, the welfare of others around you, or the society as a whole. Risky behaviors that expose adolescents to danger and inflict harm on others but increase dominance in social hierarchies and leverage access to mates are a case in point. Risky behaviors are not maladaptive if the expected benefits outweigh the expected costs. An evolutionary analysis focuses on the deeper roots of behavior and calls attention to the instrumental nature of both high-risk (e.g., aggressive, dangerous) and low-risk (e.g., cooperative, nurturing) social strategies; both function to control resources (i.e., getting what you want, getting attention from others, wielding influence).

Other than the prenatal period, adolescence is the phase of the human life span when the brain and body undergo the greatest sexual differentiation. Mating behavior emerges in adolescence and is fundamentally connected to risk taking. Because variation in reproductive success was substantially greater among men than women during human evolution, sexual selection favored more high-risk behavioral strategies in adolescent males than females. Delinquent and risky behaviors (e.g., crime, rule-breaking, fighting, risky driving, drinking games) often have signaling functions that enhance reputations for bravery and toughness and increase status, especially in males. Young, disenfranchised males, who have little to lose and much to gain from high-risk behaviors, display markedly elevated levels of violence and unrest.

The other side of the coin is that social support is a critically important resource for adolescent girls. Humans are a cooperatively breeding species, and women in traditional societies depend on an extended social network, including both mates and female allies, to help raise very energetically expensive offspring, obtain and share resources, and provide protection. Over evolutionary history, adolescence may have been a critical time for girls to develop their social base and relationship skills. For this reason, I hypothesize that selection favored heightened sensitivity to threats and opportunities regarding formation of social relationships in adolescent girls. Increasing levels of anxiety and depression in girls may reflect high susceptibility to negative social evaluations during the adolescent transition.

Life history theory provides a conceptual framework for analyzing variation in risky adolescent behavior. Much of this variation falls along a continuum of slow-to-fast life history strategies. Slow life history strategies are inherently low risk, focusing on producing relatively few high-quality offspring that are likely to survive and reproduce; the slow life history strategist is a long-term planner, delaying immediate gratification in the service of future eventualities. In contrast, fast life history strategies are comparatively high-risk, focusing on mating opportunities and producing a greater number of offspring with more variable outcomes; the fast life history strategist is a short-term planner, taking benefits opportunistically with little regard for long-term consequences. Because different risk-taking strategies are potentially adaptive or maladaptive, depending on context, the optimal life history strategy (in fitness terms) for one individual may not be the same for another. Natural selection thus favors risk-taking strategies that are contingent upon reliable and valid cues to environmental conditions. A critically important context that shifts adolescents toward faster (high-risk) strategies is the *perception* (conscious or unconscious) that life is short, the future is unknown, and your own actions cannot control or prevent hazards in the world around you. Exposure to unpredictable, changing environments is another critical factor shifting adolescents toward high-risk behaviors. These different forms of environmental stress do not so much disturb development as *direct or regulate* it toward strategies that are *adaptive* under the relevant stressful conditions (or at least were adaptive during our evolutionary history).

Evolutionary models suggest that fluctuating selection pressures have maintained differential susceptibility to environmental influence. Differential susceptibility means that the main effects of rearing conditions on adolescent development are typically modest in size. Whereas some individuals conditionally adapt development to match local contexts, others are more resistant to environmental conditions and experiences. Thus, both exposures to harsh and unpredictable environments can be expected to have variable effects on development of life history strategies in adolescence and associated risk-taking behaviors.

Because evolutionary processes have no foresight and can only adapt organisms to their current environments, our brains and bodies have been shaped by natural selection to solve recurrent problems faced by our ancestors. Adaptations can become misfire, however, when the developing person experiences environments outside of the species-typical range. For example, abnormally long periods between sexual maturation and adulthood; reduced contact with immediate and extended family; increasing influence of peers, social networking, and media in defining normative behavior; disrupted sleep cycles associated with artificial light exposure and electronic media; a high ratio of omega-6 to omega-3 PUFA; and age-segregated rather than age-mixed socialization can all dysregulate adolescent development. Such pervasive changes may have increased the intensity and ramifications of the adolescent transition in Western and Westernized cultures, with substantial implications for risky adolescent behavior. The apparent increases in aggressive behavior and reductions in prosocial behavior in adolescents as a result of pervasive age-segregation are a paradigmatic example.

The evolutionary model has myriad implications for designing prevention-intervention programs for adolescents (Ellis et al., 2012). It suggests practical solutions and new directions for research that have not been forthcoming from a developmental psychopathology perspective. The evolutionary model moves beyond psychopathology to consider "What's in it for the kids?" and, accordingly, models how natural selection shaped the adolescent brain to respond to environmental opportunities and challenges encountered at the adolescent transition. In presenting this perspective, it is my hope that new knowledge concerning the causes of risky adolescent behavior will be uncovered, and that developmentally appropriate programs and niches can be fostered that work with adolescent goals and motivations to more effectively address the problems associated with risky behavior in the second decade of life.

NOTES

1. This model is not intended to be all encompassing, as there are genuinely pathological conditions (e.g., genetic abnormalities, neurotoxins, head injury) that interfere with the ability of individuals to use adaptive strategies in a variety of contexts, particularly under stress.
2. In evolutionary biology the term "strategy" denotes an organism's realized phenotype among a set of possible alternatives. The term does not imply conscious planning, deliberation, or even awareness; low-level physiological mechanisms such as hormonal switches or modifications of genetic expression can implement a "choice" between phenotypic strategies (even behavioral ones).

REFERENCES

Allen, N.B. and Badcock, P.B.T. "The Social Risk Hypothesis of Depressed Mood: Evolutionary, Psychosocial, and Neurobiological Perspectives," Psychological Bulletin 129 (2003): 887–913.

Allsworth, J.E., Weitzen, S., and Boardman, L.A. "Early Age at Menarche and Allostatic Load: Data from the Third National Health and Nutrition Examination Survey," Annals of Epidemiology 15 (2005): 438–444.

Andersen, S.L. and Teicher, M.H. "Stress, Sensitive Periods, and Maturational Events in Adolescent Depression," Trends in Neurosciences 31 (2008): 183–191.

Andrews, P.W. and Thomson Jr., J.A. "The Bright Side of Being Blue: Depression as an Adaptation for Analyzing Complex Problems," Psychological Review 116 (2009): 620–654.

Angold, A., Costello, E.J., Erkanli, A., and Worthman, C.M. "Pubertal Changes in Hormone Levels and Depression in Girls," Psychological Medicine 29 (1999): 1043–1053.

Angold, A., Costello, E.J., and Worthman, C.M. "Puberty and Depression: The Roles of Age, Pubertal Status, and Pubertal Timing," Psychological Medicine 28 (1998): 51–61.

Archer, J. "Does Sexual Selection Explain Human Sex Differences in Aggression?" Behavioral and Brain Sciences 32 (2009): 249–311.

Aron, E., Aron, A., and Davies, K.M. "Adult Shyness: The Interaction of Temperamental Sensitivity and an Adverse Childhood Environment," Personality and Social Psychology Bulletin 31 (2005): 181–197.

Bakermans-Kranenburg, M. J., and van IJzendoorn, M. H. "Differential Susceptibility to Rearing Environment Depending on Dopamine-Related Genes: New Evidence and a Meta-Analysis," Development and Psychopathology 23 (2011): 39–52.

Beinhocker, E. 2006. The Origin of Wealth: Evolution, Complexity, and the Radical Remaking of Economics. Cambridge, MA: Harvard Business Press.

Belles, S., Kunde, W., and Neumann, R. "Timing of Sexual Maturation and Women's Evaluation of Men," Personality and Social Psychology Bulletin 36 (2010): 703–714.

Belsky, J. "The Determinants of Parenting: A Process Model," Child Development 55 (1984): 83–96.

———. "Variation in Susceptibility to Rearing Influences: An Evolutionary Argument," Psychological Inquiry 8 (1997): 182–186.

———. 2005. Differential susceptibility to rearing influences: An evolutionary hypothesis and some evidence, in *Origins of the Social Mind: Evolutionary Psychology and child Development*, edited by B. Ellis & D. Bjorklund. New York: Guildford, pp. 139–163.

Belsky, J. and Pluess, M. "Beyond Diathesis-Stress: Differential Susceptibility to Environmental Influence," Psychological Bulletin 135 (2009): 885–908.

Belsky, J., Schlomer, G.L., and Ellis, B.J. "Beyond Cumulative Risk: Distinguishing Harshness and Unpredictability as Determinants of Parenting and Early Life History Strategy," Developmental Psychology 48 (2012): 662–673.

Belsky, J., Steinberg, L., and Draper, P. "Childhood Experience, Interpersonal Development and Reproductive Strategy: An Evolutionary Theory of Socialization," Child Development 62 (1991): 647–670.

Belsky, J., Steinberg, L., Houts, R.M., Halpern-Felsher, B.L. "The Development of Reproductive Strategy in Females: Early Maternal Harshness⮕Early Menarche⮕Increased Sexual Risk-Taking," Developmental Psychology 46 (2010): 120–128.

Blair, C. "Early Intervention for Low Birth Weight Preterm Infants: The Role of Negative Emotionality in the Specification of Effects," Development and Psychopathology 14 (2002): 311–332.

Blakemore, S. and Choudhury, S. "Development of the Adolescent Brain: Implications for Executive Function and Social Cognition," Journal of Child Psychology and Psychiatry 47 (2006): 296–312.

Boyce, W.T. and Ellis, B.J. "Biological Sensitivity to Context: I. An Evolutionary-Developmental Theory of the Origins and Functions of Stress Reactivity," Development and Psychopathology 17 (2005): 271–301.

Brody, G.H., Beach, S.R., Philibert, R.A., Chen, Y.F., and Murry, V.M. "Prevention Effects Moderate the Association of 5–HTTLPR and Youth Risk Behavior Initiation: Gene x Environment Hypotheses Tested via a Randomized Prevention Design," Child Development 80 (2009): 645–661.

Bronfenbrenner, U. "Contexts of Child Rearing: Problems and Prospects," American Psychologist 34 (1979): 884–850.

Brownell, K.D., Puhl, R.M., Schwartz, M.B., and Rudd, L. 2005. Weight Bias: Nature, Consequences, and Remedies. New York: Guilford Press.

Brumbach, B.H., Figueredo, A J., and Ellis, B.J. "Effects of Harsh and Unpredictable Environments in Adolescence on the Development of Life History Strategies: A Longitudinal Test of an Evolutionary Model," Human Nature 20 (2009): 25–51.

Brunswik, E. "Representative Design and Probabilistic Theory in a Functional Psychology," Psychological Review 62 (1955): 193–217.

Carskadon, M.A., Harvey, K., Duke, P., Anders, T.F., and Dement, W.C. "Pubertal Changes in Daytime Sleepiness," Sleep 2 (1980): 453–460.

Caspi, A., McClay, J., Moffitt, T., Mill, J., Martin, J., Craig, I., Taylor, A., and Poulton, R. "Role of Genotype in the Cycle of Violence in Maltreated Children," Science 297 (2002): 851–854.

Caspi, A., Sugden, K., Moffitt, T.E., Taylor, A., Craig, I. W., Harrington, II., and Poulton, R. "Influence of Life Stress on Depression: Moderation by a Polymorphism in the 5 HTT Gene," Science 301 (2003): 386–389.

Chisholm, J.S. "Death, Hope, and Sex: Life-History Theory and the Development of Reproductive Strategies," Current Anthropology 34 (1993): 1–24.

———. 1999. Death, Hope and Sex: Steps to an Evolutionary Ecology of Mind and Morality. New York: Cambridge University Press.

Cochran, G. and Harpending, H. 2009. The 10,000 Year Explosion: How Civilization Accelerated Human Evolution. New York: Basic Books.

Conger, R.D., Wallace, L.E., Sun, Y., Simons, R.L., McLoyd, V.C., and Brody, G.H. "Economic Pressure in African American Families: A Replication and Extension of the Family Stress Model," Developmental Psychology 38 (2002): 179–193.

Conley, C.S. and Rudolph, K.D. "The Emerging Sex Differences in Adolescent Depression: Interacting Contributions of Puberty and Peer Stress," Development and Psychopathology 21 (2009): 593–620.

Crowley S.J., Acebo, C., Carskadon, M.A. "Sleep, Circadian Rhythms, and Delayed Phase in Adolescence," Sleep Medicine 8 (2007): 602–612.

Del Giudice, M., Angeleri, R., and Manera, V. "The Juvenile Transition: A Developmental Switch Point in Human Life History," Developmental Review 29 (2009): 1–31.

Dobrova-Krol, N.A., van IJzendoorn, M.H., Bakermans-Kranenburg, M.J. and Juffer, F. "Effects of Perinatal HIV Infection and Early Institutional Rearing on Physical and Cognitive Development of Children in Ukraine," Child Development 81 (2010): 237–251.

Draper, P. and Harpending, H. 1988. A sociobiological perspective on the development of human reproductive strategies, in *Sociobiological Perspectives on*

Human Development, edited by B. MacDonald. New York: Springer-Verlag, pp. 340–372.

Durrant, R., Adamason, S., Todd, F., and Sellman, D. "Drug Use and Addiction: An Evolutionary Perspective," Australian and New Zealand Journal of Psychiatry 43 (2009): 1049–1056.

Eaton, S.B. and Eaton, S.B. "An Evolutionary Perspective on Human Physical Activity: Implications for Health," Comparative Biochemistry and Physiology Part A: Molecular and Integrative Physiology 136 (2003): 153–159.

Eaton, S.B. and Konner, M. "Paleolithic Nutrition: A Consideration of Its Nature and Current Implications," New England Journal of Medicine 312 (1985): 283–289.Eccles, J.S., Midgley, C., Wigfield, A., Buchanan, C.M., Reuman, D., Flanagan, C., and Mac Iver, D. "Development during Adolescence: The Impact of Stage-Environment Fit on Young Adolescents' Experiences in Schools and in Families." American Psychologist 48 (1993): 90–101.

Eley, T.C., Sugden, K., Corsico, A., Gregory, A.M., Sham, P., McGuffin, P., and Craig, I.W. "Gene–Environment Interaction Analysis of Serotonin System Markers with Adolescent Depression." Molecular Psychiatry 9 (2004): 908–915.

Ellis, B.J. "Timing of Pubertal Maturation in Girls: An Integrated Life History Approach." Psychological Bulletin 130 (2004): 920–958.

Ellis, B.J., Boyce, W.T., Belsky, J., Bakermans-Kranenburg, M.J., and van IJzendoorn, M.H. "Differential susceptibility to the Environment: An Evolutionary–Neurodevelopmental Theory," Development and Psychopathology 23 (2011): 7–28.

Ellis, B.J., Del Giudice, Dishion, T.J., M., Figueredo, A.J., Gray, P., Griskevicius, V., Hawley, P.H., Jacobs, W.J., James, J., Volk, A.A., and Wilson, D.S. "The Evolutionary Basis of Risky Adolescent Behavior: Implications for Science, Policy, and Practice," Developmental Psychology 48 (2012): 598–623

Ellis, B.J., and Essex, M.J. "Family Environments, Adrenarche, and Sexual Maturation: A Longitudinal Test of a Life History Model," Child Development 78 (2007): 1799–1817.

Ellis, B.J., Figueredo, A.J., Brumbach, B.H., and Schlomer, G.L. "Fundamental Dimensions of Environmental Risk: The Impact of Harsh versus Unpredictable Environments on the Evolution and Development of Life History Strategies," Human Nature 20 (2009): 204–268.

Ellis, B.J., Jackson, J.J., and Boyce, W.T. "The Stress Response Systems: Universality and Adaptive Individual Differences," Developmental Review 26 (2006): 175–212.

Ellis, B.J., McFadyen-Ketchum, S., Dodge, K.A., Pettit, G.S., and Bates, J.E. "Quality of Early Family Relationships and Individual Differences in the Timing of Pubertal Maturation in Girls: A Longitudinal Test of an Evolutionary Model," Journal of Personality and Social Psychology 77 (1999): 387–401.

Ellison, P.T. 2001. On Fertile Ground: A Natural History of Human Reproduction. Cambridge, MA: Harvard University Press.

Emaus, A., Espetvedt, S., Veierød, M.B., Ballard-Barbash, R., Furberg, A.S., Ellison, P.T., and Thune, I. "17–b–Estradiol in Relation to Age at Menarche and Adult Obesity in Premenopausal Women," Human Reproduction 23 (2008): 919–927.

Embry, D. and Biglan, A. "Evidence-Based Kernels: Fundamental Units of Behavioral Influence," Clinical Child and Family Psychological Review 11 (2008): 75–113.

Evans, G.W. and English, K. "The Environment of Poverty: Multiple Stressor Exposure, Psychophysiological Stress, and Socioemotional Adjustment," Child Development 73 (2002): 1238–1248.

Fergusson, D.M., and Woodward, L.J. "Educational, Psychosocial, and Sexual Outcomes of Girls with Conduct Problems in Early Adolescence," Journal of Child Psychology and Psychiatry 41 (2000): 779–792.

Figueredo, A.J., and Jacobs, W.J. 2010. Aggression, risk-taking, and alternative life history strategies: The behavioral ecology of social deviance, in *Bio-Psycho-Social Perspectives on Interpersonal Violence*, edited by M. Frias-Armenta & V. Corral-Verdugo. Hauppauge, NY: Nova Science Publishers, pp. 3–28.

Figueredo, A.J., Vásquez, G., Brumbach, B.H., Schneider, S., Sefcek, J.A., Tal, I.R., Hill, D., Wenner, C.J., and Jacobs, W.J. "Consilience and Life History Theory: From Genes to Brain to Reproductive Strategy," Developmental Review 26 (2006): 243–275.

Foley, D.L., Eaves, L.J., Wormley, B., Silberg, J.L., Maes, H.H., Kuhn, J., and Riley, B. "Childhood Adversity, Monoamine Oxidase a Genotype, and Risk for Conduct Disorder," Archives of General Psychiatry 61 (2004): 738–744.

Gallup, A.C., O'Brien, D.T., Wilson, D.S. "Intrasexual Peer Aggression and Dating Behavior during Adolescence: An Evolutionary Perspective," Aggressive Behavior 37 (2011): 1–10.

Ge, X., Conger, R.D., Simons, R. L., Brody, G. H., and McBride Murry, V. "Contextual Amplification of Pubertal Transition Effects on Deviant Peer Affiliation and Externalizing Behavior among African American Children," Developmental Psychology 38 (2002): 42–54.

Geary, D.C. "Evolution and Proximate Expression of Human Paternal Investment," Psychological Bulletin 126 (2000): 55–77.

Gerard, J.M. and Buehler, C. "Multiple Risk Factors in the Family Environment and Youth Problem Behaviors," Journal of Marriage and Family 61 (1999): 343–361.

Graber, J.A., Brooks-Gunn, J., and Warren, M.P. "Pubertal Effects on Adjustment in Girls: Moving from Demonstrating Effects to Identifying Pathways," Journal of Youth and Adolescence 35, no. 3 (2006): 413–423.

Gunnar, M.R., Wewerka, S., Freen, K., Long, J.D., and Griggs, C. "Developmental Changes in the Hypothalamus-Pituitary-Adrenal Activity over the Transition to Adolescence: Normative Changes and Associations with Puberty," Development and Psychopathology 21 (2009): 69–85.

Gutman, L.M., Sameroff, A.J., and Eccles, J.S. "The Academic Achievement of African American Students during Early Adolescence: An Examination of Multiple Risk, Promotive, and Protective Factors," American Journal of Community Psychology 30 (2002): 367–399.

Hankin, B.L., Abramson, L.Y., Moffit, T.E., Silva, P. A., and McGee, R. "Development of Depression from Preadolescence to Young Adulthood: Emerging Gender Differences in a 10-Year Longitudinal Study," Journal of Abnormal Psychology 107 (1998): 128–140.

Hawley, P.H. "The Evolution of Adolescence and the Adolescence of Evolution: The Coming of Age of Humans and the Theory about the Forces that Made Them," Journal of Research on Adolescence 21 (2011): 307–316.

Hayward, C., Killen, J., Hammer, L., Litt, I., Wilson, D., Simmonds, B., and Taylor, C. "Pubertal Stage and Panic Attack History in Sixth- and Seventh-Grade Girls," American Journal of Psychiatry 149 (1992): 1239–1243.

Heinrichs, S.C. "Dietary Omega-3 Fatty Acid Supplementation for Optimizing Neuronal Structure and Function," Molecular Nutrition and Food Research 54 (2010): 447–456.

Hill, J.O. "Understanding and Addressing the Epidemic of Obesity: An Energy Balance Perspective," Endocrine Review 27 (2006): 750–761.

Hodgson, G.M. and Knudson, T. 2010. Darwin's Conjecture: The Search for General Principles of Social and Economic Evolution. Chicago: University of Chicago Press.

Holm, S., Forbes, E. E., Phillips, M. L., Ryan, N. D., and Dahl, R. E. "Pubertal Maturation, Reward-Related Brain Function and Sleep in Pre/Early Pubertal and Mid/Late Pubertal Adolescents," Journal of Adolescent Health 45 (2009): 319–320.

Hrdy, S.B. 1999. Mother Nature: A History of Mothers, Infants and Natural Selection. New York: Pantheon.

———. 2009. Mothers and Others: The Evolutionary Origin of Mutual Understanding. Cambridge, MA: Belknap Press of Harvard University Press.

Huerta, R. and Brizuela-Gamino, O.L. "Interaction of Pubertal Status, Mood and Self-Esteem in Adolescent Girls," Journal of Reproductive Medicine 47 (2002): 217–225.

Ilardi, S.S. 2009. The Depression Cure: The 6-Step Program to Beat Depression without Drugs. Cambridge, MA: Da Capo.

Institute of Medicine and National Research Council. 2011. The science of adolescent risk-taking: Workshop summary. . Washington, DC: National Academies Press.

James, J. J., Ellis, B. J., Schlomer, G. L., and Garber, J. "Sex-specific pathways to early puberty, sexual debut and sexual risk-taking: Tests of an integrated evolutionary-developmental model. Developmental Psychology 48 (2012): 687–702.

Jones, M.C. "The Later Careers of Boys Who Were Early or Late Maturing," Child Development 28 (1957): 113–128.

Kaplan, H.S. and Gangestad, S.W. 2005. Life history theory and evolutionary psychology, in *The Handbook of Evolutionary Psychology*, edited by D.M. Buss. New York: Wiley, pp. 68–95.

Kaplan, H.S. and Lancaster, J.B. 2003. An evolutionary and ecological analysis of human fertility, mating patterns, and parental investment, in *Offspring: Human Fertility Behavior in Biodemographic Perspective*, edited by K.W. Wachter & R.A. Bulatao. Washington, DC: National Academies Press, pp. 170–223.

Kessler, R.C., Avenevoli, S., and Merikangas, K.R. "Mood Disorders in Children and Adolescents: An Epidemiologic Perspective," Biological Psychiatry 49 (2001): 1002–1014.

Kochanska, G., Kim, S., Barry, R.A., and Philibert, R.A. "Children's Genotypes Interact with Maternal Responsive Care in Predicting Children's Competence: Diathesis-Stress or Differential Susceptibility?" Development and Psychopathology 23 (2011): 605–616.

Konner, M. and Eaton, S B. "Paleolithic Nutrition: Twenty-Five Years Later," Nutrition in Clinical Practice 25, no. 6 (2010): 594–602.Kramer, M.S., Aboud, F, Mironova, E., Vanilovich, Platt, R.W., Matush, L., and Shapiro, S. "Breast-feeding and Child Cognitive Development: New Evidence from a Large Randomized Trial," Archives of General Psychiatry 65 (2008): 578–584.

Laursen, B., Coy, K.C., Collins, W.A. "Reconsidering Changes in Parent-Child Conflict across Adolescence: A Meta-Analysis," Child Development 69 (1998): 817–832.

Lavialle, M., Denis, I., Guesnet, P. and Vancassel, S. "Involvement of Omega-3 Fatty Acids in Emotional Responses and Hyperactive Symptoms," Journal of Nutritional Biochemistry 21 (2010): 899–905.

Lavie, C.J., Milani, R. V., Mehra, M.R. and Ventura, H.O. "Omega-3 Polyunsaturated Fatty Acids and Cardiovascular Disease," Journal of the American College of Cardiology 54 (2009): 585–594.

Lengua, L.J. "Anxiousness, Frustration, and Effortful Control as Moderators of the Relation between Parenting and Adjustment in Middle-Childhood," Social Development 17 (2008): 554–577.

Lewinsohn, P.M., Joiner, T.E.J., and Rohde, P. "Evaluation of Cognitive Diathesis-Stress Models in Predicting Major Depressive Disorder in Adolescents," Journal of Abnormal Psychology 110 (2001): 203–215.

Luthar, S.S. 1999. Poverty and Children's Adjustment. Thousand Oaks, CA: Sage.

Marlowe, F.W. "The Mating System of Foragers in the Standard Cross-Cultural Sample," Cross-Cultural Research: The Journal of Comparative Social Science 37 (2003): 282–306.

Martin, C.A., Kelly, T.H., Rayens, M.K., Brogli, B.R., Brenzel, A., Jackson Smith, W., and Omar, H.A. "Sensation Seeking, Puberty, and Nicotine, Alcohol, and Marijuana Use in Adolescence," Journal of American Academy of Child Adolescent Psychiatry 41 (2002): 1495–1501.

McLoyd, V.C. "Socioeconomic Disadvantage and Child Development," American Psychologist 53 (1998): 185–204.

McMaster, L.E., Connolly, J., Pepler, D., and Craig, W.M. "Peer to Peer Sexual Harassment in Early Adolescence: A Developmental Perspective," Development and Psychopathology 14 (2002): 91–105.

Mulvihill, D. "The Health Impact of Childhood Trauma: An Interdisciplinary Review, 1997–2003," Issues in Comprehensive Pediatric Nursing 28 (2005): 115–136.

Najman, J.M., Hayatbakhsh, M.R., McGee, T., Bor, W., O'Callaghan, M.J., and Williams, G.M. "The Impact of Puberty on Aggression/Delinquency: Adolescence to Young Adulthood," Australian and New Zealand Journal of Criminology 42 (2009): 369–386.

Nelson, C.A., Zeanah, C.H., Fox, N.A., Marshall, P.J., Smyke, A., and Guthrie, D. "Cognitive Recovery in Socially Deprived Young Children: The Bucharest Early Intervention Project," Science 318 (2007): 1937–1940.

Nesse, R.M., and Berridge, K.C. "Psychoactive Drug Use in Evolutionary Perspective," Science 278 (1997): 63–66.

Nilsson, K.W., Sjöberg, R.L., Damberg, M., Leppert, J., Öhrvik, J., Alm, P.O., and Oreland, L. "Role of Monoamine Oxidase A Genotype and Psychosocial Factors in Male Adolescent Criminal Activity," Biological Psychiatry 59 (2006): 121–127.

Obama. B. 1995. Dreams from My Father: A Story of Race and Inheritance. New York: Times Books.

Ostovich, J.M., and Sabini, J. "Timing of Puberty and Sexuality in Men and Women," Archives of Sexual Behavior 3 (2005): 197–206.

Paikoff, R.L. and Brooks-Gunn, J. "Do Parent–Child Relationships Change during Puberty?" Psychological Bulletin 11 (1991): 47–66.

Palmer, C.T., and Tilley, C.F. "Sexual Access to Females as a Motivation for Joining Gangs: An Evolutionary Approach," Journal of Sex Research 32 (1995): 213–217.

Patton, G.C., Hibbert, M.E., Carlin, J., Shao, Q., Rosier, M., Caust, J., and Bowes, G. "Menarche and the Onset of Depression and Anxiety in Victoria, Australia," Journal of Epidemiology and Community Health 50 (1996): 661–666.

Pellegrini, A.D. and Long, J.D. "A Sexual Selection Theory Longitudinal Analysis of Sexual Segregation and Integration in Early Adolescence," Journal of Experimental Child Psychology 85 (2003): 257–278.

Persico, N., Postlewaite, A., and Silverman, D. "The Effect of Adolescent Experience on Labor Market Outcomes: The Case of Height," Journal of Political Economy 112 (2004): 1019–1053.

Pluess, M. and Belsky, J. "Differential Susceptibility to Parenting and Quality Child Care," Developmental Psychology 46 (2010): 379–90.

Pollak, S.D. "Mechanisms Linking Early Experience and the Emergence of Emotions," Current Directions in Psychological Science 17 (2008): 370–375.

Quas, J.A., Bauer, A., and Boyce, W.T. "Physiological Reactivity, Social Support, and Memory in Early Childhood," Child Development 75 (2004): 797—814.

Quevedo, K.M., Benning, S.D., Gunnar, M.R., and Dahl, R.E. "The Onset of Puberty: Effects on the Psychophysiology of Defensive and Appetitive Motivation," Development and Psychopathology 21 (2009): 27–45.

Quinlan, R.J. "Human Parental Effort and Environmental Risk," *Proceedings of the Royal Society B* 274 (2007): 121–125.

Raison, C.L., Lowry, C.A. and Rook, G.A.W. "Inflammation, Sanitation and Consternation: Loss of Contact with Coevolved, Tolerogenic Microorganisms and the Pathophysiology and Treatment of Major Depression," *Archives of General Psychiatry* 67 (2010): 1211–1224.

Reynolds, M.D., Tarter, R., Kirisci, L., Kirillova, G., Brown, S. Clark, D.B., and Gavaler, J. "Testosterone Levels and Sexual Maturation Predict Substance Use Disorders in Adolescent Boys: A Prospective Study," *Biological Psychiatry* 61 (2007): 1223–1227.

Richards, M.H., Crowe, P.A., Larson, R., and Swann, A. "Developmental Patterns and Gender Differences in the Experience of Peer Companionship during Adolescence," *Child Development* 69 (1998): 154–163.

Richards, M.H., and Larson, R. "Pubertal Development and the Daily Subjective States of Young Adolescents," *Journal of Research on Adolescence* 16 (1993): 421–438.

Riediger, N.D, Othman, R.A, Suh, M, and Moghadasian, M.H. "A Systemic Review of the Roles of n-3 Fatty Acids in Health and Disease," *Journal of the American Dietetic Association* 109 (2009): 668–679.

Roff, D. 2002. *Life History Evolution*. Sunderland, MA: Sinauer Associates.

Rose, A.J., and Rudolph, K.D. "A Review of Sex Differences in Peer Relationship Processes: Potential Tradeoffs for the Emotional and Behavioral Development of Girls and Boys," *Psychological Bulletin* 132 (2006): 98–131.

Rowe, R., Maughan, B., Worthman, C.M., Costello, E.J., and Angold, A. "Testosterone, Antisocial Behavior, and Social Dominance in Boys: Pubertal Development and Biosocial Interaction," *Biological Psychiatry* 55 (2004): 546–552.

Sadeh, A., Dahl, R.E., Shahar, G., and Rosenblat-Stein, S. "Sleep and the Transition to Adolescence: A Longitudinal Study," *Sleep* 32 (2009): 1602–1609.

Sagrestano, L., McCormick, S.H., Paikoff, R.L., and Holmbeck, G.N. "Pubertal Development and Parent–Child Conflict in Low-Income, Urban, African American Adolescents," *Journal of Research on Adolescence* 9 (1999): 85–107.

Sato, S.M., Schulz, K.M., Sisk, C.L., and Wood, R.I. "Adolescents and Androgens, Receptors and Rewards," *Hormones and Behavior* 53 (2008): 647–658.

Scaramella, L.V., Conger, R.D., Simons, R.L. and Whitbeck, L. "Predicting Risk for Pregnancy by Late Adolescence: A Social Contextual Perspective," *Developmental Psychology* 34 (1998): 1233–1245.

Schaal, B., Tremblay, R.E., Soussignan, R., and Susman, E.J. "Male Testosterone Linked to High Social Dominance but Low Physical Aggression in Early Adolescence," *Journal of the American Academy of Child Adolescent Psychiatry* 34 (1996): 1322–1330.

Schuchardt, J.P., Huss, M., Stauss-Grabo, M., and Hahn, A. "Significance of Long-Chain Polyunsaturated Fatty Acids (PUFAs) for the Development and Behavior of Children," *European Journal of Pediatrics* 169 (2010): 149–164.

Sentse, M., Veenstra, R., Lindenberg, S., Verhulst, F.C., and Ormel, J. "Buffers and Risks in Temperament and Family for Early Adolescent Psychopathology: Generic, Conditional, or Domain-Specific Effects? The TRAILS Study," *Developmental Psychology* 45 (2009): 419–430.

Shomaker, L.B., Tanofsky-Kraff, M., Savastano, D.M., Kozlosky, M., Columbo, K.M., Wolkoff, L.E., et al. "Puberty and Observed Energy Intake: Boy, Can They Eat!" *American Journal of Clinical Nutrition* 92 (2010): 123–129.

Shonkoff, J.P., Boyce, W.T., and McEwen, B.S. "Neuroscience, Molecular Biology, and the Childhood Roots of Health Disparities: Building a New Framework for Health Promotion and Disease Prevention," *Journal of the American Medical Association* 301 (2009): 2252–2259.

Silk, J.S., Siegle, G.J., Whalen, D.J., Ostapenko, L.J., Ladouceur, C.D., and Dahl, R.E. "Pubertal Changes in Emotional Information Processing: Pupillary, Behavioral, and Subjective Evidence during Emotional Word Identification," Development and Psychopathology 21 (2009): 7–26.

Simopoulos, A.P. "The Importance of the Ratio of Omega-6/Omega-3 Essential Fatty Acids," Biomedical Pharmacotherapy 56 (2002): 365–379.

Simpson, J. A., Griskevicius, V., Kuo, S. I.-C., Sung, S., and Collins, W. A. "Evolution, stress, and sensitive periods: The influence of unpredictability in early versus late childhood on sex and risky behavior." Developmental Psychology 48 (2012): 674–686

Smolak, L., Levine, M.P., and Gralen, S. "The Impact of Puberty and Dating on Eating Problems among Middle School Girls," Journal of Youth and Adolescence 22 (1993): 355–368.

Stearns, S. 1992. The Evolution of Life Histories. New York: Oxford University Press.

Steinberg, L. "Impact of Puberty on Family Relations: Effects of Pubertal Status and Pubertal Timing," Developmental Psychology 23 (1987): 451–460.

———. "Reciprocal Relation between Parent–Child Distance and Pubertal Maturation," Developmental Psychology 24 (1988): 122–128.

———. "A Social Neuroscience Perspective on Adolescent Risk-Taking," Developmental Review 28 (2008): 78–106.

Stroud, L.R., Foster, E., Papandonatos, G.D., Handwerger, K., Granger, D.A., Kivlighan, K.T., and Niaura, R. "Stress Response and the Adolescent Transition: Performance versus Peer Rejection Stressors," Development and Psychopathology 21 (2009): 47–68.

Sylwester, K. and Pawłowski, B. 2010. "Daring to be darling: Attractiveness of risk takers as partners in long- and short-term sexual relationships." Sex roles 64 (2011) 695–706.Taylor, S.E., Way, B.M., Welch, W.T., Hilmert, C.J., Lehman, B.J., and Eisenberger, N.I. "Early Family Environment, Current Adversity, the Serotonin Transporter Polymorphism, and Depressive Symptomatology," Biological Psychiatry 60 (2006): 671–676.

Teunissen, H.A., Adelman, C.B., Prinstein, M.J., Spijkerman, R., Poclen, E.A.P., Engels, R.C.M.E., and Scholte, R.H.J. "The Interaction between Pubertal Timing and Peer Popularity for Boys and Girls: An Integration of Biological and Interpersonal Perspectives on Adolescent Depression," Journal of Abnormal Child Psychology 39 (2011): 413–423.

Tremblay, R.E., Schaal, B., Boulerice, B., Arseneault, L., Soussignan, R.G., Paquette, D., and Laurent, D. "Testosterone, Physical Aggression, Dominance, and Physical Development in Early Adolescence," International Journal of Behavioral Development 22 (1998): 753–777.

Udry, J. 1987. Hormonal and social determinants of adolescent sexual initiation, in Adolescence and Puberty, edited by J. Bancroft. Oxford: Oxford University Press, pp. 72–80.

van Lenthe, F.J., Kemper, C.G., and van Mechelen, W. "Rapid Maturation in Adolescence Results in Greater Obesity in Adulthood: The Amsterdam Growth and Health Study," American Journal of Clinical Nutrition 64 (1996): 18–24.

Warren, M.P. and Brooks-Gunn, J. "Mood and Behavior at Adolescence: Evidence for Hormonal Factors," Journal of Clinical Endocrinology and Metabolism 69 (1989): 77–83.

Weichold, K., Silbereisen, R.K., and Schmitt-Rodermund, E. 2003. Short-term and long-term consequences of early versus late physical maturation in adolescents, in Gender Differences at Puberty, edited by Chris Hayward. Cambridge: Cambridge University Press, pp. 241–276.

Weisfeld, G.E. 1999. Evolutionary Principles of Human Adolescence. New York: Basic Books.

Weisfeld, G.E. and Coleman, D.K. 2005. Further observations on adolescence. In Evolutionary Perspectives on Human Development, 2nd ed., edited by R.L. Burgess & K. MacDonald. Thousand Oaks, CA: Sage, pp. 331–356.

West-Eberhard, M.J. 2003. Developmental Plasticity and Evolution. New York: Oxford University Press.

Whittle, S., Yap, M.B.H., Sheeber, L., Dudgeon, P., Yücel, M., Pantelis, C., and Allen, N.B. "Hippocampal Volume and Sensitivity to Maternal Aggressive Behavior: A Prospective Study of Adolescent Depressive Symptoms," Development and Psychopathology 23 (2011): 115–129.

Wilson, M. and Daly, M. "Competitiveness, Risk Taking, and Violence: The Young Male Syndrome," Ethology and Sociobiology 6 (1985): 59–73.

Wolf, M., van Doorn, G.S., and Weissing, F.J. "Evolutionary Emergence of Responsive and Unresponsive Personalities," Proceedings of the National Academy of Sciences of the United States of America 105 (2008): 15825–15830.

Wolfson, A.R. and Carskadon, M.A. "Sleep Schedules and Daytime Functioning in Adolescents," Child Development 69 (1998): 875–887.

4 Hunter-Gatherer Adolescence

Bonnie L. Hewlett and Barry S. Hewlett

This chapter describes general features of hunter-gatherer adolescence. Most studies of adolescence in small-scale cultures have been conducted with farming or pastoral cultures, and the vast majority of cultures in the Standard Cross-Cultural Sample (SCCS), used by Schlegel and Barry (1991) in their classic adolescent study, utilize these modes of production. Farming and pastoral cultures are known for their gender inequality, strong chiefs, deference and respect of older individuals (e.g., parents, older siblings), accumulation or defense of land or herds, regular warfare, and relatively high population density. These features are rare or absent in mobile hunter-gatherers. The differences in social systems and culturally constructed niches are likely to influence the daily lived experiences and identity formation of adolescents.

An understanding of forager adolescence is also important because humans were hunter-gatherers for 75 percent or more of the history of modern *Homo sapiens*. Human adolescent bio-cultural adaptations occurred at this time, and studies of extant foragers provide one vantage point for obtaining insights into the nature of adolescence. This chapter addresses the following questions: What generalizations can be made about hunter-gatherer adolescents? How are they distinct from adolescents in other cultures with differing modes of production? Does the emotional intimacy characteristic of forager infancy and childhood persist into adolescence? How do forager values of autonomy and egalitarianism impact identity formation? How might these generalizations inform our understanding of identity, human diversity, and potential?

Four sources of data provide the material for our analysis: (1) our systematic studies of Aka forager adolescents, primarily the first author's research on health and development of sixty-five older children, adolescents, and young adults; (2) Konner's (2005, 2010) discussion of adolescents in his hunter-gatherer childhood model; (3) in-depth and systematic studies of adolescents in other forager cultures, e.g., Condon's work with the Inuit (1987) and Burbank's study of Australian aborigines (1988) and; (4) cross-cultural studies of hunter-gatherer groups coded in the SCCS.

The generalizations about hunter-gatherer adolescence are placed into three groups: (1) features that are a part of our non-human primate heritage; (2) features linked to human nature, evolution, and adaptation, and; (3) features relatively unique to foragers. The last two groups of generalizations likely built upon features in the first group and evolved during the long hunting-gathering period of human history, frequently referred to as the environment(s) of evolutionary adaptation. We provide the greatest amount of ethnographic detail about the last set of generalizations because the items in the first two sets exist in many small-scale cultures while the last group of generalizations is relatively distinct to foragers.

HUNTER-GATHERERS AND THE AKA OF THE CONGO BASIN

This chapter focuses on hunter-gatherers and often utilizes the Aka adolescents as examples, therefore before identifying and describing these generalizations, we explain common features of foragers and provide a brief ethnographic overview of Aka life.

The Aka are one of at least fifteen ethnolinguistic groups of foragers, sometimes referred to as "pygmies", living in the tropical forests of the Congo Basin. Their population density is low, less than one person per square kilometer, they have high fertility (about five to six live births per woman) and high infant and child mortality (approximately 45% for children under age fifteen) (Hewlett 1992).

Aka live in small intimate camps of twenty-five to thirty-five individuals (see Takeuchi Chapter 7, this volume). The number of people in the camp

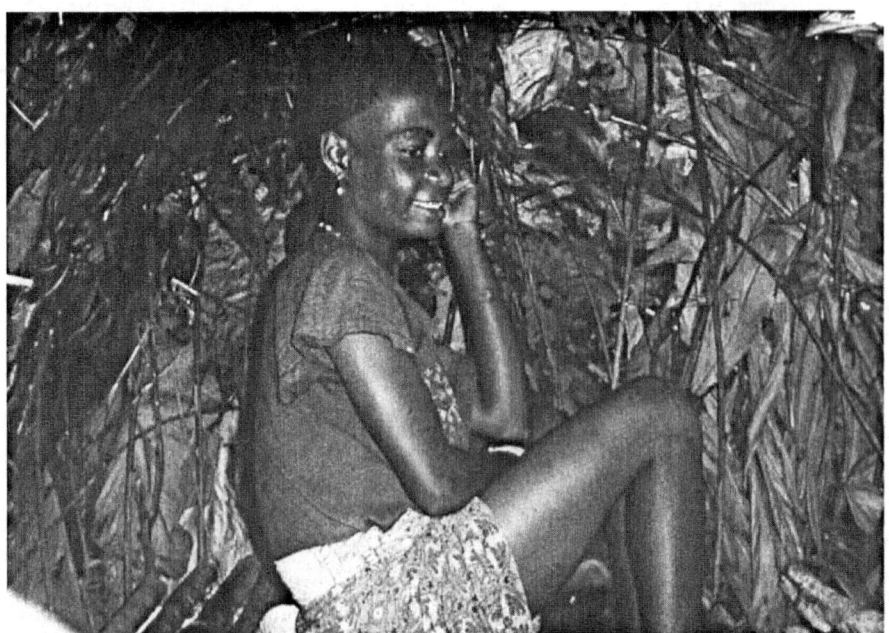

Figure 4.1   An Aka adolescent female inside her *ngondo* hut.

varies almost daily, as adolescents (and others) travel to other camps or relatives and friends come to visit. Their homes are small, at most three meters in diameter and two meters high. Inside the home is a bed of animal skins, leaves, or twigs where the family sleeps together. The *ngondo* (term for adolescent females) huts are smaller and have room enough for one or at most two inhabitants (see Figure 4.1). The bachelor lean-tos, built by the *bokola* (term for adolescent males) are usually larger, rectangular structures, able to house four to six young males.

Aka have minimal political hierarchy (a *kombeti,* male elder, is recognized but has very limited authority and no "big men" who hold authority and power over others exist); relatively high gender and intergenerational egalitarianism (no individual is given more respect simply due to their age or gender); and, weak patriclans (*dikandu*) associated with neighboring farmers. Female lines are recognized as well (*mobila*). After an initial one-year period or so of matrilocality when the husband provides brideservice, the Aka are multilocal—moving back and forth between the husband and wife's families.

Foundational Schema

Foundational schema refer to modes of thought that pervade several domains of Aka life—from subsistence activities to who sleeps together to how to organize a dance.

Four foundational schema permeate Aka life: egalitarianism, respect for autonomy, sharing/giving, and an "immediate return" mode of thought. An egalitarian way of thinking means others are respected for what they are, and it is not appropriate to draw attention to oneself or judge others as better or worse. The Aka have several cultural mechanisms to maintain egalitarianism such as rough joking and demand sharing (Hewlett 1992). For example, if an Aka child does not share, others gesture, comment, or tease the child, and young children often hear stories about how people who do not share properly face sanctions (illness, death, death of a child). Boehm (2001) calls this process, common to many mobile hunter-gatherers, "reverse dominance hierarchy."

Respect for an individual's autonomy is also a core cultural value. Men and women, young and old, are generally free to do what they want; one does not impose his/her will, beliefs, or actions on others. If an adolescent wants to travel to another camp, live with a grandparent, have sex or marry, they simply do so. A giving or sharing way of thinking also pervade Aka life; Aka share 50–80 percent of what is acquired by hunting and gathering with everyone in camp, every day.

The final foundational schema is an "immediate return" mode of thought (Woodburn 1982, 205). This means that Aka thinking and activities are oriented to the present. For instance, the time and energy invested in a day to obtain food and other resources are consumed that day or perhaps over the next few days that follow. There is a minimum of investment in accumulation, in long-term debts, obligations, or in binding commitments to specific kin or others.

Habitus and Demographic Contexts of Aka Life

The daily lived experiences, called *habitus* by Bourdieu (1977), are important for understanding how Aka children become Aka adolescents, and later adults, developing culturally specific identities, ideologies, and schema. The habitus is shaped by the foundational schema and is also the means by which infants, children, and adolescents acquire cultural knowledge. Aka habitus and demography are characterized by the following features: physical and emotional intimacy, self-motivated and directed learning, trust of others, mixed adult–child groups, and frequent play (Hewlett et al. 2011).

Physical and emotional proximity are particularly important to hunter-gatherers. Forager camps are generally very dense, often occupying a space the size of a large dining or living room in the U.S., and when Aka sit down or rest in the camp they are usually in constant physical contact with others. At night, foragers sleep very close together and rarely sleep alone.

Aka children are granted autonomy during the day whereas the neighboring farming children are subject to the control of parents and older children. Aka children of all ages decide when and what they want to do with minimal intervention from others. The development of trust is important to some degree in all cultures, but the socialization for a trust of others is particularly pronounced among the Aka. The indulgent care and resulting trust of self and others, is part of the daily life of the Aka.

Konner (2005) indicates that after weaning, hunter-gatherer children move from a relationship with the mother to relationships with children in mixed-age playgroups. Our data question his representation of hunter-gatherers and indicate that Aka parents and other adults are frequently around children and adolescents. Time with parents and other adults gradually declines with age, but by comparison to their farming neighbors foragers spend considerably less time in child-only groups. A study by Boyette found that four- to twelve-year-old Aka children spent more time in mixed-age groups, but were still within visual range of an adult 77 percent of the day, and parents and other adults were among their nearest neighbor (defined as those equally close to the child) 33.1 percent of the day (Boyette unpublished ms). At night, a co-sleeping study by the second author found that forager children and adolescents were three times more likely than farmer children of similar age to sleep with their parents or other adults. Finally, play permeates Aka adult and child life (Hewlett and Boyette in press). As mentioned earlier, several researchers have reported that hunter-gatherer children are given few responsibilities and spend most of the day playing or resting (Konner 2010).

Aka Childhood

A brief description of Aka childhood is provided here to place the preceding features into a more detailed ethnographic context and help understand precursors to adolescent development. Aka babies are held nearly constantly, often carried on the side in a sling of cloth, in constant skin-to-skin contact with their mother (or other caretaker), breast-feeding is frequent, and fussing or crying are responded to within seconds (Hewlett et al 1998).

From early infancy Aka children learn an almost "sacred" value of autonomy. Babies not only nurse on demand ("self-directed nursing," as the mother's breast is usually available), but by the third or fourth year of life are weaned when they choose to stop breast-feeding (Fouts et al. 2000). Parents rarely correct their children; when they do, discipline generally involves chastising or teasing. Although they may ask their child to do something for them (get water or help in some task), they do not punish the child if their request is ignored. Hitting a child can be cause for divorce (Hewlett 1992). Even into adolescence there are no expectations from others in terms of work or behavior save for the expectation surrounding sharing (with social sanctions for any unwillingness to share), so much of their time is spent in play, rest, or socializing with others (Boyette unpublished ms; Hewlett 1992; Hewlett et al. 2000; Hewlett et al. 2011).

Aka foragers spend a considerable amount of time playing (31.4 percent of day) and laying around idle (37.9 percent of day) (Hewlett and Boyette in press). By age ten, Aka have acquired most of the knowledge and skill necessary for life in the forest, knowing how to net hunt, fish, gather plants, honey, nuts, mushrooms, prepare food, take care of babies, build huts and baskets, and make medicines for illnesses, but interestingly they do not always put this knowledge to task (Hewlett and Cavalli Sforza 1986).

Social identity formation of Aka children from their "first taste" of exploration and interdependence leads seamlessly to increasing responsibility, power, and autonomy as adolescents (Turnbull 1982, 138). They are secure in the knowledge of self within the "circles" of kin, an identity reinforced daily through strongly maintained cultural values, practices and beliefs shared by those surrounding them. As one young Aka male related when asked of his plans for the future, (i.e. what do you "want to be or do" when you are older?) "I am," he said simply, "Aka" implying even at a relatively young age, both a sense of confidence and security of self "as" and of self "with".

Aka hunter-gatherers provide most of the data for this chapter, but many of the patterns described above are common to most mobile hunter-gatherers. Table 4.1 lists several characteristic features of hunter-gatherers. The ethnographic overview of Aka and the characteristic features of hunter-gatherers provide the broader context for understanding adolescence in these groups.

Table 4.1   Characteristic Features of Mobile Hunter-Gatherers (Lee and Daly 2004; Kelly 2007)

1. High mobility and frequent movement of camps
2. Camps consist of 25–35 individuals, and most adult camp members are not genetically related to each other
3. Lack of storage
4. Flexibility in camp composition, movement by individuals, and gender roles
5. Gender and age egalitarianism and lack of central authorities
6. Extensive sharing and giving
7. Respect for autonomy is highly valued
8. Extensive allomaternal care and provisioning
9. Low population density, high fertility and mortality

GENERALIZATIONS ABOUT HUNTER-GATHERER ADOLESCENCE

The Phylogenetic Heritage of Hunter-Gatherer Adolescence

This section briefly reviews studies of non-human primate adolescents, primarily adolescent research with three species of great apes—chimpanzees (*Pan troglodytes*), gorillas (*Gorilla gorilla*), and orangutans (*Pongo pygmaeus*). They are the largest non-human primates and have the longest periods of immaturity. Bogin (2009; Chapter 2 this volume) postulates that adolescence does not exist in non-human primates, but researchers working with primates do not hesitate to use the term "adolescence" to refer to the period between puberty, determined by a variety of ways, to the attainment of full adult weight. Due to problems of operationally defining and determining adolescence, "adolescent primates have been somewhat neglected" (Setchell 2003). Definitions and signs of adolescence in non-human primates include puberty (e.g., measured by labial swelling in females and testes growth or first full copulation in males) to the attainment of adult weight, changes in hormonal functioning, a late growth spurt, and/or changes in social interactions. Walters (1987, 358) argues, "Puberty (in non-human primates) may be defined as all the events, beginning with altered hormonal function, leading to reproductive maturation. These patterns are broadly similar in all primates." He identifies several behavioral patterns common to most non-human primate adolescents: dependence upon social learning about social and physical environments prior to reproduction, development of social bonds (play, grooming), increased aggressive behaviors, and dispersal (Walters 1987, 358–369). Setchell defines the adolescent period, between puberty and the attainment of full adult size and appearance, as a "distinct and important developmental period" in non-human primates

(2003, 1053). Accounting for a "significant proportion in a male's reproductive lifespan in highly sexually dimorphic species" as adolescent male
mandrills develop physically and developmentally, social behaviors (grooming and play) decrease, aggressive and sexual behaviors increase and males
are peripheralized (ibid.).

Pusey's (1990) study of chimpanzees indicates that adolescence, defined
as the time from puberty, marked testicular growth, and ejaculation in
males and sexual swelling in females, to the attainment of adult weight,
about four to five years later, had several characteristic features. Adolescent
males and females decreased their association and grooming time with their
mothers. Adolescent males and females began engaging in sexual activity, and adolescent females began associating with adult males. Adolescent
males associated with, and were more likely to groom, adult males and
cycling females, with a few males forming strong, long-lasting associations
with particular adult males. At this time adult male aggression toward adolescent males also increased. For both males and females time spent playing declined sharply from the juvenile period. Additionally, juveniles and
young adolescents in both sexes had friendly relations with infants, but
older adolescents rarely interacted with infants.

Adolescence is a time when individuals try to position themselves in the
dominance hierarchy and establish alliances and support networks. Adolescent chimpanzee and gorilla males, in particular, show aggressive displays
toward other males, establishing and contesting the dominance hierarchy.
Adolescent chimpanzee and gorilla males take risks and receive their first
wounds from other males as they shift their affiliations from mother to
other adult females and males. Male chimpanzee and gorilla adolescents
continually challenge adolescent females before achieving dominance over
them, even if they are smaller than the females. The rate of adult–adolescent male aggression increases as adolescents mature. But adolescent chimpanzee and gorilla males also try to seek affiliation and proximity despite
the rise in aggression toward them as they work their way into the male
dominance hierarchy and the grooming and alliance networks (Watts and
Pusey 2002).

Although the literature emphasizes male aggression and risk taking,
females are also assertive, taking risks and trying to establish their reputations as they shift affiliations with their mothers and move into dominance
hierarchies, establish relations with adult males, and obtain important
information for survival.

Among orangutans, adolescent females are the most social of all age/
sex classes and, unlike males, cannot generally be characterized as being
solitary or even semi-solitary (Galdikas 1996). Adolescent females initiate, maintain and terminate interactions with adult males, displaying an
eagerness to begin reproduction shortly after puberty and before full maturation, copulating with males at higher rates than adult females. Adolescent females are particularly social in order to increase learning—for

instance, learning how to solve social and environmental problems and how to increase foraging efficiency, and learning about resources in their home range (ibid.).

It is worth noting that researchers working with chimpanzee, gorilla, and orangutan adolescents distinguish early/young and late/older adolescents in their analysis. Younger adolescents' behavior is similar to that of juveniles (e.g., more time near and grooming by mother, less aggression) whereas older adolescents behavior is similar to adult behavior (e.g., more risk taking, aggression, and alliance building).

Although few studies exist and definitions vary, the research cited above suggests that higher primates, including humans, share the following characteristics:

1. Reputation building and increased risk taking, especially among males
2. Increase in sexual activity, beginning shortly after puberty
3. Increase in time spent around sexually active members of the opposite sex in late adolescence
4. Development of particularly close relationships and alliances with one or two members of the same sex
5. Increase in time learning complex social and subsistence skills

These are biological propensities and common in many cultures. Reputation building is a part of non-human primate adolescence as males and females try to negotiate dominance hierarchies and locate mates. Likewise, Aka adolescents have criteria for selecting mates; for example, an attractive mate is one known as a "hard worker". Both male and female adolescents try to build reputations that demonstrate that they are strong and able workers in their respective subsistence roles and activities. However, some male roles require more risk and lead to greater frequency of death. Figure 4.2 examines Aka male to female ratio of mortality by ages and demonstrates that adolescent males are particularly at risk of higher mortality. Adolescent mortality is relatively low by comparison to infant and young child mortality, but substantially more adolescent males than females die because they take greater risks to build reputations as hard workers, good hunters, strong and able men, and future providers. They may climb large trees looking for honey or fruit, or take risks on elephant or other large game hunts, e.g., volunteering to run underneath the elephant to spear it.

Unlike higher primates and humans in stratified and hierarchical cultures, reputation building among foragers does not regularly involve male-male aggression and violence due to their relatively egalitarian ethos and general disdain for competitive and aggressive individuals. Violence does occur, however, especially when older adolescent males travel great distances and have sexual affairs with, for example, married women.

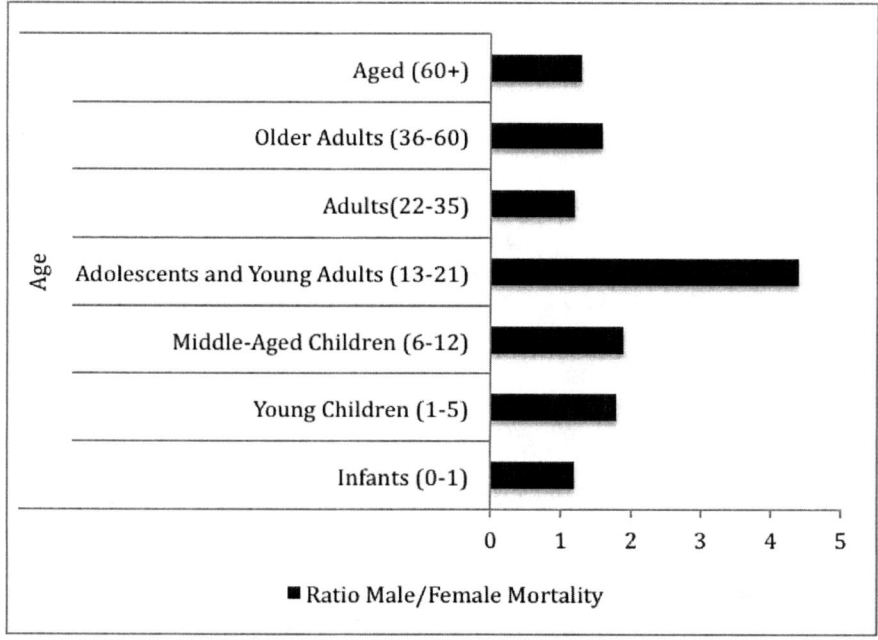

Figure 4.2   Aka male–female ratio of mortality by age.

Like other higher primates, forager adolescents begin sexual activity shortly after puberty. Timing and frequency of sexual activity varies by individual and culture, but many forager males and females have their first sexual experiences by the time they are fifteen years of age. Likewise, once past puberty and especially in late adolescence, hunter-gatherers spend more time among sexually active members of the opposite sex than they did in middle childhood and early adolescence.

Higher primate adolescents also start to spend more time with particular individuals of the same sex. Likewise, Aka adolescents develop deep friendships with one or two other adolescents/young adults of the same sex during this period. Since forager camps are small, close friends may be several years younger or older. These individuals spend much of the day together hunting, collecting, and socializing, but unlike non-human higher primates they often sleep together at night. These friendships remain important social and economic relationships well into adulthood.

Like non-human higher primates, foragers acquire more complex subsistence and social skills in adolescence. Technology and subsistence activities in humans are greater than those of higher non-human primates, and Kaplan et al. (2000) hypothesize that adolescence in humans is longer because it takes a more time to learn these complex skills. A study of Aka cultural transmission (Hewlett and Cavalli-Sforza 1986) demonstrated that most subsistence and social skills were learned by age 10, but mating skills, how to hunt large game, and knowledge about special medicine and the supernatural were acquired in adolescence.

The Human Adaptive Pattern and Hunter-Gatherer Adolescence

It is important to understand the phylogenetic heritage of human adolescence, but it is also worthwhile to briefly describe how humans are relatively distinct from non-human higher primates and how these differences impact hunter-gatherer adolescence. First, unlike non-human higher primates, humans are cooperative breeders. Chimpanzee, gorilla, and orangutan mothers may receive sporadic assistance from others, whereas allomaternal care and provisioning by many other individuals—men, other women, children—are regular and significant in humans. Although allomaternal care exists among some New World monkeys, such as marmosets, capuchins, and tamarins, it does not occur among non-human higher primates, humans' closest living relatives. Second, non-human primate mothers and others seldom, if ever, provision juveniles or adolescents after weaning. Post weaning, juveniles and adolescents subsist primarily on their own. Juveniles and adolescents in all human societies seldom, if ever, provide all of the calories they consume. This generally applies to co-sleeping as well. Young non-human primates sleep with mother until they are weaned, but they often sleep alone as juveniles and adolescents, whereas human juveniles usually co-sleep. Third, humans have relatively long-term pair-bonds with relatively high male investment (protecting, provisioning, social learning) in offspring. Finally, humans have language, an extensive symbolic system that includes beliefs in the supernatural, a substantially longer juvenile/adolescent period, and increased social cognitive learning skills. Debate continues on the extent of ape-human differences in cognitive abilities, but human's social learning abilities enable them to learn rapidly from others. Great apes are extremely intelligent and have complex tools and culture, i.e., socially transmitted and learned skills and behaviors, but they do not appear to have natural pedagogy, over-imitation, and cumulative culture.

Generalizations about hunter-gatherer adolescence that are associated with specific features of human nature, evolution and adaptation as discussed above include the following:

1. Caregiving, particularly by adolescent females, of infants and young children
2. Sexual division of labor in which adolescent males and females learn different complex tasks
3. Adults provide moderate to intensive food and care to adolescents
4. Marriage (relatively stable pair bonding) and birth of first child in late adolescence (especially females)

5. Adolescents often live with stepparents
6. Adolescents acquire in-depth understanding of supernatural beliefs

Humans are cooperative breeders; therefore, adolescents, especially females, in many societies provide important care to younger brothers and sisters. Allomaternal care is particularly pronounced in forager cultures (Hewlett et al. 2011), and adolescents, both male and female, watch, tend, and provide care for infants and young children, although as noted earlier, it is nonobligatory care. Sexual division of labor is a human universal that emerged as part of the human adaptive pattern. This, of course, occurs with the Aka and other foragers, but what is striking about foragers is the gender flexibility that exists in subsistence and other roles and tasks. For instance, men usually carry the spears and nets on hunts, but it is not unusual to see an Aka adolescent girl carry these implements as well. Taboos and sanctions on females handling hunting spears or nets do not exist (except when a female is menstruating), whereas taboos and restrictions associated with females touching hunting implements are common among farmers and pastoralists, where pronounced gender hierarchy is the norm.

Pair bonding is also part of human nature and most forager females marry and have their first child before they turn twenty. Aka, Ache, Agta, and !Kung forager girls marry between fourteen and nineteen years of age and usually have their first child two years later. Forager males tend to marry three to five years later than females, so they are usually married in late adolescence or early adulthood (i.e., by age twenty-three or so). As Takeuchi reports in Chapter 7 (this volume), social adulthood begins when Aka females give birth, and men become skilled hunters. These of course vary by indvidual. Although !Kung marriages are arranged, forager marriages are generally informal and are established by the couple living together in the same hut for some time.

Adult provisioning of children (after weaning) and adolescents is also a distinctive feature of the human adaptive pattern. Among the Aka, provisioning continues beyond the time of marriage. The first author conducted a study of adolescent food provisioning. Single and married Aka adolescents (none had children or were regarded yet as adults) were asked four times during the day, for ten random days during a month, how many meals or snacks they had consumed since the previous visit, what foods they had eaten and who provided the food. Six married adolescent Aka couples and twenty single adolescents participated in the study. Figures 4.3 and 4.4 compare provisioning in the two groups. Although married adolescents report getting substantially more of their own food, mothers continued to contribute food to their adolescents after their marriage. This was especially true for adolescent females who lived matrilocally while their new husbands performed brideservice.

The same study also looked at the number of meals or snacks eaten per day by older and younger adolescents and the number of meals or snacks

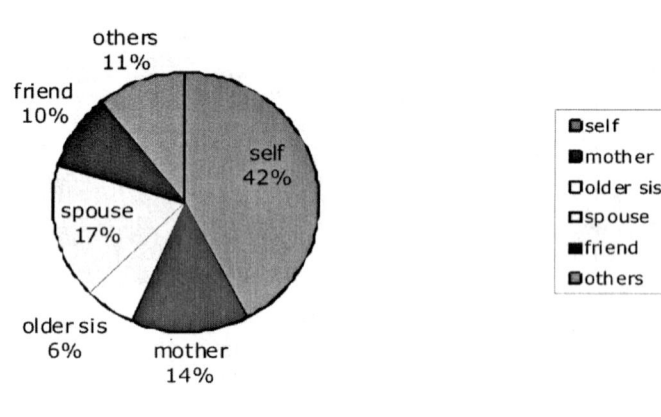

Figure 4.3   Individuals who provisioned married Aka adolescents.

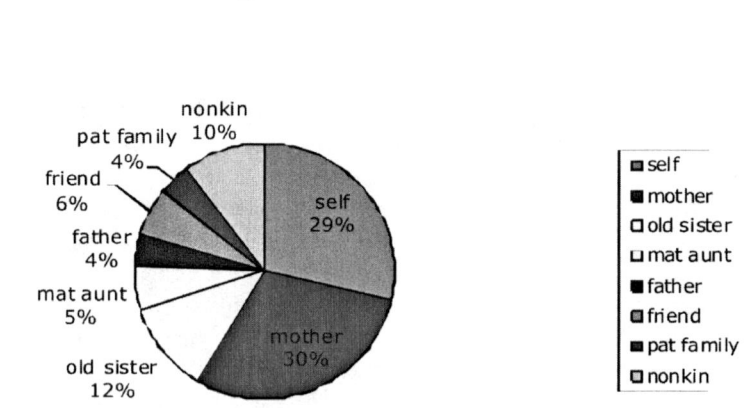

Figure 4.4   Individuals who provisioned single Aka adolescents.

eaten by married and single older adolescents. Older adolescents ate more meals or snacks per day than younger adolescents, even when marriage was controlled for in the older adolescents. The data suggest that older adolescents obtain more (and also possibly food of higher quality, i.e., meat, high carbohydrate content) meals and snacks. This is likely due to increased skill, knowledge, and motivation in building, and maintaining, a reputation as a hard worker and an able and good provider.

Young Aka adolescents are shifting from skill acquisition and low productivity in low skill tasks to high productivity and acquisition of higher skills. Kaplan et al. (2000) found this pattern among several forager groups. Generally, the increase in efficiency did not reach adult levels until age twenty or so, the age at which individuals began to establish their own households. Both sexes reached their peak rates of daily fruit acquisition in their mid to late teens. Increased skill and strength are required in the daily acquisition of more important food resources. Among the Hadza, like the Ache of Eastern Paraguay and the Venezuelan Hiwi, there is a switch from easier tasks, such as fruit collection, shallow tuber extraction, and baobab processing to honey extraction and hunting (for boys) in their mid to late teens (ibid.). Indeed, Kaplan et al. (2000) found that among the three societies, hunter-gatherer children produce little food compared to adults, and daily food acquisition rates rose dramatically in the late juvenile period, especially for males.

No children in any forager group in their study produced as many calories as they consumed until they reach their mid to late teens; by age fifteen, children in their forager sample had consumed 25 percent of their expected lifetime energy consumption but had acquired less than 5 percent of their lifetime energy acquisition (Kaplan et al. 2000, 161). This study suggests that older adolescents (i.e., over the age of fifteen) begin acquiring at a greater rate, but that younger adolescents are either provisioned or are surviving on less if not provisioned by others (ibid.). A study by Kramer (2005) argues that as humans develop, they are often "subsidized by others" not only during childhood but well into adolescence. As "consumers and producers," children and adolescents contribute more economically in childcare (allomaternal care) activities, regardless of mode of production. Their "low cost" help, although important in increasing parental reproductive success, is dependent on and varies according to the "costs and benefits specific to subsistence ecology and social organization" (2005, 224–234). Kaplan et al. suggest that juveniles and young adolescents have an "evolutionary dependency on adults to provide their daily energy needs" (2000, 161).

Step-parenting is part of the human landscape, especially in small-scale cultures, because of adult mortality and regular divorce. About one in four Aka marriages ends in divorce, and 42 percent of young adolescents (eleven to fifteen years old) and 71 percent of older adolescents (sixteen to twenty years old) live with step-parents or in single-parent households (Hewlett 1992). Similar demographic patterns exist among the Venezuelan horticultural Yanomamo

(Chagnon 1997) and we assume step-parenting is relatively common in other small-scale cultures where divorce and high adult death rates exist.

Finally, beliefs in the supernatural become pronounced in modern humans and are part of the human adaptive complex. Adolescence is a time in which learning about the supernatural world intensifies. This is due to the adolescents' enhanced cognitive abilities to hypothesize, generalize, and imagine, but it is also influenced dramatically by the physical changes of puberty and adolescents desire to learn more about the adult world. Puberty and menstrual blood, for instance, are associated with many taboos and are often entry points for learning more about the supernatural (Lewis 2008). Classic work by Margaret Mead (1928) in Manus showed that children generally have naturalistic explanations for illnesses whereas adults are much more likely to invoke supernatural causation. Beliefs in the supernatural are a characteristic feature of humanity, and it seems reasonable to hypothesize that these beliefs are integrated into young people's belief systems during adolescence.

Distinct Features of Hunter-Gatherer Adolescence

This section identifies and describes features of hunter-gatherer adolescence that are relatively unique by comparison to the lived experiences of adolescents in farming and herding societies.

Relatively High Sexual Freedom

Konner's (2005) hunter-gatherer childhood model indicates that forager adolescents have greater sexual freedom than non-forager adolescents. He finds cross-cultural support among Agta, !Kung, and Ache foragers as they value, or at least permit, premarital sexual freedom. A cross-cultural study by Textor (1967) shows sexual freedom declines with cultural complexity, and a more recent study by Korotayev and Kazankov (2003) demonstrates that premarital sexual freedom in mobile hunter-gatherers is higher than in other subsistence systems. Their study shows that it is high regardless of descent system or post-marital residence pattern, both of which are good predictors of premarital sexual freedom in farming and pastoral cultures.

Sexual freedom also exists among Aka adolescents. A favorite activity during adolescence is traveling to other camps to visit and "check out" the opposite sex. Camp dances are a good time and place to flirt and possibly get together for sex. A lot of energy and time goes into flirting and looking for a prospective mate: "At a dance, the young people flirt and get together for sex. A girl can have different boys on the same day and take turns" (young adolescent male). The visiting *bokola* (Aka male adolescent) regards the presence of an *ngondo* (Aka female adolescent) hut as signaling her readiness for sexual relations and, perhaps, marriage. If the young adolescents are interested in each other, the boy approaches the girl. If she is in agreement they may have a brief sexual liaison or begin a long-term relationship. If the two adolescents remain interested in each other, the *bokola* will stay in the girl's natal camp and perform brideservice.

Generally, as noted earlier, Aka females enter puberty at around thirteen years of age, with menarche at about fifteen to sixteen. Girls are non-fertile for several years and by age eighteen to twenty are generally married and able to sustain a pregnancy. Aka males tend to be nineteen to twenty-two or so when they first marry. Both sexes say that this stage of life is the "best" as they can now "look to marriage" and family. However, individual variation exists in the adolescents' decisions regarding when to move out of their parents' home, with whom to engage in sexual activity, and when to marry. Many adolescents mention beginning sexual activity early, although many wait until late adolescence. Some prefer multiple partners, but numerous, both male and female, do not. As with every aspect of their lives, there is great tolerance and respect for individual variation and choice.

The Aka do not value chastity highly. Whatever choices Aka adolescents may make regarding sex, such as when to engage in sexual relations, with whom, how many partners to have, and mate selection, are made without parental influence:

> The girls like to sleep in their own homes. When the breasts start coming out is when they know to build their hut and then the men start coming to ask for them . . . It's better if your parents like the boy that you like and want sex with, but we do not have to get our parents approval. (Young Aka adolescent girl)

Early sexual experimentation is not uncommon among hunter-gatherer groups. Jerome Lewis found among the Central African Mbendjele hunter-gatherers that "kids do plenty of sexual experimentation in a very free and uninhibited way" (personal communication, 2010). Early sexual activity is a way in which adolescents establish new corollary social networks and closer bonds with their peers, and find potential mates and future "helpers at the nest" prior to the adult responsibilities of significant subsistence contribution, parenting, and marriage.

Long-Distance Exploration

Most studies of forager mobility have focused on subsistence and residential movements, but here we focus on how long-distance mobility in forager adolescence impacts mating and the development of social-economic networks. Adolescents are transitioning from investment in somatic to reproductive interests and are particularly interested in finding a marriageable partner. A quantitative study of how far Aka individuals of various ages and both genders travel in their lifetime found that individuals were most likely to explore and travel long distances between ten and twenty-five years of age (Hewlett et al. 1986b). Aka travel for a variety of reasons—attend a funeral or dance, locate places to forage, and/or visit family. Traveling is important for maintaining and establishing social-economic networks and finding mates. Mating distances were calculated and a strong relationship was found between exploratory range and mating distance for males, but not females; how far an Aka male travels related to how far he had to go to find a mate.

A study comparing mating distances of foragers and farmers/herders found that foragers have significantly greater mating distances (MacDonald and Hewlett 1999). Forager population density is lower, so they have to travel farther to find a similar number of potential mates. Because foragers generally marry in late adolescence, this is the time of long-distance travel. It is important to point out that risk-taking exists during these exploratory treks. Travel is perilous, as any number of hazards can be encountered such as illness, strangers, or injuries. Travel and exploration are important in forager adolescent life as they can lead to marriage and the establishment of social-economic networks, both of which can enhance their fitness and survival.

Autonomy and Self-Directed Social Learning

Respect for autonomy is, as noted, a foundational schema among the Aka and most foragers. Forager autonomy and self-directed learning have been described for infants and children (Hewlett et al. 2011), and here we provide examples of its development and amplification during adolescence. Aka adolescents come and go as they please; travel to other camps; work or not work; begin sexual activity; build their huts; and receive scarifications for beauty—how, where, and when they want. In the Aka egalitarian society, autonomy, freedom of choice, and individual expression are vital, "sacred" ideologies fiercely upheld and valued. Young adolescents choose, for example, when to have their front teeth filed. As a young Aka girl related,

> If you are a young girl, you decide to point your teeth. Pointing the teeth is for beauty. If you do not get your teeth pointed, people will laugh at you and think you look like a chimpanzee so you get your teeth pointed to distinguish yourself. It is good to do this. If you are a man or woman searching for a wife or husband and you see someone who does not have pointed teeth, you say, 'You there, you are like a chimpanzee. You have big teeth like a chimpanzee! I do not want you.

Adolescents choose when to have their teeth pointed, but they are not, as the young Aka girl explained, simply choosing *when* to have this done; they are choosing to form a distinct social identity, different from the neighboring farmers, but similar to those immediately around them. Teeth-pointing is, as well, a way of establishing and signaling self-identity as a maturing, attractive, and available mate.

As with teeth pointing, travel, and other forms of autonomous decision making, knowledge acquisition is generally self-directed. Aka adolescents choose when and whom to follow, and this occurs within a context of continued close physical and emotional contact, an environment where trust and social-emotional security are pervasive. The social context of learning, whom the Aka are close to most of the time, and at what ages and how often they are around these "teachers" is important in understanding from *whom* learning occurs, the *way* in which self-directed learning occurs, and *what* Aka adolescents are learning. Prior to adolescence, Aka children learn through a variety of mechanisms (e.g., play, dancing, singing, exploration) cultural values, beliefs, and practices within specific and differing social and physical contexts (Hewlett et al. 2011). A good proportion of Aka social learning is early, rapid, and mostly vertical (meaning from parent to child) up to age four to five (Hewlett et al. 2011). As previously noted in the study by Kaplan, a great deal of social learning also occurs in adolescence (Bogin 2011). Emotional and physical closeness are such that parents continue to be key facilitators of cultural transmission. Adults other than parents also play important roles in adolescents' daily lives, providing the potential for both horizontal (friends and peers) and oblique (other adults) cultural transmission (Hewlett et al. 2011). Although they usually learn from their same-sex parent, as noted, knowledge acquisition is generally self-directed; and, with autonomy paramount, the adolescents choose which parent, or other knowledgeable person, to follow and to learn from: "These children need to have this knowledge and desire and they themselves decide when to learn . . . But the knowledge of each person is different, a person is not wrong in what they say and do" (Aka mother). As several adolescents told me: "My father taught me the work of women, to prepare food, and my mother taught me this too and how to hunt and kill the animal" (a young adolescent girl). "Father taught me how to care for babies, to soothe and feed them" (adolescent boy). These were not unusual cases, as learning, like earlier infant nursing and weaning, is initiated by the individual. During adolescence Aka males are learning complex rituals associated with hunting, mating, and childcare practices (see Takeuchi, this volume), whereas adolescent females learn complex subsistence, social and sexual skills, through a variety of mechanisms such as imitation, observation, and play (Hewlett et al. 2011; Hewlett 1986a).

The increasing range of adolescent social and sexual exploration, acquisition of complex subsistence skills, and increasing knowledge of the supernatural world are taking place at a distinct period of adolescent brain development, a time in which "abstract thought is possible" (Lewis 2008, 299). With some combination of these "biological changes in brain" and changes in socio-cultural contexts, "new cognitive capacities" arise (Nasir 2005; Tamnes et al. 2010). As a young adolescent Aka girl explained, "My parents did not teach me this when I was too little and did not have knowledge, but when I was older . . . I was given knowledge. This knowledge comes from both your mother and father, from grandparents to grandparents. It is passed down generation after generation."

Minimal, Nonobligatory, Responsibility for Subsistence or Baby Care

Konner's (2005) childhood model also indicated that middle childhood and adolescence were relatively "carefree" in that not much was expected or asked of them in terms of sibling care or subsistence contribution. By comparison, farmer and herder children, especially girls, are expected to be "helpers at the nest." Infant care is obligatory, as may well be other subsistence responsibilities, such as watching and managing livestock or working in the family garden or fields. This lack of responsibilities is found in the three other forager groups reviewed by Konner (2010). This does not mean that forager adolescents do not assist with childcare or subsistence. They help in a variety of ways, but their efforts are nonobligatory and generally self-motivated and directed. The exception is the Hadza whose children and adolescents provide a substantial percentage of their daily calories and are expected to help with infant care (Blurton-Jones et al. 1994). Among the Aka, sibling care (care given by siblings including juveniles and adolescents) in both matrilocal or patrilocal settings is less than other female caretakers combined (Meehan 2005, 74). Caretaking by Aka adolescent boys and girls exists, but it is infrequent.

Bahuchet's (1990, 38) quantitative study of Aka subsistence work by age found that adolescents provided 19 percent of the total work of in a camp; adult males contributed 35 percent, adult females 34 percent and elders 6 percent. Adults did most of the work to provision children, adolescents, and the elderly. Although adolescents take care of their siblings and make marked contributions to subsistence procurement, the important point is that their contribution is nonobligatory, and few or no social sanctions exist for refusal to contribute. As an older Aka woman explained, "When they (adolescents) are asked to get water or find the manioc, they refuse. They would rather do amusing things. They prefer to do what they want to do with their friends. When the parents ask, they do not do these things." This is in sharp contrast to their farming neighbors whose adolescents face physical punishment and social sanctions if they refuse to contribute to subsistence activities or sibling care.

Lack of Reliance on Specific Others for Subsistence and Health

Part of the human adaptive pattern is that adults provision their adolescents. Considerable debate exists in anthropology as to which allomaternal caregivers are particularly important for child survival—some say grandmothers (Hawkes 1998) and others say fathers (Hill et al. 1996). A study by Draper and Howell (2005) shows that no specific relative(s) had an impact on !Kung forager child growth. The first author replicated their study with the Aka but used more detailed health indicators (e.g., body mass index, mid-upper arm circumference measurement, body fat percentage, and skin fold thicknesses), and found the same—a full complement of biological relatives, or even specific kin such as grandmothers, had no overall bearing on the nutritional status and health of Aka adolescents. Both studies suggest forager ethos of giving and extensive sharing ensures that children and adolescents are fed and taken care of by many individuals rather than one or a few specific individuals (i.e., grandmother or father).

Physical and Emotional Intimacy with Parents and Other Adults

Unlike great apes, foragers do not have a dramatic break from mothers at adolescence. Aka adolescents grow up living in a physical and social world with intimate physical and emotional proximity to others to whom they are related and who know them from early infancy. Forager camps are small, living space is dense, and Aka are in near-constant physical contact and/ or visual and hearing range of one another. From birth onward, they are in nearly constant physical contact with others, being held quite regularly as two, three, and four years old (44 percent, 27 percent, and 8 percent of daylight hours) (Hewlett 2007; Hewlett et al. 2011). Older children, adolescents, and adults engaged in a wide range of activities, e.g., hunting, gathering, or working on farms, often situate themselves so they are physically close to one another. At dances or when singing, cooking, visiting, making baskets, they sit thigh to thigh or with their arms and legs intertwined.

By adolescence, foragers spent 25 percent of their time in adult–child proximity groups and 45 percent of their time in child-only proximity groups while in camp. They spend 60 percent of the day in adult social or work groups and 40 percent of day in child-only social and work groups while outside of camp (Boyette unpublished manuscript; Hewlett 1992). Continued close physical contact with parents and others in dense social context continues into the night hours, as forager children (never) and adolescents (rarely) sleep alone. Between the ages of eight and twelve, Aka children sleep with adults and others 85 percent of the time, and even by the age of eighteen, Aka adolescents are sleeping with adults or others (but not next to a sexually active family member of the opposite sex) 75 percent of the time (Hewlett 2007). As the beds are small, there is constant physical contact during the night. At the age of eleven or so (the timing is up to them), as noted, the boys and girls may decide to build their own huts. But it is not unusual for the adolescent, particularly on cold nights, to return to the small family bed of their parents or grandparents.

But it is not simply physical proximity that is important to Aka foragers. Emotional intimacy is significant as well. In a study the first author conducted on Aka foragers' and neighboring farmers' adolescent grief, it was found that Aka foragers placed an emphasis on the love and emotional bonds they had with others, which helped them work through their grief, whereas for farmer adolescents, it was the material items of the deceased they received that helped to assuage their feelings of grief (Hewlett 2005).

Physical closeness was a source of comfort in grief also, as mothers, fathers, or other kin held the young Aka as they grieved. A young adolescent boy, deeply grieved over the loss of his uncle, explained, "I loved him a lot and he went with me into the forest to hunt and walk . . . I cried a lot, and after the burial the people in camp listened to me and held me and after a while the sadness lessened. I understand that death is for all the world, and with death it is all finished." One young Aka girl sadly shared, "After the death, I was afraid for a long time. I did not eat well or sing and dance, and I cried for a long time, but then my mother held me and helped to find good food for me and amusing things to do, then the sadness diminished." For the Aka, it is within the intimate circle of family and friends that the adolescent finds comfort in the face of the finality of death and the sadness of their loss: "My family consoled me and happiness came again."

Aka adolescents are protected, held, slept with, valued, and continually surrounded by other children and adults in the intimate life of the camp while they are physically, socially, and cognitively developing. Physical and emotional proximity are "key" not only for physiological and emotional support in an environment of risk, where approximately half of all children die before the age of fifteen, but also for social learning and identity formation. This is an extension of the infant and childhood pattern but is unexpected from a Western developmental psychology perspective as generally it is thought adolescence is a time in which there is increasing identity separation from parents. This level of adolescent closeness and proximity to adults is not as common in farming or pastoral societies (Hewlett et al. 2011).

Female Initiation Ceremonies

Adolescent initiation ceremonies exist in forager and non-forager cultures in relatively similar frequencies (57 percent of forager and 55 percent of non-forager cultures in the SCCS), but foragers are much more likely to have public rituals for a girl's first menstruation than are non-foragers. Nine of eleven forager cultures and thirty-six of seventy-nine non-forager cultures with data in the SCCS have menstruation ceremonies (Fishers exact test, $p = .05$ [two-tailed]) (see also Barry and Schlegel 1980; Schlegel and Barry 1985). Why are rites of passage for girls particularly pronounced in hunting-gathering societies? Brown (1963) argues that menarche or puberty ceremonies are more likely to be found in societies with matrilocal or bilocal residence patterns, which are common to hunter-gatherers, because it is a way to mark the adolescent female's transition to adult status. By contrast, a young woman's transition to adult status in patrilocal societies is marked by her departure to her husband's household. The rites of passage, Brown suggests, help to aid the girl and her community in commemorating and adjusting to her new status and role as a reproductive adult member.

Paige and Paige tested a hypothesis somewhat similar to that of Brown and found that female menstrual ceremonies are more likely in societies with social structures that inhibit male-male alliances and strong fraternal interest groups (i.e., those with matrilocal residence or a "weak resources base" both of which are common among hunter-gatherers) in order to elicit social support for female initiates. Additionally, societies lacking a surplus of resources to support more elaborate ceremonies tend to have "simpler and less costly" menarche ceremonies (103).

For an egalitarian society such as the Aka, gender roles and tasks are fluid, and what differentiation does exist becomes pronounced in adolescence. As Turnbull (1961) describes of the Mbuti's *elima* and as Takeuchi describes in Chapter 7, girls are "presented with a dance ritual" when they reach menarche and young adolescent boys "on their first hunt receive medicine thought to possess magical properties from their fathers". Transitioning from childhood, adolescent males are taught specific hunting rituals, medicine, and techniques, and adolescent girls acquire gender-specific social-sexual knowledge. Once the young girl begins to menstruate, she is taught specific food taboos, and while she is "seeing" her monthly blood can no longer sleep in the same family bed with males that hunt (father or brothers), and in the past, touch hunting implements.

Key foundational schema are transmitted and framed around biological development, i.e., knowledge of menstruation as *ekila*, referring to "blood, taboo, a hunter's meal, animals power to harm and particular dangers to human reproduction, production health and sanity" (Lewis 2008, 299). Taboos associated with *ekila* "begin to suggest explanations for key areas of cultural practice . . . defin[ing] reproductive potential, productive activities . . . moral and personal qualities . . . shared so that group members experience good health, unproblematic childbirth and child rearing and successful hunting and gathering . . . the basic components of a good life" (ibid.). Maturing into adults, adolescents develop the cognitive ability to learn and understand "key areas of cultural knowledge, cosmological, gender and political ideology" (ibid.).

Rite of passage ceremonies prepare the way for entry into new roles, identities and knowledge as maturing individuals. The Aka, with an egalitarian ethos as part of their foundational schema, practice prestige avoidance and discourage drawing attention to particular persons, therefore rite of passage ceremonies are of a short duration and without much public display or fanfare.

Lack of Adolescent Identity Crises

Adolescent identity development as described by Erikson (1968) and Marcia (1966; 1980) is a time of conflict, crisis, doubt, confusion, insecurity, and questioning of self. These issues are rare or do not exist as characteristic features of adolescence among the Aka and other foragers (Condon 1987).

This may also be true in some farming and pastoral cultures, but due to the foundational schema and habitus described previously, these patterns are particularly less likely with foragers. There is great predictability in social relations, generally everyone is known in the community. There is a sense of belonging, trust, acceptance of individual choices, autonomy, temperaments, and personalities. Caregiving patterns throughout childhood and adolescence are consistent, indulgent, and supportive. Adults give and provide emotional, social, and economic support but they seldom, if ever, direct or intervene in the choices and lives of their adolescents. Adult contingencies, common in the West, such as "once you show me you can take on xxx responsibilities, you can have more freedom to stay out later," do not exist. The Aka and other foragers also have an immediate return mode of thought, which means concerns about where one is going, what one will do later in life, or who one will be are minimal to nonexistent among the Aka. Some may think that foragers have no "identity crisis" because they have few alternative choices available to them. However, there are other ways of being and opportunities available and known to them as they live in close proximity to farming populations and visitors from the capital city and foreign visitors as well (NGO's, missionaries, anthropologists) are frequently observed.

For the Aka, the intimate relations experienced in infancy continue into adolescence and adulthood. Through these interactions with parents and others in camp, the child learns how to survive and flourish in the tropical environment, what it means to be Aka, and what is expected of them in later life. While adolescents are traveling to different camps, working on villager farms, meeting strangers, establishing social networks independent of their parents, it is within the embrace and intimacy of the extended family. This contributes to the development of autonomy and the integration of social and personal identity. Adolescence for many, in Western psychology, is a time in which the child begins to assert his or her identity as a unique individual, but for the Aka, this process of individuation and autonomy, in a sense, began in infancy. As adolescents, the Aka do not express desires to separate from parents, nor do they have ambivalent feelings about who they once were, who they are and who they can become.

Parent–child conflict, occurring when the "wants and desires of the maturing individual no longer coincide with the expectations of the parent" (Condon 1987, 15), seldom occurs for Aka adolescents. The "wants and desires" of both the parent and the adolescent are somewhat similar—to continue and expand family bonds and the intimate relations built around the core values of a sharing and trust. All sixty-five adolescents interviewed in a study by the first author said that the most important people in their lives were parents or other family members. Adolescents also listed parents as those to whom they turned for comfort and advice, who they spent most of the day with, and to whom they felt "closest". Peers were seldom listed as the persons to whom they felt closest or turned to for comfort. This may have to do with the fact that their peer groups are small, especially in the forest camps, but in some large Aka camps where peer groups were larger, the answers were the same. Although it is often assumed that the relationship between the adolescent and parent changes in the adolescent's bid for identity and autonomy, creating conflict, these expressions of individuality, such as acting out, rebellion, and separation from parents via conflict, are rare or do not exist among the Aka. Condon (1987) describes the same among Inuit foragers.

It may be in part that the close relations are due to hunting and gathering as an activity, a social event among friends and family, in which children, adolescents, mothers, and fathers all participate together. But hunting and gathering among the Aka is also a social activity with the forest itself. The trust and confidence that they feel toward the forest, (demonstrated by the freedom and sense of security in which they travel through the environment) is similar to the confidence and intimacy they feel within the family. Human-to-human relations and human-to-nature relations are similar; there is not a dichotomy between the two (Hewlett et al. 2000). The bonds that adolescents feel toward their parents are based upon an ideology of intimacy, and sharing, ideologies that are a reflection of the bond the Aka feel toward the forest. The Aka trust in the future as they trust in forest; the future will take care of itself. The forest is an integral part of their lives, patterning behavior and ideology, and Aka adolescent social and self-identity.

It is in some ways remarkable that social-emotional security, high self-esteem, and trust in what tomorrow will bring, appear common in spite of high mortality rates in which 45 percent of Aka children die before reaching the age of fifteen (Hewlett 1992). This pattern would tend to promote low parental investment, (see Ellis Chapter 3, this volume), fear, and insecurity in the future, but Aka adolescents, surrounded by a social-emotional environment of trust, intimacy, and care, are confident, autonomous, secure individuals.

Cultural Energy, Creativity, and Play

In the context of increased cognitive abilities, reputation building, lack of subsistence obligations, substantial leisure time, forager values and social structures, and enhanced physical health, forager adolescents often take the lead in energizing the community. Forager communities are relatively small and forager subsistence is demanding. Aka adolescents are often the ones to get dances and singing going, interact vigorously with infants, and "play" on the net hunt. Foragers value autonomy, creativity, and play. While children play to learn, Aka adolescents "play" to practice and learn adult economic, social, sexual skills, to improve the success of first reproduction (Bogin 2011). The "play" continuing into adolescence often takes the form of dancing in which adolescents express ingenuity and invention, as well as learn about gender roles and sexuality. "Playful" polyphonic singing and other forms of music emphasize and transmit values of intimacy, autonomy, innovation, and creativity. A combination of these features demonstrates their interest and abilities in creativity and innovation. This is probably the most speculative of the forager characteristics, but we include it here as this has impressed us for years, many aspects of forager life amplify these features, and our informal observations of farmers and pastoralists suggest they are less pronounced in these groups although we have been unable to quantify it.

DISCUSSION AND CONCLUSION

Generalization about forager adolescence can be understood in the context the non-human primate literature, distinctive features of human evolution, and foundational schema common to foragers. Table 4.2 summarizes the features of hunter-gatherer adolescence described above. Items 1–5 are part of our non-human primate heritage and exist in many cultures, 6–11 are part of the human adaptive complex and are also common to most cultures, and items 12–20 are relatively unique to hunter-gatherers due to their foundational schema and culturally constructed niche.

The foundational schema of extensive sharing plays a role as forager adolescents are provided for by many individuals; their health and development is not impacted by a specific person, and the dramatic shift from mothers to others that occurs among higher primates does not occur with foragers or in other societies. Mothers continue to remain nearby and help provision Aka adolescents even after marriage. Consistent with the forager values of egalitarianism and respect for autonomy, adolescents have great freedom and self-direction. Adults do not have structural authority over adolescents as they do in farming and herding or other small-scale cultures.

Some features of forager adolescence are simply a matter of demography—i.e., their culturally constructed niche. Camps have twenty-five to thirty-five individuals and population densities are low. This means there may be three to four other adolescents in a camp, with one or two of the same gender. It is not surprising, therefore, that in early adolescence they develop close friendships with one or two other individuals of the same gender, that most social or "play" groups consist of children and adolescents of various ages, and that adults remain proximal. Foragers also value close physical and emotional proximity to others, they learn this in infancy and childhood, and it persists into adolescence. Adolescents continue to co-sleep with their parents and other adults (e.g., grandparents). Also, because population densities are low adolescents have to travel further to meet, and choose from, a reasonable number of alternative mates.

Mixed support exists for Bogin's hypothesis regarding the function of human adolescence. Forager adolescents do not have many obligations, have

Table 4.2 Summary of Hunter-Gatherer Adolescence

Characteristic features that humans share with other higher primates:

1. Reputation building and increased risk taking, especially among males

2. Increase in sexual activity, beginning shortly after puberty

3. Increase in time spent around sexually active members of the opposite sex

4. Increase in time with members of the same sex to develop alliances and networks

5. Increase in time learning complex social and subsistence skills

Characteristic features that emerged as part of the human adaptive complex:

6. Caregiving, particularly by adolescent females, of infants and young children

7. Sexual division of labor in which adolescent males and females learn different complex tasks

8. Moderate to intensive food and care provisioning by adults

9. Marriage (relatively stable pair bonding) and birth of first child often by late adolescence (especially for females)

10. Adolescents often live with stepparents

11. Adolescents acquire in-depth understanding of supernatural beliefs

Characteristic features relatively unique to hunter-gatherers due to their foundational schema and culturally constructed niche:

12. Relatively high sexual freedom

13. Long distance exploration

14. Autonomy and self-directed social learning

15. Minimal, nonobligatory, responsibility for subsistence or baby care

16. Physical and emotional intimacy with parents and other adults

17. Lack of reliance on specific others for subsistence and health

18. Female initiation ceremonies are common

19. Lack of adolescent identity crises

20. Cultural energy, creativity, and play

considerable free time, and experience increases in weight and BMI in late adolescence (larger body size, increasing skill in subsistence activities, consume more) consistent with hypotheses that reserve capacity building occurs. On the other hand, forager adolescents do not appear to provide much allomaternal care, or at least not that much more than middle-aged foragers. By comparison to farmers, forager adolescents, especially females, provide substantially less care of infants and young children (Hewlett et al. 2011).

How do forager data inform issues regarding U.S. adolescents? The Inuit forager versus U.S. comparison by Condon (1987) is excellent and applicable to the data in this chapter. Inuit, Aka, and other forager adolescents have a high degree of autonomy, lack of parental interference, and go and do as they please. Everyone knows everyone, strangers are few and far between, adolescents have access to any resources they can find, and do not experience an identity crisis as described earlier. Condon points out that by comparison, an adolescent's life in the urban industrialized West is characterized by movement throughout the day to substantially different social-emotional settings (e.g., school, sports events, stores, friends' houses); adolescents are often surrounded by complete strangers, or people he/she did not grow up with or know very well; low physical and emotional proximity to others; unequal access to resources; and, pronounced parental control and authority. Social hierarchy and power are important because the child learns from an early age that people are judged better or worse than others, that inequality is part of daily life. Grades in school are a classic example, but teacher–student, parent–child, supervisor–worker are other examples of daily experiences with hierarchy. By comparison, foragers have cultural mechanisms that reinforce extensive sharing and equality, that it is important to respect the autonomy and worth of each person. As Condon points out, it is not surprising that U.S. adolescents, in a world of strangers and lack of power and autonomy, are more likely to act out, rebel, and engage in risky behaviors as they try to assert individual identity (1987).

Konner argues that departure from the hunter-gathering patterns of infant and childcare may "constitute a discordance and . . . have psychological and biological consequences that merit further study" (2005, 64). This chapter identifies features unique to forager adolescence, several of which are inconsistent with characteristic features of adolescents in other small-scale and urban-industrial cultures. We are not in a position to identify psychological and biological consequences of the discordance, but agree with Konner that future research should evaluate the implications.

University libraries contain a plethora books about the nature of adolescence in Western urban industrial cultures while only a handful of books exist on hunter-gatherer adolescence. While research on hunter-gatherer children does takes place, it is generally focused on babies and young children (Hewlett and Lamb 2005). Our hope is that this chapter will encourage others to test our characterizations, determine whether the discordance between forager and urban industrial adolescence is important or not, and provide more ethnographic details of hunter-gatherer adolescence, a way of life that characterized most of modern human history.

REFERENCES

Bahuchet, S. "Food Sharing among the Pygmies of Central Africa," *African Study Monographs* 11 (1990): 27–53.

Barry, H. III and Schlegel, A. (eds.).1980. *Cross-Cultural Samples and Codes.* Pittsburgh: University of Pittsburgh Press.

Blurton-Jones, N., Hawkes, K., and Draper, P. 1994. Differences between Hadza and !Kung children's work: Original affluence or practical reason? in *Key*

Issues in Hunter Gatherer Research, edited by E.S. Burch. Oxford: Berg, pp. 189–215.

Boehm, C. 2001. Hierarchy in the Forest. Cambridge, MA: Harvard University Press.

Bogin, B. "Childhood, Adolescence, and Longevity: A Multilevel Model of the Evolution of Reserve Capacity in Human Life History," American Journal of Human Biology 21 (2009): 567–577.

Bourdieu, P. 1977 Outline of a theory of practice. Cambridge, UK: Cambridge University Press.

Boyette, A. (unpublished manuscript). "Middle Childhood among Aka Forest Foragers of the Central African Republic: A Comparative Perspective".

Brown, J.K. "A Cross-Cultural Study of Female Initiation Rites," American Anthropologist 65 (1963): 837–853.

Burbank, V.K. "Aboriginal Adolescence: Maidenhood in an Australian Aboriginal Community," Ethos 15 no. 2 (1988): 226–234.

Chagnon, N.A. 1997. Yanomamö. New York: Harcourt Brace.

Condon, R. 1987. Inuit Youth. New Brunswick, NJ: Rutgers University Press.

Draper, P. and Howell, N. 2005. "The growth and kinship resources of !Kung children," in *Hunter-Gather Childhoods*, edited by B. S. Hewlett and M. Lamb. New York: Aldine, pp. 262–281.

Erikson, E.H. 1968. Identity: Youth and Crisis. New York: Norton.

Fouts, Hillary, B. S. Hewlett and M. Lamb. 2000. "Weaning and the Nature of Early Childhood Interaction Among Bofi Foragers in Central Africa," Human Nature 12(1) (2000): 27–46.

Galdikas, M.M.F. 1996. "Social and reproductive behavior of wild adolescent female orangutans," in *The Neglected Ape*, edited by B.M.F. Galdikas, R.D. Nadler, N. Rosen, and L.K. Sheeran. New York: Springer, pp.163–182.

Hawkes, K. "Grandmothering, Menopause and the Evolution of Human Life Histories," Proceeds of the National Academy of Sciences USA 95 (1998): 1336–1339.

Hewlett, B.L. 2005. Vulnerable lives: "Death, loss and grief among Aka and Ngandu adolescents of the Central African Republic," in *Culture and Ecology of Hunter-Gatherer Children*, edited by B.S. Hewlett and M.E. Lamb. New York: Aldine, pp.322–342.

Hewlett, B.S. and A.H. Boyette. In press. "Play in hunter-gatherers," in *Evolution, Early Experience and Human Development: From Research to Practice and Policy*, edited by Narvaez, D., Panksepp, J., Schore, A., and Gleason, T. NY: Oxford University Press.

Hewlett, B.S., Fouts, H., Boyette, A., and Hewlett, B.L. "Social Learning among Congo Basin Hunter-Gatherers," Philosophical Transactions Royal Society no. 366 (2011): 1168–1178.

Hewlett, B.S. 2007. "Why Sleep Alone? An Integrated Evolutionary Approach to Intracultural and Intercultural Variability in Aka, Ngandu, and Euro-American Co-sleeping." Paper presented at the annual meeting of the Society for Cross-Cultural Research, San Antonio, TX.

Hewlett, B.S., Lamb, M., Leyendecker, B., and Scholmerick, A. "Internal Working Models, Trust, and Sharing among Foragers," Current Anthropology 41 (2000): 287–297.

MacDonald, D.H. and Hewlett, B.S. "Reproductive interests and forager mobility," Current Anthropology, 40 (1999): 501–523.

Hewlett, B.S., Lamb, M., Shannon, D. Leyendecker, B., and Scholmerick, A."Culture and early infancy among central African foragers and farmers," Developmental Psychology 34 (1998): 653–651.

Hewlett, B.S. 1992. Intimate Fathers: The Nature and Context of Aka Pygmy Paternal Infant Care. Ann Arbor: University of Michigan Press.

Hewlett, B.S. and Cavalli-Sforza, L.L. "Cultural Transmission among Aka Pygmies," American Anthropologist 88 (1986a): 922–934.
Hewlett, Barry S., van de Koppel, Jan. M.H., and Maria van de Koppel. 1986b."Causes of Death Among Aka Pygmies of the Central African Republic", in *African Pygmies*, edited by Luigi L. Cavalli Sforza. New York: Academic Press, pp. 45–63.
Hill, K. and Hurtado, A.M. 1996. Ache Life History: The Ecology and Demography of a Foraging People. Hawthorne, NY: de Gruyter.
Kaplan, H., Hill, K., Lancaster, J., and Hurtado, M.A. "Evolutionary Anthropology: Issues, News, and Reviews," 9, no. 4 (2000): 156–185.
Kelly, R. L. 2007. Foraging Spectrum. Clinton Corners, New York: Percheron Press.
Konner, M. 2010. The evolution of childhood: relationships, emotion, mind. Cambridge, MA: Harvard University Press.
———. 2005. Hunter gatherer infancy and childhood: The !Kung and others, in *Culture and Ecology of Hunter-Gatherer Children*, edited by B.S. Hewlett and M.E. Lamb. New York: Aldine, pp. 19–64.
Korotayev, A.V. and Kazankov, A.A "Factors of Sexual Freedom among Foragers," Cross-Cultural Perspective Cross-Cultural Research 37 (2003): 29–61.
Kramer, K.L. "Children's Help and the Pace of Reproduction: Cooperative Breeding in Humans," Evolutionary Anthropology 14 (2005): 224–237.
Lee, R.B. and R. Daly. Eds. 2004. The Cambridge encyclopedia of hunters and gatherers. Cambridge. Cambridge University Press.
Lewis, J. "Ekila: Blood, Bodies and Egalitarian Societies," Journal of the Royal Anthropological Institute 14 (2008): 297–315.
MacDonald, D. and Hewlett, B.S. "Reproductive Interests and Forager Mobility," Current Anthropology 40 (1999): 4.
Marcia, J.E. "Development and validation of ego identity status," Journal of Personality and Social Psychology 3 (1966):551–558.
Marcia, J.E. 1980. "Identity in adolescence," in *Handbook of Adolescent Psychology*, edited by Adelson. New York, NY: Wiley, pp. 159–187.
Markstrom, C. 2008. Empowerment of North American Indian Girls—Ritual Expressions at Puberty. Lincoln: University of Nebraska Press.
Mead, M. 1928. Coming of Age in Samoa: A Psychological Study of Primitive Youth for Western Civilization. New York: William Morrow. .
Meehan, C. "Multiple Caregiving and Its Effects on Maternal Behavior among the Aka Foragers and Ngandu Farmers of Central African Republic," PhD diss., Washington State University, 2005.
———. "Allomaternal Investment and Relational Uncertainty among Ngandu Farmers of the Central African Republic," Human Nature 19 (2008): 211–226.
Nasir, N. "Problem Solving in Technology Rich Contexts: Mathematics Sense Making in Out-of-School Environments," Journal of Mathematical Behavior 24 (2005): 275–286.
Paige, K., and J. Paige. 1982. The Politics of Reproductive Rituals. Berkeley, CA: University of California Press.
Pusey, A. "Behavioral Changes at Adolescence in Chimpanzees," Behaviour (1990): 115–121.
Schlegel, A. and Barry, H. III.1991. Adolescence. An Anthropological Inquiry. New York: The Free Press.
———.1985. Adolescent Initiation Ceremonies: a Cross-Cultural Code. World Cultures 1(2), files STDS21.COD.STDS21.DAT.
Setchell, J.M. "Behavioral Development in Male Mandrills (Mandrillus Sphinx): Puberty to Adulthood," Behavior 140 (2003): 1053–1089.

Tamnes, C.K., Ostby, Y., Fjell A.M., Westlye, L.T., Due-Tonnessen, P., and Wal-hovd, K.B. "Brain Maturation in Adolescence and Young Adulthood: Regional Age-Related Changes in Cortical Thickness and White Matter Volume and Microstructure," Cerebral Cortex 20 (2010): 534–548.

Textor, R.B. 1967. A Cross Cultural Summary. New Haven, CT: HRAF Press.

Turnbull, C.M. 1961. The Forest People. New York: Simon and Schuster.

———. 1982. "The ritualization of potential conflict between the sexes among the Mbuti," in *Politics and History in Band Societies*, edited by E. Leacock and R. Lee. Cambridge: Cambridge University Press, pp. 133–156.

Walters, J.R. 1987. "Transition to adulthood," in *Primate Societies*, edited by B.B. Smuts, D.L. Cheney, R.M. Seyfarth, R.W. Wrangham and T.T. Struhsaker. Chicago: University of Chicago Press, pp. 358–369.

Watts, D.P. and Pusey, A.E. 2002. "Behavior of juvenile and adolescent great apes," in *Juvenile Primates: Life History, Development, and Behavior*, edited by M.E. Pereira and L.A. Fairbanks. Chicago: University of Chicago Press, pp.303–314.

Woodburn, James. "Egalitarian Societies," Man 17 (1982): 431–51.

Part II

Culture and Development
Ritual, Risk, and Identity

5 Identity Development, Crises, and Continuity

Death-Defying Leaps in the Lives of Indigenous and Nonindigenous Youth

Michael J. Chandler and William L. Dunlop

AN AGENDA

This chapter is meant to say something instructive about the vexing identity problems rumored to plague so many of the world's Indigenous youth. In truth, surprisingly little hard evidence is available about such matters— a shortfall owed to the fact that, however undertheorized our collective understanding of identity formation writ large, less still is known about the identity development of Indigenous persons. Handicapped by the proverbial insolvability of equations with two unknowns, the plan here will be to proceed a step at a time by first attempting to examine some of what remains to be understood about what is thought to be common (dare one say "universal"?) to the generic course of adolescent identity development; all before going on to explore why being simultaneously young and Indigenous might constitute a kind of double jeopardy.

IDENTITY DEVELOPMENT IN THE LARGE

If there existed a high-altitude Google map laying out the presumed course of "ordinary" identity development, it would likely show an isolated archipelago of age-graded steps or stages; a train of events beginning with something hopelessly diffuse and ending with some form of "identity achievement." Following Erikson (1959, 1968) and Marcia (1966, 1980)— and more or less everyone has more or less followed Erikson and Marcia in such matters—the warp and woof of this imagined problem space consists of intersecting strands of so-called "crisis" and "commitment." Stripped to its threadbare essentials, such a minimalist fabrication comes down to a simple two-by-two matrix (see Figure 5.1) in which the imagined rows separate those who have and have not experienced any sort of identity crises, whereas the proposed columns mark off those who, crisis or no, have or have not gone on to make serious life commitments.

Beginning in the upper-left-hand corner of this imagined topologic space is a sort of shoe box meant to contain all of those who have neither

	No-Commitment	Commitment
No-Crisis	Identity Diffusion	Identity Foreclosure
Crisis	Identity Moratorium	Identity Achievement

Figure 5.1   The Identity Statuses Paradigm.

experienced an identity crisis nor forged any lasting life commitments, often, but not always because they are still too young to have legitimately done so. Call all such persons "identity diffused." Shifting to the right, one encounters a second cell meant to capture all of those who have made important life commitments, but who have, as yet, experienced no identity crises. Persons said to occupy this cell have traditionally been labeled "foreclosed," all in an effort to signal the premature nature of their having plumped for some, often traditional, even dogmatic, form of commitment without having properly tested such possibilities in the fires of personal crisis. Dropping down a row, and beginning again on the left, is a cell labeled "moratorium"—here meant to mark a place for those who, while already suffering some full-blown identity crisis, nevertheless continue to prefer the purgatory of suspended judgment for the reason that all commitments continue to be seen as perpetually premature. Finally, the lower-right-hand side of the figure is reserved for those lucky individuals that have weathered an identity crisis, and who, perhaps strengthened by it, have somehow been able to make important life commitments—individuals labeled here as "identity achieved."

"What a wonderful arrangement," you (along with a great many others who have come before) are apt to say—"what a helpful way of sorting out identity sheep from identity goats." You would be in good company in holding to such sentiments. Who can't remember a time when his or her own identity was at best diffused, and, if not, we certainly know others who are exactly like that. Most also count themselves equally familiar with those foreclosed persons who have "escaped from freedom" (Fromm 1941) by having leaped, unreflectively, into the arms of whatever waiting orthodoxy happened to be closest to hand, or, who, lost in the purgatory of moratorium, still can't make up their minds as to what they want to grow up to be. Finally, we all stand in awe of those who, despite adversity, seem to have achieved some working understanding of exactly who they are. "What a wonderful typology," we all say again, perhaps choosing to make a career out of saying it over and over again.

Although all of this may well be as good as it gets, there is, nevertheless, a rub—perhaps several rubs. Although such standard accounts include many of the more familiar and commonly told stories about young persons, similar stories could be and are similarly told about persons of almost any age. There are, for example, aging others, still diffused after all of these years, just as there are those that go to their deathbeds promoting the same take-no-prisoners moratorium rhetoric; claims first heard in their adolescent years. Perpetually foreclosed individuals are similarly a dime a dozen, and what are we to make of all of those lapsed identity achievers who, after a failed marriage or promising career, sadly, find themselves (against definitional constraints) back in some "earlier" diffused or moratorium state?

In short, although identity status accounts may have a certain descriptive ring of truth, it seems not to be a developmental truth. Nor are these statuses evidently ordered or sequenced in any theory-driven ways. There seems to be no reason, for example, why one could not leap directly from a diffused to an identity achieved status. Do young people sometimes shuttlecock back and forth between being in a moratorium period one day and foreclosed the next (it would seem that they regularly do), and how might "identity status theorists" explain away such excluded possibilities (cf. Cote and Levine 1988)? Was one's identity truly achieved if, after overcoming earlier crises and building commitments at every turn, a once seemingly perfect world manages to unravel, forcing a return to "go"? No one knows, everyone guesses, and identity status researchers seem reduced to endless *ad hoc* revisions and repeated hand-wringing.

Perhaps all of this may be ruled a bit too harsh. To give them their due, "identity status models" were always meant to be descriptive, and they were never really intended to explain, to be about process, or to justify when and why an individual might migrate from one status to another. Rather, most identity status theorists have seemed content to leave such matters to circumstance and the caprice of other people's demands for commitment. Still, it seems unlikely to have escaped the attention of serious identity status scholars that sequentiality and development appear to have gone missing, and that what comes next has been left to the vagaries of an environing world.

Among those of us who remain persuaded that there is more than coincidence at work in the fact that identity crises seemingly do pile up in the adolescent years, theories that leave all of these developmental matters to chance will hardly do. Similarly, promising opportunities to fall victim to one or another sort of identity crisis seem everywhere thick on the ground, but are often accorded little attention by most preadolescents, who fail to see in such circumstances the occasion for radical identity change. And how does all of this developing reputedly get started? Why is one identity status later abandoned in favor of some other, and why are these separate statuses imagined to be ordered in the ways that they are? When such questions of origins, or mechanisms, or sequencing have been raised (e.g., Kroger 2003; van Hoof 1999), responsibilities are usually laid at the door of some presumptively poisonous admixture of risk factors involving the supposed trials of puberty, and the imagined tribulations of mounting adult-like obligations. None of this seems nearly good enough.

Perhaps, more important still—more important than any "one-off" question about matters of origins, or mechanisms, or sequencing—is how such descriptive categories are imagined to be related to everything else that is broadly thought to be going on in the usual course of child and adolescent development. How, for example, is a young person's shifting identity status related to other equally foundational matters having to do with their social-emotional-cognitive and epistemic development? With rare but pointed exceptions (e.g., Adams, Ryan, and Keating 2000; Berzonsky 1990; Podd 1972; Rowe and Marcia 1980; Slugoski, Marcia, and Koopman 1984) such questions are seldom raised and almost never satisfactorily answered. Rather, the several identity status models that dominate the contemporary literature (e.g., Marcia 1980; Archer and Waterman 1990) have failed to properly locate the identity formation process within some broader account of the general course of adolescent development. This, we think, is a problem that needs fixing.

In light of these concerns, if we are to go on supposing the adolescent years to be some sort of especially salient moment in the course of identity development, and if Indigenous youth (or at least Indigenous youth of a particular stripe) are to continue to be understood as having more than their fair share of difficulties with such matters, then new and extended reasons for imagining why this may be so—reasons that better dovetail with what is otherwise known about the adolescent years—are obviously required. Consequently, in the space allowed for here, we will be at pains to do just that—to better situate the descriptive insights afforded by the identity status literature within a broader developmental framework. What is needed, then, we mean to argue, is not some after-the-fact tinkering, but, rather, some more radical, root-and-branch overhaul that works to preserve the descriptive richness of existing identity status models, while better situating their insights with the context of what is otherwise known about the usual course of adolescent development. Attempting something like this is what we had in mind for the paragraphs to immediately follow.

If, as just alleged, standard-issue versions of identity status theory fall dangerously short because they are neither sufficiently developmental nor properly respectful of what else is otherwise known to be going on during the adolescent years, then what clearly seems needed is some way of revisioning the course of identity development in a manner that more closely aligns with the main axes of what developmentalists usually study. A promising way to begin doing just that, we will argue, is to abandon as unhelpful any "objectivistic" account that portrays identity crises as somehow being directly brought on by haphazard turns of events in the environing world, and substitute the derivative notion of commitment for an alternative view that instead assigns responsibility for much of the usual turmoil of adolescence to a gradual awakening to the inevitability of representational diversity, and the consequent emergence of nascent skeptical doubt.

The first of these matters—the one that relocates crises in the eyes of the beholders—should not prove particularly controversial and only requires taking with utter seriousness the commonplace, two-for-a-penny idea that meaning-making is an ineluctably constructivist enterprise. On this familiar reading, the stuff of potential crises is always and everywhere thick on the ground, easily available, but only to those whose conceptual machinery is at least as structurally complex as are the issues out of which crises can be manufactured (Chandler, Boyes, and Ball 1990). Although such constructivist prospects have not been entirely overlooked by identity status theorists (e.g., Berzonsky 2004; Rowe and Marcia 1980), they have, at the very least, been seriously underutilized as a way of better understanding why it is, for adolescents, but not still younger persons, that identity crises appear to be the order of the day.

The second suggestion, the prospect of substituting doubt for commitment as the primary lever moving identity crises to adolescent center stage, is considerably less "old shoe," and successfully marketing this idea will require more in the way of convincing. Accomplishing this will hinge upon rehearsing some of what is known about so-called "representational diversity" and what will be drawn out here as the distinction between "retail" and "wholesale" doubt.

REPRESENTATIONAL DIVERSITY REDUX

To see better just how far identity status theory has drifted from the main lines of developmental study, it will prove useful to say something telegraphic, not about the entire remainder of cognitive developmental, but, more modestly, about that narrower corner of this larger enterprise that has to do with young people's changing thoughts about the possible meanings of truth and certainty. Because of its special pertinence to what might count as an identity crisis, and why youthful commitments are so illusive, we will focus attention here on adolescent's developing beliefs about belief.

So-Called "Theories of Mind"

For roughly the same quarter-century that identity status theorists have been soldiering away in an effort to understand identity crises better, more mainstream developmental theorists have been similarly hard at work elsewhere, trying (among much else) to pinpoint when and how young people first come to appreciate the representational nature of their own and others' experience. As such, the entire "theories of mind" edifice that has been thrown up since the early 1980s, along with the literatures on childhood egocentrism and social role-taking that preceded it, has been largely given over to working out the developmental pathways by means of which young persons approach some increasingly more mature understanding of the so-called "other minds problem" (Chandler 2001), or achieve some grip upon what is imagined to be similar and different about their own and others' understanding of mental life. Although such matters are not fully coextensive with identity development in any classic sense, they are certainly foundational to any understanding of the conflicts and crises thought to dominate the identity formation process.

There is not much in the way of general agreement as to when young persons first become alert to the possibility of legitimate disputes about matters of interpretation. By certain contemporary accounting strategies, the earliest turns of this epistemic wheel are thought to happen at a surprisingly young age. Infants in arms, for example, are thought to appreciate that looking and knowing are deeply related (Hyun-joo and Baillargeon 2008), and that those whose access to information has been truncated end up representing the world differently than those with a broader vision (Luo and Baillargeon 2007). Similarly, much of the landslide of research concerned with preschool children's emerging appreciation of the possibility of counterfactuals, or "false beliefs," turns upon a related set of distinctions, and contributors to this literature worry much over the threshold question of when children can be reliably shown to first appreciate that ignorance prompts misguided beliefs about the world (e.g., Onishi and Baillargeon 2005; Surian, Caldi, and Sperber 2007).

Interpretive Theories of Mind

Largely driven by the injudicious conclusion that simple false belief understanding is the same thing as holding to an "interpretive" theory of mind (Chandler and Lalonde 1996), many mainstream contributors to the theories of mind literature have been quick to argue that epistemic development begins and ends during the same preschool period; consequently, anyone substantially older than four is simply theoretically uninteresting. Although such "early onset" accounts now appear to be in at least partial eclipse, they do continue to be promulgated in the treacle-filled world of meta-analyses (e.g., Wellman, Cross, and Watson 2001) and in classroom textbooks. Elsewhere, not so much.

However precipitous the recent decline in the market value of various theories of mind stocks, at least some of these falling fortunes are likely owed to a reflexive sense of incredulity on the part of the developmental community, a kind of collective gag reflex brought on by having been repeatedly told that the whole course of epistemic development takes place during a single watershed moment in the lives of children still in short pants. Few, it would seem, not otherwise billeted within that closed compound exclusively owned and operated by so-called "theory theorists," seem to have been fully converted to such profoundly antidevelopmental views.

Over and above whatever natural aversions may exist toward developmental stories that end before middle childhood, there has also emerged a growing empirical literature given over to promoting the idea that simple false belief understanding is hardly the be all and end all of epistemic life. Pillow (1991), Carpendale and Chandler (1996), and Chandler and Lalonde (1996), among others, have, for example, made a strong case that it is not until the middle school years and beyond that young persons ordinarily gain their first understanding that personal biases and vantage point regularly intrude upon our attempts to fairly interpret what might be going on. Notwithstanding the fact that there is much to suspect about some of the more extravagant claims to emerge from the theory of mind enterprise, it is, nevertheless, also true that the well-oiled research methodologies and the carefully documented observations brought forward by the many contributors to this literature leave little room for doubt that the developmental course by means of which young persons approach a mature understanding of their own and others mental lives begins much earlier and continues much longer than many previously assumed.

What seems needed, then, as a further corrective to any holdout views to the effect that epistemic development is merely a preschool project, or the prevue of the middle-school years, is still other evidence-based accounts of what ordinarily happens next. As it turns out, seemingly unbeknownst to mainstream theory theorists, there already exists other and later-arriving parts of this unfinished story that are well supplied by the extensive research literature dealing with epistemic development during the collage years—work to which we now mean to briefly turn.

Post-Formal Reasoning and the House that William Perry Built

In ways reminiscent of theory theorists' exclusive preoccupation with infants and preschoolers, there also exists a second, equally large and equally insular, cottage industry specifically given over to the study of developing beliefs about belief, this time among college-age youth. This collective effort has largely grown out of the touchstone work of William Perry (1970). In ways that unfolded largely behind the backs of more mainstream cognitive scientists, Perry carried out a series of four-year longitudinal studies in the 1950s and 1960s; studies in which he repeatedly interviewed cohorts of Harvard undergraduate males about all manner of things concerning their changing views about the process of belief entitlement. Drawing on the interview materials he collected, Perry concluded that such students demonstrated first one and then another of a total of as many as nine distinctive epistemic levels. In the intervening years followers of Perry have whittled down this longer list to a mere five or six. The first of these is commonly said to begin with a strictly objectivistic view of the knowing process—a view according to which the truth of any matter is thought to be at least potentially available to anyone with the eyes to see reality for what it is (note the close similarity between such claims and those offered up by theory theorists about much younger preschoolers).

Across the next two of Perry's levels, this extreme objectivist position was said to be gradually qualified by the growing suspicion that others may actually distort the truth, due to their own personalized and potentially correctable biases—again a story reminiscent of claims that Pillow (1991; Pillow and Weed 1995) and others have made on behalf of five to seven-year-olds. At levels 4 and 5 Perry described a more qualitative shift—one not unlike Marcia's moratorium period, and within which certain contested knowledge claims are said to be unmasked as simple matters of arbitrary personal opinion. Finally, Perry's levels 6 through 9 described a series of sequential steps leading toward the making of reasoned commitments in an uncertain world, commitments not unlike those described by Marcia (1980) and others as hallmarks of identity achievement.

Although the full details of Perry's stage-like theory have never been examined, they have, nevertheless, come to be broadly viewed as something of a template for students' progress through the course of a liberal arts education, prompting something of a landslide of doctoral theses and published studies. The large bulk of these efforts (e.g., King and Kitchener 2004; Kitchener and King 1990) can be characterized, without serious prejudice, as an elaborate footnote to Perry's original and richly textured account. Seemingly motivated by the conviction that much of the business of postsecondary education naturally turns on the shifting course of epistemic development, such research efforts have gone on to focus on the various ways in which students' epistemic views need to be taken into account in guiding curricular reform (e.g., Hofer and Pintrich 1997); in understanding how epistemic level might influence the choice of one, as opposed to another, area of study (Paulsen and Wells 1998); and in determining whether the course of epistemic development unfolds differently in persons with and without the benefit of a college education (Kuhn 1991). Over and above such content-bearing matters, still others have explored what may or may not be unique about "women's ways of knowing" (e.g.,

Belenky et al. 1986) or in otherwise evaluating the extent to which manifestations of Perry's levels can be seen at work in the thinking of still younger persons. It is this last subset of studies, which have aimed at providing some downward extension of Perry's model, that are especially pertinent to the work of this chapter.

Adolescent Epistemology

In at least partial response to the concern that the "personal epistemologies" enterprise has done most of its looking only where the light is brightest (i.e., only among easily indentured college students), a number of investigators have brought forward evidence suggesting that many of the accomplishments and concerns featured in Perry's original account are also evident in much younger persons. Several of these studies, representing efforts of our own working group (e.g., Boyes and Chandler 1992; Chandler, Boyes, and Ball 1990), have demonstrated that more than half of the eighth through twelfth graders we have tested already show a clear appreciation of the constructivistic nature of beliefs, consistent with levels 5–9 of Perry's model, and fewer than a third responded in ways consistent with objectivist, absolutist, or naively realistic commitment to the idea that there is always some singular truth hiding behind every difference of opinion. Related studies by Oser and Reich (1987), involving groups of nine- to twenty-two-year-old Swiss youth, similarly report that recognition of the active contribution of the knower to the known begins to emerge in preadolescence, and that even the youngest of their research participants recognized the contribution of personal convictions to the knowing process. Much earlier, Broughton (1978) found similar evidence of nascent skepticism among twelve-year-olds, and reported that, by age eighteen, his respondents regularly voiced the view that knowing is a constructive enterprise guaranteed only by social convention. Clinchy and Mansfield (1985, 1986) and Mansfield and Clinchy (1997) also tracked the natural epistemologies of various groups from their preschool years through adolescence. They reported that as many as half of their seven-year-olds, and nearly all of their nine- to thirteen-year-olds believed that diversity of opinion was legitimate and "portray the knower as an active constructer, rather than a passive receiver of knowledge" (Mansfield and Clinchy 1997, 1). As they put it, "by 13, not a single objectivist was left" (ibid., 10). Finally, Kuhn and Weinstock (2002), among others (e.g., Smith et al. 2000), have also demonstrated that, particularly in domains removed from the imagined certainty of "hard" or impersonal facts, even middle school children are often quick to entertain the possibility that equally well-informed others are free to differ in their beliefs about what is right or true.

The general point being made by all of the investigators just cited is that preadolescents and adolescents do not appear obliged to hang back until they have entered college before recognizing the legitimacy of representational or interpretive diversity. Rather, this evidence, and the surprisingly similar claims emerging from the work of others studying the interpretive nature of the thoughts of late middle school children, threaten to converge in ways that strongly suggest the possibility that early insight concerning the person-relative nature of all thought is not the exclusive province of college students, but is similarly present among adolescents—the same adolescents that are so frequently troubled and so often undone by problems of identity development.

BRINGING IT ALL HOME

The argument being put forward here is meant to balance on three legs. The first of these is an account of the presumed course of identity development, one that has grown out of the pioneering work of Erikson and Marcia and that has specialized in crafting various so-called "identity statuses." On report, this account, although descriptively elegant, falls importantly short, all for the reason that it lacks any defensible (i.e., non-definitional) rationale for why the various statuses on offer are said to arise when they do, occur in the order they do, or are otherwise related to everything else that is known about the course of childhood and adolescent development. The second has been that, operating largely behind the backs of identity status theorists, a different stream of cognitive scientists has been shown to be hard at work fashioning accounts of people's changing beliefs about beliefs—a body of research that evidently bears heavily upon how and why young persons in general, and adolescents in particular, appear especially inclined to entertain troubling thoughts about their own shifting identities. Separate streams within this second research tradition (so-called "theory theorists," on the one hand, more inclined to imagine that everything of note happens early, and investigators of personal epistemologies, on the other, who have traditionally indentured their own postsecondary students as research subjects) appear, of late, to be converging. The place of this convergence is the adolescent and preadolescent years—a threshold place where newly emerging cognitive competencies serve to introduce the possibility of what we will go on to describe as "wholesale epistemic doubts"—the stuff out of which bona fide identity crises are arguably made. The third and final leg of this three-legged stool (the one now to be set in place) is to be fashioned by melding together bits of the other two.

HOLDING EPISTEMIC ANARCHY AT BAY

It would appear that most young persons, on first becoming alert to the interpretive character of the knowing process, are not automatically overcome by what Berger and Luckmann (1967) describe as the "vertigo of relativism," or immediately overtaken by what Bernstein (1983) has called "Cartesian anxiety." What is known (Chandler 1987) is that, with the gradual emergence of an interpretive theory of mind in late middle childhood, and with it a distancing of one's self from earlier epistemic stances rooted in some form of naive realism, the stage begins to be set for the onset of what we will call wholesale doubts—doubts of a caliber capable of blowing one's identity out of the water. So what are wholesale doubts, and what distinguishes them from other more run-of-the-mill retail doubts?

Wholesale Vs. Retail Doubts

Research into children's developing Theories of Mind already makes it clear enough that, by their middle-school years children have begun to shore up their flagging commitments to any earlier and more objectivistic epistemology, first by imagining how various prejudices and "idols of the mind" sometimes intrude in ways that rupture otherwise imagined links between seeing and knowing. Although it can be argued that an early appreciation of such biases may have no necessary epistemic import (Mansfield and Clinchy 1985), they evidently do introduce a wedge that eventually opens up the possibility of serious representational diversity (Flavell et al. 1990). Something like this begins to approximate what Perry (1970) labeled "objective multiplism"—a recognition of the fact that opinions differ, all without abandoning the earlier certainty that there is always a right answer in every dispute. Such a stopgap, divide-and-conquer strategy works as well as it does by comfortably fending off any otherwise impending awareness of the context-dependent character of *all* knowledge. Nevertheless, as the frequency of such attempts to finesse competing knowledge claims increase in volume and volubility, the absolute number of such competing claims— claims that can be laid off to matters of mere opinion—grows exponentially, while the residual number of ideas that are thought to be automatically fact-bearing automatically shrinks; often, it would appear, until some tipping point is reached where everything turns turtle and only opinions are left afloat. When this happens, as we will argue that it regularly does, such young people need to be seen to be playing close to the edge of the poisoned well of radical or wholesale doubt—doubts so deep that, like Kant, such young persons feel "led to the brink of madness and chaos where nothing is fixed, where we can neither touch bottom nor support ourselves on the surface" (Bernstein 1983, 18).

The Poisoned Well Principle

You are Othello, standing there confidently contemplating Desdemona's many virtues, when your trusted second-in-command, Iago, surreptitiously hands you the handkerchief you had gifted her—a personal item now reputedly discovered in the bedchamber of your lieutenant Cassio. All of this could, of course, trigger nothing more than a passive moment of mundane retail, case-specific doubt. You could, for example, doubt that the handkerchief in question was actually Desdemona's, or suppose that you yourself had absentmindedly dropped it on some previous visit. Or, alternatively, and with predictably tragic consequences, you could also fall into a pit of wholesale, generic doubt by imagining in some hyperbolic fit of lost certainty, some newfound conclusion that there was no real honor or virtue left in the world. You could, in consequence, end up killing Desdemona in a fit of jealous rage.

Because he was an adult, and so assumedly capable of viewing things in both the small or the large, Othello would have had it in him to adopt either stance. Not so with persons of a certain tender age. If Piaget had it right, then early school-age children—concrete operational children, *par example*—are typically committed, as a group, to the age-appropriate idea that all questions admit to a single right answer, and that the only repair for doubts and uncertainties is full and unencumbered access to all the relevant facts. For such young persons all doubts are necessarily of a small, retail caliber, and certainty requires running every detail to earth. To see all of this in action, engage such a child in a game of "twenty questions" where, for example, the unknown is the cause of some motor vehicle accident. He or she will want to know, not whether the weather was fair or foul or whether the car was in proper working order, but whether a bee flew in the window or the car was struck by a bolt of lightning. Othello, like other grownups, would, in contrast, likely appreciate (had he not been bitten by the green-eyed monster of jealousy) that the full atomic set of possible contributing factors is potentially infinite, and that our best hope for certainty lies along some Popperian path that works to minimize alternative prospects.

On this picture, then, the most serious sorts of doubts to which young (perhaps concrete operational) children are subject are merely retail doubts. They can, for example, doubt whether they are tall or pretty or bright enough, but what they cannot yet do, it is argued, is agonize over whether life has meaning or ultimate truth can be found. Such questions, and the wholesale and often unassuageable doubts that accompany them, would appear to require something of the caliber of what Piaget intended by talk of "formal operational" thought; thoughts that, like identity crises, appear to be the exclusive province of adolescents and still older persons (Chandler and Boyes 1982).

Nowhere in this explanation is there room for talk about commitments. That is, by working to situate such crises within the broader context of cognitive and epistemic growth, we mean to have avoided reducing identity development to a mere conditioned response triggered by mounting social responsibilities. In certain African communities children just able to walk are said to be given responsibility for their own garden plot, and almost everywhere livestock is entrusted to the care of small children (de Lange 2009). Nowhere, however, do such young children apparently become swept up in the fundamental ambiguity of all knowledge (Sass and Woolfolk 1985) or regularly risk falling into a pit of skeptical doubt. Rather, the signature problems of adolescent identity formation seem better understood as one among many manifestations of young people's ongoing struggles to construct new ways of knowing that keep pace with the rest of their growing intelligence.

THE THIRD LEG

Whatever else might be said in its favor, what the foregoing account does not do, however—or has at least not done so far—is to allow a better way of understanding why, as identity status theorists would have it, foreclosed identities must necessarily precede, rather than follow, the so-called "moratorium" period (van Hoof 1999). Definitionally, of course, a "status" that requires having suffered some identity crisis, must necessarily precede having never had such a crisis, but available data would suggest otherwise (e.g., Berzonsky and Adams 1999; van Hoof 1999), and even if it did not, that would still not be good enough.

Secret Sharers

A key to unraveling this and similarly unscheduled patterns of events is to be found in the bold insight of the German hermeneutical philosopher Hans-Georg Gadamer (1975), who reshaped continental philosophy by arguing that "both the skeptic and the dogmatist are equally guilty of creating the same pernicious binary opposition, the same misleading assumption that between absolute certainty on the one side and chaos of nihilistic relativism on the other no viable alternatives exist" (Chandler 1987, 142). By these lights, although skepticism is in some sense the dialectical antithesis of dogmatism, both are, at the same time, parasitic upon and gain their plausibility from one other. They are, to borrow Sass and Woolfolk's (1985) choice phrase, "secret sharers," in ways that promote a natural wavering between them, precisely because both are predicated on the same mistaken assumption that without absolute uncertainty everything is lost. It is for this reason, Bernstein (1983) argues, that, just as the failure of some cherished dogmatic conviction is the natural occasion for the next wave of skeptical doubt, the essential nihilism and aimlessness of know-nothing skepticism works to prepare one for conversion to some new dogmatic faith. For just such reasons, no one should be surprised on hearing (as seemingly often happens) that yesterday's skeptic is today's dogmatist or that (contrary to identity status theory) someone who once registered as being in a moratorium period subsequently measured out as being foreclosed.

Such borrowed insights also help to make plain why, between skepticism and dogmatism (read "moratorium" and "foreclosure"), it is skepticism that often proves the more illusive. Making what is, perhaps, the extreme case, Rorty (1982) argues this point by insisting that, except for the occasional cooperative freshman, essentially no one says that two incompatible options on any important topic are equally good. Although this skepticism about skepticism has a certain ring of truth, it is not entirely justified for the reason that, although skeptics may excuse themselves from believing this or that particular thing, they are, nevertheless, frequently obliged to behave either this way or that. Although committed to nothing, they can, nevertheless, still call upon various non-rational decision-making strategies by choosing to grudgingly agree to do the done thing, or through displaying their indifference by settling important question with the flip of a coin or by simply electing to act on their gut feelings (Chandler 1987). None of this appears to succeed, however, in making skepticism a comfortable option. For such reasons it is likely true that dogmatism often proves (although there is no hint of this in the Identity Status literature) to be the preferred option.

Post-Skeptical Forms of "Identity Achievement"

Finally, some closing words seem required regarding what identity status theorists choose to call "identity achievement." The dismissive undertone contained within catchphrases like "choose to call" grows out of a conviction running through this parallel account that regards words like "achieved" as far too finalistic for the circumstance at hand. To be identity achieved, at least as ordinarily understood by identity status theorists, seems to imply no take backs or the possibility of later reneging on earlier commitments. People, it would seem, are rarely like that.

If there is to be a way of extricating one's self from the entrapping dogmatism/skepticism axis just outlined, it would, in the language being developed here, likely take the form of finding a better way of understanding that (although absolute certainty may remain unobtainable) rationally guided action demands no more in the way of certainty than is humanly possible. Holders of such views would likely conclude that the price that both dogmatism and skepticism extract is simply too high to pay, would accept the ambiguity inherent in all human experience, and would commit to the existence of a kind of argumentatively redeemable truth that is justified by the force of the better argument. That is, whatever it might mean, in these terms, to be credited with having an achieved identity, it almost certainly would not mean having come to some doubtless conclusion about work and love. Rather it would depend instead on some commitment to the idea that it is still possible to become as sure about many things as certainty requires, and that some hope remains for still finding ways of clinging together against the dark.

In brief summary then, and however many pages later, we have worked here to outline a different way of understanding the course of identity development, one that: (a) attempts to situate identity formation within the context of what is otherwise broadly known about the developmental course; (b) aims for a way of better understanding why identity crises occur when they do; and (c) works to accomplish some followable account of the kaleidoscope of identity status change. What this new account has so far failed to do, however, is say anything useful about what may be unique about the course of identity development as it occurs among Indigenous youth. That will be the business of the sections to follow.

IDENTITY DEVELOMENT AMONG INDIGENOUS YOUTH

So far, we have succeeded in working our way through more than half of our page allotment having said relatively little about culture in general, or, more particularly, what might be unique about the course of identity development in young Indigenous persons. Rather, our initial focus was on what we have imagined to be common about the job of forming an identity in almost any sociocultural context. Specifically, we worked to make the case that young people in every place and time are commonly obliged to: (a) come to some understanding of how their own and others' knowledge claims might relate to events in their own environing world; (b) consider ways of accounting for and arbitrating the differences that obtain across such diverse representations; and (c) find ways of managing the doubts and uncertainties promulgated by such disparate representation, including their representations of themselves and others.

Although it has not been prominently featured so far, we have, nevertheless, quietly preceded on the assumption that, despite their similarities, different groups will have likely arrived at potentially different ways of knowing—distinct "folk epistemologies" (Chandler 2010)—that are responsible for the unique ways in which they and members of their own epistemic community routinely recognize themselves in the identities they are in the process of building. It is to some of these differences that we now mean to turn, all as part of our efforts to say something helpful about the sometimes troubled identities of Indigenous youth.

Without some sort of limits-setting, however, such a broad, looping agenda threatens to outstrip the evidence base. To avoid this, we intend to restrict the balance of this account in three ways. First we plan to draw our examples and our conclusions from a program of ongoing research focused on the identity development of so-called "First Nation" youth—residents of western Canada's province of British Columbia (BC). Second, although there is obviously more to the process of identity formation than finding some culturally sanctioned way of grasping the meaning of personal and cultural persistence in time, it is this linchpin issue that is the focus of the balance of this chapter. Finally, whereas there are evidently multiple ways to measure how young people might succeed or fail in their efforts to hammer out a sense of identity in time, one extreme way (our way) of sorting out such identity successes and failures is to proceed by picking out those young people that could no longer find themselves in their own future, and who have responded by taking their own lives. This is a grisly job. Nevertheless, and for reasons better elaborated in the following, we mean to proceed here on the assumption that youth suicide is the ultimate, "drop-dead" marker of identity development gone wrong.

As a way of beginning, we mean to quickly return to these same three ways of restricting the scope of this chapter, saying something synoptic about each in turn.

WHY THE FIRST NATION YOUTH IN BC?

The University of BC, which has served as a base camp for the program of research to be described here, sits upon a piece of unceded territory of the Musqueam First Nation, with other equally distinctive Indigenous communities relatively close to hand. A large part of the reason, then, for taking these and other of BC's Indigenous peoples as "targets" for our own cross-cultural study of identity development has, then, simply been expediency.

Pragmatic issues aside, there are, however, other and better reasons for our choice. BC is a big and diverse place, with a footprint roughly the size of Western Europe. It is also the home of some two hundred distinctive First Nation communities (or "bands"), each with their own spiritual and cultural practices; often their own Indigenous language; and, in every instance, a distinctive colonial past and present. Conveniently, for a youth-based study, approximately half of the province-wide Indigenous population is also under the age of twenty-five. Finally, as the westernmost province in Canada, BC was among the last of the country's regions to be colonized, with the result that only a modest number of generations separate contemporary First Nation persons from their vanishing precontact culture.

All of the preceding having been said, one would be dangerously mistaken to suppose that the studies reported here are about other than manifestly Westernized and bicultural youth. Just short of half of all of BC's First Nation citizens now live in urban, rather than "reserve" settings; a very large majority of these First Nation youth have English (and not some Indigenous language) as their mother tongue (Statistics Canada 2006); and the curriculum to which almost every First Nation student in BC has been exposed is Euro-American through and through, with little more than token references to Indigenous culture. By force of law, BC First Nation peoples have been assimilated almost to the brink of cultural extinction. Still, for a great many of these peoples, the present moment is often felt to be a time of special cultural renaissance (Durie 2006), and many of the hopes and efforts of BC's Indigenous communities center upon what are perceived to be the building prospects of rehabilitating important aspects of their badly savaged cultures.

WHY FOCUS ON MATTERS OF PERSONAL AND CULTURAL CONTINUITY?

Although not an easy question, there are convincing reasons to view matters of personal and cultural continuity as holding a special place of importance in the study of identity development, in general, and the study of Indigenous identity development, in particular. Among these are the facts that: (a) without some workable means of understanding one's self and one's culture as continuous (i.e., as having a necessary past and a future) the very concepts of self or personhood or culture threaten to lose all meaning; and (b) in the absence of such a sense of temporal persistence, life itself would automatically be cheapened, and many of the usual taboos against self-harm and self-appointed death would naturally fall away. The reasons for saying all of this in advance—in advance of the data to be briefly summarized here—are all long. In some cases, however, shorthand answers exists, all of which turn upon what is signaled by the so-called paradox of personal persistence and change.

The Paradox of Sameness and Change

No one, or at least no one since Parmenides (Ring 1987), has seriously doubted that change, especially personal and cultural change, is real. Clearly, our bodies change; our beliefs and desires (along with our projects, commitments, and interpersonal relationships) all change, often seemingly beyond all recognition. Notwithstanding the inevitability of change, however, sameness is likewise everywhere apparent, so much so, in fact, that we often find ourselves praying for change, even if it means change for the worst. As such, sameness, like change, is not an elective "feature" of selves and cultures, but another of their "constitutive conditions" (Habermas 1991).

There you have it. On the one hand, the usual ravages of time seem hard at work unraveling the sleeve of whatever sort of personal identity or collective culture we have been in the process of carefully knitting up. On the other, each of us is feverishly at work stitching back together those frayed parts of ourselves and of our culture that time has rent asunder. Despite the fact that sameness and change work in opposite directions, it nevertheless continues to remain the case that the fundamental logic of identity necessarily understands persons and culture as having whatever sort of persistence is necessary to allow them to be identified and re-identified as one and the same through time (Strawson 1959). Without at least this much in the way of continuity from one time to the next, responsibilities for past actions would have no meaning, and promises, responsibilities, and keeping faith would all fly out the same window. For such reasons, every concept of the self or culture that has not fallen into incoherence has done so by somehow hiding out from the natural ravages of time. The open question is how, and how successfully, various individuals and groups have done so.

Our own efforts to find answers to these fundamental questions have triggered two separate, but intertwined, lines of empirical research: one having to do with the longitudinal study of how individual young persons ordinarily think about continuities in their own lives; the other a more top-down, epidemiologic undertaking aimed at measuring continuities and discontinuities in the lives of whole cultural communities. Although described in detail elsewhere (e.g., Chandler et al. 2003), a brief recounting of each of these lines of research fills out our remaining agenda. Before that, however, why, you may legitimately wonder, study suicide—why is this an appropriate proxy for identity difficulties in the extreme?

ON CHOOSING SUICIDE (WORSE STILL, YOUTH SUICIDE) AS A MARKER OF IDENTITY DEVELOPMENT GONE WRONG

What needs to be made clear here is how each person's own future prospects, including the prospect of killing oneself, might be meaningfully associated with the successes or failures of single individuals, or whole cultural groups, to achieve a sense of ownership on their past and future. The straightforward empirical facts of the matter, repeated across what is now a long train of studies, is plain enough: self- and cultural-continuity problems are in fact strongly, that is, significantly, associated with a dramatically heightened risk of suicide in both culturally mainstream youth (Ball and Chandler 1989), and, in particular, in whole First Nation communities (Chandler and Lalonde 1998).

Here are some conceptual tools for better understanding why this might be so—why, in the absence of a sense of personal and cultural continuity, life is often so cheapened that suicide becomes a live option.

FROM NORMATIVE RISK AND RESILIENCE RESEARCH

However hazardous simply growing up may otherwise be, the associated risks are necessarily magnified when developmental circumstances produce changes of a magnitude that cannot be adequately processed or when the cultural backcloth against which development naturally unfolds is rudely unraveled by adversities (Taylor 2002). Nowhere are these handicaps more apparent than in the identity struggles of many young Indigenous persons who, like all developing persons, are changing a mile a minute, but unlike most, are obliged to construct a sense of selfhood out of the remnants of a traditional way of life that harsh colonial practices have criminalized and turned into a laughingstock. In the best of circumstances, one's culture can be counted on to provide young people with some soupçon of sameness. If, instead, one's cultural resources are marginalized, or vandalized, or assimilated out of existence, then woe be upon those still transiting toward maturity. This is far too often the fate, we argue, of many Indigenous youth whose traditional culture no longer seems relevant in a contemporary world. For such young indigenous persons their paradise has been turned into a parking lot, and their once proud heritage has been remanufactured as the stuff of mascots and Saturday morning cartoons. The consequences of such personal and cultural losses are often disillusionment; lassitude; substance abuse; self-injury; and, most dramatically, self-appointed death at an early age.

Contained in this shameful history there is, however, the prospect of finding some better way of understanding why the burden of suicide falls so disproportionately on the young, and especially on some (but not other) young Indigenous persons. Our program of research tries to bring out such explanations in two ways. One of these, the one that has involved the direct assessment of individual First Nation youth, will be summarized first, saving for later our higher-altitude studies of youth suicide in whole Indigenous communities.

MEASURING SELF-CONTINUITY IN INDIVIDUAL INDIGENOUS AND NONINDIGENOUS YOUTH

Of our several studies that have involved the assessment of individual youth, two in particular are of the greatest relevance to the present account. One of these (Ball and Chandler 1989) focused attention on adolescents recently admitted to an inpatient psychiatric facility, sometimes, but not always, because of a failed suicide attempt. Each of these patients was matched with a nonhospitalized age-mate who served as a control. Hospitalized participants were further divided into two groups: those deemed to be a high risk of suicide and so on "suicide precautions," and those who were not designated as suicide risks. All of these youth were individually interviewed and given a battery of testing procedures, including those specifically designed to assess the ways in which they understood their own and others' self-continuity across periods of dramatic personal change (for a complete detailing of these measurement procedures, see Chandler et al. 2003).

The key findings to emerge from this study were that, whereas all members of the nonhospitalized control group were able to employ some strategy for warranting a sense of self-continuity, all but two of the seventeen inpatients who were on suicide precautions failed utterly in their attempts to justify how, in the face of dramatic change, they or others might continue to be the selfsame person through time. This extreme lapse in their ability to understand themselves as personally persistent, with the attendant failure of any sense of ownership of their past or investment in their own future, was taken as evidence that there is a strong relation between any loss of self-continuity and an attendant increased risk for suicidal behaviors.

Culture-Bound Conceptions of Self-Continuity

The second study reported here undertook a direct comparison of the self-continuity warranting strategies employed by First Nation and culturally mainstream youth. Here a total of 180 First Nation adolescents, matched with another ninety age-mates, drawn from the cultural mainstream, were individually interviewed and tested.

In order to understand the main thrust of our findings from this study it is important to first know how we were previously led to identify two distinct sorts of self-continuity warranting strategies employed within what had been one of those culturally mainstream samples of convenience. By far the most commonly occurring of these response strategies rested on the assumption that, inevitable wear and tear notwithstanding, we each possess certain more or less abstract, but always enduring, bits and pieces that are believed to defy or stand outside the ravages of time. In sharp contrast, however, the occasional "other" from within our predominately Euro-American samples made a rare "interpretive turn," by granting that, although nothing ever succeeds in defeating time, personal persistence can, nevertheless, be vouchsafed by those functional, process-oriented, narrative-like connections that work to make a whole—often a whole story—out of the multiple chapters that come together to form a life. Practitioners of this relational logic credited themselves with having succeeded in solving the paradox of sameness within change so long as some unbroken chain of linked circumstances could be forged that successfully bound together life's various changing moments. We labeled such self-continuity warrants "narrative" strategies.

Had we not, for other reasons, begun to apply our measurement tools to other less culturally mainstream samples we might easily have gone on regarding such occasional narrative-like approaches to the story of identity development as little more than just another "French fad." As can be seen from an inspection of Figure 5.2, however, our first systematic venture into the study of self-continuity preserving practice of First Nation youth forced a radical revision in our thinking.

As this figure makes plain, whereas the large bulk (80 percent) of the standard-issue Canadian adolescents clearly adopted an "essentialist" approach to the problem of their own self-continuity, almost three-quarters of the First Nation adolescents tested made just the opposite choice, relying

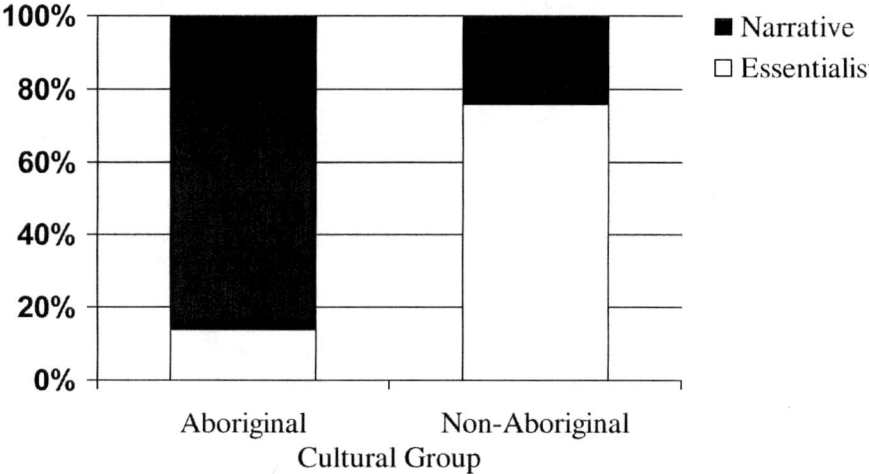

Figure 5.2 Percentage of Aboriginal and non-Aboriginal participants prescribing to a narrative and essentialist form of self-continuity.

instead upon narrative strategies in working to solve problems about their own and others' personal persistence.

Although there would seem no reason in principle to suppose that there exists some context-independent yardstick against which the absolute merits of essentialist and narrative self-continuity warranting strategies might be measured, it is easy enough to envision actual historical and cultural contexts that might advantage one or the other of these generic approaches. When, for example, stepping onto an Enlightenment era boat to explore the New World, or to escape the potato famine, there may well have been an advantage in imagining selfhood to be some weightless, featureless, but essential entity carried around in one's secret heart. Similarly, as a member of a ten-thousand-year-old, family-based Indigenous community governed by precontact oral traditions, understanding one's ongoing identity to be like a story told to an appreciative audience might well have proven to be a scenario hard to improve upon—hard unless, of course, that culture was to be savaged by invading armies of colonizers that dismissed one's traditions as childish and Stone Age, criminalized one's epistemic and spiritual conviction, and shipped one's appreciative audience off to some concentration camp–like Residential School. Something like that—a "double-whammy" composed of equal parts cultural genocide and a residual identity formation strategy better suited for a world that no longer exists—could easily make life no longer seem worth living.

Our search for better ways of more closely examining such prospects has led us to supplement our professionally sanctioned way of studying the development of individual identities with other concepts and methods fashioned for the study of still bigger units of analyses.

EXAMINING CONTINUITIES AT THE LEVEL
OF WHOLE CULTURAL COMMUNITIES

In much the same way that, in order to avoid falling into incoherence, any intelligible conception of self- or personhood requires a way of somehow binding together an individual's past, present, and future, the maintenance of any coherent culture requires some accounting strategy that allows community members to both own their traditional past and to maintain an abiding stake in their own as yet unrealized civic future. That is, or so we mean to argue, any cultural group whose traditions have been stolen away or otherwise assimilated out of existence, and that, as a direct by-product of government-inspired infantilization, has been robbed of the ways and means of properly planning for themselves and their children, would prove to be an ahistoric and futureless group, many of whose members find life no longer worth living. For such reasons, it continues to be the goal of the final program of research summarized here to attempt to glean through some various earlier individual-level insights and to test their relevance for better understanding the general lack of futurity and high rates of youth suicide that so frequently manifest themselves in the lives of whole First Nation communities.

Drawn from the research reports and commentaries that our research group has published on this topic, we mean to use the remaining pages of this chapter to distill out only three sets of findings. The first of these concern the extremely variable rates of youth suicide that characterize BC's more than two hundred First Nation communities. The second deals with what have been shown to be powerful social determinants of community-level difference in the incidence of youth suicide. The third aims to draw out some of the implications for policy and practice collectively contained in these findings.

Community-Level Variability In First Nations' Suicide Rates: Tarring Everyone With The Same Broad, Defamatory Brush

The generic story regularly told about Indigenous people in Canada is that, among other unflattering things, they are said to be an especially suicidal lot. That is, riding roughshod over the obvious differences that divide the country's more than six hundred First Nations communities, all of these culturally diverse peoples are commonly and conveniently press-ganged together and so said to collectively suffer the highest rate of suicide of any culturally identifiable group in the world (Kirmayer 1994)––rates some three to five times higher than that found for the general population. The youth version of this same apocryphal story is more tragic still. In BC, for example, Indigenous youth suicide rates are commonly said to be some five to twenty times higher than those for their non-Indigenous counterparts

(Chandler and Lalonde 1998). The problem is not that all the actuaries have somehow gotten their sums wrong, but that blithely aggregating across the enormous cultural differences that divide Canada's especially divergent Indigenous groups is, at best, deeply misleading. In order to come closer to the truth, it is necessary instead to cut considerably closer to the bone by aggregating data at a level that makes real cultural sense. That is exactly what our research group began doing in 1995, and has continued doing through what is now an ongoing third wave of data collection, a surveillance project in which suicide rates are calculated separately for each of BC's 203 First Nation bands.

The first and clearest finding to emerge from our first wave of data collection (belatedly covering the period from 1987 to 1992) was that, whereas suicides by non-Indigenous persons did not vary from place to place across the entire province, just the opposite was true for First Nation youth. As can be seen from an examination of Figure 5.3, the rate at which young First Nation persons took their own life was wildly saw-toothed, piling up dramatically in some communities and not at all in others.

More than half the province's bands are shown, for example, to have suffered no youth suicides at all during this first six-year study period, whereas in other communities rates were as much as eight hundred times the provincial average. Almost identical data subsequently emerged from our second wave of data collection (1992–2000), where again roughly 90 percent of the youth suicides were found to have occurred in only 12 percent of the bands, and more than half of all of these communities again suffered no youth suicides during this second reporting period.

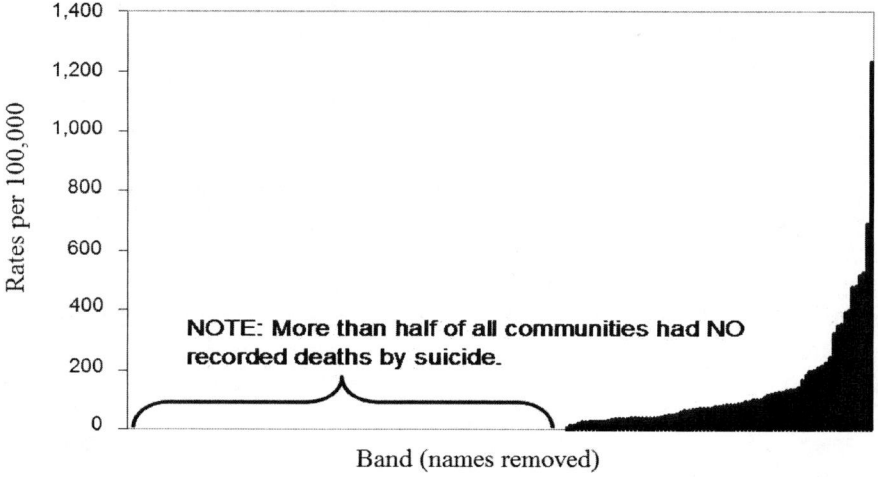

Figure 5.3 Number of youth suicides occurring among provincial bands (1987–1992).

Among much else, these large community-by-community differences make it abundantly clear that suicidality is not an attribute or defining feature of "Indigeneity" per se. The majority of First Nation communities in BC have lower rates of youth suicide than do their culturally mainstream counterparts. With any possible "race card" removed from the deck, the considerable interpretive task set by these data was to work out why youth suicide has so devastated some, but not all, First Nation communities.

Available data made it apparent very early on that the answers we were looking for did not lie in the direction of "usual suspect" variables such as "Degree of Rurality" or "Socioeconomic Status." Rather, if one is looking for an explanation for hundredfold differences of the sort already in hand, then the place to look first, we reasoned, was within those dramatic cultural differences that, as rumor had it, set various First Nation communities wide apart.

CULTURAL CONTINUITY AS A HEDGE AGAINST SUICIDE IN INDIGENOUS YOUTH

The research effort described here was predicated on the assumption that distinctive cultural groups, like individual selves, are constituted by identity-preserving practices that work to forge links to a common past and future. On this prospect, it was anticipated that Indigenous communities bereft of such culture-sustaining ties would be at special risk for suicide, whereas those that had achieved greater measures of success in preserving cultural connections would be better shielded from the slings and arrows that regularly cost young Indigenous persons, and whole groups of such persons, appropriate levels of care and concern for their own future well-being.

As before, several guiding principles directed our search for answers to the question of how best to relate community-level measures to individual outcomes. Some of these resulting questions were technical in nature, such as the need to restrict our search pattern to include only those variables for which band-level data are already available for all or most of BC's First Nation communities. Other of our reasons were more theory driven. Rather than trolling aimlessly through the mounting seas of Statistics Canada data in the blind hope of snagging something that might relate to variable suicide rates, we took our lead from our own earlier research that supports the theoretical prospect that suicide (whether measured at the individual or community level) can be understood as an outcome of the collapse of those identity-preserving practices that serve to secure some enduring sense of identity through time.

Having just demonstrated that Indigenous youth suicides are not uniformly distributed across BC's almost two hundred different First Nations Bands, but exist instead in epidemic proportion in some but not other communities, we were encouraged to attempt to find ways of indexing what we have called "cultural continuity," a concept that manifest itself at the level of whole Indigenous communities.

In pursuit of this measurement problem we began our initial 1998 study (Chandler and Lalonde 1998) by constructing a first-draft index of cultural continuity made up of six marker variables expressive of the degree to which each of BC's First Nation bands have already secured: some measure of self-government; some control over the delivery of health, education, policing services, and cultural resources; and were otherwise at work litigating for Aboriginal title to traditional lands. These proxy measures were chosen primarily because each appeared to signal something important about a community's efforts to recover its past and secure a measure of control over its own civic future. Access to information about the variables for each of BC two-hundred-plus First Nation bands made it possible to locate each of these communities along a six-point continuum ranging from low to high levels of cultural continuity. Subsequently (Chandler and Lalonde 2009) three more predictor variables were added, including measure of band-level knowledge of Indigenous languages, the proportion of women in band government, and control of child protection services.

Figure 5.4 concerns the six-year window between 1987 and 1992, and displays the suicide rates for all of those bands credited with as many as six of our original cultural continuity markers.

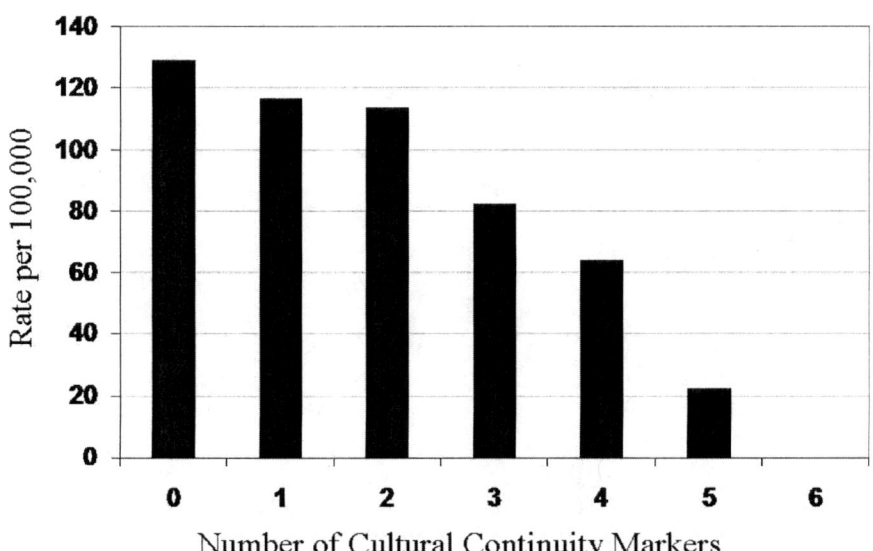

Figure 5.4 BC youth suicide rate displayed by number of continuity factors present within community (1987–1992).

As can be seen by an inspection of this figure, every band characterized by all of these cultural continuity factors experienced no youth suicides during the six-year window considered, whereas those communities lacking any of these "protective" factors regularly suffered proportionate youth suicide rates hundreds of times the national average. These data, which were closely replicated in our second wave of data collection (Chandler and Lalonde 2009), are seen to make a very strong case that the well-being of First Nation youth, as measured by community-level suicide rates, is strongly associated with the extent to which their cultural community is hard at work both rebuilding connections to its traditional past and struggling to regain control over its own future.

ACTION AND POLICY IMPLICATIONS: INDIGENOUS KNOWLEDGE, KNOWLEDGE TRANSFER, AND THE EXCHANGE OF BEST PRACTICES

What the research just reported is meant to make plain is the existence of a large but poorly appreciated source of real cultural knowledge about how the problem of youth suicide in First Nation communities might be addressed. That is, clearly contained in the finding that almost half of BC's Indigenous communities have youth suicide rates lower than the general population is the evident fact that real Indigenous knowledge about how to address this problem must already be well sedimented within these Indigenous communities. If proper attention and weight were given to such facts, then it would become necessary to radically rethink one of the government's most cherished new catchphrases: "knowledge transfer."

Knowledge transfer, as commonly understood, is a "top-down" process by means of which knowledge generated within the academy is made to "trickle down" until it eventually reaches community-level ground zero. In addition to being suspect on other grounds, such "made in Washington" or "made in Ottawa" solutions are broadly seen by Indigenous groups as disrespectful by such "served" communities and openly confirmatory of the positional inferiority commonly accorded to Indigenous cultures. By way of contrast, what the research that we have just presented suggests is that if Indigenous health knowledge is credited as being real knowledge (as the absence of youth suicide in more than half of the First Nation communities studied would suggest that it is), then, in the place of more traditional top-down approaches, what needs to be seriously explored is the possibility of a community-to-community, lateral transfer of indigenous knowledge and best practices between groups that have enjoyed greater and lesser levels of success in meeting the needs of their own children.

In short summary, then, at least two obvious action or policy implications flow from the research summarized here. The first of these turns upon exposing as false the "actuarial fiction" that it is possible to capture the diversity of a whole province's or country's Indigenous life in a single, totalizing (often statistical) gaze. The second is that, in light of the rich fund of Indigenous knowledges and practices shown to be scattered throughout the First Nations, traditional "top-down" strategies of knowledge transfer should be retired in favor of a more "lateral" transfer of "Indigenous knowledge" between these more and less successful communities.

REFERENCES

Adams, G.R., Ryan, B.A., and Keating, L. "Family Relationships, Academic Environments, and Psychosocial Development during the University Experience: A Longitudinal Investigation," Journal of Adolescent Research 15 (2000): 99–122.

Archer, S.L. and Waterman, A.S. "Varieties of Identity Diffusions and Foreclosures: An Exploration of Subcategories of the Identity Statuses," Journal of Adolescent Research 5 (1990): 96–111.

Ball, L. and Chandler, M.J. "Identity Formation in Suicidal and Nonsuicidal Youth: The Role of Self-Continuity," Developmental Psychopathology 1 (1989): 257–275.

Belenky, M.F., Clinchy, B.M., Goldberger, N.R., and Tarule, J.M. 1986. Women's Ways of Knowing: The Development of Self, Voice and Mind. New York: Basic Books.

Berger, P. and Luckmann, T. 1967. The Social Construction of Reality: A Treatise in the Sociology of Knowledge. Garden City, NY: Doubleday.

Bernstein, R.J. 1983. Beyond Objectivism and Relativism. Philadelphia· University of Pennsylvania Press.

Berzonsky, M.D. 1990. Self-construction over the life-span: A process perspective on identity formation, in *Advances in Personal Construct Psychology*, vol. 1, edited by R.A. Neimeyer and G.J. Neimeyer. Greenwich, CT: JAI Press, pp. 155–186.

———. "Identity Processing Style, Self-Construction, and Personal Epistemic Assumptions: A Social-Cognitive Perspective," European Journal of Developmental Psychology 1 (2004): 303–315.

Berzonsky, M.D. and Adams, G.R. "Reevaluating the Identity Status Paradigm: Still Useful after 35 Years," Developmental Review 19 (1999): 557–590.

Boyes, M.C. and Chandler, M.J. "Cognitive Development, Epistemic Doubt, and Identity Formation in Adolescence," Journal of Youth and Adolescence 21 (1992): 277–304.

Broughton, J. "Development of Concepts of Self, Mind, Reality, and Knowledge," New Directions for Child Development 1 (1978): 70–100.

Carpendale, J.I.M. and Chandler, M.J. "On the Distinction between False Belief Understanding and Subscribing to an Interpretive Theory of Mind," Child Development 67 (1996): 1686–1706.

Chandler, M.J. "The Othello Effect: An Essay on the Emergence and Eclipse of Skeptical Doubt," Human Development 30 (1987): 137–159.

———. 2001. Perspective taking in the aftermath of theory-theory and the collapse of the social role-taking enterprise, in *Working with Piaget: Essays in Honour of Barbel Inhelder*, edited by Anastasia Tryphon and Jacques Voneche. London: Psychology Press, pp. 39–63.

———. "Social Determinants of Educational Outcomes in Indigenous Learners," Education Canada 50 (2010): 46–50.

Chandler, M.J. and Boyes, M.C. 1982. Social-cognitive development, in *Handbook of Developmental Psychology*, edited by B.B. Wolman. Englewood Cliffs, NJ: Prentice Hall, pp. 387–402.

Chandler, M.J., Boyes, M.C., and Ball, L. "Relativism and Stations of Epistemic Doubt," Journal of Experimental Child Psychology 50 (1990): 370–395.

Chandler, M.J. and Lalonde, C.E. 1996. Shifting to an interpretive theory of mind: 5- to 7-year-olds' changing conceptions of mental life, in *The Five to Seven Year Shift: The Age of Reason and Responsibility*, edited by A.J. Sameroff and M.M. Haith. Chicago: University of Chicago Press, pp. 111–139.

———. "Cultural Continuity as a Hedge against Suicide in Canada's First Nations," Transcultural Psychiatry 35 (1998): 191–219.

———. 2009. Cultural continuity as a moderator of suicide risk among Canada's First Nations, in *Healing Traditions: The Mental Health of Aboriginal Peoples in Canada*, edited by L.J. Kirmayer and G.G. Valaskakis. Vancouver, Canada: UBC Press, pp. 221–248.

Chandler, M.J., Lalonde, C.E. Sokol, B.E. and Hallett, D. "Personal Persistence, Identity Development, and Suicide: A Study of Native and Non-Native North American Adolescents," Monographs of the Society for Research in Child Development 68 (2003): vii–130.

Clinchy, B.M. and Mansfield, A.F. 1985. "The Child's Discovery of the Role of the Knower in the Known." Paper presented that the 16th Annual Symposium of the Jean Piaget Society, Philadelphia, PA, June 5–7.

Cote, J.E. and Levine, C. "A Critical Examination of the Identity Status Paradigm," Developmental Review 8 (1988): 1–38.

de Lange, A. 2009. Child labor in Burkina Faso, in *The World of Child Labor: An Historical and Regional Survey*, edited by H.D. Hindman. Armonk, NY: M.E. Sharp, pp. 202–206.

Durie, M. 2006. "Indigenous Resilience: From Disease and Disadvantage to the Realization of Potential." Presented at the Rapu Oranga Pacific Region Indigenous Doctors Congress, Rotorua, New Zealand, December 6–10.

Erikson, E.H. "Identity and the Life Cycle," Psychological Issues 1 (1959): 18–164.

———. 1968. Identity: Youth and Crisis. New York: Norton.

Flavell, J.H., Flavell, E.R., Green, F.L., and Moses, L.J. "Young Children's Understanding of Fact Beliefs versus Value Beliefs," Child Development 61 (1990): 915–928.

Fromm, E. 1941. Escape from Freedom. New York: Rinehart.

Gadamer, H.G. 1975. Truth and Method. New York: Seabury Press.

Habermas, J. 1991. The paradigm shift in Mead, in *Philosophy, Social Theory, and the Thought of George Hebert Mead*, edited by M. Aboulafia. Albany, NY: State University of New York Press, pp. 138–168.

Hofer, B.K. and Pintrich, P.R. "The Development of Epistemological Theories: Beliefs about Knowledge and Knowing and Their Relation to Learning," Review of Educational Research 67 (1997): 88–140.

Hyun-joo, S. and Baillargeon, R. "Infants' Reasoning about Others' False Perceptions," Developmental Psychology 44 (2008): 1789–1795.

King, P.M. and Kitchener, K.S. "Reflective Judgment: Theory and Research on the Development of Epistemic Assumptions through Adulthood," Educational Psychologist 39 (2004): 5–18.

Kirmayer, L.J. "Suicide among Canadian Aboriginal Peoples," Transcultural Psychiatric Research Review 31 (1994): 3–58.

Kitchener, K.S. and King, P.M. 1990. The reflective judgment model: Transforming assumptions about knowing, in *Fostering Critical Reflection in Adulthood: A*

Guide to Transformative and Emancipatory Learning, edited by Jack Mezirow. San Francisco: Jossey-Bass, pp. 157–176.

Kroger, J. "What Transitions in an Identity Status Transition?" Identity: An International Journal of Theory and Research 3 (2003): 197–220.

Kuhn, D. 1991. The Skills of Argument. Cambridge: Cambridge University Press.

Kuhn, D. and Weinstock, M. (2002). The development of epistemological understanding, in *Personal Epistemology: The Psychology of Beliefs about Knowledge and Knowing*, edited by B.K. Hofer and P.R. Pintrich. Mahwah, NJ: Lawrence Erlbaum Associates, pp. 121–144.

Luo, Y. and Baillargeon, R. "Do 12.5-Month-Old Infants Consider What Objects Others Can See When Interpreting Their Actions?" Cognition 105 (2007): 489–512.

Mansfield, A.F. and Clinchy, B.M. 1985. "The Early Growth of Multiplism in the Child." Paper presented at the 15th annual symposium of the Jean Piaget Society, Philadelphia, PA, May 30-June 1.

Mansfield, A.F. and Clinchy, B.M. 1997. "Toward the Integration of Objectivity and Subjectivity: A Longitudinal Study of Epistemological Development between the Ages of 9 and 13." Paper presented at the biennial meeting of the Society for Research in Child Development, Washington, DC, April 3–6.

Marcia, J.E. "Development and Validation of Ego Identity Status," Journal of Personality and Social Psychology 3 (1966): 551–558.

———. 1980. Identity in adolescence, in *Handbook of Adolescent Psychology*, edited by J. Adelson. New York: Wiley, pp. 159–187.

Paulsen, M.B. and Wells, C.T. "Domain Differences in the Epistemological Beliefs of College Students," Research in Higher Education 39 (1998): 365–384.

Onishi, K.H. and Baillargeon, R. "Do 15-Month-Old Infants Understand False Belief?" Science 308 (2005): 255–258.

Oser, F.K. and Reich, K.H. "The Challenge of Competing Explanations: The Development of Thinking in Terms of Complementarity of 'Theories,'" Human Development 30 (1987): 178–186.

Perry, W.G. 1970. Forms of Intellectual and Ethical Development in the College Years: A Scheme. New York: Holt, Rinehart and Winston.

Pillow, B.H. "Children's Understanding of Biased Social Cognition," Developmental Psychology 27 (1991): 539–551.

Pillow, B.H. and Weed, S.T. "Children's Understanding of Biased Interpretation: Generality and Limitations," British Journal of Developmental Psychology 13 (1995): 347–366.

Podd, M.H. "Ego Identity Status and Morality: The Relationship between Two Constructs," Developmental Psychology 6 (1972): 497–507.

Ring, M. 1987. Beginning with the Pre-Socratics. Mountain View, CA: Mayfield Publishing.

Rorty, R. 1982. Consequences of Pragmatism. Minneapolis: University of Minnesota Press.

Rowe, I. and Marcia, J.E. "Ego Identity Status, Formal Operations, and Moral Development," Journal of Youth and Adolescence 9 (1980): 87–99.

Sass, L. and Woolfolk, R.L. 1985. "Psychoanalysis and the Hermeneutic Turn." Unpublished manuscript.

Slugoski, B.R., Marcia, J.E., and Koopman, R.F. "Cognitive and Social Interactional Characteristics of Ego Identity Status in College Males," Journal of Personality and Social Psychology 47 (1984): 646–661.

Smith, C.L., Maclin, D., Houghton, C., and Hennessey, M.G. "Sixth-Grade Students" Epistemologies of Science: The Impact of School Science Experiences on Epistemological Development," Cognition and Instruction 18 (2000): 349–422.

Statistics Canada. 2006. Aboriginal Peoples Survey 2001—Provincial and Territorial Reports: Off-Reserve Aboriginal Population. Ottawa, Canada.

Strawson, P.F. 1959. Individuals. London: Methuen.

Surian, L., Caldi, S., and Sperber, D. "Attribution of Beliefs by 13-Month-Old Infants," Psychological Science 18 (2007): 580–586.

Taylor, D.M. 2002. The Quest for Identity: From Minority Groups to Generation Xers. Westport, CT: Praeger.

van Hoof, A. "The Identity Status Field Re-Reviewed: An Update of Unresolved and Neglected Issues with a View on Some Alternative Approaches," Developmental Review 19 (1999): 497–556.

Wellman, H.M., Cross, D., and Watson, J. "Meta-Analysis of Theory-of-Mind Development: The Truth about False Belief," Child Development 72 (2001): 655–684.

6 Contributions of Ritual Expression at Puberty to Optimal Identity Formation of North American Indian Girls

Carol A. Markstrom

Identity formation of North American Indian adolescents is multifaceted, encompassing layers of influence from local, broader societal, and global levels. The local level is of primary interest in this chapter relative to the proximal sociocultural environment in which the adolescent is socialized according to the traditions, history, language, ceremonies, customs, and values associated with his/her particular culture. Identity is regarded as an attribute of the person; it is subjective in that one's self-perception is a uniquely personal experience. Nonetheless, as a personal experience, many social factors are influential as the adolescent comes to define and understand the self in a much more complex manner. One set of socio-cultural influences is those originating in rituals as demonstrated in coming-of-age ceremonies. Menarche is an experience onto which pubertal ceremonies are attached in many traditional cultures; indeed, menarche and subsequent menstrual cycles in numerous North American Indian cultures hold particular cultural significance. More specifically, the time frame in and around menarche is regarded as an especially critical or sensitive time of the life span in which the applications of poignant rituals are regarded as mechanisms of impact that yield desired outcomes, one being the ascription or assignment of a socially valued and endorsed identity (Markstrom 2008).

This chapter begins by clarifying terminology and content that is relevant according to the population of interest. Then, identity is defined with emphasis on its cultural or ethnic components. Rituals, as mechanisms of impact in identity formation, are defined along with rites of passage models. The significance of pubescence as a biopsychosocial event is articulated with attention directed toward cultural interpretations of menarche. A configuration of American Indian identity formation at the local level is presented and serves as an organizational framework to examine the influential mechanisms of rituals and ceremonies attached to the experience of menarche. Illustrations are drawn from my research among Apaches, Navajos, and Ojibwas to emphasize the impacts of rituals in identity formation.

AMERICAN INDIANS

For purposes of this chapter, *American Indians* refers to the indigenous people of the U.S. These are "The People" (Sutton 2008) who trace their origins to geographical places in North America and possess ancestral connections spanning generations prior to European contact. Today, the label *American Indian* is typically applied to those within the forty-eight contiguous states, and the term *Alaska Native* refers to the indigenous peoples of Alaska (e.g., Aleuts, Athabascans, Yuits, Inupiats, etc.). There are over 560 federally recognized American Indian/Alaska Native (AI/AN) tribes/bands, and there are hundreds of additional state-recognized and non-government-recognized tribes. The total AI/AN population is 5.2 million or 1.7 percent of the U.S. population (solely AI/AN or in combination with another race) (NCAI Policy Research Center 2011). The scope of this chapter is American Indians with some content also applicable to Alaska Natives. Further, the term *North American Indian*, when used, signifies the inclusive nature of puberty rituals across countries now known as the U.S. and Canada.

Prior to delving more directly into the topic of this chapter, it is instructive to consider actions of colonization that served to undermine North American Indian cultures resulting in the loss of numerous traditional ceremonial practices including most coming-of-age ceremonies (Duran et al. 1998). In spite of the prohibitive and destructive actions of colonization, some cultures have been able to retain or reinstate coming-of-age ceremonies; a topic I have examined relative to the functions of coming-of-age ceremonies in fostering and supporting positive development of contemporary American Indian youth and is addressed in this chapter (Markstrom 2008). Nonetheless, the statistics cannot be ignored on the high levels of social and behavioral problems (e.g., substance abuse) (Centers for Disease Control and Prevention 2003, 1070–1072) experienced by some of today's American Indian youth. The causal mechanisms behind these statistics are complex, but more generally can be linked to historical trauma stemming from long-standing colonization processes. Several labels appear in the literature that encapsulate such occurrences, such as "the Native American holocaust," "historical trauma," "intergenerational post-traumatic stress disorder," and "cultural genocide" (Duran, Duran, and Brave Heart 1998, 60–76; Evans-Campbell 2008; Tafoya and Del Vecchio 1996, 45–54; Weaver and Brave Heart 1999, 19–33).

Historically, loss of life through diseases, warfare, and genocide radically reduced the North American Indian population. Estimates of the Indigenous population in North America prior to European contact ranged up to eighteen million and even higher. Contrast that figure with that of four hundred years later in which the lowest population numbers were 228,000 American Indians in the U.S. in 1890 (Sutton 2008) and 102,000 Native people in Canada in 1871 (Indian and Northern Affairs Canada [INAC] 1996). These are sobering statistics that beg for explanation. Centuries of devastating actions of colonization undermined Native populations, traditional livelihoods, traditional tribal governing structures, expansive kinship networks, and other aspects of cultural integrity. Forced assimilation included perhaps the most destructive practice that undermined cultures: the imposition of Western-based formal education, which escalated in the late nineteenth century with the removal of Indian children from their families and cultural communities to remote residential schools. The harsh practices of these schools are now well documented in the literature, such as strict and severe discipline, imposed Western style of education, punishment for speaking one's language or practicing one's culture or religion, and generally remaking children into the appearance of White children (Brave Heart 2003; Nabokov 1999; Noriega 1992, 371–402; Tafoya and Del Vecchio 1996). The opportunity to engage young adolescent girls and boys in their cultures' coming-of-age ceremonies would not be possible within such a system of cultural isolation and imposed Western assimilation.

Forced Western-based educational practices plus lengthy absences from tribal communities served to weaken children's connections to their own cultures. Traditional cultural practices were diminished and sometimes lost with the marked absence of a younger generation upon whom traditional knowledge could be imparted. Governmental prohibitions against the practice of traditional ceremonies further undermined these practices. Within this historical legacy of intrusive forced assimilation and circumscribed lifestyles, it is remarkable that some cultures have been able to retain their coming-of-age ceremonies. Ceremonial practices of a variety of forms have experienced resurgence only in the past forty years through eras of social activism and the advancement of Native Nations sovereign rights. American Indian activism asserted and demanded the rights of tribes to exercise their sovereignty as Nations and openly participate in and perpetuate their cultural practices including their languages.

This brief overview of damaging actions of colonization serves as an explanatory framework for historical trauma with youth problems being one expression of such trauma. The focus of the present chapter, however, takes a very different approach and emphasizes the importance of cultural participation through coming-of-age ceremonies as protective mechanisms that yield positive outcomes to youth development most particularly according to strong ethnic or cultural identity. Indeed, writers have asserted the influence of enculturation as a protective factor for today's American Indian youth (Whitbeck 2011, 121–150; LaFromboise et al. 2006, 193–209). The next section situates the focus of this chapter further by careful articulation of the construct of identity followed by discussion on the role of rituals as mechanisms of impact in identity formation of American Indian adolescents.

ADOLESCENT IDENTITY FORMATION

The subject of adolescent identity formation has been considered from varying perspectives, some of which are more fully articulated in other chapters in this book (e.g., Chandler and Dunlop, Chapter 5). For the purposes of this chapter, however, Erik Erikson's (1968) psychosocial theory is a starting point for discussion. Based on Erikson's work, scholars have delineated identity according to two major distinctions of personal identity and social identity (Schwartz 2001, 7–58). Personal identity, as an internal structure of the ego, reflects unique goals, values, and beliefs of the individual that become apparent in life choices, such as occupation, politics, and religion. Social identity is also regarded as an internal structure of the ego, but is linked to self-definition relative to connections to others, such as an ethnic group or some other social group. A further distinction between personal and social forms of identity is that personal identity is self-selected or achieved; social identity is more typically ascribed to the individual, such as occurs with one being born a member of an ethnic group. However, ascribed social identity has varying levels of salience or meaning for members of a particular group. For instance, some individuals may be more invested or interested in connections to their ethnic social group than other members of the same group (Phinney 1992, 156–176; Phinney and Ong 2007, 271–281).

There is some adherence to Erikson's psychosocial theory and writings on identity across disciplines, such as in both developmental psychology and anthropology as explained by Markstrom and colleagues (1998, 337–354), who delved into particular linkages between these disciplines. The notion that ethnic identity encompasses salient features of social group membership is firmly embedded in developmental psychology and is typically referred to as ethnic identity, as in the works of Jean Phinney (Phinney 1992; Phinney and Ong 2007). A parallel term of "cultural identity" is frequently employed in the anthropological literature (Sökefeld 1999, 417–447); therefore, for the purposes of this chapter, both *ethnic identity* and *cultural identity* refer to the same aspect of social identity. Further, both developmental and anthropological scholars acknowledge the pioneering work of Erikson in advancing the study of identity formation (Hoare 1991, 45–53; Schlegel 1995, 15–32; Sökefeld 1999). For instance, the quality of self-sameness is a core psychosocial trait of a healthy identity as explained by Erikson: "The term 'identity' expresses such a mutual relation in that it connotes both a persistent sameness within oneself (selfsameness) and a persistent sharing of some kind of essential characteristics with others" (1980, 109). The latter aspect of this definition resonates with anthropological writings on identity as explained by Sökefeld: "Here it pointed not simply to selfsameness but to the sameness of the self with others, that is, to a consciousness of sharing certain characteristics (a language, a culture, etc.) within a group. This consciousness made up a group's identity" (Sökefeld 1999, 417).

Hoare regarded Erikson's conceptualizations as prominent in discussion of the fit between identity and culture, explaining that identity is "constructed from within the person and culture in which it is forged" (1991, 48). Certainly there are varied meanings of self and identity across cultures, depending on cultural preferences for self-understanding. For instance, autonomy is a value congruent with the highly individualistic American society; hence, personal identity constructions would be more salient due to an orientation toward the self (Phinney 2000, 27–31). As a counter-consideration, the social or group form of identity has been shown to be

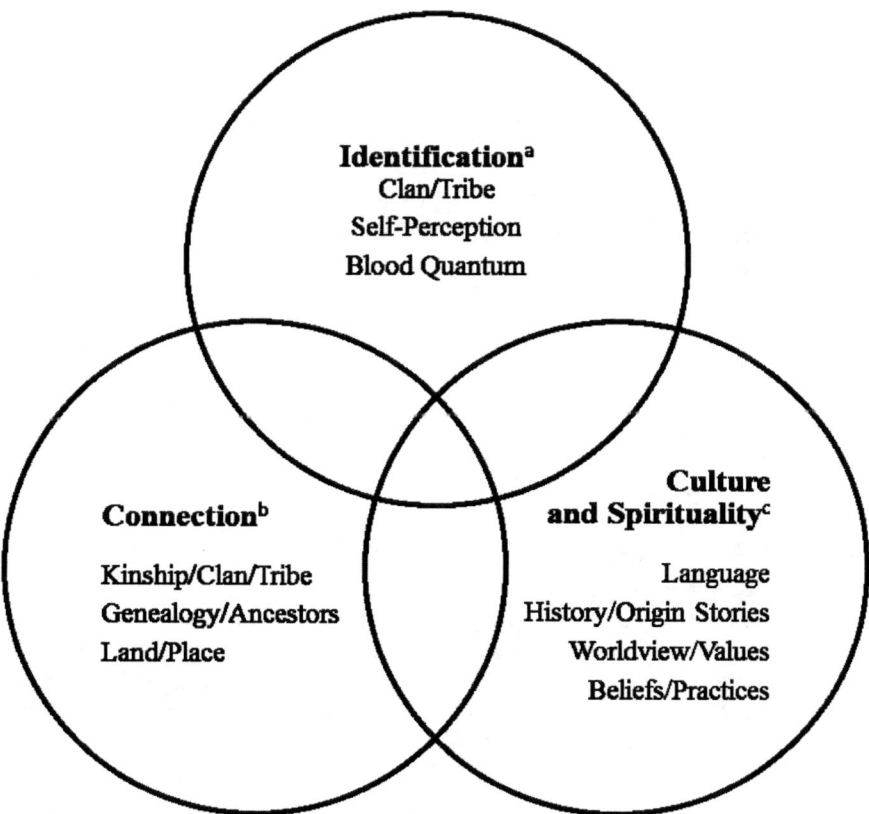

Figure 6.1   Dimensions of American Indian identity.
Source: Markstrom (2011a, 521).
[a]*Horse, 2001; Lee, 2006; Peroff & Wildcat, 2002; Pewewardy, 2002; Strum, 2002; Trimble, 2000.*
[b]*Basso, 1996; Brown and Cousins, 2001; Cooper, 1998; Deloria, 1994, 1999; DeMallie, 1998; Fogelson, 1998; Garroutte, 2003; Horse, 2001; Kawamoto and Cheshire, 1999; Markstrom, 2008; St. Pierre & Long Soldier, 1995; Weaver, 2001.*
[c]*Garroutte, 2003; Horse, 2001; Lee, 2006; Markstrom, 2008; St. Pierre and Long Soldier, 1995.*

more relevant among members of some ethnic groups and non-Western groups characterized by collectivist societies in which the individual understands the self more so according to his or her connections and relationships (Hoare 1991). American Indian cultures are more reflective of the latter with connection serving as a prominent theme as depicted in Figure 6.1 relative to other major themes of identification and culture/spirituality (Markstrom 2011a, 521). Further, a strong sense of ethnic identity is associated with more desirable adjustment outcomes for American Indian adolescents (Jones and Galliher 2007; Newman 2005, 734–746; Rieckmann, Wadsworth, and Deyhle 2004, 365–382; Whitesell, Mitchell, and Spicer 2009, 38–50). American Indian identity is complex and multidimensional, and is more fully examined in this chapter relative to rituals at pubescence or what is sometimes called coming-of-age. In particular, the present work is interested in rituals as mechanisms of influence in identity formation, as the next section illustrates.

RITUALS AS MECHANISMS OF INFLUENCE IN IDENTITY FORMATION

The formation of identity according to the dimensions in Figure 6.1 is influenced by inculcation of cultural values and beliefs through socialization processes, such as day-to-day interactions with family members, oral traditions that are imparted by respected elders in the extended kin network, and tribally based education that teaches language and culture. Additionally, adolescents learn about their culture's beliefs and traditions through their engagement and participation in culturally based rituals. Markstrom and Iborra (2003, 403) suggested that rituals at menarche serve as influential mechanisms of impact in identity formation processes: "The ritual aspect of rites of passage is argued to be the key element that links to the psychosocial conception of identity formation. It is the performance and repetition of rituals that occur throughout the rite of passage ceremony that advance the outcomes of optimal identity development." *Optimal identity formation* is a phrase used throughout the present work and is derived according to four elements found in the writings of Erikson encompassing: (a) a subjective sense of comfort according to one's becoming and feeling most like him/herself; (b) a sense of direction in life; (c) a sense of sameness and continuity of the self from the past, to the present, and to the future; and (d) the affirmation of a significant social community who values the identity being developed and expressed by the young person (Erikson 1987, 631–643; Erikson 1968).

Prior to more careful examination of the roles of rituals as mechanisms of impact in identity formation, it is necessary to define terminology of relevance to this topic. Rituals are highly symbolic interconnected actions that form a coherent ceremonial event yielding particular anticipated outcomes. They are defined as: "prescribed formal behavior for occasions not given over to technological routine, having reference to beliefs in mystical beings or powers" (Turner 1967, 19). Social conveyance from one life stage to the next (e.g., childhood to adolescence) is an illustration of one type of outcome from performances of interconnected rituals. Any particular ritual has its greatest meaning when understood in connection with the totality of the ceremonial event to which it is attached (Markstrom 2011b). For instance, rituals associated with a change of clothing accentuate a physical presence representative of the traditional regalia of an initiate's culture that may have been specified in oral traditions. The psychological salience of dressing in a prescribed manner, such as occurs at a girl's puberty ceremony, is further heightened through subsequent rituals, all of which reinforce the awareness of who she is becoming within her culture. Change in clothing signifies presumed internal changes and anticipated associated behavioral changes that will be exhibited through performance of socially valued roles and responsibilities as well as desired character traits (Markstrom 2008).

Coming-of-age ceremonies are particular kinds of ceremonial recognitions that occur in the transition from childhood to adolescence or adulthood. They characterize a type of initiation, but initiations can occur at any time in the life span whenever an individual is incorporated into a new social role or group. Puberty, as the obvious biopsychosocial event of adolescence, is a common time for the adolescent coming-of-age ceremony (Markstrom 2011b). The definitive event of menarche in girls is a ready cue to signal the timing for a coming-of-age ceremony. The biology of puberty may serve as the cue for a coming-of-age ceremony for girls, but it is the sociocultural arenas of significance that epitomize the meanings and purposes of these ceremonies. Relative to purposes of this chapter, Table 6.1 lists some of the common functions of adolescent initiation or coming-of-age ceremonies found across cultures.

Coming-of-age ceremonies can be understood within the rites of passage framework as conceptualized by Arnold van Gennep in his classic work titled *The Rites of Passage* ([1908] 1960) and Victor Turner's (1969) further delineation of the rites of passage model as a stage sequence of events. *Rites of passage* refers to both rituals that accompany the person from one social status to another (e.g., from childhood to adolescence or adulthood) and rituals that mark the passage of time (e.g., a solstice). The former type is pertinent to the present discussion on rites of passage as formalized ceremonial events that bring recognition, meaning, and significance to life transitions, such as birth, coming-of-age, marriage, and death. According to the van Gennep model, in undergoing a rite of passage, the individual progresses through a sequence of three phases in transitioning to the next stage of life (i.e., separation, transition, and incorporation, which is also called aggregation or reincorporation). More specific to the focus of this chapter, Schlegel and Barry (1980, 698) specified rites of passage during

Table 6.1   Functions of Adolescent Initiations and Rites of Passage Found in Various Cultures of the World

---

- Inculcation of cultural values, beliefs, and practices
- Adoption of desired social roles
- Exhibition of discipline, maturity, and social responsibility
- Inculcation of desired character traits related to disposition and temperament
- Tested and developed physical strength
- Longevity
- Expected social and behavioral changes conform to physical changes
- Reproductive viability or fertility
- Ascription of a socially valued identity
- Solidification and strengthening of kinship and other social bonds
- Spiritual enhancement or transcendence
- Announcement of girls' marital eligibility
- Recognition and celebration of change of status

Source: Markstrom (2011b, 155).

adolescence as: "some social recognition, in ceremonial form, of the transition from childhood into either adolescence or full adulthood."

The major psychosocial task of adolescence, namely, identity formation (Erikson 1968), has direct bearing on this discussion because the social conveyance function of a rite of passage implies changes in self-perception as well as changes in others' perceptions of the initiate. The implications for identity formation are far-reaching and have been articulated in Dunham and colleagues Ritual Process Paradigm (RPP)—an extension of van Gennep's three major sequences of separation, transition, and incorporation (Dunham, Kidwell, and Wilson 1986, 139–154). The RPP is explicit to identity transformations that occur over the course of rites of passage with the inclusion of a phase of preparation prior to the separation phase. Dunham, Kidwell, and Wilson (1986, 140) explain that rites of passage are "formalized social interactions with a phasing which separates individuals from their previous identities, carries them through a period of transition to a new identity, and incorporates them into a new role or social status." Hence, the RPP is particularly relevant to the present work due to its identity applications.

The first phase of the RPP, *preparation*, does not have a parallel in the van Gennep model as a sequence in a rite of passage. However, recognition of this phase demonstrates that the rite of passage is not a discrete event; rather, the individual's life course has been leading to the impending rite of passage at the proper time. Preparation encompasses childhood socialization by family and significant others that have taught the individual about herself within the context of group identifications along with the social roles, personal traits, and affective or cognitive features that will be transformed during the rite of passage. Menarche is the cue that the individual is ready for the rite of passage, which advances the initiate to the next phase of *separation*.

In the transition from preparation to separation, it is useful to consider Erikson's statement "identity formation begins where the usefulness of identification ends" (1968, 159). In other words, childhood identifications were sufficient for the child's situation of the self within the framework of the social group, but, at adolescence, identity becomes the more significant entity because it entails deeper psychological processes with an anticipated result of a coherent, stable, and meaningful sense of self. Separation encompasses physical and psychological components in which routine aspects of everyday life are suspended as the person is brought into a sphere of exceptionality. The initiate is symbolically and/or physically removed, either individually or in groups (Markstrom 2011b). For example, in some American Indian and other traditional cultures of the world, girls are physically separated at menarche, frequently for several days and, in some cases, up to two years as occured in some subarctic indigenous cultures (Markstrom 2008). Initiates may be required to perform extensive physically demanding rituals, such as engagement in fasting, sleep deprivation, and running long distances. The initiate is separated from a former known secure identity without the comforts of the new identity having yet been absorbed; hence, psychological states of distress, insecurity, and uncertainly are typical of the present ambiguous "liminal" status (Turner 1969). In essence, separation exposes the initiate to new requirements and responsibilities for which internal resources for managing such challenges have not yet emerged.

The isolated and distinctive status of separation is continued into the next stage of *transition*, as explained by Turner, individuals "are at once no longer classified and not yet classified" (1969, 6). The liminal "betwixt and between" status is still evident because a new identity has not yet been incorporated. However, some of the emotional discomforts of separation have diminished as the initiate is more fully engaged in her rite of passage and has yielded to ritual demands accompanied by a willingness to be guided. Awe, openness, and flexibility may be characteristic of transition during which time feelings of insecurity, uncertainty, and anxiety are replaced by relief, joy, and even ecstasy (Dunham, Kidwell, and Wilson 1986).

The last phase of *reincorporation* allows the individual to return to a state of stability as she transitions back into her society, but with significant alterations due to having undergone the rite of passage (Turner 1969). A public ceremony may occur with celebration solidifying the reincorporation of the individual back into society. The initiate and others recognize that the old identity has been relinquished and a new identity is emerging along with associated roles and responsibilities. The initiate's social group continues to support and encourage her in the absorption of a new socially recognized and valued identity that is consistent with the life stage she has now achieved.

Reincorporation can be understood according to Sebald's (1992) suggestion that initiation ceremonies or rites of passage serve three primary functions—informing, announcing, and emotionally anchoring. *Informing* is social presentation of the initiate to demonstrate she is prepared, trained, or indoctrinated according to the new rights granted by her culture. A public *announcement* may be given to the tribe, community, or society to alert others that they should alter their own behaviors toward the initiate to be consistent with the new status she has attained. Initiation ceremonies also function to *emotionally anchor* the individual firmly within the community, and such anchoring should be observed through responses of loyalty, fidelity, and commitment according to societal approval and endorsement of the initiate's new roles.

As previously stated, pubescence is a significant time frame for the application of rites of passage. The next section more specifically probes the biopsychosocial experience of pubescence with particular attention to cultural responses to this stage of development.

THE SIGNFICANCE OF PUBESCENCE

The onset of adolescence begins with pubescence, which is a highly transitional phase in the life span involving various processes. The changes of pubescence are initially hidden and unknown to everyone, but ultimately become apparent to all those in association with the physically changing adolescent. It is interesting to consider that the inhibition of hormones permits childhood to occur, but the release of the gonadotropin-releasing hormone (GnRH) pulse generator serves as the "pubertal trigger" (Shirtcliff 2009, 99) ushering in a series of hormonal and physical processes with the release of androgens stimulating the earliest signs of puberty (Shirtcliff, Dahl, and Pollak 2009, 328). Puberty begins at the end of childhood and conveys the child to adult size, shape, and sexual potential. The ages of eight for girls and nine for boys are given as the traditional ages for the beginning of normal puberty development (Susman and Rogol 2004, 19). Puberty consists of (a) maturation of reproductive capacity, including primary sex characteristics, i.e., sex organs that are directly involved in reproduction; (b) development of secondary sex characteristics (i.e., visible features of femaleness or maleness, which for females includes breast budding, growth of pubic hair, and widening of hips, etc.); (c) development of the sex drive; and (d) maturation in shape and size.

It is significant that, at pubescence, the child has not experienced changes in growth and sexual development of this magnitude since the fetal stages (Susman and Rogol 2004, 18–44), and the impacts reverberate into social and psychological domains, making this a biopsychosocial event (Berenbaum 2011, 95–104; Petersen, Leffert, and Graham 1995; Susman and Rogol 2004). The biopsychosocial approach has been used to consider the multiple dimensions of change and development occurring over the course of puberty and the interrelated nature of these changes. For instance, social reactions by families, peers, and others relative to the observable changes in the adolescent can subsequently impact the adolescent's behaviors (Shirtc-liff, Dahl, and Pollak 2009, 327–337; Susman and Rogol 2004). Likewise, a culture's response to the biological event of menarche has strong social and cultural salience according to the application of ritual actions with one purpose being changes in social and psychological domains of adolescent development. Specifically, the cultural component is of primary interest in this chapter, particularly according to the experience of menarche as a definitive event in the pubertal process that serves as a cue for the application of pubertal rituals in American Indian societies. The interconnected rituals of rites of passage originate in oral traditions thereby demonstrating the strong spiritual significance of these ceremonies. Accordingly, the adolescent coming-of-age ceremony not only facilitates transition into the next stage of life, but is also a transition into the spiritual realm (Markstrom 2008). The social and spiritual functions of these ceremonies are discussed with greater depth in later sections.

This overview of rituals, rites of passage, and the cultural significance of pubescence among North American Indians serves as a basis for discussion of the identity implications of coming-of-age ceremonies. The methodology according to which this research was conducted is first reviewed.

OVERVIEW OF RESEARCH METHODOLOGY

I have conducted field research in Apache, Navajo, and Ojibwa cultures explicit to the topic of girls' coming-of-age ceremonies (Markstrom 2008; Markstrom and Iborra 2003). Ethnographic and case study research designs were applied. Relative to ethnography, culture was the driving force to understand the influence of rituals in identity formation of North American Indian adolescents. The case study approach yielded in-depth analyses of puberty customs in the identified cultures. The sampling for the research was purposeful and was directed toward Apache and Navajo pubescent girls at the time of their coming-of-age ceremonies or who had recently undergone such ceremonies. Girls were engaged in semi-structured interviews and, frequently, their parents, grandparents, or other relatives anywhere up to eighteen months after the ceremony. In addition, other cultural experts, such as medicine men and women, were interviewed from Apache, Navajo, and Ojibwa cultures.

I also engaged in participant observation at Apache and Navajo puberty ceremonies. Participant observation involved attending a sequence of events over a number of days to observe and participate in numerous phases of the puberty ceremony. Observations were committed to memory and later recorded in audiotapes or notebooks at a convenient time. The participant observer role permitted engagement in as many rituals as were permissible over the course of the coming-of-age ceremony. For instance, I ran with Navajo girls during running rituals as part of the Kinaaldá. On many occasions, family members and close associates of the initiate requested that I participate in rituals expected by adult women in attendance, including wearing the traditional regalia of the culture. In addition to observations from the participant observer role, knowledge was obtained through countless informal conversations at ceremonies and subsequently entered into audiotaped or written field notes.

Audiotaped semi-structured interviews of initiates, their parents, and other adults were conducted. An interview guide was developed to pose questions to interviewees on: (a) perceived purposes and functions of coming-of-age ceremonies for initiates, their families and communities, and the world; (b) preparation for coming-of-age ceremonies; (c) perceived positive outcomes and contributions to identity formation and to the development of contemporary young women; and (d) initiates' understanding of the meanings and symbolism underlying the complex rituals with which they were engaged.

Extensive review of indigenous, historical, anthropological, and psychological literatures on puberty customs of North American Indians served as additional sources of data. Examination of physical artifacts and aspects of material culture, such as traditional regalia worn by initiates, also supplied data. Photographs were taken when permission was obtained from families and those officiating at ceremonies. These photographs were later examined to establish sequence and substance of events. Preexisting films were used to gather additional information on the ceremonies of interest.

Sources of data were examined in a triangulated manner (e.g., observations of the investigator vis-à-vis interviews). This approach advanced interpretative analysis of the multiple data sources. Corroboration was sought across sources, and salient themes of meaning were derived. An example of a theme would be the belief that the success of a coming-of-age ceremony is dependent on, in part, the pubescent girl's personal investment in the ceremony. Discrepancies between data sources also were considered thereby prompting deeper probing of a particular ritual or interpretation. Themes and conclusions were subjected to "member checking." That is, the investigator engaged in an ongoing process of discussion with cultural insiders according to interpretations and conclusions and to clarify points of uncertainty. The final written products were also read by cultural insiders for validity. In short, the final themes and conclusions emerged through an iterative process of observation, analysis, clarification, and refinement.

Prior to more careful examination of rituals as mechanisms in identity formation, it is useful to consider the question concerning the number of Apache and Navajo girls who undergo coming-of-age ceremonies today. A specific number is not available, but some Western Apaches have suggested to me that close to half of the girls experience the Sunrise Dance. As well, both Apache and Navajo informants explained these ceremonies have greatly increased in performance in recent decades (Markstrom 2008; Markstrom and Iborra 2003). The Apache Sunrise Dance and the Navajo Kinaaldá reached their lowest numbers in the 1960s, but have steadily increased since that time quite likely due to the American Indian activism and cultural resurgence that escalated in the late 1960s and 1970s (Markstrom 2008). Nonetheless, not all pubescent girls undergo ceremonies. One reason is that some families adhere to particular forms of Christianity that do not sanction participation in traditional ceremonies. As well, lower-income families may find it a financial strain to sponsor these events. However, many Apache and Navajo families of modest to low incomes somehow find the means to sponsor their daughters' ceremonies, particularly with support from extended family and others in the community. Further, with the Apache Sunrise Dance, there are more limited and less costly one-day and two-day forms as opposed to the typical four-day event. Still, some girls may choose not to undergo a puberty ceremony, and my impression is that in most of these cases, they are not forced to do so. Nonetheless, it is quite frequent that reluctant initiates may acquiesce to family desire. Childhood enculturation seems to be an important factor in preparing girls for their ceremony; specifically, being reared in a family and kin context in which the traditional culture is valued and taught to the younger generation. Younger girls are always in attendance at the ceremonies of older girls and learn of future expectations for themselves (Markstrom 2008).

RITUALS AND THE MULTIDIMENSIONAL IDENTITY MODEL

There are numerous influences on ethnic or cultural identity formation of American Indian adolescents (e.g., parenting, socialization, culturally based education, experiences). Of interest in this chapter are influences from rituals and ceremonies that occur at or around the time of menarche. Figure 6.1 demonstrates the multidimensional nature of American Indian identity. Table 6.2 is organized around these broader three categories of American Indian identity, but with examples of ritual and ceremonial components meaningful to each form of identity. It is important to remember that the circles overlap in Figure 6.1, which is echoed in the multiple applications of some ritual elements (e.g., oral traditions) to more than one form of identity in Table 6.2. For additional elucidation, the ceremonial illustrations in Table 6.2 are organized around four phases of rites of passage as articulated in the RPP (Dunham, Kidwell, and Wilson 1986) Table 6.3 is included to show likely outcomes for identity formation from participation in a coming-of-age ceremony. The following sections provide description of content in Figure 6.1 and Tables 6.2 and 6.3.

Table 6.2   Influences from Rituals and Ceremonies on American Indian Identity Formation as Organized around Phases of Rites of Passage (ROP)

	Dimensions of American Indian Identity		
Phase of ROP	*Identification*	*Connection*	*Culture/Spirituality*
Preparation	• Childhood socialization • Ethnic identification/labeling • Menarche cue for ROP	• Understanding of self in relation to kin and tribe • Awareness of broad-based connections to others and all creation • Coalescing of kin to support ceremony	• Childhood socialization according to the customs, beliefs, values, and language of the culture.
Separation	• Dressing rituals • Relocation to traditional structure • Emerging identification with female mentor • Awareness of personal significance of female archetype of oral tradition	• Selection of female mentor • Influence of mentor on initiate—verbally and through actions • Dressing rituals that connect initiate to her mentor and female archetype • Oral traditions/origin stories told that reinforce both vertical and horizontal dimension of connection	• Historical consciousness • Oral traditions/origin stories told • Initiate is immersed within her culture's customs and language • Imposed isolation of vision quest
Transition	• Identification with female mentor and female archetype • Alterations in self-perception through rituals	• Oral traditions/origin stories told • Performance of physically demanding rituals • Female mentor massages/shapes initiate (identification by absorption)	• Oral traditions/origin stories told • Rituals produce spiritual transformations • Initiate empowered and responds to request for blessings/prayers • Acquisition of spirit helper through vision quest
Reincorporation	• Role performances that heighten cultural identifications • Postceremonial reflection on acquisitions from ceremony	• Naming rituals ascribe aspects of identity • Social recognition and reinforcement of change in status • Expectations to fulfill inherent responsibilities toward the well-being of others and all creation	• Role performances • Others request blessings/prayers from initiate • Celebration—singing, dancing, partaking of traditional foods • Interpretation of vision

Table 6.3   Outcomes of Coming-of-Age Ceremonies According to Dimensions of American Indian Identity

Dimensions of American Indian Identity		
Identification	*Connection*	*Culture/Spirituality*
• Altered self-perception • Greater comfort with the self in terms of who she is becoming • Identification with female role models of culture, including female archetype • Heightened awareness of ethnic identification and ethnic label with tribe and possibly clan • Emerging ethnic identity and feelings of ethnic pride • Feeling of sameness and continuity from earlier childhood identifications to more internalized self-awareness with expectations for oneself into the future	• Affirmation of initiate's emerging identity by significant social community • Greater sense of direction in life as reinforced through social connections • Heightened sense of group identity • Greater sense of relatedness with others and the surrounding creation—with inherent responsibilities toward the well-being of these entities • Greater awareness of expected social roles and performance of such roles	• Spiritual awareness and embeddedness • Greater knowledge of cultural beliefs and practices • Incorporation and expression of culturally valued character traits and behaviors • Hope for the future through accomplishment of a complex ceremony that advances strength and longevity

Identification

Identification encompasses labeling as American Indian, in order words, whether and how one labels the self as American Indian as well as the implications of this label for self-perceptions. Identification is the starting point in children's awareness of their ethnic identification including self-categorization and labeling (Phinney and Ong 2007). In this respect, the phase of preparation in the RPP encompasses earlier life socialization of the child, which would be inclusive of ethnic self-identification and self-labeling as foundations upon which identity is further ascribed and understood through the coming-of-age ceremony and over the course of adolescence. Social group membership and identifications to one's tribe (sometimes including clan within a tribe) serve to foster identity formation and ultimately shape self-perceptions (Horse 2001, 91–107; Pewewardy 2002, 22–56; Trimble 2000, 197–222), including ethnic or cultural identity.

Self-perception is an aspect of understanding clan and tribal membership according to how the adolescent girl regards herself as a member of her group. Rites of passage alter self-perceptions (see Table 6.3) according to the initiate's status prior to (phase of preparation) and after completing the event (phase of reincorporation). In some cultures, the initiates are directed to engage in self-reflection for a number of days after the coming-of-age ceremony to consider the significance of what they have undergone and what has been acquired. Interviews with initiates who had experienced the Apache Sunrise Dance yielded very telling statements suggestive of the changes in self-perception and reinforcement of connections to one's tribe and clan. Acquisitions reported by initiates include: "learn about my culture," "have respect for my culture," "feel better about myself," "proud of myself," "know who I am as an Apache," "support my culture and tribe" (Markstrom 2008). These statements signify that culturally desired impacts of the Sunrise Dance were perceived by initiates and are indicative of the advancement of ethnic self-identification and ethnic/cultural identity (see Table 6.3).

Identification is reinforced in dressing rituals that frequently are part of the separation phase of a rite of passage at puberty (see Table 6.2). A series of events that occur earlier in portions of both Navajo and Apache coming-of-age ceremonies at menarche surround the initiate's change of clothing (dressing may be assisted by an adult female role model) to emulate the appearance of her cultural heroine of oral tradition. For instance, Apache girls are dressed in traditional regalia reflective of their cultural role model, White Painted Woman. Each ornament possesses symbolic meaning believed to contribute to the success of the broader rite of passage and the success of the girl's future. An eagle feather fastened to the initiate's hair symbolizes what is perhaps the primary objective of this ceremony, namely, longevity or long life for the initiate (Markstrom 2008). The white and gray of the eagle feather represents the color of hair that comes with old age. The purposes would not be known to outsiders unless deeper probing into the meaning of this symbolic ornament is conducted (Turner 1969).

The separation phase of a rite of passage also has application to identification in terms of the type of dwellings girls inhabit during separation (see Table 6.2). Typically these are the traditional forms of lodging of the initiate's culture thereby further reinforcing significant cultural components during her coming-of-age ceremony. Such structures include wickiups for Apaches, tepees for Lakotas/Nakotas/Dakotas, wigwams for Ojibwas, hogans for Navajos and so on (Markstrom 2008). Such physical structures may not be in widespread use for contemporary housing, but may continue to be used for ceremonial purposes. The physicality of construction of the structure may be significant; for instance, Western Apache girls are required to build their wickiups with their own hands. The symbolic meanings of such structures, however, possess the greater significance. The sense of separation is accentuated through the requirement that the initiate reside in such a structure during various phases of her coming-of-age ceremony. Like dressing in traditional regalia, the lodging structure emphasizes the distinctiveness of her status as well as identification with traditional aspects of her culture. The structures also are visual reminders of origin stories and oral traditions within which formative and foundational events may have occurred. For instance, the Navajo hogan is said to represent the first hogan of oral tradition (Lincoln 1981).

Blood quantum, or the degree of Indian blood one has inherited, is shown as one dimension of identification in Figure 6.1 and becomes particularly relevant with tribal and federal governmental policies that set blood quantum levels (percentages) required for certain services for American Indians (Fogelson 1998, 40–59; Horse 2001; Lee 2006, 79–103; Peroff and Wildcat 2002, 349–361). The identity implications of blood quantum to American Indian coming-of-age ceremonies are not so directly apparent. Indirectly, however, an application can be drawn to the lineal and descent patterns of a culture. In matrilineal cultures, inheritance patterns, including clan names, follow the female lineage. Markstrom and Iborra (2003) elaborated on such a matrilineal connection of Navajo culture, observing that the Ideal Woman or the adult female mentor serves as the bridge between the female archetype of the culture, Changing Woman, and the initiate. In this case, the significant component of the connection is cultural and spiritual rather than blood; nonetheless, it is a female lineage that indicates connection to the female cultural heroine (see Tables 6.2 and 6.3).

Coming-of-age ceremonies serve to reinforce childhood socialization processes during the preparation phase in which the adolescent is told of her social position relative to culture, tribe, and kin. Identification implies connection—both of which are reinforced and strengthened through the rituals of coming-of-age ceremonies as illustrated in the following discussion on the connection component of Figure 6.1.

Connection

Connection in Figure 6.1 demonstrates the broad-based value for relationships in American Indian cultures that encompass human and nonhuman entities. Horizontally, connections extend to other humans as well as nonhuman elements of the surrounding creation (e.g., animals, plants, physical features in the environment) with which the self is interdependent. Vertical connections span generations, reflective of lineage and one's ancestors. Therefore, connection encompasses kinship/clan/tribe, genealogy/ancestors, and land/place—a delineation consistent with Fogelson's (1998) historical contextualization of American Indian identity according to three interrelated prerequisites of community, blood and descent, and land.

Social connection is foremost in American Indian identity, according to connections to family, kin, clan, tribe (DeMallie 1998, 306–356; Fogelson 1998; Horse 2001; Kawamoto and Chesire 1999, 94–104; Lee 2006; Pewewardy 2002; Weaver 2001, 240–255), and is reinforced at the preparation phase of a rite of passage. *Group identity* is a related term to signify identity as defined according to belonging to a group or tribe (Horse 2001). Kinship strikes at the core of American Indian identity and encompasses commitment to connection and belongingness as well as the social responsibility associated with these connections (Garroutte 2003). This *is* social identity as the individual comes to regard the self according to the "we" or "us" in relationship to others. In regards to connection and social responsibility, it is instructive to review findings from Schlegel and Barry's (1980) global, cross-cultural examination of puberty customs based on data from the Standard Cross-Cultural Sample (SCCS). Among North American indigenous societies, the primary focus of adolescent initiation ceremonies was found to be socialization of responsibility, defined as "impressing upon the initiate the importance of taking adult duties, usually productive ones" (Schlegel and Barry 1980, 708). Certainly this focus is apparent in the instruction of initiates and role performances that are ritually performed with the expectation that later these will be part of her repertoire of behaviors (see Tables 6.2 and 6.3).

Coming-of-age ceremonies for girls are kinship-sponsored and kinship-supported events. The broader kinship network is called upon to provide material, physical, and social support to acquire the needed resources to host such an event, which will more firmly establish the initiate within connectional social systems. Esteemed family and clan members frequently are identified to play integral roles in the girl's coming-of-age. A common theme across North American Indian coming-of-age ceremonies is the influence of an older, respected woman (or women) to mentor and instruct the initiate along with frequent admonitions to the initiate from such a mentor to be industrious because her behavior at this time will affect her future roles as an adult woman (Markstrom 2008). The selection of such a mentor occurs in preparation and separation phases of the rite of passage. In Navajo culture this is the Ideal Woman, previously identified, who is typically a relative of the initiate, such as a grandmother or aunt. In the case of the Apache Sunrise Dance, the adult female mentor (*na ihł esn* or "she makes her ready" or "she prepares her") is a nonrelative who is identified for her respectable and admired behaviors and disposition. The Sunrise Dance, therefore, builds fictive kin in a culture that highly values kinship, as the adult mentor becomes the girl's "godmother," as she is referred to by some Apaches. The relationship is reported to extend beyond the ceremony with the godmother maintaining a significant role in the initiate's life for years to come (Markstrom 2008).

In Navajo and Apache cultures, the female mentor performs rituals designed to impact the initiate according to desired outcomes, such as massaging rituals in order to impress on the initiate desired physical and character traits (see Table 6.2). The adult mentor is herself regarded for her qualities of physical strength, health, beauty, ambition, and character, and displays of mastery of desired skills, such as rug weaving in Navajo culture

(Markstrom and Iborra 2003). She has established herself and is well positioned to impact the initiate by means of mutually engaged rituals. Clearly, the adult female mentor is in the position as shaper of identity, and her agencies of influence are socialization through instruction. In addition, in a more mystical sense, traits of the female mentor are transferred on to the initiate through such ritual actions as massaging. Such rituals of shaping are particularly pertinent to the transition phase of a rite of passage and have been referred to as "identification by absorption" (Reichard 1977), signifying that the initiate is being compelled to identify and absorb the desired traits of her female mentor via the physical actions of rituals.

Genealogy/ancestors refer to the vertical connections that span time demonstrating the continuity of lineages across generations. Naming rituals at coming-of-age ceremonies serve as illustrations of bringing continuity to connections (see Table 6.2). In such cases, a new name may be assigned to the young person serving to ascribe features of identity. Naming ceremonies are highly symbolic relative to identity conceptions, and the one who has the power to bestow or ascribe the name could be regarded as the one empowered with shaping the identity of the young person. Pubescence, as a transitional phase in life, is a prime time for a new name that signifies a change in status. To enhance intergenerational connections, the young person may be named after esteemed relatives, elders, or ancestors (alive or deceased) with the hope that he/she will pattern the attributes of the original name holder. An example of Lakota naming occurs within the context of Hunkapi, or Making of Relatives Ceremony, which is one of the seven rituals the Lakota derived from the sacred teachings of White Buffalo Calf Woman. The ceremony not only formally connects the person to human relatives, past or present, but to all physical and spiritual beings (Markstrom 2008; Pierre and Long Soldier 1995). In today's version of this ceremony, older relatives assign pubescent girls names of deceased relatives who possessed desirable qualities. Identity is ascribed through numerous ritual actions including the assignment of a name of someone it is expected the girl will emulate. More broadly across cultures, the assignment of a new name may occur near the end of successful completion of a rite of passage or during reincorporation. It serves to signify that the recipient has achieved a new social status with associated role expectations. In essence, naming imparts a social identity, and the assignment of a subsequent name informs the person and his or her social network that an important transformation has occurred (Alford 1988).

An additional aspect of connection particularly significant to group identity is meaning and power attached to geographical places of significance to one's people. Hence, connection to land/place brings meaning and substance to one's self-understanding as understood through one's group's situation relative to geographically consequential places of oral tradition. Land/place may be significant in the origin stories upon which the coming-of-age ceremony is based. The Diyin Dine'é, or Holy People, in Navajo ceremonials serve central roles in curing, purifying, and blessing. For instance, the

Kinaaldá or girl's puberty ceremony is part of the Blessing Way complex with the figure of Changing Woman (*Asdzáá Nádleehé*) of central importance. In Navajo oral tradition, Changing Woman was found by First Man and First Woman on Gobernador Knob, which is located just east of the present day Navajo Nation. The first Kinaaldá was formulated by the Diyin Dine'é especially for Changing Woman on the twelfth day of her life when she reached womanhood (Roessel 1981). Changing Woman's Kinaaldá is the prototype for subsequent coming-of-age ceremonies for Navajo girls at menarche. The telling of this and other aspects of Navajo origin stories is linked to places such as Gobernador Knob and serve as visible reminders that inform people who they are and from where they are derived (Markstrom 2011a).

In the telling and retelling of origin stories, sense of place is firmly established as events and cosmological constructions about instructive personages are impressed upon listeners. Further, the initiate and other listeners are reminded of who they are in relation to a complex cosmology as well as a broad-based natural world that encompasses fundamental elements as well as plants, animals, and geographical places (Markstrom 2011a also see Table 6.3). Each of these entities, likewise, is regarded according to their inherent identities and associated forms of power. In this respect, identity, then, is not just a human possession, but is attributed to a variety of animate and inanimate entities with which humans share the world and are in relationships. The following quote by Fogelson (1998, 48) encapsulates these sentiments: "Native American identity was connected to the land as a site of origination in narratives of ethnogenesis, as a home area where life was lived, and as the final resting place of mortal remains."

In summary of this section on connection, one of the most impressive aspects of American Indian coming-of-age ceremonies that I have observed is the social affirmation and support received by initiates. For a period of several days, scores of people are invested in the promotion of the initiate's attainment of a healthy, long life. Her significant social community clearly values the identity that is being ascribed to her and, likewise, she embraces and expresses components of that socially valued identity (see Tables 6.2 and 6.3). This observation is congruent with remarks of identity theorist Erikson, who observed that an optimal identity, in part, is an identity that is valued and affirmed by the social community of the adolescent (Erikson 1968, 1987). Such a sentiment is consistent with the communal orientation of North American Indian societies in which connections to others and all entities of the creation are integral aspects of one's sense of self and identity.

Culture/Spirituality

The significance of history and origin stories was introduced in the previous section on connections, but there are further aspects to examine in this section in the four facets of culture/spirituality that might be regarded as the substance of ethnic or cultural identity. Culture/spirituality encompasses dimensions of language, history/origin stories, worldview/values, and beliefs/practices as shown in Figure 6.1. Cultural components are integral aspects of identity and perpetuated through oral traditions in which origin stories are told and rituals are performed (Horse 2001; Lee 2006; Peroff and Wildcat 2002). It is apparent that practices of culturally based rituals contribute to the ongoing maintenance and stability of a culture because these events provide opportunities to practice and express cultures—oral traditions are told and performed, significant songs are song, prayers are prayed, traditional foods are prepared and consumed, traditional regalia is worn, and the language of the tribe is spoken and sung (Markstrom 2008; Markstrom 2011a).

Historical consciousness is also implicit to various dimensions in Figure 6.1 (Fogelson 1998; Garroutte 2003) and is imparted through oral traditions that enlighten listeners to their culture's origins (see Table 6.2). It is during separation and transition phases of the coming-of-age ceremony when the imparting of oral traditions is particularly significant. For instance, in Lakota/Nakota/Dakota oral tradition, the girl's puberty ceremony, called Išnati Awicalowanpi, or what is also called the Buffalo Ceremony, is said to come from instructions of White Buffalo Calf Woman, who told the people to remember her through the White Buffalo Calf Ceremony (coming-of-age) (Markstrom 2008). Additional components of historical consciousness are sensibilities that link to particular geographical places affixed to oral traditions that tell people about themselves as members of a group that has endured over time (Fogelson 1998; Garroutte 2003). An illustration of such a place for Navajos is Gobernador Knob as illustrated in the previous section.

To bring greater specificity to this section, closer examination of the Apache Sunrise Dance or *na ih es* or "getting her ready" is particularly illustrative of the dimensions of culture/spirituality, including telling of origin stories, re-creating a setting resembling earlier Apache camp life, preparing and serving traditional foods, singing and drumming traditional songs, wearing of traditional regalia, and so on (see Table 6.2). Weekend after weekend in the warmer months, these ceremonies are practiced among Western Apaches for individual girls with hundreds of people in attendance. Clearly, these events are meaningful and reinforce what is valued and regarded as the substance and core of Apache culture. The Sunrise Dance is a long-standing practice of the Western Apaches; however, related versions are practiced by other Apache groups including Mescaleros and Jicarillas.

The origin story of Western Apaches provides context and meaning for this ceremony and the rituals of which it is comprised. The following frequently cited quote is descriptive of the Apache origin story: "White-Painted Woman said, 'From here on we will have the girl's puberty rite. When the girls first menstruate you shall have a feast. There shall be songs for these girls. During this feast the Gahe shall dance in front. After that there shall be round dancing and face-to-face dancing'" (Opler 1942, 15). White Painted Woman is a supernatural being in Apache cosmological beliefs, similar to Changing Woman of the Navajos, and, indeed, she is sometimes called Changing Woman. There are numerous parallels in the origin stories of these two cultures of the same northern Athabascan environs who migrated to the Southwest centuries ago. It is the identity of this supernatural personage who is the role model for initiates and into whom the rituals facilitate transformation, as explained in oral tradition: White Painted Woman never gets too old. When she gets to be a certain age, she goes walking toward the east. After a while she sees herself in the distance walking toward her. They both walk until they come together and after that there is only one, the young one. Then she is like a young girl all over again (Markstrom 2008).

The transformation of Apache and Navajo girls into the significant female figure of oral tradition solidifies the perception that initiates are in special, sacred statuses and, accordingly, they are sought as sources of blessings. There are particular rituals within the Apache Sunrise Dance and the Navajo Kinaaldá in which initiates may be approached by others for prayer and blessings. For example, during the Kinaaldá the Navajo initiate runs her hands along the sides of attendees in a ritual called "stretching," which brings blessings to adults and aids children in their development (Markstrom and Iborra 2003). Rituals similar in sentiment were also observed in numerous cultures of the past. For instance, the Ingalik had a purifying ritual for boys to cleanse them from substances that might compromise hunting expeditions. In this case, during their year of seclusion, pubescent girls could provide such needed purification to boys with whom they were related or friendly (Osgood 1958).

The special quality of menarche and the proper application and performance of required rituals at this time of life might be regarded as key ingredients that facilitate such empowerment. The initiate's empowerment may be regarded as a form of public property, as in cases of Apaches and Navajos wherein blessings become possible for others. Transformation and empowerment of initiates can be particularly linked to transition and reincorporation phases of a rite of passage because clearly the initiate no longer is regarded in her status prior to the onset of the ceremony. She is viewed as the recipient of desired qualities made possible by her life stage and the accompanying ritual actions. In the North American Indian tradition, the initiate's sphere of influence may be perceived to extend to the world as broader life-giving properties are perpetuated that sustain and re-create all forms of life. As explained by an Apache medicine woman, "that four day period, she (the initiate) is putting the whole world on her shoulders" (Markstrom 2008, 350).

One type of adolescent coming-of-age experience not yet discussed is the vision quest—a practice prevalent across Native North America, sometimes for girls, but more frequently for boys. Depending on the culture, a vision quest might have occurred at any time in life, but puberty was regarded as particularly timely in tribes of several cultural areas of Native North America (Markstrom 2008). Ojibwas regard the vision quest as a significant experience for both boys and girls, sometimes beginning in limited forms earlier in childhood, as well as having applicability for girls at menarche. As with other rites of passage, preparation begins in childhood with socialization according to Ojibwa customs. Separation begins the vision quest and the individual is brought to a remote place by a respected and knowledgeable adult. Then, the initiate remains alone, four days being a frequent length of time, but sometimes shorter or longer. This type of separation facilitates the phase of transition during which time the initiate fasts and prays for a vision with the goal of obtaining a spiritual helper who will be a guide and protector for the life span. A successful vision quest results in such an acquisition. During the reincorporation phase, the vision may be interpreted by informed mentor(s) to enlighten the adolescent recipient. Sometimes a new name, a sacred name, is assigned to the young person based upon the content of the vision (Markstrom 2008).

The dimension of beliefs and practice in Figure 6.1 is clearly integrated throughout the rituals of coming-of-age ceremonies (see Tables 6.2 and 6.3). Some rituals involve role performances, which are additional illustrations of the reincorporation phase of a rite of passage. In countless North American Indian cultures of the past, and several today, ritual actions are performed by initiates that are demonstrative of roles of adult females of their cultures, such as sewing, beadwork, and quill working as in Lakota/Nakota/Dakota cultures (Markstrom 2008; Markstrom and Iborra 2003). Corn grinding occurs in Navajo, Hopi, and Zuni cultures. In Apache culture, initiates prepare four traditional breads. These and other gender-linked tasks of industry reflect useful skills of the past that may have continued utility in the present day. Girls may have observed and performed these tasks in a limited fashion in childhood, but there is a stronger expectation supported by explicit instruction that occurs at the time of coming-of-age, as explained by Markstrom: "the coming-of-age event serves as a culmination of earlier experiences that are embellished in the present context with an expectation that targeted behaviors will continue into the future" (2008, 350–351). The repetitive quality of ritual performances possess strong functions of reinforcement of desired and expected adult female roles.

The preparation and baking of traditional breads by Apache girls is suggestive of a broader theme across coming-of-age ceremonies and that is the ceremonial inclusion of special food sources. In the Southwest cultural area, corn is a common such item as discussed relative to corn grinding rituals. By way of further illustration, a major component of the Navajo Kinaaldá is the preparation and baking of a corn cake (Schwarz 1997). In this case, corn is a metaphor for Changing Woman, in particular, her life-giving and life-sustaining properties. Corn is a central food source across numerous American Indian cultures and many oral traditions encompass stories of the Corn Mother or other figures from which corn was derived. Corn is reflective of food, fertility, and life in the broadest sense and, therefore, serves as a metaphor for the present state of the initiate and the life-giving properties represented by menarche. The buffalo in Lakota/Nakota/Dakota cultural traditions is a parallel item of central component in the girls' coming-of-age rituals, traditionally called Išnati Awicalowanpi (Markstrom 2008).

Spirituality is an integral aspect of culture and is intricately linked to every aspect of the North American Indian coming-of-age experience. The spiritual significance of American Indian coming-of-age ceremonies cannot be understated. It was previously explained relative to Schlegel and Barry's (1980) cross-cultural analysis of adolescent initiation ceremonies that the primary focus of these ceremonies was socialization of responsibility. However, a further focus was found to be the promotion of future physical and spiritual well-being of initiates. These findings were born out in my research on the Apache Sunrise Dance and Navajo Kinaaldá in which purposes were shown to be multifaceted. For instance, the spiritual transformation of the Apache initiate into the female archetype of her culture, White Painted Woman, is perceived as a critical connection made possible by the timing of menarche and the application of specified rituals. Such a connection advances other desired outcomes of the ceremony, most notably longevity and strength for the initiate and the possibility for a good life (see Table 6.3). Certainly the acquisition of cultural knowledge and adoption of desired cultural traits and social roles are advanced through the ceremony (see Table 6.3). Most certainly, celebration of the initiate's change of status and life potentials also is recognized (Markstrom 2008).

A fitting way to end this section on culture/spirituality is to emphasize the fact that, in addition to other functions identified, coming-of-age ceremonies are celebrations and frequently conclude with feasting, singing, and dancing. Such celebration reflects the reincorporation of a rite of passage—the initiate has successfully negotiated a series of physically and psychologically demanding rituals over a matter of days or sometimes years. Gift giving may bring substance to the celebration, as occurs in Navajo and Apache cultures, as well as rituals of Lakota/Nakota/Dakota coming-of-age ceremonies that conclude with feasting and giveaways (i.e., presenting gifts to those who are important in the girl's life and/or contributed to the ceremony) (Markstrom 2008). In summary, there are countless illustrations of the distinctive features of coming-of-age ceremonies across numerous North American Indian cultures. Ritual practices of any particular tribal culture will link to specific beliefs and oral traditions of that culture all of which inform the young person of their social position and identity. Adolescent girls acquire a greater sense of belonging and pride as they undergo coming-of-age ceremonies that teach about their culture, its origins, and its beliefs and practices.

COMING-OF-RITUALS IN THE TWENTY-FIRST CENTURY

This chapter considered the identity implications of rituals performed in conjunction with coming-of-age ceremonies at puberty, particularly at menarche, for American Indian girls. It is the impressionable and amenable state of the pubescent along with the proper applications of the appropriate rituals that are believed to yield desired outcomes (Markstrom 2008). The fact that some cultures have retained or reinstated these traditions in spite of the prohibitive and oppressive nature of colonization attests to the fact that these ceremonies continue to serve functions for initiates and their societies. It is justified to ponder the question about the significance of these ancient rituals for girls of the globalized media era of the twenty-first century. Preparation for adulthood is one apparent theme of coming-of-age ceremonies across cultures according to culturally applicable instruction of initiates on expectations for their future role fulfillment. The inculcation of desired cultural values, beliefs, and practices contributes to an understanding of self as embedded in one's culture; hence, the connection to ethnic or cultural identity is apparent. Rituals also may be performed to produce strength and endurance—purposes than span place and time.

Overall, coming-of-age ceremonies have impacts across domains of development in addition to identity formation, including the sexual self and reproduction, social relationships, role responsibilities, cognitive maturation, and spirituality (Markstrom 2011b, 154–155). In short, Markstrom and Iborra explained that "rituals bring definition and meaning to culturally prescribed values and principles that correspondingly set the young person on a trajectory toward adulthood. The rituals of coming-of-age ceremonies are embedded in cultural values, beliefs, and practices and the reinforcement of the rituals during the ceremony leave the young person with a strong impression of her importance" (2003, 404).

Enculturation as a process of learning and absorbing one's culture is clearly evident at all phases of pubertal rites of passage. As explained earlier in this chapter, enculturation has been shown to be a protective factor for contemporary American Indian adolescents. In a broader sense, enculturation implies that the continuity of cultures is advanced as young people are socialized according to the values, beliefs, and practices of their cultures with an implicit expectation that they, in turn, will continue the process of cultural perpetuation. Consistent with this statement, elsewhere in this book, Chandler and Dunlop address the topic of personal and cultural continuity and provided evidence that risk for suicide was linked to the absence of such forms of continuity. Erikson provided a theoretical perspective to this topic in his writings on optimal identity formation as including a sense of self than spans the past, present, and future (Erikson 1967, 1987) and is explained in one of my previous works in this respect: "there should be a perception that strands of sameness and continuity connect the self from the past to the present and to the anticipated future. Continuous socialization processes reinforce these strands of continuity, and ultimately the initiate begins to understand the purposes of the rituals according to the totality of her life span" (Markstrom 2008, 7). Therefore, it is asserted that the continuity of practice of puberty rituals serve a protective function both for the individual's personal sense of continuity but also according to that person's self-understanding within the continuity of one's culture.

In summary, the multidimensional nature of the American Indian at the local cultural level was delineated in Figure 6.1. Puberty rituals, within the framework of rites of passage, were applied to this conceptualization and, in Table 6.2, were interpreted according to their influential mechanisms of impact on ethnic/cultural identity formation of American Indian girls. The outcomes of these rituals were articulated in Table 6.3. Rituals have been presented as valuable cultural and psychosocial resources to facilitate optimal identity formation. They are meaningful because they are embedded in a cultural community reflective of cultural continuity and with a shared history. Further, rituals symbolize, represent, and reinforce meaningful cultural constructs and values. For instance, Navajo and Apache puberty ceremonies serve to embed girls within their cultural communities, and these communities provide both implicit and explicit forms of cultural socialization and reinforcement, as explained by Markstrom:

> Her significant social community shares the celebration and provides social reinforcement, affirmation, and acknowledgement. The shared value of a successful rite of passage likely compels the initiate to a deeper level of personal value and self-understanding. All the rituals performed are meaningful, and many connect in some way to her expected future roles as a woman of her culture. In this respect, ethnic identity is reinforced, as is another aspect of optimal identity formation, namely, the acquisition of a greater sense of direction in life. (2008, 350)

Upon completion of coming-of-age ceremonies, these young adolescent girls continue to be engaged in processes of identity formation. The fact that they have participated in meaningful, socially endorsed rituals is suggested to contribute to this desired outcome. Of particular consequence is that the significant social and cultural community may have provided childhood socialization leading up to the adolescent rite of passage (i.e., preparation of the RPP) (Dunham, Kidwell, and Wilson 1986), and in most cases this same community will provide continued social support and cultural reinforcement long after the conclusion of the rite of passage (i.e., reincorporation of the RPP). Therefore, although culturally based and community-embedded rites of passage are designed, in part, to incorporate young people into expected roles and responsibilities and to facilitate spiritual transcendence, the strong ethnic identity that is advanced through these rituals may better equip adolescents to negotiate potentially conflicting and confusing sources of influence from the broader society and globally. In addition to positive outcomes of these ceremonies for identity formation, the well-being of the local community or the tribe is advanced because one of its young has been groomed to one day fulfill valued and needed roles for her community, such as in leadership or nurturance of the younger generation. Finally, coming-of-age ceremonies of North American Indians, historically and as practiced in some cultures today, are spiritual events embedded in oral tradition that provide meaning and purpose of life as a culture's cosmological beliefs are remembered and expressed.

REFERENCES

Alford, R.D. 1988. Naming and Identity: A Cross-Cultural Study of Personal Naming Practices. New Haven, CT: HRAF Press.

Basso, K. H. 1996. *Wisdom Sits in Places: Landscape and Language among the Western Apache.* Albuquerque, NM: University of New Mexico Press.

Berenbaum, S. 2011. The importance of puberty in adolescent development, in *Biosocial Foundations of Family Process*, edited by A. Booth, S.M. McHale, and N.S. Landale. New York: Springer, pp. 95–104.

Brave Heart, M.Y.H. "The Historical Trauma Response among Natives and Its Relationship with Substance Abuse: A Lakota Illustration," Journal of Psycho-active Drugs 35 (2003): 7–13.

Brown, J. E. and Cousins, E. 2001. *Teaching Spirits: Understanding Native American Rreligious traditions.* New York, NY: Oxford University Press.

Centers for Disease Control and Prevention. "Tobacco, Alcohol, and Other Drug Use among High School Students in Bureau of Indian Affairs-Funded Schools—United States, 2001," Morbidity and Mortality Weekly Report 52 (2003): 1070–1072.

Cooper, T. W. 1998. *A Time Before Deception: Truth in Communication, Culture, and Ethics.* Sante Fe, NM: Clear Light Publishers.

Deloria, V., Jr. 1994. *God is Red: A Native View of Religion* (updated edition). Golden, CO: Fulcrum Publishing.

Deloria, V., Jr. 1999. *Singing for a Spirit: A Portrait of the Dakota Sioux.* Santa Fe, NM: Clear Light Publishers.

DeMallie, R.J. 1998. Kinship: The foundation for Native American society, in *Studying Native America: Problems and Prospects*, edited by R. Thornton. Madison: University of Wisconsin Press, pp. 306–356.

Dunham, R.M., Kidwell, J.S., and Wilson, S.M. "Rites of Passage at Adolescence: A Ritual Process Paradigm," Journal of Adolescent Research 1 (1986): 139–154.

Duran, B., Duran, E., and Brave Heart, M.Y.H. 1998. Native Americans and the trauma of history, in *Studying Native America*, edited by R. Thornton. Madison: University of Wisconsin Press, pp. 60–76.

Erikson, E.H. 1968. Identity: Youth and Crisis. New York: Norton.

———. 1980. Identity and the Life Cycle. New York: Norton.

———. 1987. Late adolescence (1959), in *A Way of Looking at Things*, edited by S. Schlein. New York: W.W. Norton, pp. 631–643.

Evans-Campbell, T. "Historical Trauma in American Indian/Native Alaska Communities: A Multilevel Framework for Exploring Impacts on Individuals, Families, and Communities," Journal of Interpersonal Violence 23 (2008): 316–338.

Fogelson, R.D. 1998. Perspectives on Native American identity, in *Studying Native America: Problems and Prospects*, edited by R. Thornton. Madison: University of Wisconsin Press, pp. 40–59.

Garroutte, E.M. 2003. Real Indians: Identity and the Survival of Native America. Berkeley: University of California Press.

Hoare, C.H. "Psychosocial Identity Development and Cultural Others," Journal of Counseling & Development 70 (1991): 45–53.

Horse, P.G. 2001. Reflections on American Indian identity, in *New Perspectives on Racial Identity Development*, edited by C.L. Wijeyesinghe and B.W. Jackson III. New York: New York University Press, pp. 91–107.

Indian and Northern Affairs Canada. 1996. "Report of the Royal Commission on Aboriginal Peoples." On http://www.ainc (accessed May 15, 2007)

Jones, M.D. and Galliher, R.V. "Ethnic Identity and Psychosocial Functioning in Navajo Adolescents," Journal of Research on Adolescence 17 (2007): 683–696.Kawamoto, W.T. and Cheshire, T.C. 1999. Contemporary issues in the urban American Indian family, in *Family Ethnicity: Strength in Diversity*, 2nd ed., edited by H.P. McAdoo. Thousand Oaks, CA: Sage Publications, pp. 94–104.

Kawamoto, W. T. and Cheshire, T. C. 1999. *Contemporary issues in the urban American Indian family, in Family Ethnicity: Strength in Diversity*, 2nd ed., edited by H.P. McAdoo. Thousand Oaks, CA: Sage Publications, pp. 94-104.

LaFromboise, T.D., Hoyt, D.R., Oliver, L. and Whitbeck, L.B. "Family, community, and school influences on resilience among American Indian adolescents in the Upper Midwest," Journal of Community Psychology 34 (2006): 193–209.

Lee, L. "Navajo Cultural Identity: What Can the Navajo Nation Bring to the American Indian Identity Discussion Table?" Wicazo Sa Review 21 (2006): 79–103.

Lincoln, B. 1981. "Emerging from the Chrysalis: Rituals of Women's Initiations. New York: Oxford University Press.

Markstrom, C.A. 2008. Empowerment of North American Indian Girls: Ritual Expressions at Puberty. Lincoln: University of Nebraska Press.

———. "Identity Formation of American Indian Adolescents: Local, National, and Global Consideration," Journal of Research on Adolescence 21 (2011a): 519–535.

———. 2011b. Initiation ceremonies and rites of passage, in *Encyclopedia of Adolescence*, vol. 2, edited by B.B. Brown & M.J. Prinstein. San Diego: Academic Press, pp. 152–159.

Markstrom, C.A., Berman, R.C., Sabino, V.M., and Turner, B. "The Ego Virtue of Fidelity as a Psychosocial Rite of Passage in the Transition from Adolescence to Adulthood," Child and Youth Care Forum 17 (1998): 337–354.

Markstrom, C.A. and Iborra, A. "Adolescent Identity Formation and Rites of Passage: The Navajo Kinaaldá Ceremony for Girls," Journal of Research on Adolescence 13 (2003): 399–425.

Nabokov, P. 1999. Native American Testimony: A Chronicle of Indian–White Relations from Prophecy to the Present, 1492–2000. Rev. ed. New York: Penguin Books.NCAI Policy Research Center. 2011. Demographic Profile of Indian Country. Washington, DC: National Congress of American Indians.

NCAI Policy Research Center. 2011. *Demographic Profile of Indian Country*. Washington, DC: National Congress of American Indians.

Newman, D.L. "Ego Development and Ethnic Identity Formation in Rural American Indian Adolescents," Child Development 76 (2005): 734–746.

Noriega, J. 1992. American Indian education in the United States: Indoctrination for subordination to colonialism, in *The State of Native America: Genocide, Colonization, and Resistance*, edited by M.A. Jaimes. Boston: South End Press, pp. 371–402.

Opler, M. "Myths and Tales of the Chiricahua Apache Indians," Memoirs of the American Folk-Lore Society 7 (1942): 15.

Osgood, C. "Ingalik Social Culture," Yale University Publications in Anthropology 53 (1958): 1–289.

Peroff, N.C. and Wildcat, D.R. "Who Is an American Indian?" Social Science Journal 39 (2002): 349–361.

Petersen, A.C., Leffert, N. and Graham, B.L. "Adolescent Development and the Emergence of Sexuality," Suicide and Life-Threatening Behavior 25 (1995): 4–17.

Pewewardy, C. "Learning Styles of American Indian/Alaska Native Students: A Review of the Literature and Implications for Practice," Journal of American Indian Education 41 (2002): 22–56.

Phinney, J.S. "The Multigroup Ethnic Identity Measure: A New Scale for Use with Adolescents and Young Adults from Diverse Groups," Journal of Adolescent Research 2 (1992): 156–176.

———. "Identity Formation across Cultures: The Interaction of Personal, Societal, and Historical Change," Human Development 43 (2000): 27–31.

Phinney, J.S. and Ong, A.D. "Conceptualization and Measurement of Ethnic Identity: Current Status and Future Directions," Journal of Counseling Psychology 54 (2007): 271–281.

Pierre, M.S. and Long Soldier, T. 1995. Walking in the Sacred Manner. New York: Simon and Schuster.

Reichard, G.A. 1977. Navajo Religion: A Study of Symbolism. Princeton, NJ: Princeton University Press.

Rieckmann, T.R., Wadsworth, M.E., and Deyhle, D. "Cultural Identity, Explanatory Style, and Depression in Navajo Adolescents," Cultural Diversity and Ethnic Minority Psychology 10 (2004): 365–382.

Roessel, R.W. 1981. Women in Navajo Society. Rough Rock, AZ: Rough Rock Demonstration School.

Schlegel, A. "A Cross-Cultural Approach to Adolescence," Ethos 23 (1995): 15–32. Schlegel, A. and Barry, H. "The Evolutionary Significance of Adolescent Initiation Ceremonies," American Ethnologist 7 (1980): 696–715.

Schwartz, S.J. "The Evolution of Eriksonian and Neo-Eriksonian Identity Theory and Research: A Review and Integration," Identity: An International Journal of Theory and Research 1 (2001): 7–58.

Schwarz, M.T. 1997. Molded in the Image of Changing Woman. Tucson: University of Arizona Press.

Sebald, H. 1992. Adolescence: A Social Psychological Analysis. 4th ed. Englewood Cliffs, NJ: Prentice Hall.

Shirtcliff, E.A. 2009. Biological underpinnings of adolescent development, in *Adolescent Health: Understanding and Preventing Risk Behaviors*, edited by R.J. DiClemente, J.S. Santelli, and R.A. Crosby. San Francisco, CA: Jossey-Bass, pp. 95–113.

Shirtcliff, E.A., Dahl, R.E., and Pollak, S.D. "Pubertal Development, Correspondence between Hormonal and Physical Development," *Child Development* 80 (2009): 327–337.

Sökefeld, M. "Debating Self, Identity, and Culture in Anthropology," *Current Anthropology* 40 (1999): 417–447.

St. Pierre, M. and Long Soldier, T. 1995. *Walking in the Sacred Manner.* New York, NY: Simon and Schuster.

Strum, C. 2002. *Blood Politics: Race, Culture, and Identity in the Cherokee Nation of Oklahoma.* Berkeley, CA: University of California Press.

Susman, E.J. and Rogol, A. 2004. Puberty and psychological development, in *Handbook of Adolescent Psychology*, 2nd ed., edited by R.M. Lerner and L.D. Steinberg. Hoboken, NJ: John Wiley and Sons, pp. 18–44.

Sutton, M.Q. 2008. An Introduction to Native North America. Boston: Allyn and Bacon.

Tafoya, N. and Del Vecchio, A. 1996. Back to the future: An examination of the Native American holocaust experience, in *Ethnicity and Family Therapy*, vol. 2, edited by M. McGoldrick, J. Giordano, and J.K. Pearce. New York: Guilford Press, pp. 45–54.

Trimble, J.E. 2000. Social psychological perspectives on changing self-identification among American Indians and Alaska Natives, in *Handbook of Cross-Cultural and Multicultural Personality Assessment*, edited by R.H. Dana. Mahwah, NJ: Lawrence Erlbaum, pp. 197–222.

Turner, V. 1967. The Forest of Symbols: Aspects of Ndembu Ritual. Ithaca, NY: Cornell University Press.

———. 1969. The Ritual Process. Structure and Anti-Structure. New York: Adline Publishing.

van Gennep, A. [1908] 1960. The Rites of Passage. Translated by Monika Vizedom and Gabrielle Caffe. Chicago: Chicago University Press.

Weaver, H.N. "Indigenous Identity: What Is It, and Who Really Has It?" American Indian Quarterly 25 (2001): 240–255.

Weaver, H.N. and Brave Heart, M.Y.H. "Examining Two Facets of American Indian Identity: Exposure to Other Cultures and the Influence of Historical Trauma," Journal of Human Behavior in the Social Environment 2 (1999): 19–33.

Whitbeck, L.B. 2011. The beginnings of mental health disparities: Emergent mental health disorders in Indigenous adolescents, in *Health Disparities in Youth and Families: Research and Applications*, edited by G. Carlo, L.J. Crockett, and M. .A. Carranza. New York: Springer, pp. 121–150.

Whitesell, N.R., Mitchell, C.M., and Spicer, P.P. "The Voices of Indian Teens Project: A Longitudinal Study of Self-Esteem, Cultural Identity, and Academic Success among American Indian Adolescents," Cultural Diversity and Ethnic Minority Psychology 15 (2009): 38–50.

7 Food Restriction and Social Identity of Aka Forager Adolescents in the Republic of Congo

Kiyoshi Takeuchi

INTRODUCTION

In many ethnic groups throughout the world, individuals may avoid consuming certain edible plants and animals. This phenomenon is known as a food taboo or food restriction and arises not from individual preferences but from sociocultural factors. This topic has been the subject of research in the fields of anthropology, social psychology, and nutrition. Symbolic theorists report that restricted foods and those who are prohibited from eating both are situated in boundaries of folk classification systems (Leach 1964; Douglas 1966; Sperber 1996). From the perspective of sustainable use of animal and plant resources, food restrictions are thought to have adaptive value (McDonald 1977; Colding and Folke 1997). A universal reason for the existence of food restriction has yet to be determined (Meyer-Rochow 2009). However, theorists do agree on the way that food restrictions reflect the characteristics of a society and are deeply related to social identities (Whitehead 2000). In any ethnic group, if the food restriction applies to a particular person, it identifies that person as being within a particular social category such as menfolk, women, parents of young children, adolescents, and so on.

Hunter-gatherers who live in the tropical rain forest zones of the Congo Basin are known to consume various wild animals as part of their diet. It has also been reported that these communities restrict members who are pregnant or are of a particular age or gender from eating certain species of animals. The Mbuti, for example, who reside in the eastern Democratic Republic of the Congo and the Baka in eastern Cameroon, avoid eating 84 percent and 76 percent of wild food mammals, respectively (Ichikawa 1987; Hattori 2008).

This chapter examines the food restrictions that exist among the Aka, a hunting and gathering society residing in the tropical rainforests of northeastern Republic of the Congo. First, the general characteristics of food restrictions among the Aka will be discussed, followed by a focus on food restrictions of wild animals specifically for adolescents. Furthermore, these food restrictions will be used to investigate the social identities of adolescents in the Aka society.

THE AKA

In the African tropical rainforest belt, several ethnic groups are often termed, in a somewhat discriminatory manner, "Pygmy" because of their short physical stature. The Aka are one of these groups, and they reside within a 70,000 square kilometer region located on the eastern banks of the Ubangi River. The Aka population is estimated to be in the range of thirty thousand to forty thousand people (Bahuchet 1999). Since 1988, I have conducted surveys on the Aka society living in the northeastern part of the Republic of Congo (Figure 7.1).

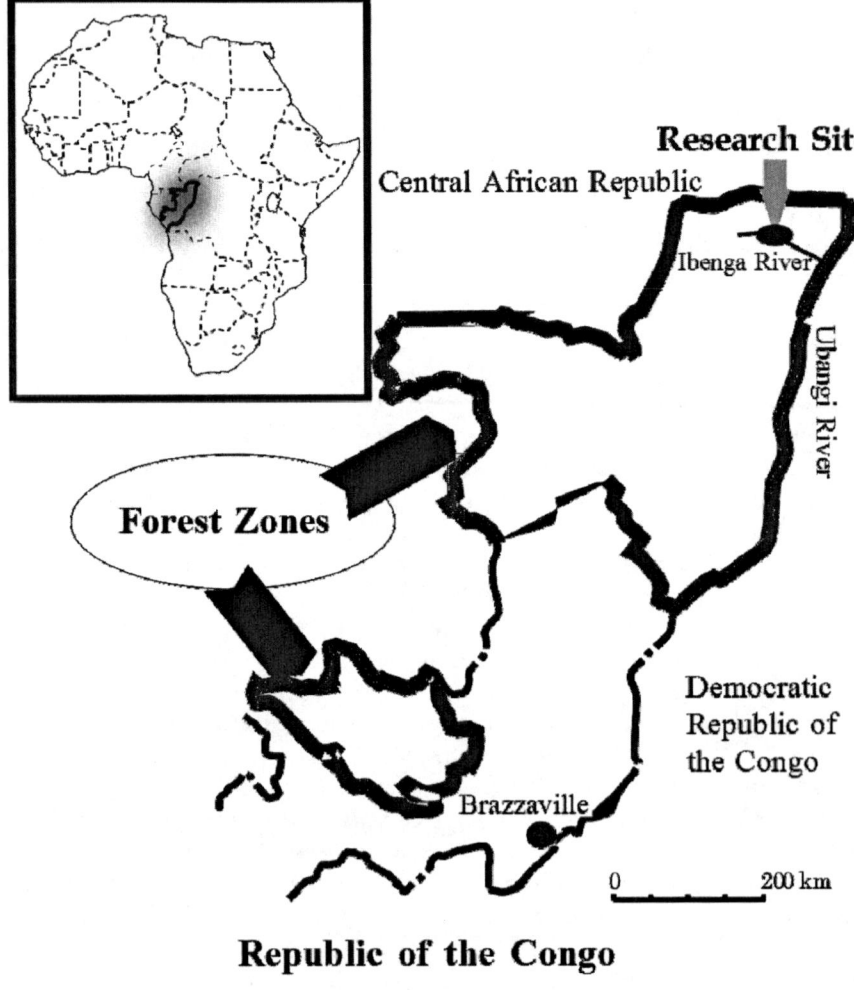

Figure 7.1   Research site.

The living unit of the Aka is generally composed of an elderly man, his married sons, married daughters, and their children. This arrangement usually results in an extended family ranging from ten to thirty people. They camp deep in the forest during the dry season to hunt and fish by bailing. Their camp may comprise a single extended family or it may include a gathering of extended families, increasing to a scale of more than one hundred people. The Aka society is egalitarian. A single specified person does not wield complete political power. Relationships between adult individuals are cordial, and adult women enjoy and often engage in gossip. Men sometimes purposely enlist other men to help in tasks that could easily be accomplished alone.

RESEARCH SITE AND METHODS

Research was conducted with the Aka who reside in the northern region of Likouala, Congo, near the Ibenga River that flows into the Ubangi River. The Aka live in proximity to the Moumpoutou village of Bantu-speaking, slash-and-burn horticulturalists. Results were obtained from a participant survey conducted over six months from January to June 1989 and two weeks in March 2010.

The location that this research was conducted at lies almost directly on the equator (2°59′N, 17°29′E). Annual rainfall ranges from 1,700 millimeters to 1,800 millimeters. There is a dry season from December to February when monthly rainfall is below 100 millimeters, and a rainy season from March to November when monthly rainfall is above 100 millimeters. The average annual temperature is 25.6 degrees Celsius, and there is little change in average monthly temperature throughout the year. There are varieties of vegetation in this area, ranging from riverine swampy forests to inland evergreen forests made of *Gilbertiodendron dewevrei*. However, most of the area is mixed forests composed of semi-deciduous trees, where the Aka people build settlements and set up camps.

Research was based in the Moumpoutou village, where approximately 260 Bantu-speaking horticulturalists resided in 1989. The Aka settlements are scattered around this village in an arc formation. As of May 1989, approximately six hundred Aka people lived in this area (see Figure 7.2).

The focus of this research was a settlement located in the southern area of the Ibenga River. This settlement was composed of four extended family groups. The population fluctuation in the settlement is very high; during research conducted in 1989 the highest recorded number of people was 105, including fifty-five women and fifty men. This settlement made use of small-scale slash-and-burn horticulture; however, they retained their nomadic lifestyle as a hunting and gathering society. During the dry season, multiple Aka settlements banded together to set up hunting camps in the forest, forming temporary camps covering an area of 10 kilometers where they conducted net hunts (Figure 7.3).

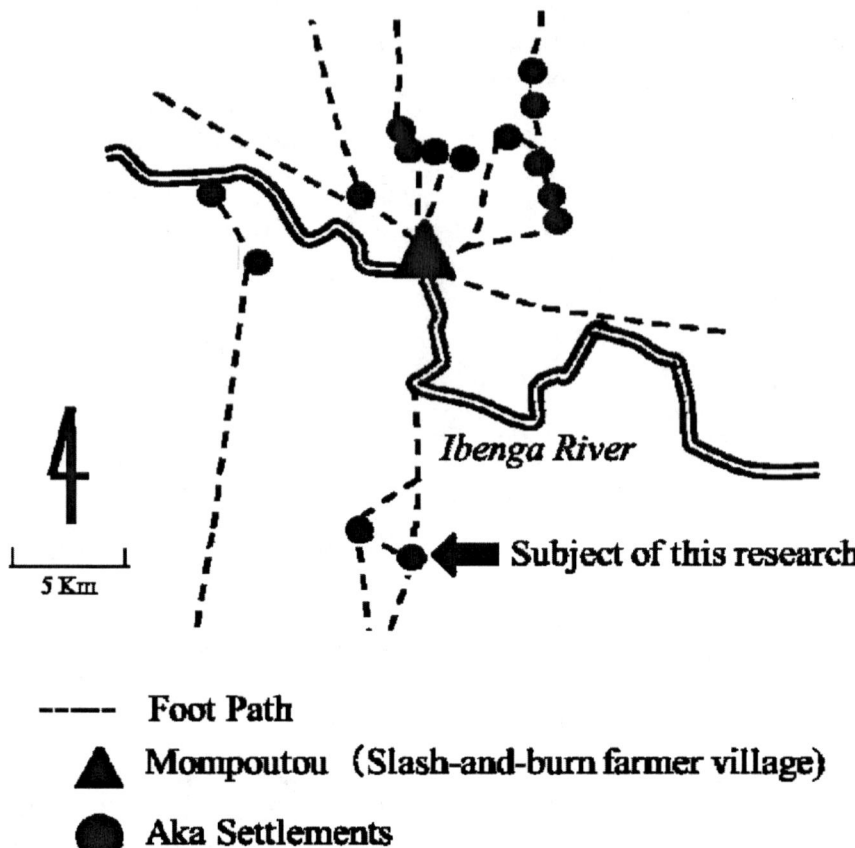

Figure 7.2 Farmers village and Aka settlements (1989).

The 1989 survey began with the intention of clarifying the roles of gender and generation in the Aka society. As a follow-up, informants were interviewed about the wild animal and plant species that comprised their diet, and they were also asked about their reasons for not eating a known food species. Nine men and nine women were interviewed for a total of eighteen informants from three extended families.

In 2010, another survey was conducted on the same settlement using the same list of wild animal and plant species as the 1989 survey. Seven men and seven women were interviewed. Additionally, five Aka adolescents who lived 40 kilometers north in a village of logging laborers were also interviewed. As most of the informants from the earlier research had moved out from the settlement or were deceased, the informants from the 1989 survey were not included.

Figure 7.3   Hunting camp.

SUBSISTENCE ACTIVITES AND GENERATION ROLES

The settlement in the present study conducts small-scale slash-and-burn agriculture and provides labor for cultivation and removal of weeds for the Moumpoutou village. In the forest, they hunt wild animals and collect tubers and nuts. Net hunting is the primary form of hunting conducted during the dry season between January and March. The members of the settlement reside in hunting camps in the forest until about July. The primary animals targeted in net hunting are six species of duikers. The hunters tie together several nets that are 10 to 30 meters wide in the shape of an arc and enclose a set area of the forest in order to capture duikers. In addition to hunting, the Aka frequently gather tubers of *Dioscoreophyllum cumminsii* and eight species of yams of the *Dioscorea* genus. During research conducted at a hunting camp in May of 1989, tubers comprised 54 percent of foodstuff in the evening meals, as hunting camps generally rely on wild plants rather than wild animals as a food supply.

Hunting is primarily conducted by men, and gathering is an activity primarily of women. However, participation in these activities by either women or men is not tightly restricted. An equal number of women may participate in net hunting by fixing the nets or by capturing or butchering the animals. Men are knowledgeable in techniques employed in gathering wild plants and sometimes aid their wives. Only men participate in spear hunting and during this time they may also gather yams. Men make digging sticks used for gathering yams such as *Dioscorea semperflorens* that grow perpendicularly in the ground. Women gather branches and lianas that their husbands or fathers may use for making hunting nets or spears. Subsistence roles in the Aka society are not clearly divided into hunting for men and gathering for women, but represent a complementary collaboration between men and women.

Once food supplies are obtained, married women prepare and cook the meals, and the food is then divided among the immediate kin who live nearby. The Aka describe the process as "dividing plates" (*ba kabanye sembe*). Sharing meals among closely related families is a daily activity. However, male adults and adolescents do not dine with the women and children. Men who are closely related to each other eat together on a bench, and the wives and mothers deliver the food to them.

The living units among the Aka consist of several families of about ten to thirty people who "divide plates" with each other. The family group acts together and lives in close proximity within the settlements. They also travel together to the Moumpoutou village or hunting camps. The extended family group includes one adult man called the *kombeti* and his married sons, daughters, and other relatives. Although the Aka people have a word that designates an extended family, the name of the *kombeti* is used in conversation to refer to a specific family group. In settlements and hunting camps, the *kombeti* of each family group meets together to discuss net hunting strategies and relocation possibilities. The wife of the *kombeti*, as well as other older women, has influence over the relationships and marriages of younger women. A case was observed in which a woman did not approve of the man with whom her daughter had spent the night. When the daughter confessed that she wanted to marry this man, the mother and a group of the mother's friends vociferously scolded the daughter until she fled in tears.

Although the Aka society is egalitarian among adults, as no single specified person wields a commanding amount of political power, older, well-experienced men and women do possess substantial leadership abilities and have influence over others in the camp.

LIFE STAGES

The generational life stages of the Aka people are displayed in Figure 7.4. Childhood is divided into three stages. The child is called *mo.lepe* for the first few months, and when the child is able to crawl and waddle, he or she is then called *jenga*. *Mo.na* is the name used for children from the time they learn how to properly walk until about ten years of age. Aka infants receive intimate skin-to-skin contact from their parents and others and are treated with indulgence (Hewlett 1991).

When a girl reaches menarche, the adult females perform a dance ritual called *e.waya*. After the ritual has been completed, the girl is called *ngondo*, signifying she has reached the adolescent stage. When a boy learns how to

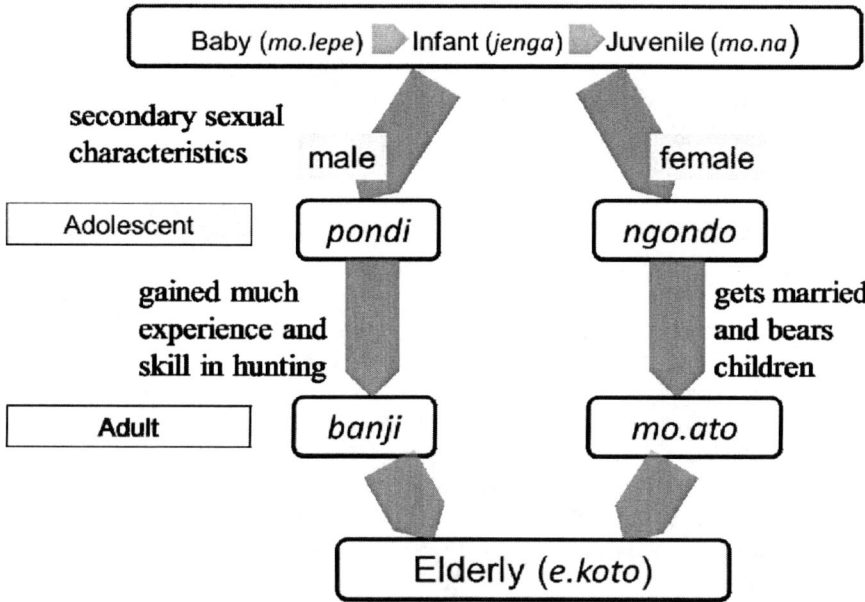

Figure 7.4 Life cycle of the Aka.

hunt and kill with a spear he is called *pondi*. During this time, the father will cut the boy's arm with a knife and rub a magical hunting drug called *mombili* or *dombi* into the wound. This drug is made from a mixture of several types of bark, leaves, and palm oil; the exact type of shrub used is a secret among adult men. The boys who have completed this process will then be considered adolescents. In Aka society, adolescent boys and girls move out of their parent's huts; adolescent boys sleep in an assembly hut for men called an *mbanjo*, and adolescent girls sleep in small huts built in proximity to their parent's huts. Aka adolescents aid in daily chores and activities under the supervision of the elders. For example, adolescent boys set up the nets used for hunting under the supervision of older men, and unmarried adolescent girls help gather and carry food such as yam tubers under the watchful eyes of older women.

When they give birth, women are accepted as adults and become *mo.ato*. Men are accepted as adults and become *banji* when they become skilled at hunting. Even a man who is married and has children is still considered as part of the *pondi* group if he does not have sufficient hunting experience. A skilled male hunter who can provide an ample source of protein for the family group is considered a "complete man," and a woman who can give birth and raise children to provide kinship resources is considered a "complete woman." In these terms, the male (*moto.pai*) and female (*mo.ato*) gender divisions are highly dependent on generational life stages.

When men and women reach old age, they are both referred to as *e.koto*. They do not actively participate in net hunting or gathering activities and usually spend the day weaving nets together or making baskets at the settlement or camp. Although they do not aid in many of the daily activities, their experience gives them some influence over the younger generations.

FOOD AND NONFOOD SPECIES

Fifty species of mammals have been confirmed to be native to the research area. The dwarf galago and the mole are the only two species that were said to be avoided as food by all eighteen informants because they were considered to be "not food for humans." Mammals generally not eaten include the potto, tree hyrax, palm civet, and flying squirrel. The owl, touraco, and alethe are among the species of bird out of thirty-six species not eaten. Many informants stated that these animals were also considered "not food for humans"; however, others said that these animals are in fact edible. It should be noted that the eating of a palm civet was observed in the settlement during the research period in 1989. Cultural rules that govern the boundaries between edible and inedible food resources are not clearly delineated. The boundaries are dependent on individual recognition and preference and thus are vague. Freedom of choice and individual preference is also a factor in food restrictions and will be discussed later in this chapter. Resources were considered as Aka food species if more than two respondents stated that they consumed it and those who answered that they would not consume it still considered it "food suitable for humans"; for example, some animal species are avoided by Aka women during pregnancy, but we would consider these species as food, because others would eat them. By this account, food species in the Aka diet include: forty-eight wild mammal species; thirty-five bird species (identified species); nine reptile species; thirteen fish species; and twenty-four invertebrate species. There are forty-seven wild plant species consumed by the Aka; among these are ginger, consumed as both a leaf and fruit, and honey.

Sheep and goats owned by the agriculturalists in Moumpoutou village are considered "village animals" (*nyama mboka*) and are not consumed by the Aka. It could be said that this reflects the separate ethnicities between the two groups (Takeuchi 2005), but in reality there are no opportunities for the Aka to share meals with the Moumpoutou villagers. The Aka refer to the weaver as the "village bird" (*nyodi mboka*), and four out of eighteen informants answered that they would not eat it. A few chickens are raised in the Aka settlements, but all female informants responded that they would not eat these because they are "village animals." Older men gave the same reason for not eating chickens. It would appear that this sentiment arises from the fact that raising chickens was originally undertaken as labor for the villagers. However, no informants answered that they would not eat agricultural products such as cassava or plantain.

Food Avoidance And Food Taboo

Out of forty-seven wild plant food species, eight species were avoided by at least one informant, and out of 128 wild animal food species, 105 species were avoided by at least one informant. In terms of the rate of avoidance, invertebrate species were least likely to be avoided; mammals, birds, reptiles, and fish were all subject to avoidance to varying degrees (Table 7.1). Although most mammals native to the area are consumed as food, 88 percent of species are not eaten at some point by various members of the Aka for reasons related to life stages or social conditions. The next sections will focus on the relationship between life stages and food restrictions on wild mammal species.

Aka individuals do not eat certain foods; this may depend on a specific situation or the life stage of the person. The Aka call these food restrictions *e.kila*. This system of food restriction can be divided into two types: food restrictions with high individual discretion and restrictions that represent respect to specific practices and beliefs, obligations that, if not followed, are met with social sanctioning. Obligatory food restrictions are those connected to hunting activities. Women during menstruation or the early stages of pregnancy and parents of newly born infants are not allowed to participate in hunting because it is believed that the prey will smell their blood and flee. Additionally, these individuals cannot consume animals caught in hunts. However, if a leaf of the fragrant African ginger is attached to a female's raffia skirt to hide her scent, she may participate in hunting, although she is still not allowed to partake in eating the meat. Consuming larvae of weevils found in the trunks of palm trees with meat is considered to bring a poor catch in hunts, and it is therefore not permitted the night before a hunt. If an individual breaks these restrictions and a hunt goes poorly, the person will be blamed for this misfortune. Hereafter, food restrictions dependent on individual discretion and not accompanied by social sanctions will be referred to as *food avoidances*, and obligatory food restrictions accompanied by social sanctions will be referred to as *food taboos*.

Food Avoidance And Cognition Of Wild Animals

The Aka avoid eating various food resources according to an individual's life stage. Food species avoided by all individuals in the same life stage are not uncommon, but food avoidance is generally an individual choice. Out of five parents with newly born infants, more than one parent avoided some forty-three wild mammal food species. However, only sixteen species were avoided by all parents.

Table 7.1 Percentage of Avoided Food Species

	Number of Food Species	Number of Avoided Species by more than One Person	Percentage of Avoided Species
Wild Animals			
Mammals	48	42	88
Birds	34	34	100
Reptiles	9	9	100
Fish	13	11	85
Invertebrates	24	9	38
Subtotal	128	105	82
Wild Plants	47	8	17

Aka believe that diseases or disorders will result from even the accidental consumption of avoided foods. The Aka recognize this phenomenon in the following way; eating animals implies not just the consumption of nutrients, but also the incorporation of the morphological or behavioral features of these animals into the human body. If humans have a weak resistance to the characteristics of the animals that may be considered "strange" or "savage," they will assume these characteristics and suffer various disorders as a consequence.

In other words, food avoidance practices are determined by human resistance correlated to the intensity of the features of the consumed animal. Furthermore, adults are considered to have a higher degree of resistance than children. As such, the degree of food avoidance in the consumption of wild animal species by a member of the Aka depends on generational or age-related factors.

Bahuchet (1985), who researched the Aka living in Central Africa, cites the earth pig, flying squirrel, and leopard as examples of avoided food animals. These animals possess distinct morphological and behavioral characteristics. The earth pig lives underground, the flying squirrel has ambiguous traits of both birds and animals, and leopards and other carnivores have black spots. The Aka believe that these characteristics are related to supernatural powers (Motte-Florac, Bahuchet, and Thomas 1993). Food avoidance by the Aka certainly illustrates an awareness of an unusual characteristic of an animal's body or behavior. For example, if an infant's parent eats a monkey, it is believed that the infant will catch "monkey's disease" (*bokono wa makako*). This is because the face of an infant suffering from spasms caused by a high fever is similar to that of a monkey baring its teeth. During the span of this research study, two infants developed spasms, and the reason given by the Aka for these illnesses was that the mothers had eaten either De Brazza's or colobus monkeys.

At the root of food avoidances practiced by the Aka, there is a visual or behavioral connection between the symptoms thought to be caused by consumption of certain foods and an animal's characteristics. However, there are times when identical characteristics of the same animal can be interpreted differently. For example, with regards to the aggressive behaviors of gorillas, some believe that eating them will cause children to act violently when they grow up, whereas others believe it will make the children stronger. It was also common for informants to cite different characteristics of an animal as reasons for not consuming it. One parent avoided eating water chevrotains so her child's buttocks would not split apart, whereas another parent avoided these animals so her child's skin would not turn white. When an extended family group was asked the reason for not eating earth pigs, a mother explained that eating earth pigs, which live underground, would return her infant to the womb. Another member believed that it would result in her infant being unable to walk because earth pigs waddle when walking on land (see Figure 7.5).

Even within the same extended family or settlement, the recognition and interpretation toward characteristics of avoided animals are not always shared. Food avoidance by the Aka is based upon individual perceptions of abnormal characteristics in animals. The reason for avoiding a certain animal is different in each individual case. Whereas the Aka perceive abnormalities in wild animals and relate them to their own personal life stages, they base their actions on individual contexts and voluntarily avoid eating certain animal species. Therefore, there are occasions when they eat animals that they had previously avoided consuming. Social sanctions against this act are not observed.

Figure 7.5 Earth pig.

There were six mammal species out of forty-eight that all informants did not avoid as food. The six species include the blue duiker and Peter's duiker, which are frequently captured during net hunting. During forty-eight days of observation on net hunts in 1989 and 1990, a total of 162 animals were captured. Of the animals captured, blue duikers were the most important, comprising 69 percent of the total numbers captured, and Peter's duikers were next at 20 percent of the total animals captured. The porcupine, the main target of snare traps; the white-nosed monkey and forest elephant, often killed when hunting with a farmer's "entrusted" gun or rifle; and the bush pig, a main target of spear hunting, are all examples of animals the Aka do not avoid. They are their primary food resources, and most likely because they see them frequently and are familiar with them, the Aka do not see them as possessing abnormal traits or characteristics.

FOOD AVOIDANCE AND LIFE STAGES

Food avoidance by the Aka is an individual choice aimed at preventing the incorporation of "abnormal" characteristics through the consumption of meat. The strength of immunity each individual possesses against these abnormalities determines the number of avoided species. According to the Aka, infants or *mo.lepe* are not considered to be complete humans and in fact are thought to be wandering in a very vulnerable existence somewhere between life and death. Aka do not name a child for as long as half a year after birth. This may be due to the high infant mortality rate or because the care and protection of a parent is provided for an infant who is suspended at the edge of the human world between life and death. Therefore, infants are thought to be highly susceptible to risk and their parents must avoid certain animal foods. Parents are thought to be invisibly connected to their child through blood and sperm and as such must exercise animal food avoidance for the protection of their child. For example, infants will develop black skin rashes if their parents eat members of the feline family that have spotted coloration, and infants will develop chimpanzee-like mouths (protruding, large, and abnormal) if their parents eat chimpanzees. Children (*mo.na*) are not completely independent from their parents until they reach adolescence and are not considered to be fully resistant to foods from animal sources. Their parents are also susceptible to risk that can be passed on to children. For the good of infants and juveniles, who are considered incomplete humans, a total of forty-two animal species are avoided by Aka parents. These include species avoided by other Aka generations as well.

When children begin to develop secondary sexual characteristics and spend their daily lives in places remote from their parents, the young males (*pondi*) and young females (*ngodo*) select certain species considered to be risky and begin to avoid consuming them. This practice ushers in the selection of a particular species at the rising of each new moon and is referred to as *songe songe*. *Songe* means moon in the Aka language; however, the selection of new animal species by adolescents does not follow the actual lunar cycle. Species subjected to food avoidance by the young Aka remained rather constant during my investigation period. Adolescent boys tended to select small animals such as field mice, whereas adolescent girls tended to select carnivores; these animals are also avoided by adult men and women. Furthermore, when young girls experience menarche and become women they avoid fifteen *nyama moto.pai* or "men's animals." According to Aka cosmology, "men's animals" are animals that depict a savage or powerful image, such as carnivores or gorillas (see Table 7.2). When Aka women eat "men's animals," they believe that they will be overwhelmed by the animal power and break out in rashes. Women from puberty to menopause refrain from eating these "men's animals."

However, out of the nine female informants, all avoided only six of the fifteen food species, and individual differences between women were large. Two unmarried women were the only informants who avoided all fifteen species, and the only woman to avoid only nine species was the oldest woman in camp. There is an increased margin for individual selection of food avoidances as a woman experiences pregnancies and begins child rearing.

In contrast to "men's animals," there are several food species that only women consume. Among these are the plant species *Microdesmis puberula*, *Palisota hirsute*, and *Pycnobotrya nitida* and the larvae of *Lepidoptera* known to the Aka as *mo.nguangua* (unidentified). These species are eaten after giving birth and are boiled together in a meal believed to aid in recovery from delivery.

As previously mentioned, a woman becomes recognized as an adult, or *mo.ato*, when she marries and bears children. A man is acknowledged as an adult, or *banji*, when he gains experience and skill in hunting game. The Aka believe that reaching adulthood means completing one's growth as a human. Aka adults do not need to avoid animals that they avoided in their youth. However, when Aka men marry and have children, the consumption of many species of animals is avoided for the benefit of their children. Wives must additionally incorporate these men's food avoidances into their own diet.

Adult men state that field mice, small squirrels, and snakes are *nyama moke* or "small animals" and sometimes refer to them as "children's snacks." Men claim these small animals are not fit for the adult male diet. There were hardly any individual differences in the types of these avoided species. The pride in hunting larger game with spears may be expressed in this food avoidance. However, some men added, "If I were extremely hungry and there was nothing else to eat, I would eat field mice," or "If my wife cooked a snake very well, I would eat it."

Table 7.2 "Men's Animals" Avoided by Nine Women

Animal	Number of Women Avoid
Carnivores	
Leopard	9
Golden cat	9
Genets	9
Black-legged mongoose	9
Marsh mongoose	9
Civet	8
Spotted-necked otter	8
Palm civet	8
Ratel	4
Noncarnivores	
Tschego chimpanzee	9
Oustalet's red colobus	8
Western Sitatunga	8
Hippopotamus	5
Western gorilla	5
Dwarf forest buffalo	5

In the Aka society, gender is not a factor in life stages related to aging. Men and women are both addressed as the elderly or *ekoto*. Although the elderly may be physically diminished, their existence is never considered as weakened. They are considered to have the highest resistance against the forces in the external world because of their accumulated experience gained over the years. Moreover, the elderly need not practice food avoidance for their children. Women who have undergone menopause and have completed the life stages involved in achieving the status of an elderly woman can eat "men's animals." Therefore, when an Aka becomes elderly, both men and women can eat all food animal species, including the potto and tree hyrax, which other generations avoid eating (see Figure 7.6). These animals that are only eaten by the elderly are called "animals for the elderly" or *nyama e.koto*. In practice, the elderly may continue to avoid eating some animal species they once shunned.

Aka individuals who have lost their marriage partners or their children select a few species from bush pig, duikers, yams, and honey and avoid eating them while in mourning.

Figure 7.7 displays the avoidance rates of wild mammal species by the eighteen informants in order of their age. Using this figure, the characteristics of sex and generation on food avoidance will be described. In all

Figure 7.6   Tree hyrax.

generations, women have higher food avoidance rates. This is because, as noted earlier, women avoid the group of animals classified as "men's animals." Food avoidance rates in adolescent females are higher than in adolescent males, and adolescent females' rates are comparable to women with newborn children. Adolescent girls are influenced by their mothers and other close female relatives in their selection of animal species to avoid during the *songe songe*. These selections generally include "men's animals" or animals avoided by adult or pregnant women. For example, an adolescent girl (a in Figure 7.7) avoided thirty-two mammal species of the thirty-four species that her mother (b) avoided. In contrast, adolescent boys tend to only select "children's animals" during the *songe songe*. However, these selections both indicate that adolescents are already incorporating the food avoidances of adults on their own accord. There were two individuals who had an exceptionally low food avoidance rate. One individual was a woman who had not given birth to a child although she had been married for some time, and the other individual was a man who fell sexually impotent. The woman did not avoid foods that were believed to harm pregnancies or infants. The man ate foods considered to be "animals for the elderly" or *nyama ekoto*, such as the potto or tree hyrax. These food restrictions reflect how these two individuals viewed themselves. Food avoidances are behavioral representations of each individual's self-perceived position of their condition in life.

Aka adolescents do not need to avoid foods that are dangerous when raising children, and, similar to the elderly, adolescents have a relatively high degree of freedom in choosing which foods to avoid. However, adolescents mimic several adult food avoidances, which indicates that they are aware of their stage in life.

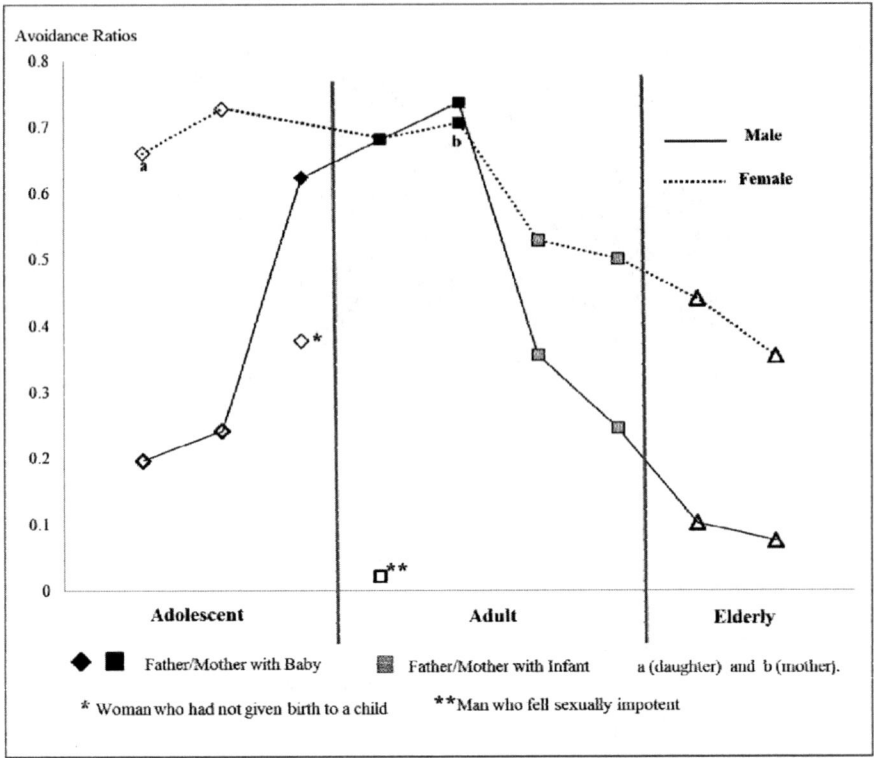

Figure 7.7   Avoidance ratios and generation.

CONTINUATION AND CHANGES
REGARDING FOOD AVOIDANCES

The responses of wild mammal food avoidances of twelve informants, six men and six women, who were surveyed in 2010, are displayed in Figure 7.8. It is evident that food avoidances according to life stages have not changed. The food avoidance rates of five adolescent boys who work as laborers in a village of loggers 40 kilometers north of Moumpoutou is lower than food avoidance rates of the elderly in Aka settlements. All of them do not avoid eating *nyama moke* or "small animals" such as field mice. Four of these six boys responded that they only avoid tree hyraxes, flying squirrels, and water shrews. These boys also ate a potto, which is avoided by most of the Aka living near Moumpoutou village.

These adolescents came from east of Moumpoutou and were working in a logging village in order to earn cash. It can be surmised that their food avoidance rates are low because they are not exposed to the food avoidances of adult males on a daily basis.

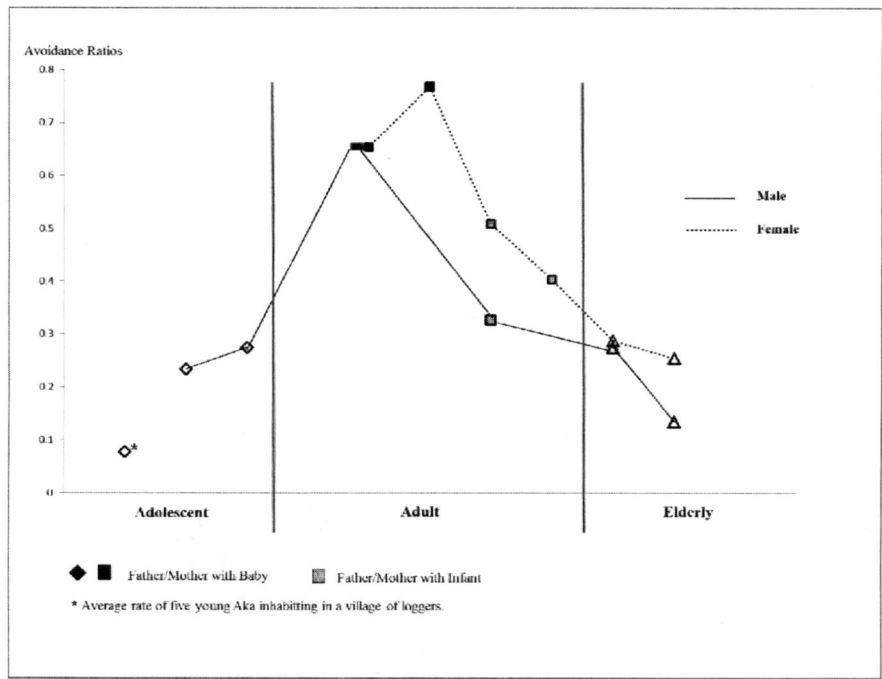

Figure 7.8   Avoidance ratios and generation (2010).

Food Taboos Among Adolescent Boys

Food taboos are obligatory and are subject to social sanctions. It was previously mentioned that they are related to hunting, but the food taboos for young men during hunting activities are especially strict. As opposed to the kind of food avoidances that have been discussed so far, adolescent boys are subjected to food taboos related to meat taken from hunted animals. Game captured by adolescent boys using hunting gear (e.g. spears, shotguns, crossbows, snares) is not allowed to be eaten by these men regardless of the type of species.

When Aka adolescents come of age, they often go hunting with adults. When the arm of a young man is bruised, his father or a close kin of elderly status will treat the wound using a medicine with presumed magical properties called *mo.mbili* or *dombi*, which is derived from various plants. This practice is recognized by the Aka to be a symbol of the treated young man developing from a parent-dependent "weakling" to a "strong adult."

It is believed that when a young man eats game that he has caught, poisons from the "magical" medicine transfer from the treated arm to the hunted game and can cause the death of the young man or lead to misfortune in hunting. This abstinence, in which extreme strict adherence to the common rules is practiced, is different from the other findings of food avoidance. On several occasions, I have personally witnessed young Aka men who would not touch food cooked with game they had captured despite their obvious appetite.

This food taboo has potential consequences for more frequently hunted animals. From an ecological perspective, this food taboo restricts the access of the young men to animal protein sources. Furthermore, this taboo is uniformly applied to young men and does not allow any room for individual choice. Adult men possess the authority over this taboo, which establishes the social context of the Aka. In other words, this taboo symbolizes the "complete power" of the adult men or *banji* as opposed to the "incomplete power" of the young men or *pondi*. It expresses the generational status of the adult men in shouldering the central roles of decision making regarding hunting activity and the group as a whole. The poison of the medicine applied on the arm of a young Aka man is diluted by every game animal killed, and thus eventually through successful hunting the poisons will be nullified. A young man comes to be recognized as a full-fledged hunter through experience and time. Following this period of maturity, he attains adulthood and the status of a "complete man."

CONCLUSION

Several reports have been published regarding the correlation between food restrictions and generational life stages of hunter-gatherer groups in the Congo Basin (Ichikawa 1987; Pagezy 1993; Sato 1993). However, previous research has not focused on the individual diversity. The high level of independence within the Aka society is expressed in the high level of individual variability due to an individual's ability to select restricted foods. Aka individuals assess their own positions in various stages of life and take into account the unique characteristics of wild animals when making decisions regarding which foods to avoid. In the Aka society, there are no group divisions on the basis of age or gender. Therefore, food avoidances observed in the Aka society are expressions of individual confirmations of social identities.

In many societies around the world there are foodstuffs, clothing, and behaviors that adolescents use to express social identities. These expressions can be forced upon individuals by society or expressed on one's own accord. A characteristic of Aka food avoidance is that adolescents can express their social identities by choosing which foods to avoid.

According to Hewlett's research on the Aka who live in central Africa, Aka adolescents act with a large sense of freedom and autonomy while maintaining a close relationship with their families and learning what is expected of them (Hewlett 2004). The main difficulty in the current research was that adolescent boys would leave the settlement for prolonged periods of time in order to meet females of their age in other settlements.

Girls are presented with a dance ritual when they reach menarche, and boys on their first hunt receive medicine thought to possess magical properties from their fathers. These are rites of passage that represent the transition from childhood to adolescence. After these rites, adolescents move on to the next life stage and express these changes through food avoidances. Adolescent boys actively choose and avoid "children's foods," and adolescent girls under guidance of their mothers and close relatives avoid "men's foods" and dangerous food for children. Lewis (2008) points out that food restrictions among Mbendjele hunter-gatherers serve to justify key cultural distinctions between male-related outward activities, such as hunting, and female-related inward activities, such as caring for children. Food avoidance among Aka adolescents is part of the social learning process of gendered roles in Aka society.

Adolescent boys are also subject to food taboos connected to the eating of game animals they caught themselves. This taboo expresses the weakness of young hunters and the strength of experienced adult male hunters. Through this taboo an adolescent is faced with the task of becoming a "complete man." The presence of two types of food restrictions displays the two dimensions of Aka society. There is a highly independent and informal dimension, as well as a dimension that displays the central role of adult men in hunting and continuing the nomadic lifestyle. However, as shown in the data from the 2010 survey, adolescent boys who have moved away from their family groups do not have similar food avoidances. It likely will be difficult for these adolescents to obtain the sense of being an adult male.

Erikson refers to adolescence as a crucial period of time when an individual confirms a new identity (Erikson and Erikson 1987). Aka society features two mechanisms that are central to the development of adolescent boys from indulged children into adults. Adolescent boys actively participate in preparing for the next stage in life by selecting which food to avoid, and they also abide by societal rules and recognize their future role in providing meat for their families. The food restrictions of the Aka presented in this chapter display the current state of Aka adolescents within the context of modern society.

ACKNOWLEDGMENTS

This study was supported by the Grant-in-Aid for Scientific Research, "A Study of Ecological Anthropology on the Consistency and Change of Traditional African Societies" (No.63041072) and "Comparative Study on Marginalization among Indigenous People in Tropical Forest Zones of Africa" (No. 18251014) from the Ministry of Education, Science, Sports, and Culture, Japan. I thank for Dr. Jiro Tanaka, Dr. Tadashi Tanno, Dr. Hideaki Terashima, and Dr. Mitsuo Ichikawa for mentoring; Dr. Jerome Dinga-Reassi and Ministry of Scientific and Technical Research of the

Republic of the Congo for research permission; Dr. Paul Sita for the identification of my plant specimen; and the Aka people for their tolerance and companionship.

REFERENCES

Bahuchet, S. 1985. Les Pygmées Aka et la Forêt Centrafricaine. Paris: SELAF.
———. 1999. Aka Pygmies, in *The Cambridge Encyclopedia of Hunters and Gatherers*, edited by Richard B. Lee and Richard Daly. Cambridge: Cambridge University Press, pp. 190–194.
Colding, J. and Folke, C. "The Relations among Threatened Species, Their Protection, and Taboos," Conservation Ecology 1, no. 1 (1997). http://www.ecologyandsociety.org/vol1/iss1/art6/ (accessed .October 18, 2011).
Douglas, M. 1966. Purity and Danger: An Analysis of Concepts of Pollution and Taboo. New York: Routledge and Kegan Paul.
Erikson, E.H. and Erikson, J.M. 1987. The Life Cycle Completed. New York: Norton.
Hattori, S. 2008. "Conservation of Tropical Rainforests and the Culture of the Forest People: The Case of Baka Hunter-gatherers in Southeastern Cameroon." PhD diss. Kyoto University (in Japanese).
Hewlett, B. L. 2004. "Aka and Ngandu Adolescents of the Central African Republic: An Exploration of the Inter-and Intracultural Variability of Socio-Emotional Development, Responses to Loss and Health Status." PhD diss. Washington State University.
Hewlett, B.S. 1991. Intimate Fathers: The Nature and Context of Aka Pygmy Paternal Infant Care. Ann Arbor: University of Michigan Press.
Ichikawa, M. "Food Restrictions of the Mbuti Pygmies, Eastern Zaire," African Study Monographs, Supplementary Issue 6 (1987): 97–121.
Leach, E.R. 1964. Anthropological aspects of language: Animal categories and verbal abuse, in *New Directions in the Study of Language*, edited by E.H. Lenneberg. Cambridge, MA: MIT Press, pp. 23–63.
Lewis, J. "*Ekila*: Blood, Bodies, and Egalitarian Societies," Journal of the Royal Anthropological Institute 14, no. 2 (2008): 297–315.
McDonald, D.R. "Food Taboos: A Primitive Environmental Protection Agency (South America)," Anthropos 72 (1977): 734–748.
Meyer-Rochow, V.B. "Food Taboos: Their Origins and Purposes," Journal of Ethnobiology and Ethnomedicine 5, no. 18 (2009): 18–27. http://www.ethnobiomed.com/content/5/1/18 (accessed November 19, 2010).
Motte-Florac, E., Bahuchet, S., and Thomas J.M.C. 1993. The role of food in the therapeutics of the Aka Pygmies of the Central African Republic, in *Tropical Forests, People and Food*, edited by C.M. Hladik, A. Hladik, O.F. Linares, H. Pagezy, A. Semple, and M. Hadley. Paris: UNESCO, pp. 549–560.
Pagezy, H. 1993. The importance of natural resources in the diet of the young child in a flooded tropical forest in Zaire, in *Tropical Forests, People and Food*, edited by C.M. Hladik, A. Hladik, O.F. Linares, H. Pagezy, A. Semple, and M. Hadley. Paris: UNESCO, pp. 365–380.
Sato, H. "Food Restriction on Elephants among the Baka Pygmies in the Northwestern Congo," Bulletin of Hamamatsu University School of Medicine (Liberal Arts) 7 (1993): 19–30 (in Japanese).
Sperber, D. "Why Are Perfect Animals, Hybrids, and Monsters Food for Symbolic Thought?" Method and Theory in the Study of Religion 8, no. 2 (1996): 143–169.

Takeuchi, K. 2005. The ambivalent symbiosis between the Aka hunter-gatherers and neighboring farmers, in *Culture Conservation and Development in African Rain Forest (Research Report of MEXT Grant-in-Aid for Scientific Research)*, edited by Kiyoshi Takeuchi. Toyama: University of Toyama, pp. 11–28.

Whitehead, H. 2000. Food Rules: Hunting, Sharing, and Tabooing Game in Papua New Guinea. Ann Arbor: University of Michigan Press.

8 "The Bullet is Certain"
Armed Children and Gunplay on the Streets of Haiti

J. Christopher Kovats-Bernat

"Bal la se sèten," the boy tells me. The bullet is certain.

It is March 2010, shortly after the magnitude-seven earthquake that leveled Port-au-Prince. I am squatting on the pavement with a gaggle of street boys in a broken neighborhood in the sprawling Cité Soleil slum, discussing the recent shooting death of a boy they knew. The name of the dead child was Chouchou, and the consensus among these boys is that he was around the age of fifteen at the time of his death. His killer—Frèjean—was a street boy, also fifteen, and known to the victim because the two slept and worked in the same neighborhood and occasionally sniffed glue together. There had been an argument, my friends tell me, but over what they are not sure. What is known is this: heated words led to punches thrown, and then the boys parted ways. A few nights later, Frèjean blasted Chouchou in the chest as he slept with a small-caliber round from a handgun. He had allegedly borrowed the weapon from an older cousin associated with one of the many gangs who have partitioned armed control of Cité Soleil among themselves.

I have worked in Haiti for over seventeen years, conducting ethnographic research with street kids in the capital, and in that time I have grown as accustomed to child morbidity and death as I suppose one could. I have recorded all too many tales of kids dying violent deaths on the streets of Port-au-Prince, some likely true, some not. So I would have been cautiously skeptical of this account had I not known a few of the boys telling the story as well as I do. Moreover, although the incident was not reported in the newspapers (the violent demise of a street boy is far from newsworthy here), word of the killing had in recent days been circulating through the neighborhood's eerily reliable gossip mill. Besides this, I have recorded enough killings of street kids by other street kids to recognize this incident as more than plausible. The details of this particular case conformed very closely to an emergent pattern of violence among street children that I had been observing since at least 2000. Whereas in the past physical altercations rarely escalated to lethal consequences, confrontations were now increasingly resolved by the summary execution of one child by another with a handgun.

"How many times did the two fight with one another before Frèjean killed Chouchou?" I asked.

"Yon sèl fwa. Premye fwa," one of the boys answered. "Just once. Only that first time."

That's when another boy spoke up, preempting my next question. "Pwen yo pa serye. Bal la se sèten," he says.

"Fists are unreliable. The bullet is certain."

ARSENAL HAITI

Haiti is overarmed and heavily militarized. There are an estimated 250,000 small arms and light weapons in the Republic of Haiti (Gun Policy News 2011; MINUSTAH DDR 2005; Muggah 2005), and the vast majority of these are concentrated in the capital of Port-au-Prince. The range of weapons is broad, although most prevalent are small arms, including pistols, shotguns, and semiautomatic assault rifles. In the slums of the capital, neighborhoods are awash in handguns, many of which are so-called "creole" weapons cobbled together from the assorted parts of old or damaged firearms, or crafted from scratch by local blacksmiths. Although these guns are rudimentary and often misfire, they are relatively inexpensive to own (they can be had for as little as U.S.$20), are even cheaper to "rent" from an entrepreneurial owner, and can be just as deadly as a factory-manufactured firearm.

This arsenal is distributed across a bewildering array of formal and informal armed groups. State forces (including police paramilitary units such as the riot control unit, the tactical response unit, the antinarcotics unit, and the antigang unit), and MINUSTAH (the United Nations Stabilization Mission in Haiti) account for roughly 10 percent of all small arms in the country. The remainder of the firearms (upwards of two hundred thousand guns) are in the hands of civilian individuals and groups (Small Arms Survey 2011; Agència Catalana de Cooperació al Desenvolupament 2008; Muggah 2005). These include private citizens from across the demographic spectrum; members of armed popular organizations; gang members involved in narcotics trafficking as well as intimidation and extortion; neighborhood and village strongmen; so-called "resistance front" movements made up of demobilized soldiers and their supporters; "vigilance brigades" (*brigad vigilanz*) organized and armed by local residents and shop owners for self-defense; prison escapees (many of whom cache their weapons prior to incarceration); private security companies; bodyguards for wealthy civilians and politicians; and the *zenglendo* ("glassbacks"), the *chimère* ("ghosts"), and the *rat* ("rats")—euphemisms for the heterogeneous lot of predatory bandits, entrepreneur assassins, and drive-by specialists responsible for the periodic outbreaks of explosive gun violence in certain urban areas (UNDDR 2011).

A complex history of dictatorship, paramilitarism, and corruption; persistent problems associated with disarmament; chronic insecurity and crime; and the generally permissive and casual culture of gun possession in Haiti are together responsible for the country's plague of firearms. Legal transfers of weapons in the form of military aid commenced with the end of the U.S. Marine occupation of Haiti (1915–1934) and the establishment of the *gendarmerie*, the predecessor to the modern Haitian Army; small arms flowed continuously into the country until the military coup of 1991–1994, during which an international embargo was imposed and after which the import of arms resumed (Stockholm International Peace Research Institute [SIPRI] 2007). In 1995, the government of then-president Jean-Bertrand Aristide disbanded the army but failed to disarm them. As a result, some eighty-seven hundred small arms and light military weapons held by the fifty-five hundred demobilized soldiers disappeared into the civil sector (Muggah 2005). U.S. military aid to Haiti has continued steadily since then in support of the Haitian National Police (HNP), organized in the army's stead. Weapon stockpiles reached their present-day high by 2000, and a steady leakage of guns into Port-au-Prince's civil society has stubbornly persisted since then.

In February 2004, an armed uprising by paramilitary rebels against the second Aristide government nearly succeeded as insurgents overran HNP barracks across the country, routing the police from their posts and commandeering their weapons, body armor, uniforms, identity cards, and badges. Days after the campaign began, over 70 percent of the country had slipped out of government control. As the rebels descended on the capital, government agents distributed thousands of assault rifles, shotguns, and pistols to pro-Aristide street gangs in order to counter the impending assault, which was only averted by Aristide's eleventh-hour resignation and exile (Girard 2010; Dupuy 2007).

Whereas small arms transfers to Haiti have declined precipitously in recent years, illegal gun imports have been traced to more than a dozen countries, although most are smuggled from Miami, Pompano Beach, and Ft. Lauderdale (Bergman and de Granados 2004). Jamaica and the Dominican Republic are also notorious sources.

Despite several coercive and voluntary initiatives to disarm the civil society, and despite Haiti's establishment in 2005 of a National Commission on Disarmament, neither the Haitian state nor the UN stabilization mission has had much of an effect on small arms proliferation throughout the country. In fact, a guns-for-cash buyback program implemented by MINUSTAH in 2005 resulted in the collection of mostly unserviceable weapons, likely turned in for cash that could then be used to purchase better firearms on the black market (International Crisis Group [ICG] 2005; Muggah 2005). Although there has been some progress toward disarmament in recent years (Small Arms Survey 2011; Cockayne 2009; Dziedzic and Perito 2008), the devastation of the 2010 earthquake and the surge of over twenty-five thousand foreign troops to assist in relief and rebuilding are perhaps largely responsible for any quell in the violence.

STATE OF SEIGE

Haiti's gun woes today represent the single greatest impediment to human development throughout the country, nowhere more so than in Port-au-Prince. The tens of thousands of weapons that have drained into the civil society in the past five years, and the failure of the Haitian state to secure a legitimate monopoly on violence, have fostered a state of siege in the capital. Street gangs known locally as "clans" (the most significant bene-factors of small arms proliferation) have systematically seized control of entire slum districts throughout Port-au-Prince. Most, like the Cannibal Army (*Lamè Kanibal*), the Red Army (*Lamè Rouj*), and the Army of the Motherless (*Lamè San Manman*), have long been backed by political factions. Most however lack national notoriety and are little more than groups of young men and boys brandishing G3s and Glock handguns, roaming the rutted paths of their ghetto neighborhoods, extracting trib-ute or trafficking drugs while professing to provide a service of protec-tion. Still others are associated with syndicates of triggermen-for-hire, contracted by clans to carry out brazen executions that few others would hazard. A handful of these have achieved a special infamy for their brash style and unrepentant brutality, and are known far and wide simply by their *nom de rue*: Dieusibon. Ti Loulou. Pouchon. Chyencho. Don Féfé. Patatou. Labanyè. Colibri. The fluid loyalties of these men and their rela-tionships to political parties and the drug trade are considered of second-ary concern to most Haitians, who regard their wanton mayhem, whether motivated by profit or politics, as a menace to society.

In some areas, clans have utterly substituted the legitimate authority and serve as de facto governing entities. The Cité Soleil slum is one such area. Founded in the 1960s on a stagnant floodplain on the edge of Port-au-Prince and home to almost a half-million people, Cité Soleil's exceptional destitution and marginalization have made it rife for exploitation. The dis-trict had been regarded since the early 1990s as a region of staunch support for Aristide's *Fanmi Lavalas* party, its loyalty ensured by the predominance of pro-Aristide strongmen and their followers who resided throughout the shantytown. As the Aristide regime crumbled in 2004, the area erupted in violence, fueled by the sudden influx of arms to both pro- and anti-Aristide factions. Cité Soleil was subdivided among competing gangs into balkan-ized territories separated by free-fire zones that were frequently the scene of explosive shootouts (Wilman and Marcelin 2010). As pitched firefights raged through 2006 and 2007, MINUSTAH troops were ordered into the slum to restore order. Armed confrontations between the clans and UN peacekeepers and the National Police became routine. Despite the arrest of over eight hundred gang members, Cité Soleil remains beyond the control of both MINUSTAH and the Haitian state.

UNICEF (2009) estimates that there are over one thousand children employed by the clans as messengers, mules, scouts, intermediaries, gun-carriers, errand-runners, stone-throwers, lures, spies, and armed soldiers. They guard kidnap victims, frequently children their own age. They act as sentinels for the gangs, raising the alarm when UN or National Police personnel are operating in their area. In 2004, children were among the participants in *Operasyon Bagdad*—a campaign of beheadings of HNP officers by antigovernment gangs throughout Port-au-Prince. In 2007, two children were used by gangs to slip beneath and cut the brake lines of UN tanks during antigang operations in Cité Soleil (UNHCR 2008). Sometimes the clans shut down thoroughfares with barricades of burning debris to deter police activity in their areas of influence; when they do, street children can be found excitedly feeding tires into the flames for a few American dollars dispensed by street toughs decked out in torn pants and ostentatious bling and with assault rifles slung over their shoulders. Haiti's street children constitute a reserve of young and willing labor whose loyalties can be easily costed in proportion to their individual degree of desperation. The complicity of some can be ensured over extended periods with the regular distribution of modest rations of food, alcohol, or glue.

In many ways, the clans serve as acceptable, even desirable, substitutes for the shelter otherwise afforded by a home. In a context of extreme poverty and insecurity, gang leaders are apt to be perceived as effective providers and protectors, especially when the success of their local dealings is contrasted against the impotent rhetoric of the elected bureaucracy. Accordingly, clan strongmen are typically ascribed parental status by adolescent recruits, who refer to them by the deferential kin terms *tonton* ("uncle") or *papa* ("father").

As gang warfare and armed insecurity have proliferated throughout Port-au-Prince, entire regions of the capital have become socioeconomic dead zones. Residents are fearful of sending their children to school. Vendors are unable to sell their wares on streets riddled with strife. Commodity prices have escalated, and traditional exchange networks have been compromised by firefights in market areas. Public services have been crippled as violence has disrupted the provision and maintenance of electricity and water to neighborhoods. Hospitals, clinics, schools, and churches are often forced to close their doors when stray rounds pound into their walls.

The pervasion of gun violence and its consequences was already lending credence to Haiti's claim as "the world's first permanent failed state" (ICG 2006) when the earthquake struck in January 2010 and effectively ensured that Haiti would not be "succeeding" anytime soon. The epicenter was in Léogâne, 15 miles to the west of the capital. Although the primary ground shock would last less than a minute, the aftermath was nothing short of apocalyptic. In the time it takes to read this paragraph, over 220,000 Haitians were killed; three hundred thousand maimed; one million left homeless; and over two million more displaced, orphaned, or missing. Three hundred thousand commercial buildings in the capital were leveled, and a quarter of a million homes were lost. The Presidential Palace, the National Assembly, thirteen of the government's fifteen ministries, the Palace of Justice, the Supreme Court, the National Art Museum, National Police headquarters, the UN Mission, the offices of the World Bank, City Hall, the seaport, the Catholic Cathedral—all of these and more were reduced to rubble. The National Penitentiary broke, and 5,409 inmates escaped after commandeering the prison arsenal and descending into the slums of the capital.

SUFFER THE CHILDREN

It would be an understatement to say that Haiti did not need this. Long the poorest and most volatile country in the Western Hemisphere, Haiti has the highest under-five mortality rate in the Americas, making it one of the most inhospitable and unhealthy places in the world for a child to live. Here, adolescent morbidity and death threaten from all quarters of everyday life. Sickness, scarcity, and physical pain are ubiquitous among the poor, who here constitute an overwhelming majority of the whole—a full 70 percent of Haitians live in abject poverty. Pediatric infections and nutritional deficiencies are normative, and it is not uncommon for children to die of malnutrition, starvation, or dehydration. Less than half the population has access to clean water, and a mere 20 percent use sanitation facilities that ensure that human excreta are disposed of in a way that prevents it from contaminating food and water resources (UNICEF 2011b). Diarrhea—the doppelgänger of child death worldwide—is the number one killer of Haitian children, closely followed by respiratory illness, malaria, tuberculosis, and complications resulting from AIDS (nineteen thousand children are seropositive for HIV, and antiretroviral drugs are almost nonexistent). Typhoid, malnutrition, dysentery, hepatitis A/B/C, measles, yaws, elephantiasis, rabies, and even leprosy claim the lives of tens of thousands of Haitian children annually. Assault and homicide are the leading causes of death among adolescents aged ten to nineteen (PAHO 2009), in part due to the proliferation of small arms over the past half century.

Although estimates vary widely, there are conservatively ten thousand and as many as fifty thousand children or more working, eating, sleeping, socializing, loving, fighting, killing, and dying on the streets of Port-au-Prince, Cap Haïtien, and other towns and villages throughout Haiti (UNICEF 1999, 2011a; Save the Children 2011; Kovats-Bernat 2010, 2006a, 2006b; Bernat 1999). Although some of these children number among the country's 380,000 orphans, most street kids have living kin and know where to find them; they elect to live on the street. Forced out of the home to work in support of the household economy, they spend ever-increasing amounts of time away until they stop going back altogether, preferring to support themselves on the street with the money they make rather than take it home and receive only a portion of it in return (Kovats-Bernat 2006b). For them the street is home. And to be sure, the challenges to child health and survival are more aggravated for those who have been displaced from their homes and onto the streets, where they subsist and survive wholly in a world of violence, scarcity, and uncertainty. As one boy explained to me, "*Blanc*, it is easy enough for anyone to die here."

Since 1994 I have conducted ethnographic research with an ever-shifting population of street children in Port-au-Prince, most of them boys between the ages of five and twenty. Defining the street child population presents a number of problems because of the almost limitless ways that adolescents might comport themselves to the street, to say nothing of the highly variable amount of time they spend there and the multiplex ways in which they use it (Kovats-Bernat 2006b). However these children identify with the street, they rarely call what they do there 'living.' *Nou sufri lari*, they say; "we suffer the street." They run low-grade fevers most of the time and cope with frequent bouts of diarrhea. Their bodies are raked with edge wounds, gouges that reach down into deep tissue. Their frames are bent and broken from breaks and fractures that have gone unset. On the bodies of some are the dented mottle-scars of gunshot wounds. Dogs bite them, flies pester them, rats and roaches swarm them when they sleep. Cars hit them; passersby revile them; and the police kick them, beat them, and occasionally shoot them. Always there is the threat of another kid's rock or razor.

Kinship and sharing are their only effective defense. Street children work a variety of jobs—shining shoes, selling foraged things, washing cars, stealing, drug dealing—and they usually do this labor alone or in twos or threes. As the sun sets each evening, they return to their respective "home bases" (*baz fouaye*), where they congregate with perhaps a dozen or so of their closest friends and allies to share what they have pilfered, begged, won, or earned from the day: coins and crumpled bills; a mango or an egg; cigarettes half-smoked; tinned fish and some rice; fried plantain in oil-soaked newspaper; candies, to be sure. They pool their net resources and hand them back out again so that each has what she or he requires for the night. They joke and shove and call one another "my sister" and "my brother." It is in this way that they negate their poverty each night with what they share among themselves. When darkness falls, they disperse in even smaller groups to sleep in secret spaces, and they awaken with the day to suffer the street again.

AN EYE FOR AN EYE

With so many unsupervised children (two-thirds of them boys) hashing out a livelihood on the streets of Port-au-Prince, it should be unsurprising that conflict is frequent, taunting is normative, and fistfights are commonplace. Occasionally, altercations escalate to the brandishing of razors or the throwing of rocks, but rarely are these confrontations lethal, and they are almost never intended to be so. That is not to say that street children do not try to kill one another. Indeed, I have known a few children who were killed by their street peers, and many others—usually teenage boys—whom I know to have killed or are believed to have done so, but this never has been, nor is it presently, the norm. To the contrary, the overwhelming majority of the hundreds of street kids with whom I have worked exercise great restraint in fighting with one another, which they do within the bounds of a semi-structured system of confrontation that both regulates and limits the extent to which violent acts impinge upon their everyday lives.

Elsewhere (Kovats-Bernat 2006b) I have discussed at length the manifold motivations for violence among street kids in Port-au-Prince (including altercations over insults or injury, fistfights over work territory, sexual assaults at razor-point, and predatory attacks in the line of robberies), and so will not do so here. Like any population anywhere, street children resort to violence when their physical or economic security is at stake, their dignity is compromised, or their lives are threatened. Most of these violent encounters carry little meaning for them beyond immediate utility or necessity, and some even speak with casual indifference about acts of almost indescribable brutality: the beating of a child with a length of lumber in order to steal his radio; the disfigurement of a street boy by a girl who slashed his face with a razor in the haze of a glue-sniffing high; the rape of a prepubescent boy behind a tomb in the National Cemetery. Violent acts like these indeed occur, but most kids living off the street struggle to make an honest living free from conflict and will in most instances avoid at all costs a potentially volatile encounter with another youth, especially when there is the possibility that such an encounter might interfere with their work.

That said, it is not the infrequent (however appalling), one-off instances of brutality that carry the greatest weight of meaning for Haitian street kids. Every child who lives on the street is aware of the fact that they could be victimized in a savagely senseless attack by another youth, but they rarely seem any more preoccupied with this possibility than they are with the possibility that they will be struck by a car, or bitten by a dog, or detained by the police, or overwhelmed with roaches as they sleep. Isolated instances of violent victimization are an accepted risk of life on the street and are frequently regarded as remote possibilities that are, should they eventuate, as unavoidable as an act of God and therefore merit little if any preoccupation.

This is not to argue that street kids do not concern themselves with the possibility of being attacked by one another. Many of their individual and group efforts as friends and allies tied to a particular *baz* suggest that they peremptorily defend themselves against that very eventuality: they hide themselves when sleeping and do so in groups; they sleep *je klè* (lightly, "with one eye open"), prepared to wake easily in order to confront a threat. There are times, however, when a child will find herself or himself enmeshed in a protracted conflict with another youth for which there is little effective defense or promise of a compromise. In such instances, animosities erupt in a series of punctuated acts of violence that find no resolution and only promise future altercations. As time goes on, these confrontations escalate in frequency and brutality—fists give way to rocks, and then razors. Anger gives way to rage. Vengeance grows insuppressible, and retaliation begets more of its kind, or worse. Blood is let once, then again and again—a cracked lip, a busted nose, a slashed forearm. A climate of fear and sickening anticipation descends, as both parties are gripped with anxious hypervigilance. The violence becomes a preoccupation, a state of being, and a condition of its own reproduction.

These are the conflicts that carry the heaviest symbolic and affective load for kids bound to the street, because they are emblematic of the kind of lethal trouble that can emerge from the sorts of interactions that define everyday life for a street child. An accidental injury, an inadvertent affront, or an unintentional slight leads to a fistfight. Subsequent encounters freshen the insult of the original confrontation, leading to more violent encounters. Then comes a nighttime attack while the victim sleeps, the opening salvo of a kind of ritualized violence that street kids call *lagè domi*—"sleeping wars." As a systematic series of tit-for-tat attacks between two children with a history of persistent violent encounters that repeatedly fail to find resolution, the sleeping war accomplishes what the prior altercations could not: a conclusive end to hostilities. When the war begins, both actors bend desperately and irretrievably toward an absolute and final solution to their differences.

I first documented the sleeping wars in the late 1990s. Then as now, the weapons of choice were rocks, melted plastic, chunks of concrete, razors, or lengths of lumber used to target the feet, knees, and legs of a child adversary (less frequently his head or chest) as he sleeps unawares until the moment of attack. The violence, enacted always at night and while the victim sleeps, becomes systemic and cyclical. A child's wounding by his adversary marks a moment of choice. If he so elects, the conflict can end with his own victimization; he may opt to forgo a counterattack as revenge for his wounds, and so the war ends with a single blow. Or he may opt to continue the war, seeking out his attacker and exacting his vengeance under the cover of night, likewise to his own victimization. His hope in retaliating is to inflict an injury sufficiently painful or debilitating to his adversary so as to deter him from returning the violence. As a first assault, a child might heat a plastic juice bottle to melting and shove it into the bare sole of the foot of his sleeping enemy, who might retaliate nights later by inflicting razor cuts to the feet and legs of his sleeping attacker, now the victim. Next might come a chunk of concrete dropped onto the enemy's ankles, waist or chest. Eventually the face or head might be targeted, but until recently the wars rarely reached this point, most ending after a second or third nonlethal assault. That was when the handgun existed as an alien fetish of ghetto power, something often seen but rarely touched, like cocaine or amphetamines. Street kids stick to glue and alcohol because the more potent stuff is beyond their means; it used to be that way with guns, too.

It is the escalating fear on the part of both parties, and a mutual desire to put a conclusive end to the terrible tension of what is to come that ultimately leads youths enmeshed in a sleeping war to ever-intensified acts of brutality against one another. Each child so embroiled genuinely believes that the only event that can end the hostilities, and the terrible pain inflicted in the dead of night and slumber, is the terrorization of his opponent into leaving him alone. That terrorization may come as a profound maiming or a final deathblow, although the latter had almost always been, until recently, an inadvertent consequence of the killer's miscalculation of the delicate ratio of maximal-impact-to-minimal-harm. Overshooting the mark becomes a likelier outcome as time and fear impel the actors to ever-greater acts of morbidity.

I have argued previously that the wars seem to conform to larger economic imperatives that demand a conclusive end to animosities between antagonists as soon as possible, that fearful vigilance and incapacitation quickly hamper the labors of the fighters, who must work each and every day with minimum distraction in order to survive (Kovats-Bernat 2006b). That given, all that is required to get back to the business of unfettered and unconcerned street work is the concession of victory to one's enemy by not protracting the conflict beyond one's own victimization—and I have found that few street kids value their egos over their economic survival. As a result, maiming assaults that impact a child's ability to work have customarily been regarded as sufficient, because hunger and helplessness compel begging, a practice generally viewed as humiliating. When a killing did occur, the perpetrator was apt to be marginalized from his *baz*, stigmatized and feared as aberrant, capricious, and unrestrained in his willingness to kill, whether that was his intention or not. Shut out of his network of reciprocity and social support, he would find himself in the most dread of circumstances: alone on the street.

ZERO-SUM

That was all before the injection of large numbers of small arms into Port-au-Prince's slum communities in the early 2000s, when warring political factions turned the streets of the capital into a battleground. Although the 2004 insurrection lasted all of a few weeks, it marked a shift in the balance of power away from MINUSTAH and the Haitian state. Heavily armed rebels patrolled the ghettos with impunity and in defiance of UN patrols. Neighborhood strongmen directed squads of fighters brandishing Galils and R4s to launch attacks on the police.

Most street kids remained ill at ease in the presence of guns; others clearly relished handling them. For the first time in a decade, I could find the occasional street kid swaggering about with a revolver shoved into his waistband, almost comically dragging his pants down. Almost. Hand-me-down pistols from older street youth who had moved into the ranks of the clans circulated among groups of younger kids. I came upon a gaggle of boys who had come into possession of a .38 in just this way. They were dry-firing it at one another's heads, seemingly oblivious to the potential consequences of error. They told me that it was now fairly easy to "borrow" or "rent" a gun by the hour or the day, and at rates within their means.

It was immediately apparent that the sleeping wars now had an increased potential for lethality, both because of the real possibility that a gun might be had by a child and because of the heightened sense of urgency to put a quick end to animosities as a result. Since 2000, I have recorded over a dozen instances of firearm homicides among street youth, each at the hands of a fellow street kid. In the six years before then, I had recorded none. In all but two of these instances, the killings were carried out within the context of a sleeping war, usually one so brief as to barely merit the label. The sleeping wars were now starting, or very shortly thereafter ending, with a fatal deathblow by any means, including but not limited to a gun blast. As small arms increased in prevalence throughout their communities, street kids grew proportionately fearful of being shot to death early in a sleeping war. Some sought to preempt their own victimization by killing their adversary at the very outset of the war, as a first and final volley.

Chouchou never had a chance. Frèjean shot him as an opening salvo to the war. He is the first such homicide that I know of since the earthquake. He surely won't be the last.

I wondered if the proliferation of small arms was changing the fundamental nature of violence among street kids in some way. Could it be that they had given up on restraint, that they would have a long time ago had they had the easy access to firearms that they do now? The stigma of killing among street kids has certainly diminished a great deal in the past ten years. They still speak with dread and click their tongues in disapproval when the subject of a sleeping war ending in a fatal gunshot comes up, but no one talks about ostracizing the killer anymore. Many can identify with his desperate measure, even feel sorry for him because now he has to carry the weight of his sin for the rest of his life. Kill or be killed is what they say. It's not like it used to be, when one had more options, when the life of a child was not so cheap.

Frèjean still works and sniffs glue with the same crowd of kids he always has. The consensus is that he did what anyone would do. After all, Chouchou was an addict. Chouchou could have gotten a gun first. It was a matter of personal security, one boy tells me. And that I think is at the very heart of the matter.

A CONTAGION OF VIOLENCE

In June 2003, a conference of scholars and nongovernmental organizations concerned with small arms proliferation was held in Port-au-Prince to discuss the relationship of youth and small arms in Haiti. It was the first meeting of major international small arms NGOs and researchers to focus exclusively on the matter of gun violence in that country. The report that emerged from that conference concluded that individuals and groups in Haiti primarily regard guns as tools to be used as a guard against insecurity. As such, they have an almost exclusively utilitarian value in that they are used by people to lessen their fear of violent threats and to increase their sense of security in the face of scarcity, poverty, and corruption. Individuals and groups arm themselves not simply because of the power and deference that comes with carrying a gun (a common perception throughout Haitian society and among many scholars), but because of the palpable vulnerability of the communities in which they live. In short, the use of small arms is driven by chronic shortages of basic physical needs, work, land, education, and access to the political process. The result, however, is ever-greater insecurity as social cohesion breaks down, infrastructure is destroyed, investment is frightened away, and development is thwarted (James 2010; American Friends Service Committee Haiti Program 2003).

If this conclusion is correct (and I believe that it is), then we should find that those populations most fraught with gun violence are those among whom scarcity is most profound, and we in fact do. Despite the fact that the entire city of Port-au-Prince is awash in small arms (gunmen are a fixture of everyday life throughout the city), with occasional exception rampant gunplay is primarily confined to the slum districts. Even during the 2004 rebel uprising, when weapons were being distributed almost everywhere (had been, in fact, for weeks before), the heaviest armament was carried out in places like Cité Soleil, Carrefour, La Saline, Ti Bwa, Krisroi, Nan Beny, and parts of Delmas—poor neighborhoods whose gangs have taken advantage of community insecurity to assume de facto control. As an assault on the capital threatened and anarchy obtained throughout the city, I stood across the street from the Presidential Palace and watched as government functionaries handed assault rifles—scores of them—through the Palace gates to young men who then recruited street kids to help them load the weapons into the bed of a pickup truck bound for Cité Soleil.

Among street children—whose lack of virtually everything is remarkable even amid the abject poverty and scarcity of Port-au-Prince—insecurity is even more acute. Perhaps this is why some have taken so readily to the use of guns in adjudicating conflict among themselves. In addition to their daily struggle to secure the basic needs of survival, street children are alienated from the education system and the political process (in fact are virtually unrepresented in that arena); marginalized within even the most destitute of communities; criminalized and often abused by the police; compete fiercely among themselves for work; and, except for their identification with their respective *baz*, enjoy little or no association with a protective group. But most significantly, they are children, whose small stature and relative powerlessness in an adult world possesses them of a keen sense of vulnerability, heightened still by the fact that they exist in a very public world of utter exposure. Little wonder that they adopt, innovate, and maintain strategies among themselves for the avoidance, diversion, minimization, and quick resolution to threats and conflicts that intensify their sense of insecurity. This includes the channeling of their conflicts into the rubric of the sleeping wars (where at least a modicum of expectation and control is imposed on violence), as well as the use of firearms in those wars—despite the ironic fact that their adoption of such weapons for such purposes only increases their chances of dying under circumstances that in the past might not have been lethal.

CERTAINTY AND INDIFFERENCE

The lives of street children in Haiti are anything but easy to understand, and attempts to impose a system of logic onto everything that they do is doomed to failure at least most of the time. It is true that the kids with whom I have worked have demonstrated a capacity to rationally assess and cope with the violence that characterizes so much of their existence. Their explanations of the dangers they face are veridical, and the tactics they deploy to defend against them are often reasonable and practical. They recognize that they are vulnerable to a great deal of unpredictable danger, and both individually and as groups do what they can to obviate or (having failed this) manage it when it occurs. The sleeping wars are emblematic of this. Admittedly unsettling, the sleeping war is a pragmatic solution for dealing with chronic conflict on the street, and the "rules" for its conduct are not only a novel way of leveling the playing field between antagonists but demonstrate a degree of reason that goes a long way toward dispelling the myth that street kids are little more than passive, unenculturated victims of larger social dynamics.

The lethal impact that guns have had on the sleeping wars may be predictable, and the explanation given—that the use of firearms has increased the insecurity of street kids at the same time that they have adopted them as a means to reassert, reassure, and defend themselves against insecurity—may not make much sense; but then again it doesn't have to. Insensible is not the same as meaningless. Most street children are not capriciously violent, nor do they regard the maiming or killing of another child thoughtlessly. To the contrary, they think quite deeply about these things and ruminate on their moral culpability when they are involved in such acts. Morbidity and death may not make sense to these children, but they surely do mean something to them.

The behavior of street kids, like that of all groups, is as often reactive and contradictory as it is predictive and logical, and more frequently than not is a product of adaptation to a given set of circumstances. In much the same way that the apparent absurdity of the clumsy design of the human anatomy makes little sense except in light of how it evolved, so too does the apparent absurdity of violence among street kids make little sense except in light of its history of emergence. Street kids live in a world that is largely indifferent to their suffering. If it is true that their embrace of guns has only heightened their insecurity, it is also true that a child compelled to arm himself does so not because the irony is lost on him, or because he cannot comprehend the consequences, or because he is amoral, or because he has no choice. He does so because in the dead of night, reason is not always reliable. But the bullet is certain.

REFERENCES

Agència Catalana de Cooperació al Desenvolupament. 2008. Haiti: Country Report.

American Friends Service Committee Haiti Program. 2003. A Summary of Lessons on Small Arms Demand and Youth. Geneva.

Bergman, J. and de Granados, O.Z. 2004. "Guns Smuggled from South Florida Arming Haitians," Sun-Sentinel, March 2.

Bernat, J.C. 1999. "Children and the Politics of Violence in Haitian Context: Statist Violence, Scarcity, and Street Child Agency in Port-au-Prince," Critique of Anthropology 19, no. 2 (1999): 121–138.

Cockayne, James. 2009. Beyond Market Forces: Regulating the Global Security Industry. New York: International Peace Institute.

Dupuy, A. 2007. The Prophet and the Power: Jean-Bertrand Aristide, the International Community, and Haiti. Lanham, MD: Rowman and Littlefield.

Dziedzic, M. and Perito, R. 2008. Haiti: Confronting the Gangs in Port-au-Prince. Special Report 208 (September). United States Institute for Peace.

Girard, P. 2010. Haiti: The Tumultuous History—From Pearl of the Caribbean to Broken Nation. New York: Palgrave Macmillan.

Gun Policy News. 2011. "Haiti—Gun Facts, Figures and the Law." On http://www.gunpolicy.org/firearms/region/haiti (accessed July 6, 2011).

International Crisis Group. "Haiti's Transition: Hanging in the Balance," Latin America/Caribbean Briefing 7 (February 2005).

———. 2006. "Haiti after the Elections: Préval's 100-Day Challenges." Media Release (May). Port-au-Prince.

James, E.C. 2010. Democratic Insecurities: Violence, Trauma, and Intervention in Haiti. Berkeley: University of California Press.

Kovats-Bernat, J.C. "Factional Terror, Paramilitarism and Civil War in Haiti: The View from Port-au-Prince (1994–2004)," Anthropologica 48, no. 1 (2006a): 117–139.

———. 2006b. Sleeping Rough in Port-au-Prince: An Ethnography of Street Children and Violence in Haiti. Gainesville: University Press of Florida.

———. "Haïti Chérie," Childhood 17 (2010): 426–429.

MINUSTAH DDR. 2005. Public Information and Sensitization Strategy for the DDR Process in Haiti. Mimeo. Port-au-Prince: MINUSTAH.

Muggah. 2005. Securing Haiti's Transition: Reviewing Human Insecurity and the Prospects for Disarmament, Demobilization, and Reintegration. Geneva: Small Arms Survey.

PAHO. 2009. HAITI. PAHO Basic Health Indicator Data Base.

Save the Children. 2011. "Haiti—Projects." On http://www.savethechildren.ca/haiti/haiti—projects (accessed July 7, 2011).

Stockholm International Peace Research Institute. 2007. United Nations Arms Embargoes: Their Impact on Arms Flows and Target Behaviour. Uppsala, Sweden: SIPRI.

Small Arms Survey. 2011. Small Arms Survey 2011: States of Security. Geneva: Small Arms Survey.

UNDDR. 2011. Haiti: Country Programme. On http://www.unddr.org/country-programmes.php?c=80 (accessed July 10, 2011).

UNHCR. 2008. Child Soldiers Global Report 2008—Haiti. May 20. On http://www.unhcr.org/refworld/docid/486cb10528.html (accessed July 7, 2011).

UNICEF. 1999. Haiti Faces Major Education Challenge. On http://www.unicef.org/newsline/99pr19.htm (accessed July 9, 2011).

———. 2009. The State of the World's Children 2009: Maternal and Newborn Health. New York: UNICEF.

———. 2011a. Residential Care Centre Provides a Refuge for Street Children in Cap-Haitian. Special Report (15 February). Onhttp://www.unicef.org/infoby-country/haiti_57670.html (accessed July 9, 2011).

———. 2011b. The State of the World's Children 2011: Adolescence—An Age of Opportunity. New York: UNICEF.

Wilman, A. and Marcelin, L.H. "'If They Could Make Us Disappear, They Would!' Youth and Violence in Cité Soleil, Haiti," Journal of Community Psychology 38, no. 4 (2010): 515–531.

Part III

Globalization
Tradition, Modernity, and Identity

9   Multiple Identifications of Multicultural Adolescents

Dialogues between Tradition and Postmodernity in a Global Context

Toon van Meijl

This chapter examines the shifting identities of adolescents growing up in multicultural societies, especially in the Pacific. In the postmodern era, the constitution of their cultural identity is not only compounded by rapid cultural changes that are associated with globalization, but also by the paradoxical revival of cultural traditions that the large-scale compression of time and space has incited in many societies, especially those with a colonial history (Meyer and Geschiere 1999). As a consequence, young people are increasingly caught in dilemmas that emerge from the diversity of cultural circumstances in which they are growing up. At home they are expected to abide by traditional customs, but loyalty to their parents and family background is increasingly challenged by enticing images dominating public spaces that are supposedly conflicting with their upbringing.

The main question I seek to address in this chapter is how the identity of adolescents growing up in multicultural societies is constituted in and through cultural differences. More specifically, how do multiple forms of difference, such as traditional and postmodern expressions of culture, intersect within the self of individuals? How may we conceive of individual selves who are not unified but torn between a number of different, possibly conflicting, identifications? In other words, how can multiple differences within individuals be acknowledged without representing their identifications as negative, damaged, or in crisis? Before these questions can be examined, however, it is essential to delineate the historical, ethnographic, and theoretical parameters of this chapter in more detail.

Adolescence is a cultural concept, commonly distinguished from puberty, the process of physical maturation, and therefore it signifies by definition cultural variation in the transition from childhood to adulthood (Herdt and Leavitt 1998). The widespread view in Western societies that associates adolescence with mood swings and the turning away from parents toward peers, for example, has been challenged in cultural anthropology since the publication of Margaret Mead's *Coming of Age in Samoa* (1928). Notwithstanding the critique this book received from Derek Freeman (1983), it demonstrated that adolescence is not necessarily an inherently conflictual process of internal distress and external rebellion (Shankman 2009).

Aside from the cultural differences in the social and psychological development of young people, a common denominator in the transition to adulthood may be, as Erik Erikson (1968) suggested, that around the globe "society" replaces the "family" as the context of identity formation for adolescents. Indeed, the living space of adolescents gradually expands as they grow up. Erikson's influential perspective, however, is currently compounded by the rise of globalization, which has deeply changed the makeup of contemporary societies. Although peoples have, of course, always been on the move (Wolf 1982), the enhanced mobility and massive migration enabled by revolutionary innovations in information and communication technology that characterizes globalization seems unprecedented. Thus, globalization is complicating social relationships within multicultural nation-states that are slowly becoming more diverse than ever before, which at the same time implies that an increasing number of adolescents are coming of age at a time of great socioeconomic; linguistic; and, last but not least, cultural changes.

Apart from the fact that more and more young people are growing up in a bilingual environment (e.g., Doerr 2009), globalization and its related mobility of peoples, goods, ideas, and values generally entails fundamental social and economic changes in the lives of many adolescents. In view of the rising importance of the service sector in the neoliberal economies around the globe, which generally implies a decreasing number of unskilled jobs, young people are increasingly forced to stay in school much longer than in the past. As a consequence, adolescence in global economies tends to become longer as fewer young people are able to become economically independent at an early age. Their money is rarely sufficient to live on by themselves, and many adolescents, especially those who extend their education, have to rely on the resources of their parents until well into their twenties (Montgomery 2009, 208). The tension that this involves is often reinforced by the impact of television and marketing on the growing desire to participate in global consumption patterns of music, fashion, and information technology. Furthermore, the cultural meaning of global gadgets is not infrequently believed to represent a lifestyle that may contradict the moral content of cultural traditions that migrated families seek to uphold in their new surroundings.

Thus, this chapter focuses on the life course of adolescents who find themselves betwixt and between different cultural environments, in migrated families and in wider societies that are characterized by cultural difference. Until recently, the study of migration patterns focused on the transition from rural to urban areas, whereas international migration was analyzed in terms of a shift from developing countries in the "Global South" to metropolitan centers in the metaphorical West (van Meijl 2007). Underlying this approach was the widespread assumption that links migration waves generally with a transition from tradition to modernity. As a rigorous distinction between tradition and modernity is deeply embedded in the history of social sciences (Bendix 1966), the cultural changes that parallel the long-term process of globalization tend historically also to be analyzed in terms of a dichotomy between tradition and modernity, or, for some, postmodernity (Vertovec and Cohen 1999). This perspective, in turn, is founded on the belief that changes can take place in one direction only, invariably involving declining traditionality and rising modernity. For the analysis of the lives of adolescents growing up in culturally diverse contexts, this view implies that the transition from childhood to adulthood, during which the family is gradually replaced by the multicultural society as the predominant frame of reference, is paralleled by a sudden shift from tradition to postmodernity (Nilan and Feixa 2006).

The aim of this chapter is to disprove that assumption by showing that the dislocation of adolescents growing up in a multicultural environment puts them in an ongoing, everyday, multidimensional process of negotiation between the so-called "traditional" milieu at home and the cultural practices of the "new" society beyond the bounds of the family. Although the positioning of young people and the appropriations they make of both "old" and "new" cultural discourses and practices take place within settings that some would qualify as inauthentic (Jolly 1992), being neither genuinely "traditional" nor truly "postmodern," in this chapter they are considered as creative agents of cultural change. By reconstituting their cultural identity in global societies made up of mixed cultures, they often borrow foreign cultural meanings that simultaneously enable them to put new meanings into old shells (Jourdan 1995). Thus, they manipulate the best of both worlds, and for that reason too, multicultural adolescents must not necessarily be regarded as victims of cultural ruptures, but instead as motors of change and perhaps also as flywheels of cultural continuity.

The liminal position of multicultural adolescents and the mediation of multiple identifications within their self shall be analyzed with the psychological theory of the dialogical self. Dialogical self-theory is based on the Bakhtinian notion of dialogue among a multiplicity of different cultural position, in combination with William James's view of the interlinkages between self and other (Hermans and Kempen 1993). The assumption of dialogical self-theory is that the self is a society of mind, reflecting the dilemmas of localization and globalization, of tradition and postmodernity, within the self of individuals, sometimes leading to identity confusion, but often also lifting the self up to a hybrid level of integration (Kinnvall and Lindén 2010).

Empirically, this chapter examines the hybridization of multicultural adolescent identities in two case studies from Pacific societies, which are not only historically young, but also demographically youthful (Herdt and Leavitt 1998, 8). Like many developing countries, those of the Pacific have populations whose average age may be in the teens or twenties, and it goes without saying that a reversed population pyramid has far-reaching implications for relationships between generations. One case study focuses on Maori youngsters who face difficulties identifying with the cultural renaissance in their society prescribing them to follow traditional protocol. The other case study provides a glimpse of the lives of Tongan youngsters who were born and bred in Australia and New Zealand, but who are nevertheless expected *not* to change Tongan customs and *not* to adjust to Western values. Maori and Tongan adolescents share with each other that they have great difficulties to express their cultural identities in terms of traditional aspects of culture, such as language and ritual, yet they cannot discard their ethnicity and therefore attempt to recombine traditional and postmodern aspects of their mixed cultural environments in daily life. I begin with a brief sketch of the setting of global changes in the Pacific.

A SEA OF ISLANDS

Representations of the Pacific have been ambivalent since first European contact in the eighteenth century. For tourists, the region evokes images of white beaches and waving palm trees, yet for locals international contacts have induced a desire to "develop" and achieve living standards similar to those in the home countries of the thousands of travelers visiting the region each year. Recently, however, the Tongan intellectual Epeli Hau'ofa (1994, 1998) responded to pessimistic views of the Pacific horizon by drawing attention to the enormous opportunities of Pacific people. In a famous dictum, he proclaimed that the Pacific should be viewed as "a sea of islands" instead of a group of "islands in a far sea." He considered this perspective as consistently in line with historical patterns that were characterized by mobility. The dynamic past of the Pacific clearly shows, according to Hau'ofa, that it is wrong to focus on the alleged limitations of geographical, national, or economic boundaries. In his view, borders are a mere legacy of colonialism as the ocean was boundless before Captain Cook's apotheosis. Large numbers of ordinary Pacific Islanders were crisscrossing the ocean for centuries, enlarging their worlds in search of challenging opportunities. In essence, contemporary migration patterns suggest that these age-old processes are still ongoing, which caused Hau'ofa (1994, 151) to argue that "Oceania is not small," but "huge and growing bigger," and that those who focus on the geographical size of most Pacific islands suffer from a "small" state of mind and therefore fail to understand the meaning of the endless ocean for the people of Oceania.

Indeed, the impact of migration is nowhere near as pervasive as it is in the Asia-Pacific region, which accounts for almost 40 percent of the millions of people who cross national borders each year (Goss and Lindquist 2000). The tiny countries and territories of Polynesia and Micronesia, especially, have contributed to substantial migration due to limited prospects for economic growth, and the pressure for further international migration is still increasing under the impact of climate change. As a consequence, the life courses of most island people, present or absent, are increasingly embedded in international ties, and given the small size of island populations the impact of transnational connections is magnified in the Pacific region.

In the Pacific, much of the largest migration streams have been from Polynesia, notably Samoa and Tonga, whereas there is currently also increasing migration from the independent Micronesian states that were once linked closely to the U.S. Altogether, half a million of Polynesians are living abroad today, which is about 25 percent of the total population. Approximately 250,000 of those are living in New Zealand, where they make up almost 7 percent of the total population. Because roughly two-thirds of all Pacific Islanders in New Zealand are concentrated in the suburbs of Auckland, this city is often labeled the Polynesian capital.

Migration from the Pacific Islands to New Zealand began after World War II, but has increased since the 1970s. In consequence, six out of ten Pacific Islanders living in New Zealand were born in their new home country. Furthermore, it is interesting that for some groups, such as Cook Islanders, Niueans, and Tokelauans, the numbers resident in New Zealand exceed, often considerably, those resident in the origin societies (Macpherson, Spoonley, and Anae 2001). The transnational connections between Pacific people in New Zealand and their places of origin, in many cases the distant places of origin of parents and grandparents, make this a fascinating field for research into the nature and content of linkages and networks between Pacific communities across borders. In addition, it shows that an increasing number of diasporic adolescents are growing up between two or more shores, developing multiple identifications with more than one place in and beyond New Zealand.

Because migrants from Samoa and Tonga make up the largest Polynesian groups in New Zealand, their situation has been investigated in some detail (Anae 1997, 2001; Lee 2003, 2004). As mentioned earlier, some 60 percent of Pacific peoples resident in New Zealand were born there, but continue to be raised in the Pacific style by parents who were born overseas. In New Zealand, these migrant children are generically identified as Samoans or Tongans, although within Samoan and Tongan communities a distinction is gradually being made between those who were born in the Pacific and those who were born in New Zealand. In both cases, however, the main label of identification continues to refer to a territory that is far removed from the country in which they are growing up, a phenomenon that has been described as deterritorialization by the influential anthropologist Arjun Appadurai (1996). It goes without saying that this paradoxical relationship between the customary label of someone's identity and the circumstances in which a person is raised generates confusion. The Samoan anthropologist Melani Anae (2001, 106) has encapsulated the perplexity following this mix-up in the following verse:

> I am a Samoan—but not a Samoan. To my aiga in Samoa, I am a Palagi. I am a New Zealander—but not a New Zealander. To New Zealanders, I am a bloody coconut at worst, a Pacific Islander at best. To my Samoan parents, I am their child.

The confusion begins when someone's Samoan identity is challenged by island-born members of one's extended family (*aiga*) or church community, which are rather influential in Pacific Islander communities, while at the same time one's identity as a New Zealander is challenged by *Papalagi*, New Zealanders of European descent. For many adolescents, these emotional challenges to their identity as both Samoan and New Zealander entail not only confusion, but also insecurity and lack of control. It reinforces their awareness that some social and cultural attitudes and behavior derived from their new world are opposed to prior behavioral and sociocultural norms proceeding from the Pacific.

The prime source of identity confusion among Pacific youngsters growing up in New Zealand, Australia, and the U.S. is the inability to speak the first language of their parents and grandparents. Although many might be able to understand their "mother tongue," their lack of proficiency prevents them from participating in activities organized by the extended family or other institutions that are founded on a Pacific Island basis, such as churches. For that reason, too, many young people no longer think of themselves as "real Pacific Islanders," nor are they viewed as such by their parents and other family members whose first language is not English. Thus, the level of fluency in a Pacific language becomes a sign for which dimension of an adolescent's upbringing is more dominant: those more fluent in a Pacific Island language than in English are still regarded as real Pacific Islanders, whereas those who prefer to communicate in English are frequently considered as more New Zealander, Australian, or American.

The question of whether Pacific youngsters are torn between two cultures or whether some sometimes successfully manage to constitute a balanced identity "between two shores" has been examined most extensively for Tongan youngsters living in Australia by Helen Lee (2003). She demonstrates in great detail that young people are increasingly able to shift between identities in different contexts. These shifts may involve significant transformations in appearance (clothing, hairstyle, etc.) and behavior according to whether they are at home, church, or school, or socializing with peers. However, some are more successful than others. Lee (ibid., 137) mentions a young women by the name of Vika, who blended two different styles of dress by shortening a *puletaha*, a Tongan-style women's dress that is normally knee-length and worn over a long skirt. She hastens to add, however, that more youngsters are struggling to combine different roles that are expected of them in different domains of society: "One minute you're a Tongan and the other, you are stepping out of that circle to join the rest of society" (ibid.).

The dilemmas with which young Pacific Islanders growing up in countries around the Pacific Rim are confronted make it difficult for many to strike a balance, especially when parents are unwilling to adjust to new circumstances. One young man compared the situation with walking a tightrope:

> At home, my parents were very strict and imposed a Spartan, rough life style that demanded complete obedience and respect for elders. Then I would go to school where they taught me to question authority and be an individual that can stand alone in the world. What I finally realized as being important was that I had to find some sort of balance between the two cultures . . . In order to successfully walk the rope of life, the new-age Tongan must balance what is good in the Tongan culture with what is good in the American culture. If he/she concentrates too much on one or the other, then they will lose balance and not be able to survive in both environments (Lee 2003, 141–2).

In this context, it is important to realize that these intercultural dilemmas of young migrants coincide with adolescence, and so they take place at a crossroads in their course of life. Many adolescent migrants are going through a period of distancing themselves from their parents, which is not uncommon at their age, but in the specific circumstances of migration the process of becoming more independent of their parents is reinforced by cultural differences between the situation at home and at school. This also entails that many do not always succeed in meeting the different expectations of the contrasting contexts in their lives. The pressure of peers, from a variety of cultural backgrounds, including Tongan, other Pacific Islands, and Pacific Rim countries, seems to override the pressure from parents to respect Tongan customs:

> If I had to be born again I wish I was never Tongan, because you're taught to be someone that you're not. It's hard to live up to. Because emotionally I don't think I'm built to be a Tongan, I mean I can't—all the criticism, people criticize you for what you try to do and to be, so if you make a mistake, it's "no you're meant to be this person" (Lee 2003, 140).

Obviously, the interest of young Tongans overseas in issues relating to Tonga is not infrequently outweighed by their concern with diasporic issues that affect them much more in their daily lives. This generates conflicts at home, where cultural differences not infrequently lead to a form of estrangement between adolescents and their parents. A central issue in this debate is "the Tongan way," *anga fakatonga*, which is an all-encompassing and multiply defined concept that most youngsters have struggled with from an early age. Interestingly, definitions of *anga fakatonga* given by those born overseas are rather similar to the views of the older generations to a great extent, with a focus on "blood," "language," and "heart." A significant difference, however, is that young people are more willing to allow for a lack of language, poor knowledge of the Tongan way, and even lack of Tongan blood (Lee 2003, 138).

The dilemmas faced by Tongan youngsters born overseas but raised in a Tongan family that continues to abide by Tongan traditions are in many ways similar to the cultural dilemmas of young Maori people who are at odds with the traditional culture that is currently being revived in contemporary New Zealand (van Meijl 2002). The Indigenous population of New Zealand is largely locked in a vicious circle of poverty that many feel can only be unlocked by good education because the main cause of most socio-economic problems is thought to be the fact that many Maori boys and girls drop out of school without any qualifications. Subsequently, they have few options left, except special education to improve their skills for the labor market. One of the assumptions of the special training programs for disadvantaged Maori adolescents is that they leave school mainly because of the monocultural climate there that is not amenable to children with a different cultural background (cf. Rata 2011). Related to this is the conviction that young Maori people feel more at ease on a *marae*, a ceremonial center that is normally considered as the cultural hearth of Maori people. In the cultural practices on the *marae*, however, it appears that not all Maori youngsters feel comfortable in the traditional center.

The cultural background of many deprived Maori adolescents is characterized by a marked lack of knowledge and familiarity with *marae* protocol for ceremonial gatherings and the associated ritual speechmaking, chants, and dances. Most youngsters rarely visit *marae* and do not speak a word of Maori. Their training on the *marae* therefore entails a first encounter with classic Maori culture, which is reinforced by *marae* etiquette, which prescribes everyone present to participate in its practices. To meet this demand the youngsters are not only trained in practical skills, but also in Maori language and "culture," which sadly brings about strong feelings of embarrassment and of alienation from a culture that is ideologically considered to be theirs yet far removed from their personal experiences (van Meijl 2006).

Maori adolescents are like the Tongan youngsters described earlier in that both are inclined to acknowledge the need to maintain cultural traditions, but they also think traditions are archaic and therefore unnecessary to survive in the contemporary world. Yet it would be unfair to criticize these adolescents for being contradictory or inconsistent. They are facing an irresolvable dilemma that is increasingly common in the present day because more and more people are constantly moving across cultural landscapes. People for whom multiculturalism is the order of the day have no option but to mediate their multiple identifications that can no longer be integrated into a coherent whole. Precisely this unprecedented predicament for adolescents in particular raises the questions formulated at the beginning of this chapter: To what extent is the process of maturation complicated by cultural dilemmas in the lives of young people growing up in multicultural societies, especially in the Pacific? How do they deal with the ambiguities if not contradictions that may emerge from their crossings of various cultural landscapes?

TOWARD A THIRD SPACE

The differentiation of the self of adolescents growing up in multicultural circumstances is not a general effect of migration, but it seems to be concentrated among those who are disadvantaged in society, in this case, young, usually unemployed Indigenous people or Pacific Islanders living on the Pacific Rim. Jameson (1991) argued that their alienation in modern society has been displaced by the fragmentation of their self in postmodern society. Recent developments nevertheless indicate that some youngsters seem to be moving successfully beyond the differences between so-called "traditions" and "modernity" that characterize their multiple identifications. Many youngsters talk about having 'time-out' periods in order to come to terms with the identity confusion (Anae 2001, 111). This involves rejecting both Western and parental authority structures and leaving the church. Adolescents of Pacific descent tend to leave the cocoon of family, school, and church in order to "get a life" including experimentation with drugs, alcohol, and marginal lifestyles.

During time-out periods, many Tongan and Samoan youngsters whose relationship to the traditional territory of their parents and other ancestors is changing and becoming more fragile take on a "PI" persona, as Pacific Islander. This construction of a translocal identity enables them to temporarily formalize the estrangement from the 'territorial' identity of their parents and to experiment with different identifications and lifestyles at the same time. An identity as "Pacific Islander" has been well documented (e.g., Small 1997). Children of Pacific migrants may take on a generic "PI" identity in a new social space in which elements of their parents' culture and society are combined with elements of others found in the city to produce a new patois, new music, new fashion, new customs, and new practices that mark their distinction. A common "PI" identity, however, implies that crucial aspects of Pacific Island culture are not shared to the extent that they differ between various societies. This has important implications for the continuity of the cultural dimensions with regard to language, church, genealogical connections, respect for separate systems of hierarchy, and associated values and expectations. Moreover, "PI" identification during time-out periods is still very much a youth phenomenon, and for that reason, too, it is unclear what the long-term consequences are of these temporary stages in cultural identifications.

212 Toon van Meijl

It is also significant to note that the development of a generic identity seems not the most logical outcome of multicultural interaction in cosmopolitan space because those in control of authentic or primordial identities continue to marginalize people who choose to negotiate their identity depending on context, whether traditional or nontraditional. This is most apparent in the struggles faced by youngsters of mixed descent who attempt to achieve a new, unified identity, but rarely find sanctuary in either the society of their mother or in the society of their father because both continue to define them as hybrid or "half-caste" others who are different and inferior (Webber 2008). As indicated in the preceding, the identifications of Pacific Islanders living on the Pacific Rim and Indigenous adolescents living on the margins of Maori society in New Zealand or Aboriginal society in Australia are invariably engaged in a dialogue with hegemonic views of "authentic" ethnicity, which is associated with fixed indicators. People of mixed descent or multicultural youngsters whose identifications are characterized by a double heritage do not necessarily look, speak, or live in accordance with these fixed indicators and therefore they are frequently deemed not to be "real," at least as far as their cultural identification is concerned.

The hegemony of authentic or primordial identity works against the interests of hybrid adolescents by creating a divide between the authentic and the inauthentic. The latter are generally unable to speak their mother tongue, or their "father's tongue" for that matter, and they may not be familiar with the genealogical connections linking them to the territory to which their dominant identifications refer. At the same time, their daily practices may differ from the way in which they are expected to behave by their parents and extended family. Indeed, the hegemony of authentic identity marginalizes most people of mixed descent and those living on the margins of their so-called traditional society. As a consequence, they perforce occupy "in-between" positions and they necessarily have to negotiate innumerable "border crossings." Because these adolescents are forced to choose only one identity whereas their daily lives are characterized by cultural diversity, the marginalization of "modern" aspects of their identity by the hegemonic form of authentic culture invariably results in difficulties to articulate multiple identifications.

The dilemmas and difficulties associated with hybrid identities of many adolescents growing up in multicultural circumstances may to some extent be associated with colonial desires for assimilation. For that reason, too, it is essential to re-appropriate the negative representation of multiple identifications as hybrid, as inauthentic and unreal, as damaged and in crisis, from the racial discourses dating from the colonial era. Homi Bhabha (1998) was among the first to elaborate on the impossibility of culture's containedness and to acknowledge the existence of "partial," "in-between" cultures, which are both baffling like those they spring from, and yet different. Accordingly, he attempted to innovate the concept of hybridity as superseding partial cultures and potentially enabling the construction of new visions for dynamic cultural identifications he labeled a "third space":

> The importance of hybridity is not to be able to trace two original movements from which the third emerges; rather hybridity . . . is the "third space" which enables other positions to emerge. This third space displaces the histories that constitute it and sets up new structures of authority, new political initiatives, which are inadequately understood through received wisdom . . . the process of cultural hybridity gives rise to a something different, something new and unrecognizable, a new area of negotiation of meaning and representation (1990, 211).

The strength of Bhabha's vision is his early appreciation that globalization, transnationalism, and the extension of cultural connections across boundaries all imply that cultural boundaries are becoming increasingly permeable, which makes it necessary to study cultural processes on the contact zones. More importantly, he was among the first to recognize that cultural contact across boundaries does not necessarily lead to division and separation, but that instead it may generate positive outcomes and energy for people whose life experiences have likewise multiplied. The weakness of Bhabha's approach, however, is that he does not provide a lead to understand the struggle between different cultural positions within the self of individual adolescents, who need to balance the multiplicity of meanings and practices they encounter in diversifying cultural spaces. Are their lives riddled with confusion about contradictory experiences or do they manage to create a so-called "third space"? Dialogical self-theory offers a comprehensive framework for the analysis of the large impact of the process of globalization on the development of adolescent identities in multicultural societies.

SOCIETY AND SELF

Indeed, the increasing cultural complexity that is associated with the distribution of cultural meanings, practices, and forms across populations has also far-reaching implications for the identification of individuals and their self, especially for adolescents who are growing up in between different cultural spaces. Because cultural complexity is closely related to multiplicity and interlinkages between different cultural positions in the lives of individuals, the concept of the dialogical self offers a sophisticated analytical framework for the analysis and appreciation of the multiple identifications of adolescents living in multicultural societies. The dialogical self is a useful construct for the analysis of multicultural identifications because it relates plural, competing conceptions of identity to the notion of a person as a composite of multiple, often contradictory, self-understandings.

In short, the dialogical self may be described as a dynamic multiplicity of *I*-positions in the landscape of the mind, intertwined as the mind is with the minds of other people (Hermans, Kempen, and van Loon 1992; Hermans and Kempen 1993). Dialogical self-theory is inspired, on the one hand, by Bakhtin's ([1929] 1984) metaphor of the polyphonic novel, which allows for a multiplicity of positions among which dialogical relationships may be established, and, on the other hand, by William James's (1890) classic distinction between *I* and *me*. James described the *I* as "the self as knower," as the observing agent. The *me*, on the other hand, was portrayed as "the self as known," as the object of self-observation. On the interface between these traditions, Hermans and Kempen (1993) have argued that the *I* has the possibility to move from one spatial position to another in accordance with changes in situation and time. The *I* fluctuates among different and even opposed positions, and it has the capacity to endow each position with a voice so that dialogical relationships between positions can be developed. Thus, it may be argued that Tongan adolescents growing up in multicultural Australia or Maori trainees enrolled in vocational training on a traditional *marae* are all involved in a dialogue between different conceptions of their cultural identity. The contrasting voices speaking in their self, function like interacting characters in a story, involved in a process of agreement and disagreement. Each of them has a story to tell about his or her own experiences, both from the viewpoint of traditional culture and from the viewpoint of adolescents who seek to distance themselves from the traditional lifestyle of their extended families. As different voices, these characters exchange information about their respective *me*'s, resulting in a complex, narratively structured self.

Bakhtin (1981, 360) especially proves very useful for the purpose of acknowledging the dialogue in which multicultural adolescents find themselves. He describes "hybrids" as having two voices, two languages, two consciousnesses, two epochs; being situated at "the collision between differing points of view on the world" but also "profoundly productive historically" and "pregnant with potential for new world views." Thus, Bakhtin creates the possibility for the self to be conceived of as a dynamic multiplicity of different and even contrasting positions or voices that allow mutual dialogical relationships.

Hermans (2002) has also drawn attention to the similarities between self and society, both functioning as a polyphony of consonant and dissonant voices because there is no essential difference between the positions a person takes as part of the self and the positions people take as members of a heterogeneous society (see also Hermans and Hermans-Konopka 2010). As a consequence, the dialogical self may be considered a "society of the mind" (Hermans 2002) to the extent that different and contrasting cultures are represented in the diverse repertoire of collective voices playing a part in a multivoiced self. This insight, in turn, raises questions regarding the mixing of cultural positions or voices. Should we conceptualize of different cultural identifications of people living in multicultural societies as two separate cultural positions that are available and between which a person shifts from time to time, or, alternatively, is a third position emerging that may be a mixture of two original positions? And if a third space emerges for the construction of a new, hybrid self, do the original positions retreat or even vanish, or do they continue to be accessible in their original form depending on changes taking place in spatial positions?

For several reasons, the conception of the self as multivoiced and dialogical has proved a valuable device for the analysis of the dynamic connections between the global and the local at the level of personal identifications (Hermans and Dimaggio 2007). First, in a globalizing world people are no longer living in bounded and relatively isolated societies that are radically different from other societies. Instead, an increasing number of people are living on the interfaces between societies, implying intimate contact with different cultural customs. And the increasing interconnectedness of societies and peoples does not only lead to an increasing contact between different cultural groups, but also to an increasing contact between different cultural conceptions within individual persons. As demonstrated in this chapter, this compounds the development of adolescents growing up "between two shores" in particular. Intercultural contact leads to the emergence of a multiplicity of cultural positions or voices coming together in the self of single youngsters. And such positions may become engaged in mutual negotiations, agreements, disagreements, tensions, and conflicts. The global–local nexus is, in other words, not just a reality outside the individual, but it has penetrated the self of multicultural adolescents that have no option but to engage in a dialogue between their various cultural positions.

In contrast to societies in the past that tended to be more isolated, bounded, and perhaps also homogeneous, at least to some extent, contemporary societies are increasingly characterized by strong cultural differences, contrasts, and oppositions. These require dialogical relationships in order to strike the right balance within society. When the world becomes more heterogeneous and multiple, however, the self of individuals making up that world also becomes more heterogeneous and multiple. Again, this applies especially to the maturation of young people, who can only cope with differences, contrasts, tensions, and uncertainties by developing dialogical relationships between the various dimensions of their lives. This requires a conception of the self in which processes of question and answer, agreement and disagreement, and negotiations between different parts of the self are recognized as intrinsic features of dealing with diversity.

A third reason why a dialogical conception of the multicultural self is required to orchestrate the dynamic relationship between local and global institutions, and between traditional and postmodern values and views in the multiple identifications of adolescents, is intertwined with the necessity for multicultural youngsters to interact with people from a different cultural background by recognizing and accepting their alterity. This is unavoidable in a world in which divisions between different cultures can only be bridged by means of dialogical exchange. After all, only dialogue may contribute to making cultural differences meaningful and comprehensible (Hermans and Kempen 1998). Because other persons and groups with different cultural customs are increasingly part of an extended self in terms of a multiplicity of contradictory voices or positions, a dialogical conception of the self seems therefore also indispensable.

Here, it is important to highlight that a multiplicity of *I* positions is to be distinguished from a number of possible selves, which still featured in the groundbreaking work of William James. The difference is that a number of possible selves are generally assumed to constitute part of a multifaceted self with one centralized *I* position, whereas the dialogical self "has the character of a decentralized, polyphonic narrative with a multiplicity of *I* positions" (Hermans, Kempen, and van Loon 1992, 30).

Another important feature of dialogical relationships between self and other is dominance, which Hermans and Kempen (1993, 73) exemplify with reference to the relationship between self and community. If the self is defined as a multiplicity of different *I* positions, it may be argued that the community is not only able to address the self in a variety of identifications, but also to let the self know how these identifications, and the way the self functions in them, are approved. This also exactly occurs in multicultural societies when young people are unable to express their cultural identity in terms of their parent's cultural background and likewise fail to subscribe to ideological notions of authenticity. In those situations, the self of adolescents growing up in multiple settings is usually monitored by the community approving or disapproving of their behavior and concomitant construction of an ethnic identity. Thus, communities also have the capacity to make some identification more dominant than others. And the dominance of cultural communities in the identification process not only organizes, but also restricts the multiplicity of possible identifications in the public arena of multicultural societies. An important implication of this form of cultural dominance is that some identifications are strongly developed, whereas others are suppressed or even disunited from self. Indeed the prevalence of one identification implies the necessary neglect or suppression of another identification. Specific experiences, particularly negative experiences, may lead to the active suppression or even splitting of unwanted identifications, which slow down the dialogical movements between different identifications. Dominance of one identification over another, however, rarely excludes dialogical exchange (van Meijl 2006). For that reason, too, it may be argued that the inescapable dialogue between multiple identifications of self will continue to characterize adolescents' constructions of multicultural realities as well as the position of their own self within it.

The dialogical self, then, is not a substance or an essence in its own right as it exists only in a tensile relationship with all that is other and, most importantly, with other selves (see also Gardiner 1992, 73). For the same reason, the dialogical self is not a whole or a unified composition, but instead it is based on the assumption that there are many *I* positions that can be occupied by the same person. At the same time, the dialogical self is intensely social, not in the sense that a self-contained individual enters into social interactions with other outside people, but in the sense that other people occupy positions within the multivoiced self (Hermans, Kempen, and van Loon 1992, 29).

The implications of this view of the—dialogical—self for our understanding of the development of adolescents growing up in multicultural societies are rather fundamental. Contrary to the individualistic conception of the self, the most important implication of the dialogical perspective on the self is that it is not an intrapsychic but a relational phenomenon that transcends the boundaries between the inside and the outside, between self and other. Methodologically this view has been elaborated in the form of an analogy between, on the one hand, the spatialization of the dialogical relations between the different *I* positions and, on the other hand, the simultaneity of voices within a self's discourse. This compelling perspective on the self has been extraordinarily influential over the past two decades because it makes a decisive contribution to the process of transcending individual identity, which is especially significant for understanding how young people deal with cultural diversity in their daily lives in multicultural societies.

CONCLUDING REMARKS

Globalization, migration, and multiculturalism have challenged essentialist notions of culture and identity as being bounded and nationally defined. In multicultural societies, people are facing the challenge of adapting not only to traditional, if not "local" culture, but also to modern, if not postmodern, culture. Adolescents growing up in multicultural societies are usually among the first who have no option but to deal with the inevitable multiplication of their identifications in the New World: part of their identity remains rooted in the so-called "traditional" culture of their families, but another part is more attuned to the global situation beyond the bounds of their home. Because traditional cultures are increasingly challenged as a result of globalization, some young people feel at home in neither the local situation nor in the global situation, and for them multicultural societies bring about identity confusion (Vestel 2009). Others may successfully combine elements of traditional and postmodern situations at home and, for example, at school, and they may develop a hybrid identity (Ibrahim 2008). All adolescents in multicultural societies, however, share the challenge of swiftly changing societies that are highly diverse, so they perforce develop mechanisms to cope with cultural complexity.

Global societies are characterized by cultural complexity because they are increasingly composed of various parts that are intricately interlinked in a large variety of relations and meanings (Hannerz 1992). For the identity of adolescents growing up in multicultural circumstances this implies that their self is more and more characterized by multiplicity (van Meijl 2010). The articulation of different narratives within their self also entails that the multiple identifications of adolescents are characterized by ambiguity. The cultural meaning of the various parts of which the multicultural self is made up is no longer fixed or self-evident because the meaning of one part is determined by the flux and variation of other parts. For the same reason, in global societies characterized by multiculturalism a super-ordinate voice is no longer available for resolving contradictions between the parts (Gressgård 2010). Information associated with one part or another is generally insufficient to deal with conflicting information in a conclusive manner. As a corollary, multicultural adolescents increasingly lack control of future developments, and the horizons of their existence are more and more characterized by unpredictability (Hermans and Hermans-Konopka 2010).

In this chapter, I have argued that the connections between local and global influences, between traditional and postmodern cultural influences in the self- development of adolescents coming of age in multicultural societies require a dialogical approach. In a global world, individuals and groups are increasingly living on the interfaces of cultures, and these cultures come together and meet not only in the public domain, but also within the self of one and the same individual. As shown in the preceding, this compounds particularly the maturation of adolescents growing up in culturally diverse circumstances. Their self is often engaged in mutual negotiations, agreements, disagreements, tensions, and conflicts, implying that different cultural voices are involved in various kinds of dialogical relationships, which may produce either negative or positive meanings. In other words, the self of multicultural youngsters is becoming dialogical to the extent that it incorporates the local–global nexus.

The dialogicality that characterizes the multicultural self of adolescents who are raised within traditional families but growing up in global societies reflects the cultural contrasts, heterogeneity, and multiplicity of postmodernity. As historical and cultural differences within the global world require a dialogical capacity in order to achieve workable solutions to contemporary problems and challenges, the parallel with individual selves makes it so a dialogical conception of the self is required in order to become sensitive to the processes of question and answer, agreement and disagreement, and negotiations between different self-positions of adolescents living in "between two shores" who have to resolve cultural ambiguities in their daily lives. Finally, dialogues only come about when individual participants are able and willing to recognize the perspective of others and, further, when they are willing to revise and change their initial views by taking preceding messages conveyed by the cultural other into account. Needless to say, adolescents generally are still endowed with the flexibility to engage in dialogue with cultural otherness, which is indispensable in the contemporary world. For that reason, too, adolescents may be considered crucial agents of cultural change; therefore, it is highly important to enhance insight into the dialogical self of multicultural adolescents.

REFERENCES

Anae, M. "Towards a NZ-Born Samoan Identity: Some Reflections on 'Labels,'" Pacific Health Dialog 4, no. 2 (1997): 128–137.
———. 2001. The New "Vikings of the Sunrise": New Zealand-borns in the Information Age, in *Tangata O Te Moana Nui: The Evolving Identities of Pacific Peoples in Aotearoa/New Zealand*, edited by C. Macpherson, P. Spoonley, and M. Anae. Palmerston North: Dunmore Press, pp. 101–121.
Appadurai, A. 1996. Modernity at Large: Cultural Dimensions of Globalization. Public Worlds, vol. 1. Minneapolis: University of Minnesota Press.
Bakhtin, M.M. 1981. The Dialogical Imagination: Four Essays. Translated by C. Emerson and M. Holquist. Edited by M. Holquist. Austin: University of Texas Press.
———. [1929] 1984. Problems of Dostoevsky's Poetics. Translated and edited by C. Emerson. Introduced by W.C. Booth. Minneapolis: University of Minnesota Press.
Bendix, R. "Tradition and Modernity Reconsidered," Comparative Studies in Society and History 11 (1966): 292–346.
Bhabha, H.K. 1990. Nation and Narration. London: Routledge.
———. 1998. Culture's in between, in *Multicultural States: Rethinking Difference and Identity*, edited by D. Bennett. London: Routledge, pp. 29–36.
Doerr, N.M. 2009. Meaningful Inconsistencies: Bicultural Nationhood, the Free Market, and Schooling in Aotearoa/New Zealand. New York: Berghahn.
Erikson, E.H. 1968. Identity, Youth and Crisis. New York: Norton.
Freeman, D. 1983. Margaret Mead and Samoa: The Making and Unmaking of an Anthropological Myth. Harmondsworth: Penguin.
Gardiner, M. 1992. The Dialogics of Critique: M.M. Bakhtin and the Theory of Ideology. London: Routledge.
Goss, J. and Lindquist, B. "Placing Movers: An Overview of the Asian-Pacific Migration System," Contemporary Pacific 12, no. 2 (2000): 385–414.
Gressgård, R. 2010. Multicultural Dialogue: Dilemmas, Paradoxes, Conflicts. New York: Berghahn.
Hannerz, U. 1992. Cultural Complexity: Studies in the Social Organization of Meaning. New York: Columbia University Press.
Hau'ofa, E. "Our Sea of Islands," Contemporary Pacific 6, no. 1 (1994): 148–161.
———. "The Ocean in Us," Contemporary Pacific 10, no. 2 (1998): 392–410.
Herdt, G. and Leavitt, S.C. 1998. Introduction: Studying adolescence in contemporary Pacific Island communities, in *Adolescence in Pacific Island Societies*, edited by G. Herdt and S.C. Leavitt. Pittsburgh: University of Pittsburgh Press, pp. 3–26.
Hermans, H.J.M. "The Dialogical Self as a Society of Mind," Theory and Psychology 12, no. 2 (2002): 147–160.
Hermans, H.J.M. and Dimaggio, G. "Self, Identity, and Globalization in Times of Uncertainty: A Dialogical Analysis," Review of General Psychology 11, no. 1 (2007): 31–61.
Hermans, H.J.M. and Hermans-Konopka, A. 2010. Dialogical Self-Theory: Positioning and Counter-Positioning in a Globalizing Society. Cambridge: Cambridge University Press.

Hermans, H.J.M., and H.J.G. Kempen. 1993. The Dialogical Self: Meaning as Movement. San Diego: Academic Press.

———. "Moving Cultures: The Perilous Problems of Cultural Dichotomies in a Globalizing Society," American Psychologist 53, no. 10 (1998): 1111–1120.

Hermans, H.J.M., Kempen, H.J.G., and van Loon, R.J.P. "The Dialogical Self: Beyond Individualism and Rationalism," American Psychologist 47, no. 1 (1992): 23–33.

Ibrahim, A. "The New Flâneur: Subaltern Cultural Studies, African Youth in Canada and the Etiology of In-Between," Cultural Studies 22, no. 2 (2008): 234–253.

James, W. 1890. The Principles of Psychology, vol. 1. London: Macmillan.

Jameson, F. 1991. Postmodernism, or, the Cultural Logic of Late Capitalism. London: Verso.

Jolly, M. 1992. "Specters of Inauthenticity," Contemporary Pacific 4, no. 1 (1992): 49–72.

Jourdan, C. 1995. Masta Liu, in Youth Cultures: A Cross-Cultural Perspective, edited by V. Amit-Talai and H. Wulff. London: Routledge, pp. 202–222.

Kinnvall, C. and Lindén, J. "Dialogical Selves between Security and Insecurity: Migration, Multiculturalism, and the Challenge of the Global," Theory and Psychology 20, no. 5 (2010): 595–619.

Lee, H.M. 2003. Tongans Overseas: Between Two Shores. Honolulu: University of Hawai'i Press.

———. 2004. All Tongans are connected: Tongan transnationalism, in Globalization and Culture Change in the Pacific Islands, edited by V.S. Lockwood. Upper Saddle River, NJ: Pearson Prentice Hall, pp. 133–148.

Macpherson, C., Spoonley, P. and Anae, M., eds. 2001. Tangata O Te Moana Nui: The Evolving Identities of Pacific Peoples in Aotearoa/New Zealand. Palmerston North: Dunmore Press.

Mead, M. 1928. Coming of Age in Samoa: A Psychological Study of Youth for Western Civilization. Foreword by F. Boas. New York: Morrow.

Meyer, B. and Geschiere, P., eds. 1999. Globalization and Identity: Dialectics of Flow and Closure. Oxford: Blackwell.

Montgomery, H. 2009. An Introduction to Childhood: Anthropological Perspectives on Children's Lives. Malden: Wiley-Blackwell.

Nilan, P. and Feixa, C., eds. 2006. Global Youth? Hybrid Identities, Plural Worlds. London: Routledge.

Rata, E. "Theoretical Claims and Empirical Evidence in Maori Education Discourse," Educational Philosophy and Theory 43, no. 4 (2011): 1–13.

Shankman, P. 2009. The Trashing of Margaret Mead: Anatomy of an Anthropological Controversy. Madison: University of Wisconsin Press.

Small, C. 1997. Voyages: From Tongan Villages to American Suburbs. Ithaca, NY: Cornell University Press.

van Meijl, T.V. 2002. Culture and crisis in Maori society: The tradition of other and the displacement of self, in Politics of Indigeneity in the South Pacific: Recent Problems of Identity in Oceania, Novara Contributions to Research on the Pacific, vol. 1., edited by E. Kolig and H. Mückler. Hamburg: Lit Verlag, pp. 47–71.

———. "Multiple Identifications and the Dialogical Self: Maori Youngsters and the Cultural Renaissance," Journal of the Royal Anthropological Institute 12, no. 4 (2006): 917–933.

———. "Beyond Economics: Transnational Labour Migration in Asia and the Pacific," International Institute for Asian Studies Newsletter 43 (2007): 17.

———. 2010. Anthropological perspectives on identity: From sameness to difference, in The Sage Handbook of Identities, edited by M. Wetherell and C.T. Mohanty. London: Sage, pp. 63–81.

Vertovec, S. and Cohen, R. eds. 1999. Migration, Diasporas and Transnationalism. Cheltenham: Elgar Reference.

Vestel, V. "Limits of Hybridity Versus Limits of Tradition? A Semiotics of Cultural Reproduction, Creativity, and Ambivalence among Multicultural Youth in Rudenga, East Side Oslo," Ethos 37, no. 4 (2009): 466–488.

Webber, M. 2008. Walking the Space Between: Identity and Maori/Pakeha. Wellington: New Zealand Centre for Educational Research.

Wolf, E.R. 1982. Europe and the People without History. Berkeley: University of California Press.

10 Traditional Dress in Kuwaiti Adolescents' Drawings
Relations to Social Attitudes

Ramadan A. Ahmed and Judith L. Gibbons

Adolescents in Kuwait share the developmental tasks and challenges of adolescents worldwide, including adapting to changes in body shape and size, navigating the social worlds of peers and family, forging a personal identity, and planning for the future. In the context of globalization, many adolescents are forging dual, hybrid, or multicultural identities, based in part on their traditions and cultural heritage, but also on their incorporation of the values, ideals, and practices of an international youth culture (Arnett 2002; Jensen 2003, Lan 2009; Schlegel 2000).

THE SETTING OF KUWAIT

Kuwait is a low-lying, mostly desert nation on the Arabian Gulf, bounded by Saudi Arabia and Iraq. Almost all (98 percent) of the population lives in cities, and most all Kuwaitis (99 percent) are Muslim (Central Intelligence Agency 2011). However, among the workforce in Kuwait are thousands of non-Kuwaiti Christians. Kuwait has one of the highest average income levels in the world, derived primarily from the natural resource oil. According to a report by the United Nations Children's Fund (UNICEF 2011) the gross national income (GNI) per capita is $43,930, and, according to the United Nations Development Programme (UNDP 2010), it is even higher, $55,719. By either measure, Kuwaitis are among the wealthiest people in the world. Kuwait is classified by the UNDP as a high human development country in terms of life expectancy, education, and GNI. In the past thirty-five years, life expectancy has markedly increased from an average of sixty-six to seventy-seven years (Ahmed and Al-Khawajah 2007). Kuwait's human development lags somewhat behind its wealth (UNDP 2010).

The Islamic cultural heritage forms the basis of the moral value system in Kuwait. Islam assumes that the Koran contains the true, ultimate, and unchanging word of God as revealed to the Prophet and messenger Mohammed. The Koran contains a corpus of religious beliefs, prescriptions, and laws that order social and political institutions, social relationships, and especially the family. Male and female roles are sharply differentiated. The social ethic of Islam stresses humility, solidarity, equality, piety, charity toward the less fortunate, and rejection of sin. Orthodox and fundamentalist movements in Islam have emphasized that God alone decrees, in the Koran, what is morally right. Creative ethical choice by humans is thereby deemphasized. Although Sunni Muslims predominate in Kuwait, about 30 percent of the population is Shi'ite (adapted from Ahmed and Al-Khawajah 2007, 562).

Most people in Kuwait have good access to technology. According to UNICEF (2011), there is approximately one telephone per person, but the UNDP (2010) puts those figures even higher, with an average of 1.26 telephones per person. Kuwait was one of the first countries of the Middle East to allow access to the Internet (Alqudsi-Ghabra 2003). Today, Internet users are estimated to be between 34 percent and 38 percent of the population, and it is likely that usage is even higher among adolescents (UNDP 2010; UNICEF 2011).

As a nation Kuwait is ranked as 144th in terms of the under-five mortality ranking, an overall indicator of children's well-being. Its rank is similar to that of the U.S. (ranked 149th). The adult literacy rate is 95 percent, and 57 percent of the population over twenty-five has at least a secondary education. Those percentages are slightly higher than the average for countries classified as having high human development (UNDP 2010).

Gender inequalities with respect to life expectancy, health, and education are small, and Kuwait's Gender Inequality Index is slightly less than the average for the world, indicating greater gender equality than in most nations (UNDP 2010). Kuwait enjoys the rank of 105 in gender equality in education, and is second among Arab countries in this context (*Al-Watan* 2010).

However, women are greatly underrepresented in the public and political sphere. Women in Kuwait gained the right to vote only in 2005, and they are represented in miniscule numbers among elected officials. In 1993, the first Arab female university rector was appointed at Kuwait University. In 2005, the first female minister was appointed to Kuwait's cabinet.

Most Kuwaitis express satisfaction with their jobs (89 percent of employed persons), with their health (89 percent), and with their standard of living (77 percent). Most also report that they have a purposeful life (97 percent), that they are treated with respect (91 percent), and that they experience social support (86 percent) (UNDP 2010).

ADOLESCENTS IN KUWAIT

Adolescents in the Arab world, including Kuwait, face some common developmental challenges and societal expectations (Arnett 2002; Booth 2002). In Arabic there seems to be no exact word for "adolescence" that is in common use, and available translations may emphasize sexuality (Booth 2002), connote immaturity and imperfection (Mahdi 2003), or relate to pressure (Almubayei 2010). Kuwaiti law, rooted in the Islamic religion, treats individuals under the age of twenty-one as minors. Kuwaiti society in general may consider adolescence as a stage that lasts between about thirteen until about twenty-one years of age. In a survey conducted by Ahmed (2006), a sample of university students reported that the adolescent period extends from age twelve to nineteen for boys and from age eleven to eighteen for girls. The word "adolescent" in Kuwait is frequently used to refer to people who show unusual behavior, dress, and appearance, or to describe someone who is active, energetic, and dynamic.

Davis and Davis (1989) have reported that a successful transition from adolescence to adulthood in Morocco requires the young person to acquire *aql* (reason and the ability to smoothly navigate complex social relationships). Similarly, Booth (2002) argues that the attainment of adulthood in the Arab world requires "reflective, mature participation in society, maintaining the primacy throughout life of family ties, connectivity, and mutual responsibility" (207). This concept of adolescence as an immature stage that occurs prior to responsible adulthood may also hold for Kuwaiti society; mental maturity forms the basis of responsible adulthood in Kuwait.

Adolescents (defined as ages ten through nineteen) make up 14 percent of the population of Kuwait (UNICEF 2011). This percentage is lower than that for the Middle East and North Africa (20 percent) and for the world overall (18 percent). Thus, compared to other nations, Kuwait is not experiencing a population bubble of adolescents; so Kuwaiti adolescents are protected from the consequences of an excess of teenagers, such as overcrowding in schools and diminished job possibilities after completing their education (Simonsen 2005). The UNICEF (2011) data also show that 100 percent of children who begin primary school finish schooling at the primary level, a very high achievement for any nation. As noted earlier, there are no or very small gender differences in school attendance and school attainment. The literacy rate for youth (ages 15 through 24) is 98 percent for males and 99 percent for females (UNICEF 2011).

Education in Kuwait is compulsory through the sixth grade. In Kuwait, there are different kinds of schools: government-run (public) schools (almost free of cost) and private schools (that usually charge high tuition fees). The latter include Arab private schools, with Arabic as the language of instruction, and English/Pakistani/Indian schools, with English as the language of instruction. Whereas government-run or public schools adopt gender segregation in all precollege education levels (i.e., primary, intermediate, and secondary schools' levels), Arab and non-Arab private schools allow coeducation (or mixed education) where boys and girls attend classes together. Some researchers have pointed at the lower quality of education in public schools compared with private schools, especially American and British private schools (*Al-Qabas* 2011). Schooling is an important part of life for Kuwaiti adolescents (Alqudsi-Ghabra 2003). In a recent study, acceptance and warmth by teachers significantly predicted the psychological well-being of Kuwaiti adolescents, especially for adolescent girls (Ahmed, Rohner, and Carrasco 2012).

Scholars emphasize the importance of Islam to most Arab adolescents (e.g., Arnett 2010; Booth 2002; Mahdi 2003), but also stress that practices and traditions with respect to religion vary greatly among different nationalities, communities, and individuals.

In Kuwait, at the age of six, children start to learn about religion, and they are required to behave according to its dictates. Through early socialization, children adopt religious values and norms, which later on shape their behavior. Children are first required to pray five times a day and keep the fast of Ramadan when they reach puberty (for boys) and menarche (for girls). In Bedouin areas and in more traditional and more religious families, girls are required to wear *hijab* at an early age (seven or eight), but by the age of twelve to thirteen wearing *hijab* is mandatory for daughters in almost all families. In some well-to-do and more liberal families, girls are not asked or forced to wear the *hijab* (adapted from Ahmed and Al-Khawajah 2007, 563).

In a sample of almost one thousand Kuwaiti adolescents, three measures of religiosity were positively correlated with physical and mental health, happiness, and satisfaction and negatively correlated with anxiety (Baroun 2006). The author suggests that religion plays a protective role for Kuwaiti adolescents. The relationship between religiosity and happiness was replicated with a sample of Kuwaiti university students (Abdel-Khalek and Lester 2009). Religion may also play a role in the rejection of physician-assisted suicide by the great majority of Kuwaiti university students (Ahmed, Sorum, and Mullet 2010). For a very few students, physician-assisted suicide is sometimes acceptable; they use a judgment rule similar to that used by European laypeople. Religion was also a factor in willingness to forgive among Kuwaiti males and females between twelve and fifty-five years of age (Ahmed, Azar, and Mullet 2007).

Another phenomenon that extends across Arab nations is the patriarchal and paternalistic nature of the family (Alqudsi-Ghabra 2003; Arnett 2010; Booth 2002). In this system "power rests with elders, particularly males" (Booth 2002, 213). The greater power of men is instantiated in government regulations, such as those of the military, the National Guard, and Ministry of the Interior in Kuwait. For example, in order to obtain a passport or travel abroad Kuwaiti persons under twenty-one must have permission from their father or another male relative. Recently, women were granted the right to obtain a passport without their husband's permission, but a husband can still prevent his wife's departure from the country for twenty-four hours (Embassy of the United States Kuwait 2011). According to Islam, women inherit only half of what men inherit, and in civil courts of law, the testimony of two men is equivalent to the testimony of one man and two women.

In patriarchal Arab societies, children and adolescents are expected to demonstrate obedience and respect for their parents and grandparents, especially for fathers and grandfathers (Achoui 2006). Scholars have investigated the perceptions of Arab children, adolescents, and young adults with respect to parental acceptance and rejection, using Rohner's theoretical framework and measures (Rohner, Khaleque, and Cournoyer 2008). Findings showed that Arab (including Kuwaiti) male subjects tended to perceive their fathers as having less acceptance, more aggression, more neglect, and more rejection compared with their female counterparts (Ahmed 2008). In a recent study of Kuwaiti high school students and their parents, attitudes toward cleanliness and bodily functions were shown to be more similar between adolescents and their fathers than between adolescents and their mothers (Al-Fayez et al. 2009). The results were explained in terms of the dominant role of the father in the family.

The life stage of adolescence for Middle Eastern and Arab adolescents may also be highly gendered, with different lifestyles and expectations for girls and boys (Arnett 2002; Booth 2002; Davis and Davis 1989). Although both genders are expected to live up to moral and social standards, boys enjoy more liberty and flexibility in the rules than girls. For example, male adolescents in Kuwait may socialize outside the home without close supervision, but this is not the case for females (Ahmed and Al-Khawajah 2007).

According to Kuwaiti society's expectations, girls have to show feminine characteristics, such as kindness and tenderness, whereas boys have to be ready for manhood's responsibilities and demonstrate the ability to make decisions and to display firmness and power. Through socialization, both sexes are trained to perform their expected gender roles. Reputation and chastity are particularly important for girls (Alqudsi-Ghabra 2003). According to the Prophet Mohammed's teachings, boys and girls aged five years or older should sleep in separate beds. Families are often very concerned about this matter, and affluent families devote separate rooms to each son and daughter (adapted from Ahmed and Al-Khawajah 2007, 563).

The strict gender rules might sometimes be violated. In a study of the use of the Internet by youth in Kuwait, Wheeler (2003) reported that young people often used the Internet, especially chat rooms, to make contact with the opposite sex, a phenomenon she called gender transgression. Young Kuwaitis reported that the Internet offered opportunities for cyberdating, for accessing taboo information, and for feeling connected with the rest of the world. Some adults saw Internet use as undermining traditional values and threatening family life; the solitary nature of computer use was seen as jeopardizing opportunities for Kuwaiti families to spend time together (Wheeler 2003). Along with the Internet, Kuwaiti adolescents use cell phones to subvert the strict rules of their schools and parents (Almubayei 2010). Other gender transgressions in Kuwait may involve acting or dressing like the opposite sex. For example, *boyat* are girls with short hair who display masculine behaviors (ibid.). Adolescents who overstep gender boundaries in terms of dress or behavior may be considered disordered, abnormal, or deviant, with their behavior attributed to corrupt Western influences and to their family's failure to enforce moral standards (ibid.). In a recent newspaper report, thirty teenage boys had their heads shaved by the Kuwaiti police for harassing girls at a local school (Toumi 2010). In sum, the gender boundaries in Kuwaiti culture are clear-cut and strongly enforced, but nevertheless sometimes violated.

As mentioned in the preceding, technology may play an important role in the lives of many Kuwaiti adolescents. Research reveals both benefits and costs of Internet usage. A Kuwaiti study on the relationship between Internet use and isolation/alienation (Al-Kandari and Al-Qashan 2001) showed that the more time spent by Kuwaiti adolescents using electronic mail and chat, the greater their feelings of loneliness and self-estrangement. Studies summarized by Ahmed and Al-Khawajah (2007, 571) on the purposes and time spent on Internet use in samples of Kuwaiti university students showed that 40 percent of the participants used the Internet for acquiring information, with fewer using newspapers, magazines, or libraries. Another study (summarized in Ahmed and Al-Khawajah 2007, 571) showed that: (a) students spent an average of four hours daily using the Internet; (b) there were no differences between male and female students concerning time spent or purpose of Internet use; (c) there was no relationship between Internet use and students' academic performance; (d) the primary reason for Internet use among Kuwait university students was to further social relationships, such as contacting relatives and friends, approaching entertainment programs, and filling free time; and (e) the use of the Internet by university students in Kuwait was reduced or even halted when students graduated and became involved in a job or career. A recent study on Internet use among 909 Kuwaiti high school students (Al-Hashemi et al. 2011) showed that Internet use in Kuwait had dramatically increased between 2000 and 2010 (633 percent increase). The prevalence of Internet addiction among students was estimated at 10.9 percent, and was slightly higher among females (12.3 percent) than males (8.6 percent). Finally, although results showed that Internet addiction in Kuwaiti high school students was not associated with health problems (i.e., obesity or being overweight), it was associated with lower academic performance.

A number of scholars have viewed the tensions that Arab adolescents experience as representing a collision between the traditional and the modern. The subtitle of one chapter on Arab youth was "Enduring Ideals and Pressure to Change" (Booth 2002). A chapter on the Saudi family was titled, "The Saudi Society: Tradition and Change." Egyptian youth are said to face a similar tension, torn between "the need to modernize and keep up with the global economy" and preserving Egypt's values and traditions (Ibrahim and Wassef 2000, 161). In an article titled "The Mosque and the Satellite," Davis and Davis (1995) pointed out that although Moroccan adolescents feel tension between the modern and the traditional, the real hope of many is to have the best of both worlds—access both to modern technology and to traditional Islamic structures. The conflict between modern and traditional or a creative integration of the two poles may be central to the inner worlds of Kuwaiti adolescents and may be instantiated in their individual perspectives, as well as in their public behavior.

ADOLESCENT'S VIEWS OF THE IDEAL
MAN AND THE IDEAL WOMAN

One window into the inner world of adolescents is through their views of the ideal man and ideal woman (Gibbons and Stiles 2004). Those ideals reflect adolescents' values, gender ideologies, and views of the future. A study of over eight thousand adolescents from twenty countries around the world revealed that adolescents hold idealistic and mostly positive views; the most important quality of the ideal person was that he or she be kind and honest. Adolescents from wealthy, individualistic countries rated the importance of being fun and sexy more highly than did adolescents from collectivistic countries. Adolescents from low-resource, collectivistic countries were more likely than adolescents from wealthy, individualistic countries to report that it is important that the ideal person be intelligent, have a good job, and like children (ibid.). Although Kuwait was not among the countries in the study, nor was it part of Hofstede's (2001) study that identified the dimension of individualism–collectivism, Kuwaitis' emphasis on family and group identity are consistent with a collectivist orientation (Abdel-Khalek and Lester 2009; Al-Fayez et al. 2009).

Particularly revealing are adolescents' drawings of the ideal person (Gibbons and Stiles 2004). Although children's drawings have been most often used to assess their emotional state (Koppitz 1984) or their intellectual development (Goodenough and Harris 1963), researchers have also evaluated adolescents' drawings to reveal their social attitudes and life circumstances (Abdel-Hamid 1998; Badri 1965, Badri and Dennis 1964; DiCarlo et al. 2000; Stiles and Gibbons 2000).

In the large international study, adolescents' drawings of the ideal man and ideal woman differed by gender of the adolescent drawer, gender of the ideal, and culture of the ideal (Gibbons and Stiles 2004). For example, adolescent boys were more likely to depict the ideal man working, whereas girls were more likely to draw the ideal woman working. Adolescents from wealthy, individualistic countries were more likely to depict brand names or images, such as the Nike swoop on shoes (ibid.).

One feature of drawings that has received little attention is that of the clothing or dress of the person drawn. However, for adolescents clothing and style of dressing may serve many symbolic functions, reflecting values and social class, as well as identification with a particular group or clique (Almubayei 2010; Kaiser 1997). The clothing worn by adolescents is, in part, a reflection of their identity (Bhui et al. 2008) and may be part of a communication process in which they display who they are and by which others categorize them. In one study in the U.S., "nerds" were distinguished by their out-of-style clothes and "freaks" by their leather and black clothing (Eicher, Baizerman, and Michelman 1991). In two public discourses, the clothing of adolescents has been the focus of controversy—that over school uniforms (Brunsma and Rockquemore 1998) and the use of the veil in Islamic societies, particularly the banning of Muslim headscarves in French schools (CBC News Online 2004). Like other adolescents around the world, Kuwaiti adolescents may categorize or stereotype others based in part on clothing style. In a study among Kuwaiti adolescents, one high school clique was labeled *hijabiz* (veiled) and another was labeled *Ladiyat* (femme lesbian) on the basis of the use of the hijab in the first group, and dressing in a pretty and fashionable manner in the second (Almubayei 2010). Two early studies categorized the human figure drawings of children from the Sudan according to whether a man was drawn in traditional clothing consisting of headgear and a loose flowing garment, or in modern Western dress, such as shirt and trousers, necktie, belt, or collar (Badri 1965; Badri and Dennis 1964). In four communities differing in level of industrialization, ten- and eleven-year-old boys were more likely to draw a man in modern clothing in the industrialized communities. According to the authors, the clothing depicted in children's drawings reflected the values of their communities (Badri 1965; Badri and Dennis 1964).

CLOTHING STYLES IN KUWAITI ADOLESCENTS' DRAWINGS

The depiction of tradition or modern Western clothing in Kuwaiti adolescents' drawings of the ideal man or ideal woman may reflect their ideas and values with respect to tradition and modernization or globalization, just as do other behavioral markers, such as use of the Internet (Wheeler 2003) and use of English versus Arabic (Almubayei 2010).

The present report is based on a secondary analysis of a data set collected by the first author in the year 2006.

PROCEDURE

Kuwaiti adolescents (975, including 488 males and 487 females) attending twelve public schools (located in all Kuwait's regions) completed questionnaires anonymously. Their ages were from eleven to eighteen. The measures included ratings of ten qualities of the ideal man and ideal woman (Gibbons and Stiles 2004, adapted from Clifford, Grandgenett, and Bardwell 1981), the Historico-Socio-Cultural Premises Scale (HSCP; Díaz-Guerrero 1972), and scoring of drawings of the ideal man and the ideal woman (Stiles and Gibbons 2000).

On the ideal man/ideal woman scale, participants rated the importance of each of ten items on a seven-point Likert scale from "not at all important" to "extremely important." The items were: "he/she likes children," "he/she has average height and weight," "he/she is very intelligent," "he/she has a lot of money," "he/she is kind and honest," "he/she is fun," "he/she is popular," "he/she has good looks," "he/she is sexy," and "he/she has a good job." These ten items have been shown to show reliability and validity among adolescents of twenty different countries (Gibbons and Stiles 2004). Each participant rated and drew both the ideal man and the ideal woman. The drawings were scored according to an established system developed by Stiles and Gibbons (2000), in which the interrater reliability of the scores ranged from .57 to 1.00, with most values in the acceptable to good range. For the purposes of this report, the drawings were rescored for the presence of traditional (Islamic) clothing, including head covering and loose attire, and modern (Western) clothing, such as suits and pants for men and dresses and skirts for women. Some drawings could not be classified. Thus, there were three possible scores: (1) traditional attire, (2) modern attire, or (3) undetermined. To test for the coding reliability of this new score, a second rater independently coded one hundred randomly selected drawings. The interrater reliability as measured by Kappa for the attire in drawings of the ideal man was .94 and for the ideal woman .95, both in the excellent range.

Although the HSCP was designed to tap the values and assumptions of Mexican families, it has shown utility for samples of international adolescents (Gibbons, Stiles, and Shkodriani 1991). On the HSCP, participants rated each of twenty-nine phrases on a four-point Likert scale from "strongly disagree" to "strongly agree." Sample items include, "it is not right for a married women to work outside the home" and "it is more important to respect your father than to love him." High scores represent more traditional beliefs. In the present study, the Cronbach's alpha for the scale was .79 (very good). To analyze the data, the scores of participants who drew modern attire were compared to those who drew traditional attire with respect to the other variables, using either t-tests or chi-square.

RESULTS

Most adolescents' drawings were detailed and thoughtful and revealed their thoughts about family and values. An example is shown in Figure 10.1. A twelve-year-old boy wrote, "It is a duty for parents to love their children. It is a duty for children to love their parents."

When the drawings were scored for whether the ideal was shown in traditional or modern clothing, about one-third fell into each category: traditional, modern, and indeterminate. Those results are depicted in Table 10.1.

Figure 10.1   A typical drawing by a Kuwaiti adolescent.

Participants who drew the ideal woman in traditional attire were significantly more likely to draw the ideal man similarly attired, r = .465, *p* < .001.

Examples of depiction of the ideal man and ideal woman in traditional clothing are shown in Figure 10.2.

Examples of depictions of the ideal man and ideal women in modern clothing are shown in Figure 10.3, and those with indeterminate attire in Figure 10.4. Note the sunglasses on the modern ideal man and the stylish dress of the modern ideal woman.

When the HSCP scores of adolescents who drew the ideal man in traditional attire were compared to the scores of those who drew the ideal man in modern attire, there was no significant difference. However, when the HSCP scores of adolescents who drew the ideal women in traditional attire (X = 3.26) were compared to the scores of those who drew the ideal

Table 10.1   Distribution of Drawing Scores for Clothing of the Ideal (N = 957)

	Traditional	Modern	Unknown
Ideal Woman	28.7%	27.5%	43.8%
Ideal Man	30.5%	29.7%	39.8%

Figure 10.2   Drawings of the ideal man and ideal woman in traditional clothing.

woman in modern attire (X = 3.12), there was a significant difference, *t* (526) = 2.419, *p* < .05. Although the Kuwaiti sample overall endorsed relatively traditional values on the HSCP, this was more true of those who drew the ideal woman in traditional clothing.

Table 10.2   Differences According to Attire in Ratings of the Qualities of the Ideal Man and Woman (Scale from 1 to 7 with Higher Ratings Indicating Greater Importance)

	Ideal Man		Ideal Woman	
Quality	Traditional Clothing	Modern Clothing	Traditional Clothing	Modern Clothing
He/She is kind and honest	6.6 ± 1.0	6.6 ± .9	6.7 ± .8	6.6 ± 1.1
He/She likes kids	6.0 ±1.4*	5.8 ± 1.5	6.3 ± 1.3	6.1 ± 1.3
He/She is fun	5.7 ± 1.5*	5.9 ± 1.3	5.7 ± 1.4	5.7 ± 1.4
He/She has a good job	5.7 ± 1.5	5.9 ± 1.4	4.9 ± 1.9	5.1 ± 1.8
He/She is very intelligent	5.4 ± 1.7	5.6 ± 1.4	5.3 ± 1.7	5.2 ± 1.6
He/She has good looks	4.8 ± 2.0	5.0 ± 1.8	4.7 ± 2.0	5.0 ± 1.8
He/She is of average height and weight	4.5 ± 2.1*	4.9 ± 1.8	4.4 ± 2.1*	4.9 ± 2.0
He/She is sexy	4.4 ± 2.0*	4.7 ± 1.8	4.6 ± 2.2*	4.9 ± 1.9
He/She is popular	6.3 ± 1.2	6.3 ± 1.2	6.2 ± 1.2	6.3 ± 1.2
He/She has a lot of money	4.0 ± 1.9*	4.3 ± 1.7	3.4 ± 1.9	3.4 ± 1.8

Notes: Cell entries represent mean ratings ± standard deviations.
* = p<.05, ** = p<.01, *** = p<.001, differences by clothing depicted.

Figure 10.3   Drawings of the ideal man and ideal woman in modern clothing.

In the next step of the analysis, the ratings of the qualities of the ideal man were compared for participants who drew the ideal man in traditional attire with those who drew the ideal man in modern attire, and the same procedure was followed for drawings and ratings of the ideal woman. The results are depicted in Table 10.2. It can be seen that those who showed the ideal man in traditional clothing rated liking children as more important for the ideal. Those who drew the ideal man in modern clothing rated being fun, being of average height and weight, being sexy, and having a lot of money as more important. For the ideal woman, those who drew her in modern clothing rated it as more important that she be of average height and weight and sexy.

In the third stage of the data analysis, drawings depicting the ideal in traditional or modern clothing were compared for other features of the drawings by means of chi-square analysis. Table 10.3 depicts those results. There were many significant effects. Adolescents who drew the man in traditional attire were more likely to mention religion or depict religious images on the drawings, to show the ideal person with others (see Figure 10.1), and to show the ideal man in feminine gender roles (such as caring for

Figure 10.4   Drawings with indeterminate attire.

children). They were less likely to show the ideal man doing paid work, in masculine gender roles, in a leisure activity, or to depict weapons or fighting or brand names or insignia in the drawings. On drawings of the ideal woman, those depicted in traditional clothing were more likely to mention religion or depict religious images, to be shown with others, to be shown performing adult responsibilities, or to be depicted doing homemaking or childcare, or in feminine gender roles. They were *less* likely to be depicted doing paid work, in masculine gender roles, as physically mature, with sexual emphasis, in a leisure activity, or wearing brand name clothing.

DISCUSSION AND CONCLUSIONS

The tension between traditional and modern does seem to occupy the thoughts of adolescents in Kuwait. In this study, tradition was strongly associated with religion; the traditional drawings manifested both religious images (such as men praying) and comments about religion. A thirteen-year-old girl wrote, "The ideal man is going to the mosque to pray." A fifteen-old girl wrote, "The ideal woman is praying to God based on Islam's teaching 'praying is better than sleeping.'" On his drawing, a fifteen-year-old boy wrote, "You will go to the mosque to pray to God." And a twelve-year-old girl depicted the ideal man as one who "teaches others how to read the holy Koran." The ideal man in traditional clothing was not only religious, but he also was more likely to cherish children, to be shown in a

Figure 10.5   A seventeen-year-old girl's drawing of the ideal man.

Table 10.3   Differences by Type of Attire in Drawings of the Ideal Man and Ideal Woman

Feature	Ideal Man		Ideal Woman	
	Traditional Clothing	*Modern Clothing*	*Traditional Clothing*	*Modern Clothing*
Religion	19.1***	4.7	17***	2.7
Helping others	18.4	14.7	36.9**	25.2
Inner qualities mentioned	21.9	20.8	18.8	13.2
Shown with others	36.9***	20.8	42.8***	29.8
Adult responsibilities	59.3	53.4	65.3**	53.7
Paid work activity	29.2*	34.8	14.8**	19.8
Homemaking and childcare	13.5*	7.9	45.4**	29.5
Masculine gender roles	25.2***	38.9	4.1**	10.9
Feminine gender roles	7.7***	5.1	52.2**	40.7
Physical maturity	42.0	44.0	26.3***	45.5
Sexual emphasis	11.1	8.2	7.0*	13.2
Smiling	67.4	66.3	71.9	70.8
Appearance mentioned	11.1	11.1	11.4	14.3
Achievement and success	5.9	5.0	.7	2.7
Money and wealth	3.5	3.9	2.2	4.3
Leisure activity	17.0*	24.4	9.6**	17.8
Smoking, drinking, drugs	1.4	1.1	.4	0
Weapons or fighting	.3***	6.1	0	.4
Brand names or insignia	1.0***	6.1	0**	3.1

Notes: Cell entries represent percentages of drawings.* = p<.05, ** = p<.01, *** = p<.001, chi-square showed significant differences between drawings of different clothing types.

"feminine" gender role, with others and doing homemaking or childcare. The iconic image of the ideal man in traditional attire showed him caring for children. A seventeen-year-old girl drew the picture in Figure 10.5 of the ideal man with children and wrote, "The father tells his children, 'my children, we will go to make the world flourish and progress.'" So, in this example, the traditional image emphasizes not only the family, but modernization and progress. This suggests that some Kuwaiti adolescents, like young people in Morocco, are striving to integrate progress and globalization with traditions of strong families and religion.

The opposite pole from the traditional is the modern ideal man who spends more time alone, in masculine gender roles, in both paid work and leisure, and is associated with the military, fighting, and brand names. It is

Figure 10.6   A twelve-year-old boy's drawing of the ideal man.

Figure 10.7   A sixteen-year-old boy's drawing of the ideal woman.

important that he be sexy, of average height and weight, and have a lot of money. This man working in an office epitomizes this perspective (Figure 10.6), but there were also many drawings of the modern ideal man playing soccer or serving in the military.

The traditional woman is associated with endorsing items such as "it is not right for a married woman to work outside the home" on the HSCP. Like the traditional ideal man, the traditional ideal woman is also religious. She is likely to be depicted with others, helping them, in feminine roles, and engaged in homemaking and childcare. This drawing (Figure 10.7) by a sixteen-year-old boy explicitly defines the ideal woman as a mother. "The best thing in a mother is that she is kind."

The modern woman, on the other hand, is more often depicted as engaged in paid work or at leisure, as physically mature, with sexual emphasis. It is more important that she be of average height and weight and sexy. Figure 10.8 depicts a sexy modern woman, "the ideal woman should be attractive and beautiful." Note that another feature associated with modern drawings, the depiction of brand names, is present on this drawing. The girl who drew this originally labeled the car as a Ferrari, but then changed it to a Lamborghini instead. The hourglass figure of the woman in this drawing may also point to a risk of globalization for adolescent girls. There may be greater exposure to the thin ideal, putting them at risk for eating disorders (Trainer 2010).

There was evidence in the drawings of some Kuwaiti adolescents that they are striving to keep their valued traditions and yet embrace the positive aspects of modernity and globalization, especially with respect to women's roles. The twelve-year-old boy who drew the traditionally attired ideal woman in Figure 10.9 wrote, "A woman could work. Working is not prohibited for women."

Figure 10.8   A seventeen-year-old girl's drawing of the ideal woman.

Figure 10.9   A twelve-year-old boy's drawing of the ideal woman.

In sum, dress is an external characteristic that may have intrapsychic and complex meanings for young people. We can get clues as to adolescents' inner thoughts by examining the correlates of the different features of their drawings.

Other authors have pointed out that the dimension of traditional versus modern is an important one among Arab adolescents and young adults (Booth 2002; Davis and Davis 1995; Gregg 2007). Alqudsi-Ghabra (2003) describes Kuwaiti adolescents as presenting conflicting images, "Teens, both boys and girls, are generally stylish and modern, yet conservative" (109). Our study has shown that traditional versus modern is a salient dimension for adolescents in Kuwait, and that, for them, attire is an indicator of a cluster of values that accompany the external representation.

Our scoring method (traditional attire, modern attire, or undetermined), with an analysis of the differences between those who drew the ideal person in traditional and modern dress, highlighted the polarity of the two positions. However, there is evidence that some adolescents were attempting to integrate the traditional and modern. A twelve-year-old boy wrote, "[The ideal] woman can be veiled or not veiled. A woman is free in her behavior."

Both girls and boys described dual roles for the ideal woman: "She has to take care of her family and her business affairs," and "The ideal woman should take care of her home and keep her children clean, and at the same time, work outside her home." A fifteen-year-old boy drew the ideal woman in stylish high-heeled boots, with dramatic makeup, taking care of her children. A sixteen-year-old girl drew a pretty woman in modern attire, thinking mostly of men in her thought bubble, "my father, my mother, dad, dad, my father, my husband."

ADOLESCENCE AND MODERNIZATION/GLOBALIZATION

Globalization may be one factor that provokes a tension between the traditional and the modern (Jensen 2003). Furthermore, adolescents may be on the forefront of globalization and societal change (Skovgaard-Petersen 2005). And depending on the context, the specific cultural traditions, and the type of experiences with modernization and globalization, the consequences can be beneficial or harmful to adolescents' well-being and development.

There are many examples from other cultural settings of varying consequences of modernization and globalization for adolescents. An interesting case study comes from Belize of a young woman "Maria" who watched the Oprah TV show and concluded that she had been abused and was suffering from post-traumatic stress disorder (PTSD). She subsequently received the PTSD diagnosis, heretofore unknown in her community (Anderson-Fye 2010). The diagnosis may have conferred advantages for Maria in terms of treatment, but Maria's use of global media is a vivid example of how adolescents can exploit the international media to interpret their personal experiences.

The use of media to form a global identity may provide essential information and insights to adolescents that will prepare them for global citizenship and modernization, and in some contexts might facilitate healthy development. Researchers in Hong Kong hypothesized that adolescents who held more individualistic Western values would be at greater risk for suicide than those who held traditional values, such as obedience and respect for elders. The findings did not support the hypothesis; adolescent boys who held more individualistic values were at lesser risk for suicide and there was no relationship for girls. In a study of two communities in Nigeria—one that held to traditional ways and another that was rapidly modernizing—Hollos and Leis (1989) found that there was less conflict and more intergenerational cooperation in the modernizing village. The authors concluded that in the modernizing village adolescents and their parents shared modern values. In rapidly changing societies as well (those that Mead [1970] termed prefigurative or cofigurative cultures) adults learn from young people. Because young people may be on the forefront of change, parents may look to them for knowledge and skills.

On the other hand, adhering to traditional cultural values may be advantageous for adolescents in some contexts. A study among adolescents in Delhi,

India, revealed that adolescents who adhered to traditional values were less likely to use tobacco than those who identified with "Western" culture (Stigler et al. 2010). Adolescents who adhere to religious values and participate in religious practices are buffered against drug use in general (Chitwood, Weiss, and Leukefeld 2008). Adolescents who spend less time on the Internet might receive more social support from close family members (Al-Kandari and Al-Qashan 2001; Wheeler 2003). In addition, traditional preferences for a rounder body shape may prevent girls' preference for the thin ideal, and thereby protect them from eating disorders (Anderson-Fye 2004).

"Being modern," of course, is multifaceted and can have contradictory consequences (Trainer 2010). It can mean eating fast food, using cars, and employing servants and at the same time being exposed to Western thin ideals. Trainer (2010) found high rates of being overweight and obesity in Kuwait. In this case a traditional preference for a round body was protective against eating disorders, but also led to unhealthy obesity. A contributing cultural factor mentioned by many Arab women was they were not permitted to exercise without a male relative to accompany them. In sum, traditional and "modern" values and practices interact in complex and sometimes contradictory ways.

In conclusion, the drawings of Kuwaiti adolescents provide windows into the developmental challenges they face as they affirm traditional religious and family values and at the same time anticipate the positive opportunities of technological innovation and modernization. For adolescents in Kuwait the distinction between the traditional and modern is a salient one, indexed by the type of clothing worn, and associated with complex sets of attitudes and values. For Kuwaiti adolescents, tradition is associated with an emphasis on religion and the family, and on endorsement of feminine rather than masculine gender roles for both sexes. The ideal was more often shown taking care of children than working at a job. Modern values were associated with the importance of being sexy and good-looking, having a job, and for women, having a mature body shape.

In today's societies adolescents need to navigate the social changes associated with modernization and globalization (Bennani-Chraibi 2000). Young people are on the forefront of social change, especially with respect to technology; they are the harbingers of the future and will construct the world of the future (Skovgaard-Petersen 2005). We end with a quote by a sixteen-year-old Kuwaiti adolescent boy, "The ideal woman says the world is changed."

ACKNOWLEDGMENTS

The authors would like to thank Carrie M. Brown, Alyssa Gurgul, and Claire T. van den Broeck for their help in the research reported here. A report based on this research was presented at the annual meeting of the Society for Cross-Cultural Research, New Orleans, 2008.

REFERENCES

Abdel-Hamid, S. 1998. Children's drawings, in *Psychology in the Arab Countries*, edited by R.A. Ahmed, and U.P. Gielen. Shibin el Kom, Egypt: Menuofia University Press, pp. 97–113.

Abdel-Khalek, A.M. and Lester, D. "A Significant Association between Religiosity and Happiness in a Sample of Kuwaiti Students," Psychological Reports 105 (2009): 381–382.

Achoui, M.M. 2006. The Saudi society: Tradition and change, in *Families across Cultures: A 30-Nation Psychological Study*, edited by James Georgas, John W. Berry, F. van de Vijver, J.R. Kagitcibasi, and Y.H. Poortinga. Cambridge, UK: Cambridge University Press, pp. 435–457.

Ahmed, R.A. 2008. Review of Arab research on parental acceptance-rejection, in *Acceptance: The Essence of Peace: Selected Papers from the First International Congress on Interpersonal Acceptance and Rejection*, edited by F. Erkman. Istanbul: The Turkish Psychology Society (Istanbul Branch), pp. 201–224.

Ahmed, R. A. 2006. Kuwait University students' perception of the adolescence stage. Kuwait University, Kuwait (Unpublished manuscript).

Ahmed, R.A., and Al-Khawajah, J.M. 2007. Kuwait, in *International Encyclopedia of Adolescence: Middle East and Africa Volume 1*, edited by J.J. Arnett. New York: Routledge: Francis and Taylor Group, pp. 562–574.

Ahmed, R.A., Azar, F., and Mullet, E. "Interpersonal Forgiveness among Kuwaiti Adolescents and Adults," Conflict Management and Peace Science 24 (2007): 159–170.

Ahmed, R.A., Rohner, R.P., and Carrasco, M.A. 2012. Relationships between psychological adjustment and perceived parental, sibling, best friend, and teacher acceptance among Kuwaiti adolescents, in *Proceedings of the 3ʳᵈ International Congress of the International Society for Interpersonal Acceptance and Rejection*, edited by K. Ripoll-Nunez and C.M. Brown, pp. 1–10.

Ahmed, R.A., Sorum, P.C., and Mullet, E. "Young Kuwaitis' Views of the Acceptability of Physician-Assisted Suicide," Journal of Medical Ethics 36 (2010): 671–676.

Al-Fayez, G., Awadalla, A., Arikawa, H., Templer, D.L., and Hutton, S. "Body Elimination Attitude Family Resemblance in Kuwait," International Journal of Psychology 44 (2009): 410–417.

Al-Hashemi, A., Abdulaziz, A., Jumaa, I., Gaafar, A.M., Al-Khadhari, A., and Al-Jassar, M.A. 2011. "Internet Use among High School Students in Kuwait." Paper presented at the 7th Annual Forum: Psychological and Social Health and Society. Department of Sociology and Social Work, College of Social Sciences, Kuwait University, Kuwait, March 29–31 (in Arabic).

Al-Kandari, Y.Y. and Al-Qashan, H.F. "The Relation between Internet Use and Social Isolation of Kuwait University Students," Journal of Humanities and Social Sciences (The United Arab Emirates) 17 (2001): 1–45 (in Arabic).

Almubayei, D.S. 2010. "Articulations of Identity within Kuwaiti High School Cliques: Language Choices in 'boyat' and 'emo' Filipino Youth Groups." PhD diss. University of Texas at Arlington. On http://dspace.uta.edu/bitstream/handle/10106/4871/Almubayei_uta_2502D_10583.pdf?sequence=1 (accessed March 27, 2011).

Al-Qabas. 2011. A Kuwaiti daily newspaper. April 2 (in Arabic).

Alqudsi-Ghabra, T. 2003. Kuwait, in *Teen Life in the Middle East*, edited by A.A. Mahdi. Westport, CT: Greenwood, pp. 101–116.

Al-Watan. 2010. A Kuwaiti daily newspaper. October 13 (in Arabic).

Anderson-Fye, E. "A 'Coca-Cola" Shape: Cultural Change, Body Image, and Eating Disorders in San Andres, Belize," Culture, Medicine and Psychiatry 28 (2004): 561–595.

————. 2010. Ethnographic case study: Maria—cultural change and posttraumatic stress in the life of a Belizean adolescent girl, in *Formative Experiences: The Interaction of Caregiving, Culture, and Developmental Psychobiology*, edited by C.M. Worthman, P.M. Plotskky, D.S. Schechter, and C.A. Cummings. New York: Cambridge University Press, pp. 331–343.

Arnett, J.J. "The Psychology of Globalization," American Psychologist 57 (2002): 774–783.

————. 2010. Adolescence and Emerging Adulthood: A Cultural Approach. 4th ed. Upper Saddle River, NJ: Prentice Hall.

Badri, M.B. "Influence of Modernization on Goodenough Quotients of Sudanese Children," Perceptual and Motor Skills 20 (1965): 931–932.

Badri, M.B. and Dennis, W. "Human-Figure Drawings in Relation to Modernization in Sudan," Journal of Psychology 58 (1964): 421–425.

Baroun, K.A. "Relations among Religiosity, Health, and Anxiety for Kuwaiti Adolescents," Psychological Reports 99 (2006): 717–722.

Bennani-Chraibi, M. 2000. Youth in Morocco—an indicator of a changing society, in *Alienation or Integration of Arab Youth: Between Family, State and Street*, edited by Roel Meijer. Richmond, Surrey, UK: Curzon Press, pp. 143–160.

Bhui, K., Khatib, Y., Viner, R., Klineberg, E., Clark, C., Head, J., and Stansfeld, S. "Cultural Identity, Clothing and Common Mental Disorder: A Prospective School-Based Study of White British and Bangladeshi Adolescents," Journal of Epidemiology and Community Health 62 (2008): 435–441.

Booth, M. 2002. Arab adolescents facing the future: Enduring ideals and pressures to change, in *The World's Youth: Adolescence in Eight Regions of the Globe*, edited by B.B. Brown, R.W. Larson, and T.S. Saraswathi. Cambridge: Cambridge University Press, pp. 207–242.

Brunsma, D.L. and Rockquemore, K.A. 1998. "Effects of Student Uniforms on Attendance, Behavior Problems, Substance Use, and Academic Achievement," Journal of Educational Research 92 (1998): 53–62.

CBC News Online. 2004. "France's Hijab Ban." September 7. On http://www.cbc.ca/news/background/islam/hijab.html (accessed April 11, 2011).

Central Intelligence Agency. 2011. The World Factbook. On https://www.cia.gov/library/publications/the-world-factbook/geos/ku.html (accessed March 25, 2011).

Chitwood, D.D., Weiss, M.L., and Leukefeld, C.G. "A Systematic Review of Recent Literature on Religiosity and Substance Use," Journal of Drug Issues 38 (2008): 653–688.

Clifford, M.M., Grandgenett, M., and Bardwell, R. 1981. Activities and Readings in Learning and Development. Boston: Houghton, Mifflin.

Davis, S.S., and Davis, D.A. 1989. Adolescence in a Moroccan Town. New Brunswick, NJ: Rutgers University Press.

————. "'The Mosque and the Satellite': Media and Adolescence in a Moroccan Town," Journal of Youth and Adolescence 24 (1995): 577–593.

Díaz-Guerrero, R. "Una Escala Factorial de Premisas, Histórico-Socioculturales de la Familia Mexicana," Revista Interamericana de Psicología 6 (1972): 235–244.

DiCarlo, M.A., Gibbons, J. L., Kaminsky, D., Wright, J.D., and Stiles, D.A. "Street Children's Drawings: Windows into Their Life Circumstances and Aspirations," International Social Work 43 (2000): 107–120.

Eicher, J.B., Baizerman, S., and Michelman, J. "Adolescent Dress, Part II: A Qualitative Study of Suburban High School Students," Adolescence 26 (1991): 679–686.

Embassy of the United States Kuwait. 2011. Bureau of Democracy, Human Rights, and Labor. 2009 Country Reports on Human Rights Practices. March 11. On http://kuwait.usembassy.gov/human_rights.html (accessed March 27, 2011).

Gibbons, J.L. and Stiles, D.A. 2004. The Thoughts of Youth: An International Perspective on Adolescents' Ideal Persons. Greenwich, CT: Information Age Publishing.

Gibbons, J.L., Stiles, D.A. and Shkodriani, G.M. "Adolescents' Attitudes toward Family and Gender Roles: An International Comparison," *Sex Roles* 25 (1991): 625–643.

Goodenough, F.L. and Harris, D.B. 1963. The Goodenough-Harris Drawing Test. New York: Harcourt, Brace, and Jovanovich.

Gregg, G.S. 2007. Culture and Identity in a Muslim Society. New York: Oxford University Press.

Hofstede, G. 2001. Culture's Consequences: Comparing Values, Behaviors, Institutions, and Organizations across Nations. 2nd ed. Thousand Oaks, CA: Sage.

Hollos, M. and Leis, P.E. 1989. Becoming Nigerian in Ijo Society. New Brunswick, NJ: Rutgers University Press.

Ibrahim, B. and Wassef, H. 2000. Caught between two worlds: Youth in the Egyptian hinterland, in *Alienation or Integration of Arab Youth: Between Family, State and Street*, edited by R. Meijer. Richmond, Surrey, UK: Curzon Press, pp. 161–185.

Jensen, L.A. "Coming of Age in a Multicultural World: Globalization and Adolescent Cultural Identity Formation," *Applied Developmental Science* 7 (2003): 189–196.

Kaiser, S.B. 1997. The Social Psychology of Clothing: Symbolic Appearances in Context. New York: Fairchild.

Koppitz, E.M. 1984. Psychological Evaluation of Human Figure Drawings by Middle School Pupils. Boston: Allyn and Bacon.

Lan, J. "The Impact of Globalization on the Values of Contemporary Chinese Youth," *Journal of Youth Studies* 12 (2009): 12–16.

Mahdi, A.A., ed. 2003. Teen Life in the Middle East. Westport, CT: Greenwood.

Mead, M. 1970. Culture and Commitment: A Study of the Generation Gap. Bodley Head.

Rohner, R.P., Khaleque, A., and Cournoyer, D.E. "Parental Acceptance-Rejection: Theory, Methods, Cross-Cultural Evidence, and Implications," *Ethos* 33 (2008): 299–334.

Schlegel, A. 2000. The global spread of adolescent culture, in *Negotiating Adolescence in Times of Social Change*, edited by L.J. Crockett and R.K. Silbereisen. New York: Cambridge University Press, pp. 71–88.

Simonsen, J.B. 2005. Introduction: Youth, history and change in the modern Arab world, in *Youth and Youth Culture in the Contemporary Middle East*, edited by J.B. Simonsen. Aarhus, Denmark: Aarhus University Press, pp. 7–9.

Skovgaard-Petersen, J. 2005. The discovery of adolescence in the Middle East, in *Youth and Youth Culture in the Contemporary Middle East*, edited by J.B. Simonsen. Aarhus, Denmark: Aarhus University Press, pp. 21–34.

Stigler, M., Dhavan, P., Dusen, D.V., Arora, M., Reddy, K.S., and Perry, C.L. "Westernization and Tobacco Use among Young People in Delhi, India," *Social Science and Medicine* 71 (2010): 891–897.

Stiles, D.A. and Gibbons, J.L. "Manual for Evaluating Individual and Social Values Expressed in International Adolescents' Drawings of the Ideal Woman and Man," *World Cultures* 11 (2000): 181–221.

Toumi, H. 2010. "Kuwait Police Shave Heads of 30 Teenagers as Punishment for Harassing Girls." On http://www.habibtoumi.com/2010/04/11/kuwait-police-shave-heads-of-30–teenagers-as-punishment-for-harassing-girls/ (accessed March 18, 2011).

Trainer, S.S. "Body Image, Health, and Modernity: Women's Perspectives and Experiences in the United Arab Emirates," *Asia-Pacific Journal of Public Health* Supplement to 22, no. 3 (2010): 605–675.

United Nations Children's Fund. 2011. "State of the World's Children 2011. Adolescence An Age of Opportunity." On http://www.unicef.org/sowc2011/pdfs/SOWC-2011–Main-Report_EN_02092011.pdf (accessed March 25, 2011).

United Nations Development Programme. 2010. "Human Development Report 2010 20th Anniversary Edition: The Real Wealth of Nations: Pathways to Human Development." On http://hdr.undp.org/en/media/HDR_2010_EN_Complete_reprint.pdf (accessed March 25, 2011).

Wheeler, D.L. "The Internet and Youth Subculture in Kuwait," Journal of Computer-Mediated Communication 8 (2003). On http://jcmc.indiana.edu/vol8/issue2/wheeler.html (accessed March 25, 2011).

11 Introduction of Television and Dominican Youth

Marsha B. Quinlan and Jenna R. Hansen

INTRODUCTION

Television plays a major role in the lives of most of the world's children and adolescents (Van Evra 2004). Children and teens in the U.S., for example, typically spend three hours a day watching television (Ad & Marketing News 2011). When U.S. television programming began in 1948 and numbers of home televisions mushroomed through the early 1950s (Mittell 2009), neither commercial nor academic researchers "undertook, while there was still opportunity to do so, a systematic study, over a period of time, of the social changes which television brought in its wake" (Bogart 1958, 333). Half a century later in 2004, as television was reaching some of the world's more remote communities, our team witnessed the introduction of television programming to a rural West Indian community. We had conducted ethnography there for several years before television arrived and continued research on and after television's arrival.

This longitudinal study examines how the advent of television affects the youth population of a rural village, Bwa Mawego, in the Commonwealth of Dominica. Along with qualitative ethnographic observations and interviews about television, we present a time allocation restudy study of village youth (ages three to seventeen). We compare a set of Instantaneous Behavior Scan data from a sample of sixteen households in the pretelevision summers of 1993 and 1994 (Quinlan 1995; Quinlan et al. 2005) with post-television data from a sample of fourteen households in the summer of 2008 (Hansen 2009). With this chapter, we respond to the myriad behavioral researchers who have found television to affect child and adolescent development (notably Van Evra 2004; Zimmerman and Christakis 2005; Murray 2007) and to Lull's call for firsthand investigations of media use that are informed by a sense of cultural and social processes (Lull 1990).

ANTHROPOLOGY AND TELEVISION

Until relatively recently in the 1980s, mass media was "almost a taboo topic for anthropology" (Ginsburg et al. 2002, 3). Earlier anthropologists perhaps perceived television and other mass media as "too redolent of Western modernity for a field identified with tradition, the non-Western, and the vitality of the local" (ibid.). However, rapid globalization and the spread of modern media along with it increasingly called attention to the sociocultural infiltrations of television, particularly in the wake of Spitulnik's 1993 synthesis, "Anthropology and the Mass Media." In the twenty-first century, radio, television, and, increasingly, the Internet (yet another vehicle for television programming) are part of everyday life in all but the very most remote parts of the world. As Ginsburg et al. (2002, 2) note, "While anthropologists are always firmly grounded in the local, we realize that certain sweeping technology and institutional changes have had irreversible consequences over the last decades." Television is prominent in this change.

Television changes local culture in terms of what people do with their time and money, how people interact, and what people believe about the world and their place in it. Reis (1998) judges that, overall, television decreases physical and social activity in villages. Also, the availability of television programming may stress socioeconomic differences between households as some families can afford to buy a television and perhaps pay additionally for service, whereas others cannot. As is true with the present case study, many of the world's new television-receiving sites may be relatively new to wage-earning work, with egalitarianism within memory. Television hence becomes a visible status symbol that may enhance status by ownership and by becoming a receptor of privileged information to be passed onto those with the medium (Kottak 1991). Watching television and discussing programs are then inseparable parts of a single social process, and television programming becomes integrated with daily conversation topics (Painter 1994; Gillespie 1995; Wilk 2002). As Spitulnik (2002) points out for radios in Zambia, televisions may also serve as vehicles for reciprocity and sharing. Television viewing is often a social, collective event. Although as language comprehension increases, television viewing may become less interactive (Davis and Davis 1995), television remains a social tool in that the programming becomes relational, as people may refer to it or draw upon it to clarify issues (Lull 1990). Television changes part of a household's functional environment in terms of house layout, as background noise and as a regulator of talk and social activity (ibid.).

Several anthropological studies of mass media focus on media's critical role in cultural hegemony, including the way that media influences individual values, and political economic views. In most of the developing world, the majority of television programming comes from the U.S. (Miller et al. 2001). The imbalance of American and European television programming inflicts a sort of postcolonial "cultural imperialism" on non-Western audiences (Schiller 1976) through which recipient countries adopt capitalist consumer values through entertainment programming and commercials (Schiller 1976; Beltrán and de Cardona 1979; Kottak

1992; Brown 2001; Regis 2001; Ginsburg et al. 2002). Consumerism, in turn, fuels capital interests (Fisherkeller 1997). Media use significantly predicts levels of consumerism (Skinner 2001), and television is particularly inciting a new wave of consumerism (Abu-Lughod 1997; Reis 1998). Researchers note the menace of foreign television programming inducing materialistic values upon traditional value systems (Fisherkeller 1997; Reis 1998; Skinner 2001; Wilk 2002). And, as sharing is the foundation of traditional Caribbean lifestyle (Macfarlan and Quinlan 2008), the change may be shocking to the local culture.

Besides affecting local economic views, television programming may broaden the new audience's worldview. Television coverage affects individual's values (see especially Gillespie's [1995] study of TV and immigrants in Southall, London, a South Asian neighborhood). Exposure to news programming may show larger national or international debates on traditional topics. Even in dramatic programming, characters may live according to Western norms, pursuing lives in which they seek non-arranged "love" marriages, have few children, criticize governments, or are sexually promiscuous. Such images introduce new, admirable, or scandalous ideas, which may affect viewers' thinking about themselves vis-à-vis global movements. Mass media hence influences the process of identity formation (Fisherkeller 1997; Reis 1998; Ginsburg et al. 2002; Wilk 2002). Television exposure creates new forms of cosmopolitanism in communities (Abu-Lughod 1997), including increased political awareness (Abu-Lughod 1997; Fisherkeller 1997; Reis 1998; Ginsburg et al. 2002; Wilk 2002); a shift in conversation topics from local to global (Kottak 1991); changes in time perspective (Levine 1997; Reis 1998; Wilk 2002); and revised thinking on gender roles (Davis and Davis 1995; Gillespie 1995; Fisherkeller 1997; Mankekar 2002). Kottak found in Bahia, Brazil, that television correlated with liberalness—as length of television exposure increased, sexist views decreased (Kottak 1991).

Global populations show an overall preference for U.S. and European television programming over local programming, likely due to the better production quality (Davis and Davis 1995; Skinner 2001; Wilk 2002). Lashley's (1995) study of U.S. television in Trinidad and Tobago, the first in the English-speaking Caribbean to acquire television in 1962, concluded that the youth viewers preferred American television over local programming, stating that "the more American the fare, the more it is preferred by the youth" (89). People nevertheless consume and understand television according to the internal logic of their home culture such that there may be culture-specific filtering of programming (Painter 1994). Television subjects provide sociocultural markers by which viewers may consider themselves and their lives like, or unlike, the people on-screen and agree or disagree with the values present in the programming (Abu-Lughod 2005). Programs that are written with one audience in mind and then consumed by another foreign audience may be perceived differently with unpredictable outcomes for the secondary foreign audience (Ginsburg et al. 2002). Miller's (1992) study of an American soap opera in Trinidad reveals an active process of societal self-production through which people incorporate television topics into their own value system.

YOUTH BEHAVIOR AND TELEVISION

Global demographic tendencies exist among the young television-watching audience. Daily hours of television viewing increase with national class, local class, household income, urban residence (Kottak 1991), age, and level of education (Davis and Davis 1995). Youth in wealthy nations use more media generally. Across the world, the more industrialized and schooled a society is, the less time people spend in household and wage labor, which opens time for other activities, including television (Larson and Verma 1999). Yet, in these schooled societies, as children age and improve their reading ability, they tend to watch less television. In the U.S., for example, school-age children's weekday television viewing declines with age as they spend increasingly more time in educational activities and reading, although weekend television viewing rates go back up (Huston et al. 1999). Although overall rates of television-watching increase with national wealth, within wealthy countries, youth's rates of television-watching decreases with increasing socioeconomic status (U.S. Department of Education 1988; Brown et al. 1990; Bianchi and Robinson 1997; Huston et al. 1999). Larsen and Verma (1999) propose that this intracultural inversion may take place in wealthy countries because once a family owns the equipment, the cost of using it is less expensive than costly leisure and enrichment activities available to those with more means. Further, families with high SES may stress more time on homework and reading, as the preceding nation-level statistics suggest.

Worldwide, boys tend to watch more television than girls (Carpenter et al. 1989; Bianchi and Robinson 1997; Robinson and Bianchi 1997; Larson et al. 2001). This slight imbalance occurs as boys watch additional action and sports programming (Larson et al. 1989; Huston et al. 1990).

As young people are less set in their ways than are adults, television may have particular transformational effects on youth culture. In terms of consumerism, researchers find that fashion and societal trends are increasingly important to young people as television serves to model current fashions (Gillespie 1995; Fisherkeller 1997; Reis 1998). Television may motivate young people to strive for upward mobility to have a "better life" based on the people they see on television (Fisherkeller 1997). Adults sometimes opine that television causes young people to desire to move away for better jobs, and may promote crime or lifestyles that can never be attained locally (Davis and Davis 1995; Reis 1998). Youths learn about new and foreign activities and situations by watching television programming that presents certain practices that are culturally prohibited locally (Davis and Davis 1995), although the home often filters learning from other cultures in young viewers' lives (Fisherkeller 1997). For young acculturating people, television is another vehicle for "switching" between cultural worlds of school and home in terms of language, political support, technology, and so forth (Gillespie 1995). Finally, as television opens up new societies and lifestyles, it also is a vehicle for social learning about coping with new situations and may provide young viewers with "imaginative strategies" for dealing with problems (Fisherkeller 1997).

SETTING

Dominica, in the Lesser Antilles (670 miles southeast of the larger Dominican Republic), is a mountainous, relatively undeveloped island nation without substantial agricultural or tourist industries. Dominica's population (approximately sixty-five thousand) is of mixed indigenous Island-Carib, African, and European descent. Most Dominicans are bilingual in Creole English and French-Patois (*Kwéyòl*).

Bwa Mawego is one of the least developed villages on Dominica's remote eastern (Atlantic) side. It has about 550 full- and part-time residents, and is secluded at the dead end of a paved lane. Isolation limits villagers' job and education opportunities. Economic opportunities are scarce and so average annual income is approximately 5,400 East Caribbean dollars (E.C.$5,400 = U.S.$2,000). Subsistence is primarily through swidden horticulture, occurring in gardens at the village periphery.

Commercial occupations include fishing, driving a "transport" (shuttle to Roseau, the capital), running a small shop for staples and rum, teaching school, and occasional wage labor. Most families cultivate and process West Indian bay leaf oil (an essential oil scent that comes from the bay rum tree, *Pimenta racemosa*), although the market is limited and seasonal. Many households receive remittances from emigrated kin. For detailed ethnography of the site, see *From the Bush* (Quinlan 2004).

MODERNIZATION AND MEDIA IN BWA MAWEGO

Bwa Mawego first got electricity (or "current") in the late 1970s. The power lines were soon destroyed by Hurricane David in 1979, and the village spent the next decade without power. Electric lines returned around 1989, and modern appliances and entertainment devices trickled into use. Modernization occurred remarkably rapidly beginning at the turn of the millennium. In the last decade the village obtained an improved paved road, a secondary school within commuting distance, piped water, television, and cell phone and Internet services.

Prior to 1955, Dominicans tuned into the Grenada Radio Service for limited news and music (Dominica Broadcasting Services [DBS] 2011). In 1971, the government of Dominica created localized radio with Radio Dominica (Honychurch 1995, 145). The government also provided transistor radios to citizens, thereby making broadcasts accessible to most of the island. Radio Dominica provided information, education, and entertainment to the public until 1975, when new governmental leadership shut the radio station down (Honychurch 1995, 145). Then, in 1979, the Dominica Broadcasting Corporation Act made provisions for "high-quality" radio and television broadcasting services in Dominica (DBS 2011). But then that same year, Hurricane David flattened the building in Morne Bruce that housed the television service and also destroyed the equipment and the majority of telephone lines laid out by Cable and Wireless. By the time Bwa Mawego regained electrical "current" service and throughout our research, Dominica has had four radio stations: one state-run (Dominica Broadcasting Corporation [DBS]), the Christian Voice of Life Radio, and two commercial stations.

Meanwhile, in 1982, Marpin Television Company brought cable television to Roseau, the capital, and out to various Dominican villages over the next two decades (DBS 2011), but not to the study site due to its remote mountainous location. Dominica never had domestic terrestrial television stations, so there was no sufficient TV reception in Bwa Mawego village before cable television became available. Between 1989 and 2004, a few villagers did, however, own televisions with video players. Videos, as well as the televisions and the players, generally were sent as gifts from relatives in other countries. Pre-cable video showings were occasional and were often social events. Shopkeepers and other television owners might place a set outside to play a movie so that many could view it.

At the turn of the millennium, a construction project brought piped water to the village and improved the road. Not having to spend time carrying water and laundry freed several hours that villagers seem to have supplanted using new entertainment and communication paraphernalia. The improved road ushered in a wave of technology that included not only cable television in 2004, but cellular phone coverage and Internet service, first in the village council, then in some homes. Around 2006, a store in Roseau began to extend credit to villagers so that they could buy televisions on time. At that time, many households obtained television sets and cable television service.

Dominica's only cable provider, Marpin Telecoms, provides fifty-two channels, including local radio stations' channels that broadcast radio along with a slideshow of local news bulletins and advertisements, the regional network Caribvision, BBC, and many U.S.-based channels. Cable instillation costs 150 East Caribbean dollars (U.S.$56) and the service costs residents E.C.$50 (U.S.$19) per month (Marpin 2008).

Rural Dominica's transition to a television-watching culture appeared to occur immediately. Youth likewise transitioned into using other electronic media equally rapidly. While collecting data for her undergraduate honors thesis, JH noted that by 2008, Dominicans in their teens and early twenties knew and used much of the same media as their same generation in the U.S.—including television, cell phones, and electronic social networking.

OBJECTIVES AND PREDICTIONS

This chapter has four objectives. The first is to understand how having (or not having) television affects village social life and order. Second, we will assess what kinds of programming Dominican children and adolescents are watching and the nature of their television viewing. Our third objective is to assess Dominican parents' opinions on television and any changes in children that they attribute to television. Parents' opinions of televisions costs and benefits are key to television's use. After all, in addition to the cost of a television set, parents apportion considerable family resources on the cable fee (around 5.5 percent of a typical $350 per month family income). Finally, we examine the effect of television's introduction on children's and adolescents' time allocation patterns. Using our qualitative and quantitative data, we will examine the following ten television-related hypotheses.

Objective 1: To assess whether and how the possibility of television ownership affects the sociocultural order of village life.
   H1: We predict that villagers with televisions (and cable service) will have higher perceived social status than those without.
   H2: As elsewhere, we predict that television consumption will correlate with liberal (less traditional) views.

Objective 2: To assess what kinds of programming Dominican children and adolescents are watching and the nature of their television viewing.
   H3: Because it is available, we predict that the Disney Channel will dominate the youth audience, as it does elsewhere.
   H4: We predict that Dominican children, as children elsewhere, will prefer cartoons.

Objective 3: To assess Dominican parents' opinions on television and any changes they regard in the children or village family life.
   H5: Because parents everywhere appear to perceive moral degradation in subsequent generations, and because television is new and externalizes fault, we predict that parents will attribute moral degradation to television.

H6: As media use imposes materialistic values and significantly predicts levels of consumerism elsewhere, we predict that parents indicate increased TV-related consumerism among Bwa Mawego's youth.

H7: Television-watching should improve knowledge of Standard English.

Objective 4: To assess the effect of television's introduction on children's and adolescents' time allocation patterns.

H8: Boys will watch more television than girls, as has been found elsewhere.

H9: Compared to children in 1993–1994 we predict that 2008 children will spend less of their leisure time playing (as they will be watching television instead).

H10: We predict that 2008 children will spend less time being frankly passive than 1993–1994 as children will instead rest/relax in front of television.

METHODS

Fieldwork for this project was conducted during eight trips to the study site between 1993 and 2008 by MQ and two trips by JH in 2007 and 2008. Ethnographic data on television use before and after cable were collected using participant-observation (P-O) and informal key informant interviews. Parents' and children's views on television were collected through semi-structured interviews and free-list tasks with adults and children. Finally, time allocation data from before and after television was gathered with instantaneous behavior scans ("spot checks").

Sample

The data from 2008 (post-TV) comes from a sample of fourteen households containing thirty-eight children during the summer of 2008 (Hansen 2009). This sample includes every family with children between the ages of three and seventeen who lived along an approximately 2 mile circular route through the central part of Bwa Mawego. We compare time allocation data from thirty-one youths (those with at least three observations, μ 5.38 observations per child) within this 2008 sample with time allocation data from a sample of sixteen households with forty-three children from 1993 and 1994, before television reception (μ 24.97 observations per child) (Quinlan 1995). Interview data are from thirty-five children in the 2008 sample and fourteen adults who were primary guardians of household children, usually the mother (actually twelve mothers, one grandmother, and one mother's brother), from each household.

Participant-Observation

P-O (DeWalt et al. 1998) was used to achieve qualitative understanding of the Dominican way of life and people's views, specifically those that deal television. Opportunities for P-O in television-watching abound in this community, as it is normal for neighbors to visit with the purpose of watching television. Parents are particularly glad for another adult to be with their children while they are busy. For this project, we remained ever curious of what people were watching on television and took note of what programming was most prevalent among community members during certain times and how people interacted during television-watching. Through television participation, we witnessed the general program preferences of the youth and heard what people had to say about the shows. Within the television-watching context we could conduct informal interviews with our fellow audience members (Bernard 2005). For example, we might ask who a favorite character was and why, or whether they had seen that particular episode before. P-O enabled us to internalize a general understanding of the nature of TV viewing among young people and family television interaction.

Semi-Structured Parental Interviews

Semi-structured interviews were conducted (by JH) in participant's homes using a predetermined interview guide of questions that were reviewed and reworded by a local consultant to reflect local dialect, thereby avoiding potential linguistic confusions (Quinlan 2004). A primary guardian was asked a series of questions pertaining to the relative time frame they acquired television and related technologies in their homes and the family's general patterns and taste of television-watching. Objectives were to gain an idea of local viewing preferences and also a grasp on the general attitudes about television among villagers.

Semi-Structured Interviews With Children

The primary aim of youth interviews was to gather information regarding children's television preferences. Children were asked (by JH) if they had a television in their own home, or where they watched TV, with whom they watched, and if they watched local or Caribbean television shows.

Free-List Interviews For Salience

During the same session in which JH conducted the semi-structured interviews, she conducted free-list interviews about television with Bwa Mawegan parents and children. Children's free lists provided quantifiable data on their favorite channels and shows. Adults' free lists offered data on guardians' views of the costs, benefits, and overall changes that they believed television had brought to village children.

In a free-list interview, an informant simply lists things in an emic category or "cultural domain" in whatever order they come to mind. The resulting list is a basic inventory of the items the informant knows or thinks of within the domain (Weller and Romney 1988; Bernard 2005). The established ethnographic assumptions of the method are threefold. First, individuals who know a lot about a subject list more terms than people who know less (geographic experts can list many countries [Brewer 1995]). Second, people tend to list terms in order of familiarity (people list the kin term "mother" before "aunt," and "aunt" before "great-aunt" [Romney and D'Andrade 1964]). And third, terms that most respondents mention indicate locally prominent items (Pennsylvanians list "apple" and "birch" trees more frequently and earlier than they do "orange" or "palm" [Gatewood 1983]).

With a parent/guardian in each of the fourteen families in the 2008 sample, JH obtained three free lists. Prompts elicited (a) the good things that watching television has done for village children, (b) any bad impacts that watching television has had on village children, and (c) changes that they had observed in village children since television came. Parents' lists were analyzed for salience to find those television-attributed changes with the greatest cognitive and cultural significance among the sample of respondents. JH obtained two free lists from thirty-five youth participants: favorite television programs, and favorite television channels.

Salience (or Smith's S, see Smith [1993]) is a statistic that accounts for an item's frequency of mention and is also weighted for list position, e.g., in the domain of English color terms, "red" is more salient—it appears more often and earlier in free lists—than "maroon" (Smith et al. 1995).

Salience analysis ranks each item in an individual's free list and divides by the number of items listed, then finds the mean salience value for every listed item across all informants to reveal the intracultural salience of each item (see Smith 1993; Quinlan 2005). Generally, items with the highest salience values are those that villagers mention more often and more immediately.

Whereas free-list prompts generally ask informants to name as many items in the domain as the informant can think of, JH instead asked each subject to "name three" items in each domain. This was done for expedience in consideration of the families being interviewed, as the concern here was not to address intracultural variation or knowledge differences, as with, say an ethnobiological study. For this reason, the data show several tied scores (rare in varied-length free lists).

Instantaneous Behavioral Scans

Children's time allocation was measured using instantaneous behavioral scans. The method was a modified version of "spot check" behavioral sampling (Hames 1992; Quinlan 1995; Johnson and Sackett 1998). A circular route that passed through every household's yard was established, and twice daily, beginning from a randomly selected point and direction, a researcher walked the entire route and recorded the name, nearest neighbors, location, activities, and time for each individual encountered.

Instantaneous sampling obtains multiple "snapshots of individual behaviors over the study period" (Paolisso and Hames 2010, 367). The spot check method is well suited to research in Bwa Mawego because daytime activity takes place in family yards, in houses with open doors and windows, and on footpaths used for moving about the village, and people are generally visible (even while watching television). In addition, villagers are accustomed to exchanging greetings and small talk with people who pass by their yards and houses. Scans were conducted on thirty days between May and August of 1993 and 1994 (by Robert and Marsha Quinlan) and on ten days in May and June of 2008 (by Jenna Hansen). The 1993–1994 Activities were coded under nine broad categories of behavior, including (1) childcare, (2) chores, (3) eat/drink, (4) hygiene, (5) transport, (6) play, (7) passive, (8) conversation, and (9) subsistence, with various subcodes under each. In 2008, "television" was added as a subcode under "passive." The first scan of the day took place at a randomly determined time between 7:00 a.m. and 12:00 p.m. The second scan started at least six hours after the first to reduce the likelihood of dependent observations. The 1993–1994 sample includes 1,074 observations of twenty-one boys and twenty-two girls between age three and seventeen. The 2008 sample contains 178 observations of thirty-one children ages three to seventeen. Although the number of observations per individual in the 2008 sample is too small for detailed time allocation profiles, it is suggestive.

Informed Consent

Prior informed consent from parents and assent for children was obtained verbally at the time of each interview and for each field season that included instantaneous behavioral scans. Internal review boards of the University of Missouri and Washington State University examined and approved human subjects protocol for the protection of the study participants. The research followed ethical guidelines adopted by the American Anthropological Association (American Anthropological Association 2009).

FINDINGS

More than half of Bwa Mawego's households own television sets, and, because many homes are part of extended family compounds, almost everyone (and each child in this sample) has regular access to television. Television viewing is a decidedly social activity in Bwa Mawego. Compared to before cable, when video-watching might be a neighborhood event, cable television-watching tends to be somewhat more private for the household, although neighbors still visit to watch television, including neighbors without televisions and neighbors (children) who are not interested in what is on their own household's set. Further, households contain several generations who share the television. It is rare for someone to watch television alone.

During the early day, adults are generally busy with food preparation, gardening, and various other work, so television-watching is for young people. By midday or afternoon, women, teens, and elders may take in a soap opera, music videos, or reality television during food preparation or folding laundry, but televisions remain dominated by children during the day. At home, during the evenings, old and young women, youth, and children form the preponderance of television viewers. In Dominica, as Spitulnik (2002) notes in Zambia, the male head of household may be absent during leisure time. Dominican males between the ages of twenty to sixty frequently spend evenings away from home (in rum shops or with friends—often watching TV there) while the rest of their family socializes with one another around the television. Because evening television-watching is a multigenerational event, families tend to watch shows that do not require close concentration, but rather lend themselves to continuous social commentary, cheering, booing, and other interaction. Game shows and competitive reality shows, soap operas, and movies aimed at general audiences are most popular for family viewing. As others have found, Dominicans will understand or filter television content using their own culture-specific logic; however, the zany, ridiculous, and comedic scenarios of the common selections in the presence of children appear to sidestep some of the potential cultural translation issues.

Television sets appear to be, as Kottak (1991) found and as posited in H1, a status symbol in ownership—both through owning the set and through the invisible but perceptible ownership of television-related knowledge, i.e., knowing about the current news or television characters, dramatic plots, and humor. Knowledge of television programming creates a sort of "in" crowd in this village that has been, until recently, mostly egalitarian with shared knowledge. Television owners enjoy the possibility of a sort of generosity—inviting neighbors without a television over to watch TV. Here television owners offer their neighbors not just the experience of watching the television at that occasion, but a window into the knowledge on the popular programs that are part of local social discourse. Television owner's statuses additionally increase not only through their generosity in television-sharing, but by their consequent status as a host. Hosting gives the TV owner authority over guests in his/her house (e.g., a TV homeowner may eject a visiting child who is not respectful of the TV owner's child, food, house, etc.).

H2 predicts that television will usher more liberal views into the cultural mix. Our ethnographic observations support this idea. Although still relatively conservative and with certain intracultural variation, rural Dominican views have become somewhat more liberal regarding gender issues. Evidence is that one now hears individuals declare the acceptability of family planning, the unacceptability of corporal discipline of children and spouses, and some consideration for tolerance of homosexuals (whereas in years past, rural villagers only voiced the opposite views). Female dress has become evidently less conservative after television exposure.

The most salient channels that Bwa Mawego's youth listed as their favorite channels were the Disney Chanel, followed by Cartoon Network (see Table 11.1), such that we cannot reject H3 (preference for Disney) nor H4 (preference for cartons). Starz (a movie channel) and BET (Black Entertainment Television) were generally a second or third choice among adolescents, whereas Boomerang (a child-oriented network) ranked second or third among young children.

Disney's *Hannah Montana*, a situation-comedy about a teenager with a secret life as a pop star, and the classic cat and mouse cartoon *Tom and Jerry*, appearing on both Cartoon Network and Boomerang, tied for the two most salient "favorite shows" (see Table 11.2 and Figure 11.1). Although adolescents tended to list *Hannah Montana* first and younger children tended to list *Tom and Jerry* first, both of these shows appeared

Table 11.1   Salience and Frequency of Channels Children Watch Most

Channel	Salience	Frequency
Disney Channel	0.65	41
Cartoon Network	0.57	36
Starz	0.18	11
BET	0.14	9
Boomerang	0.13	8

Table 11.2   Salience and Frequency of Television Shows that Youths Listed as Their Favorites—Not Shown Are Forty-Seven Titles that Were Given Only Once

Show	Salience	Frequency
Hannah Montana	0.27	17
Tom and Jerry	0.27	17
Movies	0.13	8
SpongeBob	0.10	6
Ben 10	0.08	5
That's So Raven	0.05	3

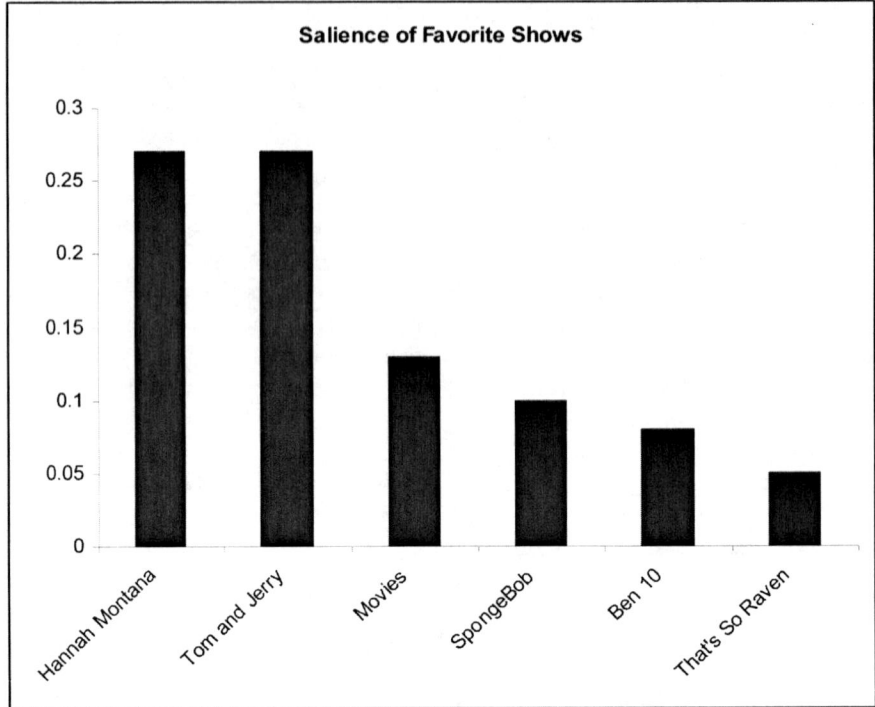

Figure 11.1   Saliences of shows children and adolescents listed as their favorites, not counting forty-seven single mentions.

Table 11.3   Salience and Frequency of Items that Parents List as Good Things that Television Does for Their Children

Good functions of TV	Salience	Frequency
Exposure to daily news	0.357	5
Good for school	0.286	4
Global awareness	0.286	4
Teaches songs and dances	0.286	4
Teaches about Bible	0.214	3
Improves language	0.143	2
Builds confidence	0.143	2
Entertains	0.071	1

on children's and adolescent's lists, which accounts for their high overall salience. Rather than name a specific program, eight youths listed that they liked to watch "movies," which may refer to feature-length Disney films and to more adult-oriented movies on the Starz network, mentioned by several teens. As a cartoon with adult-aimed humor, *SpongeBob Square Pants* appealed to both younger and older youths. *Ben 10*, a cartoon about a child hero, was then listed by younger viewers, whereas *That's So Raven*, a Disney sitcom about a musical and clairvoyant African American teenage girl, was popular among adolescents. Dominican children explained, and free lists confirmed, that they especially enjoy shows with music and cartoons.

Interviews with parents revealed mixed feelings about the changes that television has created. When asked to free list the "good things" that television does for their children, they had no problem listing benefits. Most salient were ideas related to urbaneness: television exposed youth to daily news, improved their school performance, and made them globally aware (see Table 11.3 and Figure 11.2). Some parents also noted personal educational benefits for the children, such as teaching them songs and dances, teaching them about the Bible, and improving their English and confidence. Interestingly, only one parent mentioned the children's entertainment as a benefit.

When asked about the "bad impacts" that television has for their children, parents were more reluctant to list; however, the items of concern that parents listed are also topics of parental conversations and complaints. The most salient negatives were a concern that girls have begun to dress more provocatively; that kids, especially boys, are more aggressive or rude; and

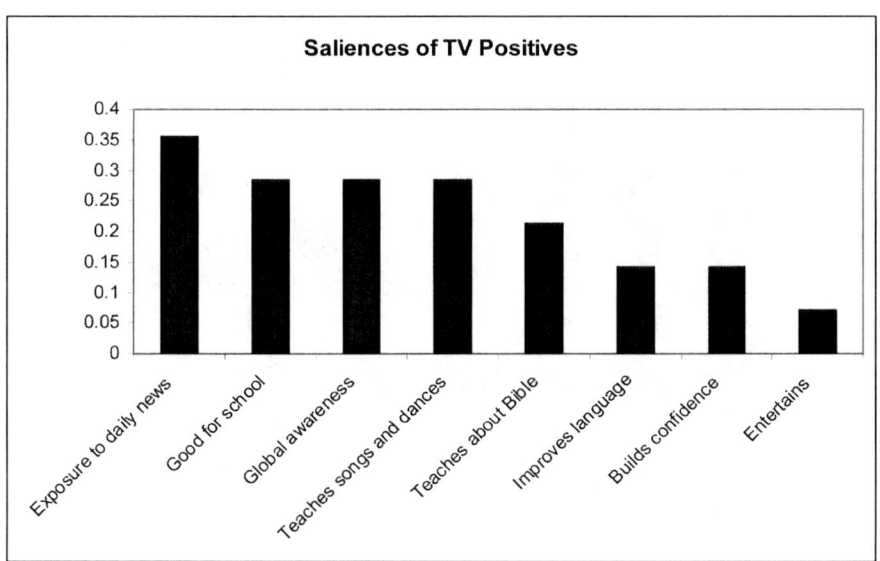

Figure 11.2   Salience of items parents listed as good things television does for children.

that boys copy American urban gangster behaviors/style (see Table 11.4 and Figure 11.3). Some parents also listed that television increases attitude problems in young children, attributing it to rude characters in cartoons, and some say that it increases "partying" in teens.

After asking about the positive and negative impacts of television, JH in effect asked parents to summarize by asking them to free list the "biggest

Table 11.4   Salience and Frequency of Items that Parents List as Bad Impacts that Television Has on Their Children

Negative impact of TV	Salience	Frequency
Provocative dressing	0.5714	8
Encourages violence/aggression	0.5	7
Introduces U.S. gang-like behaviors	0.5	7
Increases bad/negative attitude	0.2143	3
Increases "partying"	0.2143	3
Gives false impression of relationships	0.1429	2
More "dirty dancing"	0.0714	1
Bad for health (eyes)	0.0714	1
Creates unrealistic demand for things	0.0714	1

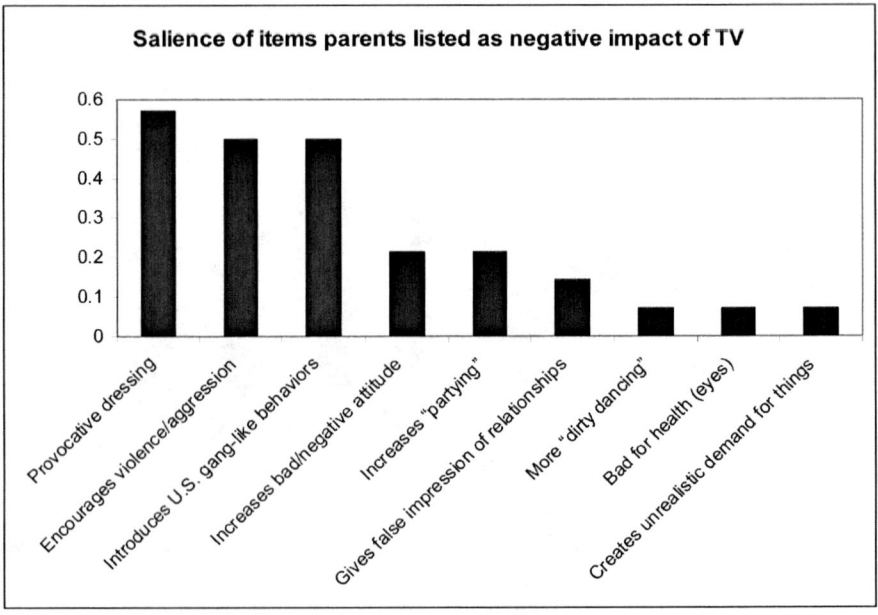

Figure 11.3   Salience of items parents listed as television's bad impacts on children.

changes" they had observed in children since television came to the village. The outcome of this list is interesting because it highlights parents' complaints (see Table 11.5 and Figure 11.4). Here, girls' provocative dress and boys' gangster style were most salient, followed by concerns about increased aggression and bad attitudes. Two parents perceived that more "partying" resulted from television. These responses provide support for H5, that parents would attribute moral degradation to television. A couple of parents noted increased seclusion as a problem, which shows at least

Table 11.5   Salience and Frequency of Items that Parents List as Biggest Changes They Had Observed in Children since Television Came to the Village

Changes listed	Salience	Frequency
Girls dress provocatively	0.50	7
Boys copy U.S. gangster style	0.43	6
More violent/aggressive	0.29	4
More bad/negative attitudes	0.21	3
More teen "partying"	0.14	2
More secluded/less social	0.14	2
More materialistic	0.07	1
More ways to show talents	0.07	1

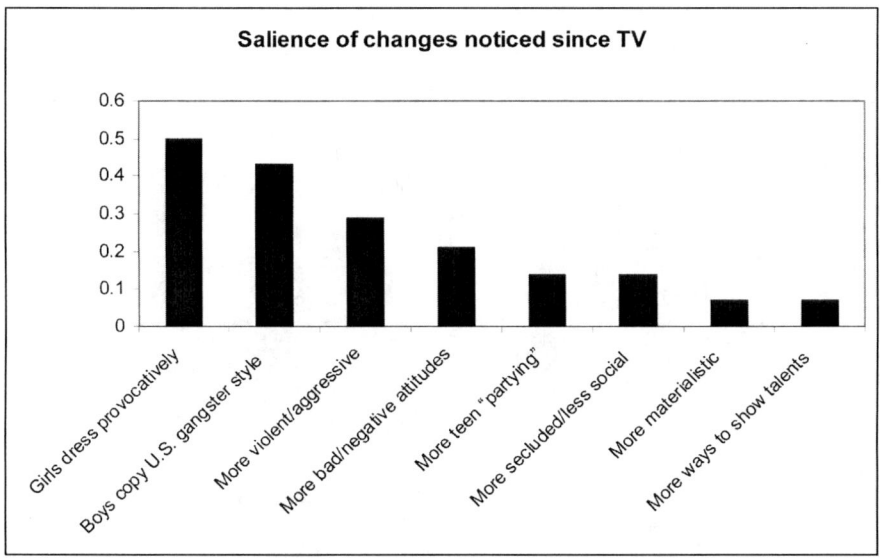

Figure 11.4   Salience of items parents listed as changes they had observed in village children since television's arrival.

some concern for that phenomenon. Only one parent mentioned television increasing children's materialism. With this small sample, we cannot reject H6, that television will increase materialism, but can say that materialism is not a prevalent concern in this community so far.

There is some support for H7, that television will increase rural Dominican youths' knowledge of Standard English. Although parents did not mention this in their assessment of "biggest changes," the increased knowledge of Standard English is likely behind several of the items that parents listed as positive impact from television. Not only did some parents specify that television "improves language," but may reflect the relationship between TV and Standard English when they note that watching television is "good for school."

Of JH's 2008 spot checks for children's time allocation between 7:00 a.m. and 7:00 p.m., forty-seven out of 175 (27 percent) observed children watching television as a primary activity, with an additional ten observances of watching television as a secondary activity (e.g., watching TV while folding laundry or having one's hair styled). Children and adolescents thus spend one-third (32.6 percent) of their day watching television in some way.

The 2008 time allocation data (see correlations in Table 11.6) finds that boys in Bwa Mawego spend less time watching television than do girls. We must then reject H8, that boys will watch more television than girls, which has been found elsewhere but is not true here. As proposed in H9, there is a strong negative correlation between play and television-watching (r = .8) such that children who watch more television spend less time playing. There is not a significant correlation between television-watching and time spent in frankly passive activity.

Multiple linear regression with data from 2008 and 1993–1994 (Table 11.7) show that, although the two are not correlated within the 2008

Table 11.6   Shows Bivariate Correlations among Time Spent in Play, Passive, and Watching TV for Twenty-Nine Children between Age Two and Seventeen in 2008

Correlations (obs = 20)	TV	Play	Passive	Age	Sex
TV	1				
Play	-0.80	1.00			
Passive	-0.04	-0.55	1.00		
age	0.36	-0.35	0.14	1.00	
sex (male = 1)	-0.24	0.43	-0.46	-0.04	1.00

Notes: The analysis shows a strong negative association between play and TV watching (r = -.80), indicating that the more time spent watching TV the less time spent playing. TV watching is not associated with time spent passive. Boys watch less TV than girls (r = -.24) and TV-watching increases with age (r = .36).

population, children before television in 1993–1994 did spend almost twice as much time being frankly passive as do the children in 2008 (Table 11.7, model A). This lends support for H10, that 2008 children will spend less time being frankly passive than 1993–1994 (as children will instead rest/relax in front of television). Although there is currently a negative correlation between television-watching and play, we nevertheless find that children's play has increased by 18 percent since 1993–194 (Table 11.7, model B) despite the availability of television (owing to other modernizations resulting in less chore time). We also find significant relationships between age, sex, and play, such that boys play 13 percent more than girls and with every additional year of age children play 3 percent less.

Table 11.7 Shows Multiple Linear Regression Models Comparing Time Spent Passive and Time Spent Playing for Children in 1993–1994 (before TV) Compared to Children from 2008

Number of observations	56	
Model A		
Prob > F	0.02	
R-squared	0.17	
Passive	*Coef.*	*Sig.*
Old = 1	0.10	0.01
Age	0.00	0.51
Sex (male = 1)	-0.06	0.10
Constant	0.10	0.11
Model B		
Prob > F	0.00	
R-squared	0.44	
Play	*Coef.*	*Sig.*
Old = 1	-0.18	0.00
Age	-0.03	0.00
Sex (male = 1)	0.13	0.01
Constant	0.64	0.00

Notes: Results show that on average children spend 10 percent of their time passively (constant in Table 11.2, model A) and children in 1993–1994 (old) spent twice as much passive time as did children in 2008. Model B shows that on average children spent 64 percent of their time playing (constant) and that children in 1993–1994 spent 18 percent less time playing than did children in 2008. There were also significant associations between age, sex, and playing such that older children play 3 percent less per year than younger children and boys play 13 percent more than do girls.

DISCUSSION

Television viewing in Dominica is a social activity. Dominicans watch TV in groups and share continuous social reactions to the programming. Davis and Davis (1995) posit that, as language comprehension increases, television viewing may become less interactive. Although it is true that rural Dominican have varying levels of Standard English comprehension, it is difficult to imagine a rural Dominica in which gatherings for laughing, talking, and socializing do not occur in some way, especially in the evenings. So far, television is being integrated into rather than replacing the essential nature of this evening "together time" tradition.

As mentioned in the section on findings, television sets appear to be status objects for their owners. However, Bwa Mawegans try to downplay the status of their televisions as they have an ethic that no one should display a noticeable interest in the accumulation of material goods. Their modesty stems from an image of "limited good," a common view among peasants that the quantity of good fortune within a community is limited so that if one resident has excessive good luck, another's luck will turn bad (Foster 1965). Bwa Mawegans diffuse their wealth of having a television by sharing the set with family and neighbors (nearby neighbors are often relatives). As more people watch television, the programs may become relational, that is, the shows become topics for conversation and comparison (Lull 1990). A child who could not discuss *Hannah Montana* or *Tom and Jerry* would become a sort of social outsider, potentially. There is no such child in our sample, however, as all kids have the opportunity to watch television with their cousins and friends, even if their household has no TV set.

As has been observed elsewhere, rural Dominican views have become somewhat more liberal regarding gender issues, such that the youths of the television generation grow up not only forming their own potentially more liberal opinions, but with some conversion going on among the parental generation. This matrifocal community with often absent or ineffectual fathers has always had a bias in female education and stressed female earning ability (Quinlan 2006); however, traditional rejection of birth control tempered the effects of those values, as mothers were encumbered by constant demands of large families. Various local health and social organizations have been promoting the idea of family planning as a correlate of female health and success. By the late 1990s a minority of women began using birth control. Television reinforced the idea of family planning as a route to success through programming in which small, relatively wealthy families, with career-having mothers are a norm. Likewise, television programming presents male physical threats over women and children as wrong or illegal, and toleration of homosexuals as normal, or at least controversial. Villagers are beginning to debate the possibilities of these liberal views. At the same time, liberal (more provocative) dress for females has entered the culture. Caribbean researchers Brown and Wilk debate whether television's acculturating impact is more positive or negative for Caribbean communities (Brown 2001; Wilk 2002).

As we hypothesized in H3, the Disney Channel was most popular among interviewed youth. In the U.S., Disney is uniquely successful in attracting very young viewers as well as teenage audiences due to its wide range of both cartoon and live-action programming, and their formula of family sit-coms is particularly efficacious to this broad youth audience (Giroux 2001). Those families in Bwa Mawego who have home television sets have one sole set, which is placed in the home's common area in order to accommodate the maximum amount of viewers. (Interior walls of Bwa Mawegan houses rarely reach the ceiling, so that rooms are stall-like, and sounds carry from one room to another. Economics aside, multiple TVs would not make sense without architectural change as well.) Therefore, it is likely that G-rated shows such as *Hannah Montana* and *That's So Raven* are regularly viewed in homes with youth of varying ages. Further, P-O of Disney Channel viewing revealed that nearly all commercials on the Dominican version of the Disney Channel are for Disney products or other Disney shows. The Disney Corporation can afford not to have exterior institutions pay them for advertising because they generate income from various Disney merchandise (ibid.). The Disney Channel is itself its own commercial, both for the channel and for all of its other enterprises from which it derives profits (amusement parks, toys, movies, snacks, etc.) (Giroux 2008). Although very few Disney products are sold in Dominica, and Bwa Mawegans will likely never travel to Disney World, these products are nevertheless attractive to Bwa Mawegan youth. This channel is the most salient in young people's minds.

Dominican children, especially younger ones, prefer animated cartoon images. This explains the salience of the Cartoon Network and Boomerang, and Disney, which blends animation with live action. The combination of bright, flashing colors; quick movements; fantasy characters; and goofy voices captivate children (Mallory 1998; Huston et al. 2007). In seamlessly merging humor and violence with quick pace and animation, cartoons that are designed for children serve to ensure the most attention and attraction to the images (Huston et al. 2007, 45).

The popularity of the cartoon *Tom and Jerry*, which tied with Disney's *Hannah Montana* for the most salient favorite show (see Table 11.2 and Figure 11.1), is a prime example of the way that cartoon violence successfully attracts children (Cantor 1998). As one of the most successful series to come out of the Hanna-Barbera limited animation technique (Mallory 1998), *Tom and Jerry* has since the 1960s featured the ever-impending tribulations that ensue during a cat and mouse chase. There are a number of factors that contribute to the show's immense popularity among the youth of Bwa Mawego. First, the cartoon's characters are recognizable to everyone in the village as semi-wild cats and mice are commonly seen rummaging through garbage piles and also lounging on doorsteps. Next, the cartoon serves to appeal to even the youngest audiences and speakers of non-Standard Dominican English Creole because it does not employ the use of dialogue in its comedic act. The absence of language allows for the avoidance of linguistic misinterpretations that would serve to lessen its comedic translation between American English and the local dialect. Last, its use of repeated and constant violence in its jokes may serve to make the show practically irresistible to young viewers (Cantor 1998).

Miller's (1992) study of American soap operas in Trinidad reveals an active process of societal self-production through which people incorporate objects into their own value system. This is evident with Dominican adults more so than children because the ridiculous or magical societies and scenarios of children's programming (e.g., talking animals, child rock stars, superhero transformations) are similarly unlikely to children in the production society. Yet, the cultural filter still pertains. An important supporting character in *Tom and Jerry*, a mostly salient show, is an African American maid caricature, Mammy Two Shoes, who remains faceless (the viewer only sees her shoes and maid's uniform) as she antagonizes both Tom and Jerry. As King et al. (2010, 395) note, "animation has historically fed on blackness, recycling caricatures—such as Mammy Two Shoes in Tom and Jerry." This negative stereotype is lost on these new Dominican children viewers, who refer to Mammy Two Shoes as "the mom," and only remark at how indulgent the "mom" is to ever allow, and even *feed*, the cat in the house.

Dominican parents' opined overall that television was educational for their children. They noted that it made the young people more aware of the world in terms of geography, current events, and science. Parents indicated that television has improved children's school performance, and mothers like that it gives children new songs and dances and new words and helps them to better "express their talents." It has been demonstrated that positive, nonviolent programming such as *Mister Roger's Neighborhood*, does develop prosocial helping behavior among children (Murray 2007). Although educational shows were not salient favorites, young children do watch educational programming, especially on Boomerang, the Disney Channel, and the Catholic channel's morning programming, and older children do watch news.

We hypothesized that television would improve children's knowledge of Standard English. Interestingly, parents realize that children are doing better in school, but do not necessarily relate the success to language skills. Villagers speak two Creole languages, French Patois (*Kwéyòl*) and Dominican English Creole (Roberts 1988). Television programming, whether presented in a West Indian, American, or British English dialect or accent, contains a standardized English grammar, which is foreign to rural Dominicans. Television should improve knowledge of Standard English. Dominican teachers lament that it is hard for children from rural schools to read and write well and to do well on national exams because rural children are not fluent in the Standard English of the educational materials. Improved fluency in

Standard English would make English reading and writing easier for these children who grow up speaking Creole versions of English and French. It explains how parents would be correct when they note that watching television is "good for school." Parents, of course, continue to communicate with their children in the Creole-language forms of the region, and do not necessarily realize that their children have developed excellent passive knowledge of Standard (particularly American) English. We American researchers do notice the difference. Researchers from the U.S. can now speak to and be understood by young Dominicans without translating into Dominican English Creole. This was not the case before there were any televisions. Throughout the 1990s, even occasional video-watching somewhat improved Dominican comprehension of American English (Quinlan 2004); however, the ability of post-cable Dominican youths to understand American field school students was unprecedented. It is not surprising that reading and writing scores would improve.

The salient "biggest changes" that Dominican parents noted were, nevertheless, all negative reactions to television. We predicted in H5 that parents would perceive moral degradation in youth and that they would blame this corruption on television. This proved true.

The most salient negative impact and change after television that parents noted was teenage girls' more provocative style of dress. This concern conforms with Caribbean parents' tradition of daughter-guarding (Flinn 1992). Before television, women usually wore dresses, although younger women often wore pants. For their most informal wear, Bwa Mawegan females wore Bermuda-style shorts (to the knee) and sleeved shirts or sleeveless shirts with coverage from the neck to the top of the arm. Now, it is common for young women to wear short skirts or short shorts and to leave their shoulders mostly bare. Elders determine that this dress is sexually risky, "inappropriate," and driven by the women's styles present on television, particularly the (mostly Jamaican) Caribbean music videos on the BET channel (those videos predictably contain several scenes in which the camera is zoomed in on the dancing, miniskirt-clad rear end of a woman). In truth, global clothing styles in "junior" sizes are simply in a more provocative trend. Whether girls get their clothes from stores in town, from local hucksters, or from Catholic Charities, short shorts and shirts with spaghetti straps abound, and likely would with or without television, although television may buttress the style as normal in the global market.

Parent's assertion that television is promoting more aggressive and violent behavior among today's youth makes sense in light of findings from the over one thousand published reports on the issue of TV and violence over the past fifty years (Murray 2007). Humans are innately interested in (even if repulsed by) violence, and children's television programs often use violence to attract audiences because it works so well (Murray 2001; Murray et al. 2006). By the time a typical U.S. child finishes elementary school he has witnessed about eight thousand murders on television (Singer et al. 1998).

Fifty years of television research indicates that televised violence does affect viewer's attitudes, values, and behavior (Hearold 1986; Murray 1994; Paik and Comstock 1994). It effects how children develop a worldview, and it often leads to more aggressive behavior later in life (Murray 2007). In investigating the effects of light versus heavy viewers, increased television consumption associates with the development of a fearful perception of the world, described as the "mean world syndrome" effect, in which children grow to believe that "greater protection is needed, that most people can't be trusted, and that most people are just looking out for themselves"(Gerbner et al. 1994, 30). Research shows that even the far-fetched realities in the cartoon universe serve to influence violent behavior, as children who view violent television programs become desensitized to violence and are more willing to tolerate aggressive behavior in others (Drabman and Thomas 1974). That increased violence and aggression was the second most listed change parents mentioned is not then surprising, even after four years or less of exposure.

Less troublesome than violence, but still vexing to parents, is an observation that children have become ruder and developed bad or negative attitudes from watching television. Parents particularly complain that the impetuous voices and attitudes of cartoon characters are more "troublesome" than comical. We have observed a few parents specifically instructing their children not to use a "cartoon voice" with them. This concurs with Lashley's finding in Trinidad and Tobago that American television influenced negative behavior in some of the youth, a phenomenon coined by some high school students as "a 'Bart Simpson' syndrome" (Lashley 1995, 91).

Television appears tied to capitalist values globally, including in the Caribbean. For example, among Jamaican high school students, Brown (1995) found a positive linear relationship between media use, consumerism, and externally driven cultural orientation. We predicted (H6) that parents would complain of increased TV-related consumerism or materialism among Bwa Mawego's youth. The rural Dominican television experience appears to contrast with this television influence elsewhere as only one parent mentioned materialism as a change since television (and that was a low-ranking response), and the one parent who mentioned it as a bad impact of television specified that television "creates unrealistic demand for things." Indeed, the products on television are largely not available in Dominica or so far out of reach for villagers that there is no real demand for such products. Bwa Mawegan youth do not hence appear to be increasingly capitalistic or materialistic as a result of television. The vast majority of parents do not indicate a consumerism trend as a negative or a change, and our observations concur. We attribute this little-affected materialism to Bwa Mawego's remoteness and relative absence from the larger market economy. Other than the typically closet-size shops that sell few supplies (e.g., matches, sugar, flour, a few canned goods, rum by the shot), there are no stores in or near the village. Jobs with wages are rare for villagers. For most people, the spending money that they earn from their bay leaf crop, odd jobs, and remittances must go directly into essentials such as protein, basic provisions, clothing, tuition, and the utilities of water, electricity, cell phone minutes, and, now, cable television.

Researchers have identified television as increasing a desire for upward mobility (Fisherkeller 1997) and causing young people to move away for better jobs. In Bwa Mawego, this phenomenon has occurred for generations, and it is difficult to say whether television itself has had any impact on the already hemorrhaging village population. Others critique that television promotes lifestyles that can never be attained locally (Davis and Davis 1995; Reis 1998). This is certainly true in Bwa Mawego; again, however, villagers experienced the relative wealth of other places through the correspondence, remittances, and returns of numerous migrating relatives long before television.

Although elsewhere boys have been found to watch more television than girls, this is not the case in Bwa Mawego. We attribute this to a local matrifocal pattern of time allocation. Males, from childhood through adulthood, spend less time at home (Quinlan et al. 2005; Quinlan 2006). Boys are out of the house playing and foraging for snacks more often than girls, who are home more than boys. Men, similarly, are out of the house, both for work in gardens at the village periphery and during leisure time when they tend to socialize with other males. Meanwhile, girls and women stay home more and do more household chores, some of which might allow one time to catch some television.

Our time allocation findings regarding television, play, and passive activity require some explanation. A comparison of time allocation to play in 1993–1994 and 2008 finds that the latter children play more despite having televisions for recreation. At first glimpse, because contemporary children are playing more than 1993–1994 children, it appears that we should reject H9 (that 2008 children with television will spend less of their leisure time playing); however, the quality and quantity of leisure time has changed dramatically. Although this chapter is about the introduction of television, television did not appear alone. Rather, as discussed earlier, television was one element in a suite of modernization that occurred in Bwa Mawego at the turn of the millennium in the wake of a piped water and road improvement project. Although the 2008 data set is small and suggestive only, it indicates some major shifts in time allocation.

On average, 2008 kids spent 32 percent of their time watching television. This is a larger time allocation than *any* 1993–1994 activity. The largest time allocation category for the old sample was 28 percent for being passive, followed by 23 percent in play. Also, children had more responsibilities that took up their time before recent modernizations. Children in our 1993–1994 sample spent 14.61 percent of their time in household chores, compared to 2.35 percent in 2008. Before piped water, every family member had to trek daily to the river to bathe and launder and go to and from the spring for drinking water. This took considerable time and energy. Once people had piped water close to home, not only did a lot of carrying end, but many families bought a type of relatively inexpensive portable plastic washing machine. Of all modern appliances, the washing machine is the one that truly results in the greatest net work savings (Cowan 1983). By washing at home, women save a lot of time and labor, thereby freeing siblings from alloparenting. Children, now freed from the water fetching and laundry of previous years, have time to watch television. Time spent in "transport" activities decreased by 3.2 percent between the studies (from to 6.6 percent to 3.4 percent). We also attribute this to modernization. First, before cell phones, children were regularly sent around the village to deliver things and messages. Now, people more often send a text message. Further, with the improved road and more frequent passing of vehicles, it is extremely common for people to wave down a local driver for a ride up the central road, which cuts time and effort from transport—again increasing leisure time. Finally, children spent 4 percent of time in childcare in 1993–1994 and 0 percent in 2008. In previous years, older brothers and, more often, older sisters cared for their younger siblings while parents engaged in other work, and this alloparenting was obvious to an observer as the older sibling was often carrying or holding the younger one. Now, with television, one observes children of all ages sitting side by side watching the television rather than engaging in an active caregiver–care-receiver interaction. Although older children are still reckoned the responsible party, sibling alloparenting has become passive and absent in appearance, and what is observable is that children are watching television.

We thus see that leisure time comprised 51 percent of children's observable time in 1993–1994, whereas in 2008 leisure activities comprise 62.86 percent of children's time. Children spent 45 percent of their leisure time playing in 1993–1994 whereas, after television, 2008 children only spend 27 percent of their leisure time playing (and 49 percent of their leisure time watching television). We cannot then reject H9, that children with television spend less of their leisure time playing. Our data provide strong support for this hypothesis. These proportions indicate that television time is, in effect, coming out of would-be playtime, thus the negative correlation between television and play. This contrasts with U.S. findings in which researchers found no relationship between time spent watching television and time in active play (Vanderwater et al. 2006).

Play is important for child development. Many researchers (see, e.g., Lillemyr 2009; Pelligrini 2009) propose that play is an adaptive, organized means by which children learn to make sense of their physical and social environment. Through mastery, rule play, and pretending—all inherent in play—children gain a feeling of control and learn to overcome fears (Hurwitz 2002). They learn to navigate groups, to share, and to self-advocate (Erikson 1985). Play stimulates "all aspects of a child's development"

(Lillemyr 2009, 8). We do not know whether there is a saturation point to the benefits of play; however, it seems that more play should be better. The exercise of active play would be particularly good for these modernized Dominican children whose daily 2008 lives require substantially less effort than the steep water-hauling, message delivering, and so forth, of previous years. Active time certainly reduces children's cortisol, leptin, and insulin levels, which are health dangers if elevated (Karacabey 2009).

Multiple linear regression with data from 2008 and 1993–1994 (Table 10.7) shows that children before television in 1993–1994 did spend almost twice as much time being frankly passive or idle (apparently resting, doing "nothing," or zoning out) as do the children in 2008. Back in 1993–1994, our observations found children passive during 54.9 percent of their free time. In 2008, not counting TV time, children were frankly passive for only 25.6 percent of their leisure time. Although television and frankly passive time are not correlated, the difference in time allocation between the two samples is substantial. If television or modernization decreases passive time, it is at modern children's detriment. Recent research indicates that individuals who are idle—who are daydreaming, "zoning out," or whose minds are wandering—exercise a crucial mental state simultaneously using "executive functioning" and "default" brain networks associated with imagination and planning more deeply than at other times. Although people are not aware of it, they are often solving problems when their minds wander (Smallwood and Schooler 2006; Belton and Priyadharshini 2007; Mason et al. 2007; Smallwood et al. 2007).

Compared to children in 1993–1994, modernized Dominican children have little responsibility, play slightly more (though proportionately less of their free time), are frankly passive less, and watch a lot of television. Television may deliver benefits to the population. It can provide opportunities for early language and concept learning not otherwise available, and early learning and experience has the potential to enhance positive developmental outcomes (Weber 2006). Watching television at ages three to five has demonstrated benefits to later reading skills (although watching before age three has detrimental effects) (Zimmerman and Christakis 2005). Further, Dominican parents note that television has improved children's school performance. Nevertheless, Dominican parents note behavioral concerns (e.g., rudeness, aggression) that are supported by literature for other populations. According to an American Academy of Pediatrics (2001) policy statement, possible negative health effects of television viewing on children include but are not limited to: violent or aggressive behavior; decreased school performance, poor body image, and obesity. In particular, data from a tri-ethnic longitudinal study in Texas found that children's body mass index is predicted by television viewing and physical activity, not by diet (Jago et al. 2005). Current and future Dominican families will have to keep these risks well in mind as their children engage in passive televised entertainment.

272   *Marsha B. Quinlan and Jenna R. Hansen*

ACKNOWLEDGMENTS

We are thankful to the Dominican people who accepted us with kindness, especially to the families who participated in this television project. Many thanks to Rob Quinlan for sharing data and offering statistical consultation. Thank you, Bonnie Hewlett, for giving us the opportunity to join this extraordinary volume.

REFERENCES

Abu-Lughod, L. "The Interpretation of Culture(s) after Television," Representations 59 (1997): 109–134.
———. 2005. Dramas of a Nationhood: the Politics of Television in Egypt. Chicago: University of Chicago Press.
Ad & Marketing News. 2011. "Time Spent Watching TV: Television Bureau of Advertising's TV Basics with Data from Nielsen Co. NTI Annual Averages." On http://adage.com/article/mediaworks/time-spent-watching-tv/227022/ (accessed April 26, 2012).
American Academy of Pediatrics. "Policy Statement, 'Children, Adolescents, and Television'(RE0043)," Pediatrics 107, no. 2 (2001): 423.
American Anthropological Association. 2009. "Code of Ethics of the American Anthropological Association." On http://www.aaanet.org/issues/policy-advocacy/upload/AAA-Ethics-Code-2009.pdf (accessed December 2009).
Belton, T. and Priyadharshini, E. "Boredom and Schooling: A Cross-Disciplinary Exploration," Cambridge Journal of Education 37, no. 4 (2007): 579–595.
Beltrán, L.R. and de Cardona, E.F. 1979. Latin America and the United States: Flaws in the free flow of information, in National Sovereignty and International Communications, edited by K. Nordenstreng and H. I. Schiller. Norwood, NJ, Ablex, pp. 33–64.
Bernard, H.R. 2005. Research Methods in Cultural Anthropology. 4th ed. Newbury Park, CA: Sage Publications.
Bianchi, S.M. and Robinson, J.P. "What Did You Do Today? Children's Use of Time, Family Composition, and the Acquisition of Social Capital," Journal of Marriage and the Family 59, no. 2 (1997): 332–344.
Bogart, L. 1958. The Age of Television. New York: Ungar Publishers.
Brewer, D.D. "Cognitive Indicators of Knowledge in Semantic Domains," Journal of Quantitative Anthropology 5 (1995): 1047–128.
Brown, A. 1995. Caribbean Cultures and Mass Communication Technology: Re-Examining the Cultural Dependency Thesis Globalization, Communications and Caribbean Identity. Dunn, Jamaica: Ian Randle Publishers.
———. 2001. Caribbean cultures, global mass communication, technology, and opportunity in the twenty-first century, in Culture and Mass Communication in the Caribbean: Domination, Dialogue, Dispersion, edited by H.A. Regis. Gainesville: University Press of Florida, pp. 169–184.
Brown, J.D., Childers, K.W., Bauman, K.E. "The Influence of New Medial and Family Structure on Young Adolescents' Television and Radio Use," Communication Research 17, no. 1 (1990): 65–82.
Cantor, J. 1998. Children's attraction to violent television programming, in Why We Watch, edited by J.H. Goldstein. Kingston, Jamaica: Oxford University Press, pp. 88–115.

Carpenter, C.J., Huston, A.C. and Spera, L. 1989. Children's use of time in their everyday activities during middle childhood, in *The Ecological Context of Children's Play*, edited by M.N. Bloch and A.D. Pelegrini. Norwood, NJ: Ablex, pp. 165–190.

Cowan, R.S. 1983. More Work for Mother: The Ironies of Household Technology from the Open Hearth to the Microwave. New York: Basic Books.

Davis, S.S. and Davis, D.A. "'The Mosque and the Satellite': Media and Adolescence in a Moroccan Town," Journal of Youth and Adolescence 24 (1995): 577–593.

DeWalt, K.M., DeWalt, B.R., and Wayland, C.B., eds. 1998. Participant Observation. Walnut Creek, CA: AltaMira Press.

Dominica Broadcasting Services. 2011. "About Dominica Broadcasting Services." On http://news.dbcradio.net/about/#page-content (accessed April 1, 2011).

Drabman, R. . and Thomas, M.H. "Does Media Violence Increase Children's Toleration of Real-Life Aggression?" Developmental Psychology 10, no. 3 (1974): 418–421.

Erikson, R.J. "Play Contributes to Full Emotional Development," Education 105 (1985): 261–263.

Fisherkeller, J. "Everyday Learning about Identities among Young Adolescents in Television Culture," Anthropology and Education Quarterly 28, no. 4 (1997): 467–492.

Flinn, M.V. 1992. Paternal care in a Caribbean village, in *Father–Child Relations: Cultural and Biosocial Contexts*, edited by B. Hewlett. New York: Aldine De Gruyter, pp. 57–84.

Foster, G.M. "Peasant Society and the Image of Limited Good," American Anthropologist 67 (1965): 293–315.

Gatewood, J.B. "Loose Talk: Linguistic Competence and Recognition Ability," American Anthropologist 85, no. 2 (1983): 378–387.

Gerbner, G., Gross, L., Morgan, M., & Signorielli, N. (1994). Growing up with television: The cultivation perspective, in Media effects: Advances in theory and research, edited by J. Bryant and D. Zillmann. Hillsdale, NJ: Erlbaum, pp. 14–71.

Gillespie, M. 1995. Television, Ethnicity and Cultural Change. New York: Routledge.

Ginsburg, F. D., Abu-Lughod, L., and Larkin, B. 2002. Introduction, in *Media Worlds: Anthropology on a New Terrain*, edited by F.D. Ginsburg, L. Abu-Lughod, and B. Larkin. Berkeley: University of California Press, pp. 1–36.

Giroux, H.A. 2001. The Mouse That Roared: Disney and the End of Innocence. Lanham: Roman and Littlefield Publishers, Inc.

Giroux, H.A. 2008. Against the Terror of Neoliberalism: Politics Beyond the Age of Greed. Boulder, CO.: Paradigm Publishers, University of British Columbia Press,

Hames, R. 1992. Time allocation, in *Evolutionary Ecology and Human Behavior*, edited by E.A. Smith and B. Winterhalder. New York: Aldine de Gruyter, pp. 203–236.

Hansen, J.R. 2009. Television and Youth in Dominica. Honors College. Pullman: Washington State University.

Hearold, S. 1986. A synthesis of 1,043 effects of television on social behavior, in *Public Communication and Behavior*, edited by G. Comstock. Orlando, FL: Academic Press, pp. 65–133.

Honychurch, L. 1995. The Dominica Story: A History of the Island. Oxford: Macmillan Caribbean.

Hurwitz, S.C. "To Be Successful: Let Them Play!" Child Education 79 (2002): 101–102.

Huston, A.C., Bickham, D.S., Lee, J.H., and Wright, J.C. . 2007. From attention to comprehension: How children watch and learn from television, in *Children and Television: Fifty Years of Research*, edited by N. Pecora, J.P. Murray, & E.A. Wartella. Mahwah, NJ: Lawrence Erlbaum Associates, pp. 41–63.

Huston, A.C., Wright, J.C., Rice, M. L., Kerkman, D., and St. Peters, M. "Development of Television Viewing Patterns in Early Childhood: A Longitudinal Investigation," Developmental Psychology 26, no. 3 (1990): 409–420.

Huston, A.C., Wright, J.C., Marquis, J., and Green, S.B. "How Young Children Spend Their time: Television and Other Activities," Developmental Psychology 35, no. 4 (1999): 912–925.

Jago, R., Baranowski, T., Baranowski, J., Thompson, D., and Greaves, K. . "BMI from 3–6 y of Age Is Predicted by TV Viewing and Physical Activity, Not Diet," International Journal of Obesity 29, no. 6 (2005): 557–564.

Johnson, A. and Sackett, R. 1998. Direct systematic observation of behavior, in *Handbook of Methods in Cultural Anthropology*, edited by H.R. Bernard. Walnut Creek, CA: AltaMira, pp. 301–332.

Karacabey, K. "The Effect of Exercise on Leptin, Insulin, Cortisol and Lipid Profiles in Obese Children," Journal of International Medical Research 37, no. 5 (2009): 1472–1478.

King, C.R., Bloodsworth-Lugo, M.K., and Lugo-Lugo, C. R. "Animated Representations of Blackness," Journal of African American Studies 14, no. 4 (2010): 395–397.

Kottak, C.P. "Television's Impact on Values and Local Life in Brazil," Journal of Communication 41, no. 1 (1991): 70–87.

———. 1992. Anthropological analysis of mass enculturation, in *A Guide for Student Anthropologists: Researching American Culture*, edited by C.P. Kottak. Ann Arbor: University of Michigan Press, pp. 40–74.

Larson, R.W., Kubey, R.W., and Colletti, J. "Changing Channels: Early Adolescent Media Choices and Shifting Investments in Family and Friends," Journal of Youth and Adolescence 18 (1989): 583–599.

Larson, R.W., Richards, M.H., Sims, B., and Dworkin, J. "How Urban African American Young Adolescents Spend Their Time: Time Budgets for Locations, Activities, and Companionship," American Journal of Community Psychology 29, no. 4 (2001): 565–597.

Larson, R.W. and Verma, S. "How Children and Adolescents Spend Time across the World: Work, Play, and Developmental Opportunities," Psychological Bulletin 125, no. 6 (1999): 701–736.

Lashely, L.M. 1995. Television and the Americanization of the Trinbagonian youth: A study of six secondary schools, in *Globalization, Communications and Caribbean Identity*, edited by H.S. Dunn. Kingston, Jamaica: Ian Randle Publishers Ltd., pp. 83–97.

Levine, R.K. 1997. A Geography of Time: On Tempo, Culture, and the Pace of Life. New York: Basic Books, Perseus Group.

Lillemyr, O.F. 2009. Taking Play Seriously: Children and Play in Early Childhood Education. Charlotte, NC: Information Age Publishing.

Lull, J. 1990. Inside Viewing: Ethnographic Research on Television's Audiences. London: Routledge.

Macfarlan, S.J. and Quinlan, R.R. "Kinship, Family, and Gender Effects in the Ultimatum Game," Human Nature 19, no. 3 (2008): 294–309.

Mallory, M. 1998. Hanna-Barbera Cartoons. Southport, CT: Levin, Hugh Lauter and Erlbaum Associates.

Mankekar, P. 2002. National texts and gendered lives: An ethnography of television viewers in a north Indian city, in *The Anthropology of Media: A Reader*, edited by K. Askew and R.R. Wilk. Malden, MA: Blackwell Publishers, pp. 299–322.

Marpin, T. 2008. "Cable Television Electronic Document." http://www.marpin.dm/support.htm (accessed September 10, 2008).

Mason, M.F., Norton, M.I., Van Horn, J.D., Wegner, D.M., Grafton, S.T., and Macrae, C.N. "Wandering Minds: The Default Network and Stimulus-Independent Thought," Science 315, no. 5810 (2007): 393–395.

Miller, D. 1992. The young and restless in Trinidad: A case of the local and global in mass consumption, in *Consuming Technologies: Media and Information in Domestic Spaces*, edited by R. Silverstone and E. Hirsch. London: Routledge, pp. 163–182.

Miller, T., Govil, N., McMurria, J., and Maxwell, R 2001. Global Hollywood. London: British Film Institute.

Mittell, J. 2009. Television and American Culture. New York: Oxford University Press.

Murray, J.P. "The Impact of Television Violence," Hofstra Law Review 22 (1994): 809–825.

———. "TV Violence and Brainmapping in Children," Psychiatric Times 17, no. 10 (2001): 70–77.

———. 2007. TV violence: Research and controversy, in *Children and Television: Fifty Years of Research*, edited by N. Pecora, J.P. Murray, and E.A. Wartella. Mahwah, NJ: Lawrence Erlbaum Associates, pp. 183–203.

Murray, J.P., Liotti, M., Ingmundson, P.T., Mayberg, H.S., Pu, Y., Zamarripa, F., Liu, Y., Woldorff, M.G., Gao, J.-H. and Fox, P.T. "Children's Brain Activations while Viewing Televised Violence Revealed by FMRI," Media Psychology 8, no. 1 (2006): 25–37.

Paik, H. and Comstock, G. "The Effects of Television Violence on Antisocial Behavior: A Meta-Analysis," Communication Research 21 (1994): 516–546.

Painter, A.A. "On the Anthropology of Television: A Perspective from Japan," Visual Anthropology Review 10, no. 1 (1994). 70–84.

Paolisso, M. and Hames, R. "Time Diary versus Instantaneous Sampling: A Comparison of Two Behavioral Research Methods," Field Methods 22, no. 4 (2010): 357–377.

Pelligrini, A.D. 2009. The Role of Play in Human Development. New York: Oxford University Press.

Quinlan, M.B. 2004. From the Bush. Belmont, CA: Wadsworth/Cengage.

———. "Considerations for Collecting Freelists in the Field: Examples from Ethnobotany," Field Methods 17, no. 3 (2005): 219–234.

Quinlan, R.J. 1995. Father Absence, Maternal Care and Children's Behavior in a Rural Caribbean Village. Department of Anthropology. Columbia, MO: University of Missouri.

———. "Gender & Risk in a Matrifocal Caribbean Community: A View from Behavioral Ecology 108, 464–479," American Anthropologist 108, no. 3 (2006): 464–479.

Quinlan, R.J., Quinlan, M.B., and Flinn, M.V. "Local Resource Enhancement & Sex-Biased Breastfeeding in a Caribbean Community," Current Anthropology 46, no. 3 (2005): 471–80.

Regis, H.A. 2001. Introduction, in *Culture and Mass Communication in the Caribbean: Domination, Dialogue, Dispersion*, edited by H.A. Regis. Gainesville: University Press of Florida, pp. 3–13.

Reis, R. "The Impact of Television Viewing in the Brazilian Amazon," Human Organization 57, no. 3 (1998): 300–306.

Roberts, P.A. 1988. West Indians and their Language. Cambridge: Cambridge University Press.

Robinson, J.P. and Bianchi, S.M. "The Children's Hours," American Demographics 19, no. 12 (1997): 20–4.

Romney, A.K. and D'Andrade, R.G. "Cognitive Aspects of English Kin Terms," *American Anthropologist* 66, no. 3 (1964): Part 2:146–170.

Schiller, H.I. 1976. Communication and Cultural Domination. White Plains, NY: International Arts and Science Press.

Singer, M.I., Slovak, K., Frierson, T. and York, P. "Viewing Preferences, Symptoms of Psychological Trauma, and Violent Behaviors Among Children Who Watch Television," *Journal of the American Academy of Child and Adolescent Psychiatry* 37, no. 10 (1998): 1041–1048.

Skinner, E.C. 2001. Empirical research on mass communication and cultural domination in the Caribbean, in *Culture and Mass Communication in the Caribbean: Domination, Dialogue, Dispersion*, edited by H.A. Regis. Gainesville: University Press of Florida, pp. 37–62.

Smallwood, J., McSpadden, M., and Schooler, J.W. "The Lights Are On but No One's Home: Meta-Awareness and the Decoupling of Attention When the Mind Wanders," *Psychonomic Bulletin & Review* 14, no. 3 (2007): 527–533.

Smallwood, J. and Schooler, J.W. "The Restless Mind," *Psychological Bulletin* 132, no. 6 (2006): 946–958.

Smith, J.J. "Using ANTHROPAC 3.5 and a Spreadsheet to Compute a Freelist Salience Index," *Cultural Anthropology Methods Newsletter* 5 (1993): 1–3.

Smith, J.J., Furbee, L.N., Maynard, K., Quick, S., and Ross, L. "Salience Counts: A Domain Analysis of English Color Terms," *Journal of Linguistic Anthropology* 5, no. 2 (1995): 203–216.

Spitulnik, D. "Anthropology and the Mass Media," *Annual Review of Anthropology* 22 (1993): 293–315.

———. 2002. Mobile machines and fluid audiences: Rethinking reception through Zambian radio culture, in *Media Worlds: Anthropology on New Terrain*, edited by F.D. Ginsburg, L. Abu-Lughod, and B. Larkin. Berkeley: University of California Press, pp. 337–354.

U.S. Department of Education. 1988. Education Longitudinal Study of 1988. First Followup. Washington, DC, National Center for Education for Longitudinal Study.

Van Evra, J. 2004. Television and Child Development. Mahwah, NJ: Lawrence Erlbaum Associates.

Vanderwater, E.A., Bickham, D.S., and Lee, J.H. "Time Well Spent? Relating Television Use to Children's Free-Time Activities," *Pediatrics* 117, no. 2 (2006): 181–191.

Weber, D.S. 2006. Media use by infants and toddlers: A potential for play, in *Play = Learning: How Play Motivates and Enhances Children's Cognitive and Social-Emotional Growth*, edited by D. Singer, R.M. Golinkoff, and K. Hirsh-Pasek. New York: Oxford University Press, pp. 169–191.

Weller, S. and Romney, A.K. 1988. Systematic Data Collection. Newbury Park, CA: Sage Publications.

Wilk, R.R. 2002. "It's destroying a whole generation": Television and moral discourse in Belize, in *The Anthropology of Media: A Reader*, edited by K. Askew and R.R. Wilk. Malden, MA: Blackwell Publishing, pp. 286–298.

Zimmerman, F.J. and Christakis, D.A. "Children's Television Viewing and Cognitive Outcomes: A Longitudinal Analysis of National Data," *Archives of Pediatrics & Adolescent Medicine* 159, no. 7 (2005): 619–25.

12 China's Emergent Youth
Gender, Work, Dating, and Life Orientation

William Jankowiak and Robert L. Moore[1]

INTRODUCTION

Youth, that long curving transition from childhood to adulthood, is a phase of life that frequently tests and challenges social convention. The new forms of behavior that emerge from youth pushing against the mature generation's preference for the familiar can result in the establishment of new practices and cultural understandings. Feeling little stake in the status quo of the adult world, and with access to sources of power new in their young lives, youth often play the role of shock troops for the latest new social or political movement, taking little for granted (Moore and Rizor 2008). The experimental propensities of the young, seen against the conservative objections of the older generations, reveal facets of cultural systems—their basic values and assumptions—that are often otherwise invisible. The efforts of youth to test and redefine conventional morality give a glimpse into the social landscapes of the future. This is especially so among wealthier societies whereby the transformation from adolescents into adulthood is being redefined less by the fulfilling of specific roles and related duties and more by the quality of personal development. This expanded definition of youth is resulting in a new emergent stage of youth (Arnett 2004). It is the period in which individuals are encouraged to explore personal, social, and economic opportunities, if for no other reason than a more thorough understanding of themselves and the economic options available to them. In this context, individuals need "more time to develop the emotional maturity, cognitive skills, and social intelligence to navigate the challenges if uneasy transitions, fluid careers, and changing families" (Arnett 2004, 15).

Not every community sees its adolescents entering into an "emergent youth" phase as a positive development. The senior generation, for example, often views the younger generation as being too wasteful in its spending on such things as fashionable clothes and travel. As often as not, the expansion of youth phase is misunderstood and usually blamed on the individual adolescent's moral failing.

The tension between the senior generation's expectation and the junior generation's ability to fulfill its desires often leads to confusion, disappointment, and moral exasperation. A forty-seven-year-old Chinese office worker's frustration over social change is evident in her comment about China's singletons (those born after 1979): "We no longer understand this generation." But the pace of change in China has quickened, it is no longer between generations, but now between age cohorts. A seventeen-year-old Chinese high school student informed us, for example, she did not recognize the slang terms twelve-year-old middle school students were using.

The new attitudes toward what is and is not appropriate behavior(s) often create a distinctive habitus, or pattern of unreflective action. In time, most people come to tolerate, if not appreciate, the new behavior. China's singletons, like the post–World War II American baby boomers, are fundamentally remaking Chinese society. They are doing this through language, fashion, and social practices. Instead of a blind adherence to social duty, China's singletons are actively engaged in the pursuit of personal development and this has resulted in a more pronounced sense of autonomy.

In this chapter, we will explore the emergence of China's youth stage as a distinctly new type of generational phenomenon as it has impacted men and women's perception of the importance of marriage, family, parenthood, and life orientation. The change is broad and it permeates various segments of society. It affects young men and women similarly and yet, in some ways, differently. Finally, we will examine the ways China's youth strive to express themselves, especially within the dating context, as socially bounded yet autonomous individuals.

ECONOMIC REFORMS, SINGLETONS, AND THE EMERGENT YOUTH

Jeffery Arnett (2004) notes that emergent youth arise whenever there is a material basis that enables youth to control subsistence—if not prosper—independently of family support. For the first fifty years of the People's Republic of China's (PRC) history, the material factors necessary to create a youth stage were absent. But ten years after the market reforms of 1978, Chinese cities began to resemble European cities in many ways. There were more economic opportunities, apartments to rent, and a pronounced change in social norms that enabled males and females to not only hang out together, but even to cohabit with one another (Moore and Wei 2011). For the first time, the material factors necessary for the creation of a youth culture had appeared. But material factors, in and of themselves, are seldom sufficient. Something else is needed. In the case of China—the emergence of a new social category—youth culture—required a political act. This came in the form of the single-child policy.

The single-child policy had numerous unintended consequences. One, it altered the way many Chinese looked at the relationship between sex and marriage. If marriage was no longer primarily for reproduction, then it followed that parenthood was no longer a primary marker of adulthood. This fact was not lost on Chinese sociologists, who pointed out that the separation of sex from reproduction contributed to making family life associated less with child rearing and more with hedonistic pleasure (cited in Zheng 2009). The redefinition of the meaning of sexuality and marriage is taking place within an emergent economy that provides China's youth with more economic and social opportunities than those available in their parental generation.

For many urban youth, migration to another locale for economic opportunity resulted in the dilution of interaction and thus parental authority. Today's youth live in work-sponsored dormitories, share a rented apartment with one or two other roommates—who may or may not be their boyfriends/girlfriends—or live alone. These structural changes provided China's singletons with an expanded cognitive horizon in which to explore, change jobs, date, and thus learn from their successes and failures. The new cultural arena further enables many youth to develop a more refined sense of responsibility and strengthen their resolve to more effectively manage their lives. The new economic opportunities also provided youth with greater financial independence. For example, a Hohhot survey found that forty-two out of ninety-eight or 43 percent of youth working in central business districts did not live with their parents (Jankowiak 2011). The Hohhot data revealed that for those youth who continued to live with their parents, even though their parents treated them as if they were still children (*haizi*), they felt, at least in their mind's eye, that they were adults. A twenty-three-year-old's comments are representative: "My parents always treat me like a child, because I am the only child in my family. Maybe they love me too much. But I still know I am an adult." In contrast to the 1980s, where marriage and parenthood, but not necessarily age, were the more salient cultural markers of adulthood, by the 2000s other more subjective factors had emerged as equal to and, in many cases, more important than the fulfillment of specific duties, obligations, and social roles.

For many, marriage and having a child are no longer the only markers of adulthood. A twenty-two-year-old woman who continued to live with her parents explained it this way: "I think self-sufficiency is the more critical factor." After a long thoughtful pause, she added, "It does not matter if you live with your parents, if you are earning an income and are responsible for yourself [i.e., your own daily affairs], then you are an adult." Her position is representative of Hohhotian youth whose financial situation often makes it difficult to rent an apartment or buy a flat, but who still consider themselves to be adults. Another young woman noted, "Working is the base of independence; without work, we cannot financially live as adults." She elaborated: "Marriage is just a stage in a person's life. It may mean or not mean you have become an adult." For her and her cohort, the more effective measure of adulthood is mastery of subjective qualities, such as the ability to be responsible and effectively manage your ordinary life. To this end, a twenty-three-year-old unmarried elementary school teacher readily admitted she considers herself an adult because she "lived alone, was financially independent from her parents, and could take care of herself." In reform era China, adulthood is increasingly assessed through one's ability to be personally responsible to oneself. In more developed Chinese cities, more youth are capable of living alone, but in economically depressed Hohhot, this is more difficult. Hohhotian youth who are unable to leave the city have redefined adulthood to mean having greater autonomy, mastery of personal responsibility, and self-expression. Today, China's youth increasingly embrace the values of personal inquiry, self-sufficiency, self-fulfillment, and happiness, all of which carry, albeit implicitly, additional attributes of adulthood: personal and social responsibility (see Fong 2004; Fong, personal communication). In this way, identity exploration, and not social position, constitutes the new criterion youth use to assess the presence or absence of adulthood.

The search for self-fulfillment is evident in the remarks of a twenty-three-year-old youth who moved from a small town in Inner Mongolia to Hohhot and who admitted that, "I struggle for a better life. It is this struggle to improve that makes life worth living. I have a kind of faith that I can make it. This belief is what makes life worth living." For him and for most of his friends, success is not only about obtaining greater material benefits; it is about the fulfillment of personal goals based on an ongoing dialogue with one's self. This desire for personal improvement is evident in a twenty-eight-year-old female sales clerk, who said, "There are days when I wonder why I could not make a sale—I get depressed. I work very hard. I always wonder how I might improve." Another twenty-two-year-old college graduate noted, "Work is an important source for self-fulfillment." A twenty-four-year-old elementary school teacher admitted that she gained a tremendous reward from teaching her students. She added, "I am often very tired but I feel so fulfilled." It is found in the satisfaction of a thirty-five-year-old mother's reflections on her ten-year-old daughter's future: "I want my child to travel and see the world. I never had the opportunity to travel—I want my child to do this." It is also found in the remarks of a nineteen-year-old man: "I want to embrace and enjoy life as much as I can. I believe in the beauty of life. [I want] to explore the world and dedicate myself to making a difference every day. I want so much to travel around the world." The thrill of involvement is found in a twenty-year-old woman, who said, "I was so excited and felt so fulfilled the day I opened my hairdressing salon. . . . I knew I was going to learn a lot and improve my position."

The ambition to improve oneself, to learn new skills, to be tested in a competitive arena, and to succeed, all aspects associated with adulthood, are found in a twenty-four-year-old male, who noted, "I could get a good job in Inner Mongolia. . . . But in Beijing life is fast. . . . I think I can make my fortune in Beijing. I can earn enough to do things, and to get a wife." He added, "I want a challenge. . . . Money isn't everything, but it is important these days." For this young man, like so many others we talked to, it was not money per se but the challenge to test his mettle in a major cosmopolitan arena that made Beijing more attractive than Hohhot. A twenty-year-old real estate saleswoman admitted that one of the reasons she liked her job was it allowed her to confront different situations. She explained, "I like the way my job challenges me and helps me explore my potential. I also learn to be more patient and how to communicate with others better." The pursuit of self-improvement is found in a twenty-five-year-old man's explanation for quitting his job at a foreign-operated hotel and taking a pay cut in order to accept a job that offered better opportunities to learn new tasks and, perhaps, to experience personal growth and happiness: "Before, I thought that money was everything. I now realize that there is more to life than consumption and the drive to earn more and more things or find the most beautiful girl."

The Hohhot findings are consistent with Vanessa Fong's (2004) research on Dalian youths' attitudes toward the future. Fong discovered that ambitious striving can produce happiness and satisfaction as well as stress and frustration. In effect, achievement and stress are different sides of the same coin (Fong, personal communication). The dilemma for Chinese youth is to achieve something beyond themselves, while in the process not losing their support network. Both male and female singletons have adopted different values and outlooks and have embraced ethics associated with individualism.

The increasing value placed on individuality is apparent in the way men and women use fashion to define themselves as distinct individuals. Jankowiak's observational survey of gender and the selection of fabric color found that, as the 1980s middle-aged women (forty-five years old plus) wore essentially darker and more somber colors, younger women were likely to wear brightly colored clothing. Unlike the 1980s, he noted that today 33 percent of young women now wear somber colors (e.g., black and gray). He also found an expansion in the kinds of colors preferred. In the 1980s women wore eight basic colors; today there are more than fourteen different colors worn in public (2). The expansion in choice of fashion coloring has also impacted men, who in the 1980s wore five dark-colored jackets (e.g., blue, green, brown, black, and gray) but now include brightly colored ski jackets and an array of colorful shirts in their wardrobes. In fashion, Hohhotian youth are no longer restrained by social convention.

The public readily accepts personal freedom to include decoration of the body. In Hohhot, it is not unusual to see young men and women with brown-, blonde-, or red-dyed hair. Also completely unknown in the 1980s were tattoo parlors, which today have grown quite popular. As in the U.S., tattoos in China used to be considered images worn by the socially marginal but today, as in the U.S., are thought to be cool. As a twenty-six-year-old woman asserted, "You should always strive to be yourself." If this means having a tattoo, then you should do it. Oprah Winfrey could not have said it more clearly.

Another way youth seek to create personalized borders is through use of special ring tones on their cell phones. In a small survey Jankowiak conducted among local twenty-year-old roommates, seventeen out of twenty-one individuals were found to have different ring tones. Individuals interviewed admit with some pride their interest in finding a ring tone that symbolizes their personality and not their social identity (e.g., junior college student). The importance of boundaries is evident in the extension of personal space. In the 1980s it was common for strangers to lean into each other on the bus, train, or at a counter. In fact, one of the easy ways for a petty theft to pickpocket was to place his arm around a stranger's shoulder and then take money from his upper jacket pocket. This was so commonplace that few people bothered to look. This is no longer the case. Unlike in the 1980s, when people literally crawled over each other to get into a bus or on a train, people today are increasingly reserved. Chinese urbanites, like the 1960s Hong Kong citizens (Watson 1997), are learning, with some fits and starts, to form lines and follow the principle that the first to arrive has seniority over others. This ethical principle is in complete opposition to the folk ideal that the first person to get to a seat or pick up an item has the right to it. The "first to arrive" principle is being adopted by the urban singletons more than it is by the senior generation, who prefer the folk ideal. The expansion of bodily space is particularly apparent when it comes to men and women interacting. Jankowiak repeatedly observed young women's expressed negative reactions whenever a male would bump into them. In these situations, men were not given the benefit of the doubt, but rather it was assumed that the men may have done so deliberately.

Another illustration of the value given to personal expression is the rise of personal photos that are sexually suggestive or teasing in allure. Girlfriends often give these photos to longtime boyfriends. The photos are seldom nude, but are sexy in the type of clothing (often showing outlines of breasts or bare midriffs) or style worn (e.g., a leather miniskirt). A twenty-year-old woman who had just taken photos she was showing to her girlfriends at the local McDonald's acknowledged, "My friends thought I was too pure and cute and I should change my style. I need to be more natural and feminine." She added, "My mother says [upon looking at the pictures] I am no longer a little girl but a young lady."

Perhaps one of the most demonstrable social changes that signify the rise of individualism is the birthday party. In the past, the only true birthday was one hundred days after a child was born. After that there were none. The one-hundred-day birthday (*chang ming bai sui*) was more a parental celebration and message to the community that their child had survived. In contrast, the birthday party in reform China is completely different in kind of participants, focus, and meaning.

The frequency with which elementary school children have birthday parties that only involve other kids today is striking. These events were witnessed at local Dairy Queen and McDonald's restaurants. In the 1980s neither of us ever observed such parties. In fact, young men and women seldom celebrated their own birthdays. At most a person's mother might sometimes make an extra long noodle on her child's birthday and put it into his or her bowl of dinner noodles. Classmates and friends seldom were aware of one another's birthday. Among the singletons, this is no longer so for children or young adults. Classmates and friends often celebrate each other's birthdays. Moreover, the worst mistake a man can make is to forget his girlfriend's birthday. Birthday celebrations can be about many things. In China, they highlight the individual as a societal good. In this way, the center of Chinese society is gradually shifting from its former exclusive focus on the family as the essential social unit to the individual, China's new arbitrator of personal autonomy and responsibility. Even the popular youth slang term *ku*, which first emerged in the mid-1990s, is marked by its identification with individualism (Moore 2005).

There are gender and class difference that have distinct and different impacts on men and women when it comes to age at marriage, becoming a parent, and obtaining career independence. On these issues of timing, young men and women differ considerably.

MALENESS AND FEMALENESS: SHIFTING IMAGES AND OPPORTUNITIES

Prior to the reemergence of China's market economy, both men and women typically worked. The Chinese family required both spouses' incomes to survive. Moreover, Chinese communist ideology held it important for both genders to work in order to achieve status and respect. For most, work in the socialist command economy was considered easy, often to the point of being downright boring. However, employment held little opportunity for self-fulfillment. In fact, people often admitted they did not like their jobs but did like having time to be engaged in their personal hobbies. In the market economy the conjugal family continues to need both sexes' income but it is now tacitly expected that the husband has the greater responsibility to support the family. This presents something of a paradox: Young females are at least as ambitious as young males, yet there is an expectation that the husband will be the more able provider in a couple. This assumption that the man has greater responsibility has placed a uniquely heavy burden on both urban men and rural men who work in the city. Not only are women actively competing with them for many jobs, but many women also expect men to have the greater share of financial responsibility for maintaining the family.

The conflicting expectations can be seen in the shift in the way urbanites perceive gender differences. Compared to Jankowiak's (1993) survey from the 1980s, there is more blurring in men and women's ranking of ideal gender features today. The distinguishing markers are not as clear-cut as they were a decade or two ago. This is evident in the increase in factors that individuals perceive as irrelevant to gender.

There are three significant shifts in the way young men and women differ from the early 1980s or their parents' generation. The first is recognition that men and women have equal intelligence (*congming*). In contrast to the 1980s where college-educated women and men were unanimous that men were smarter than women, urban youth no longer hold to this view. Intelligence is no longer the monopoly of any one gender.

The single-child policy has resulted in girls being encouraged to achieve the same as boys, a point that is amply demonstrated in classroom performance. The end result is that girls are perceived to be just as intelligent as boys. The shift in gender has also manifested in other performance domains. For example, Tianshu Pan has observed in Fudan University, an elite Chinese university, that boys are less assertive and confident than female students. He recalls that in the 1980s, this was not the case even in the English department where women outnumbered men, but men were still assertive. He adds that, "in all the courses I taught, the women tended to score higher than men and contributed more to class discussion." Furthermore, 50 percent of China's university students today are women compared to 23 percent in 1980 (Hewlett 2009). This ratio is similar to that found in the U.S., where 57 percent of all college undergraduates are women.

The second shift has to do with life's pressure (*yali*). Although men and women acknowledge that both sexes felt pressure (*yali*), it is understood that men felt the greater responsibility for the family's financial well-being and, in this regard, have more pressure. Young Chinese repeatedly asserted that men have a strong responsibility to their parents and to uphold the cultural image of being a successful man. For example, they have to get a job, an apartment, maybe a car, and support their family. They are expected to make more money and believe they are looked down upon if they do not accomplish these things. Males' heightened pressure arose from a shift in the organization of gender and cultural expectation about family life. Significantly, married women in their early thirties who had a child, felt both sexes had equal amounts of pressure and that women suffered as much as if not more than men from depression. Women in their thirties enjoyed pointing out that "behind every successful man is a woman." This qualification was absent in the gender discourse of the 1980s. Today, there is an agreement that a good marriage should be mutually supportive of life's pressures. This suggests that youth's perception of marriage is more akin to being a joint partnership in which emotional support is deemed equally important to both sexes.

Jankowiak also found in his 2000 Hohhot survey a shift among college students concerning their preferred images of maleness; gentility and cultivated politeness was no longer the preferred posture. It had been replaced by a persona that was organized around an image of forcefulness, assertion, and aggressive ambition. The ideal model was no longer the college professor but the CEO. The return of the businessman (or China's new merchant class), who is seen as someone capable of making rapid choices and is strict and opinionated, constitutes a new role model that has an impact on China's college-educated youth. Today, educated males are blending attributes found in the socialist era image of the genteel professor with a more aggressive, strong-willed, and domineering businessman persona. In the process, most singleton males strive to be less timid, more decisive, and cool in their interactions with their colleagues and their romantic partners.

The shift in folk images of what constitutes authentic masculinity is not entirely new. Throughout Chinese history, as Kam Louie (2000) observed, there have been essentially two different conceptions of what constitutes ideal masculinity ranging from *wu*, or aggressive toughness, to *wen*, or cultivated gentility based on politeness, self-control, and aggressiveness that is typically implied rather than expressed directly. During the Maoist era educated males adopted the image of the scholar official as their masculine ideal. In the 1980s some in the working class also strove to adopt this posture—although some did not. For most youth, the behavior typically expressed had more in common with a *wu* than *wen*. By the twenty-first century, educated urban males had no longer adopted the ideal of the scholar official as the preferred cultural ideal. Rather, most young males now blend elements of gentility with a touch of toughness and frank assertiveness. Moreover, as in the case of many contemporary Papua New Guinea cultures (Mageo 2005), Chinese men's newfound assertiveness is culturally recognized and valued.

The *wu* and *wen* images of masculinity both acknowledge that the ideal man should be in control and confident. Today, singletons have embraced the Western image of coolness or the belief that it is best to "always look cool (*ku*) under pressure" (Moore 2005). This does not mean that women cannot also be *ku*; some are. It does mean, however, that *ku* is not regarded as a fundamental component of femininity, whereas it is of masculinity. Moore's research (ibid.) found that for Beijing youth *ku* referenced both a degree of flamboyance and emotional distance. This is consistent with an increased celebration of an introspective focus. An individual's ability to display an emotional calmness also makes a statement of one's own internal psychological development. This contrasts with earlier personas that were organized around managing social relationships. *Ku* is not so much about the performance of social roles and the duties thereunto entailed, but is really about making a claim concerning individualistic mastery and concerning the independence of one's social position. This posture also hides an unvoiced fear of failure. Males feel an enormous responsibility or pressure to succeed as would be signified through obtaining a respected and well remunerated social position. Many strive for this ideal but few succeed in attaining it. Adopting a *ku* demeanor enables everyone, especially the more fragile males, to make a claim that they are in charge of their lives when, for many, the opposite is closer to the truth. A risk economy promotes and, at times, rewards social persona based more on performance than reality. In the case of young, contemporary Chinese males, given their ongoing concern with social success in a market as opposed to communist economy, Chow Yun-fat, Jet Li, and Jackie Chan—not the Confucian sage—provide the new ideal of proper masculinity. The image of the more assertive male is consistent with the new economy, where decisions have to be made and the bold often gain the advantage. The emergence of the new image is also taking place with the arrival of so many bright, talented, and ambitious females who are challenging men for traditionally male jobs. Significantly, outside of the work arena there is a corresponding shift whereby women have embraced a more "feminine" or sexually provocative demeanor designed to attract the male gaze. In the work context, women actively compete with men; however, within the domain of the sexual encounter, women and men continue to emphasize what they think the other sex most wants to experience.

There appears to be an underlying cultural logic present here. Men continue to value the work arena as the primary domain to express and define the self. Most women, on the other hand, although valuing work, often very highly, continue to find deeper meaning with being responsible for the family's well-being. With a few notable exceptions (e.g., women who either have a PhD or are wealthy businesswoman—see Southwell-Lee 2009), work is not the exclusive domain by which identity is defined. For most women, other considerations are equally important. For example, a twenty-five-year-old medical doctor admitted that "having a happy strong family is more important to me than having an amazing career." She further acknowledged that she liked her job a lot and enjoyed learning new things, but her job was not her life. Her opinion is fairly typical. Numerous young women readily admitted that although they enjoyed and worked hard at their job, it was not their life goal. Most women today admit that a loving marriage with a family (with an emphasis on all three words: loving, marriage, and family) is the preferred option.

This is a real dilemma for contemporary Chinese woman. A married woman who decides to raise her child often discovers that she has shifted her orientation from valuing work as an end in itself to valuing the child. This does not mean that women do not enjoy working or that they do not do it very well. This is clearly not the case. It does mean that women's fundamental sense of self-worth is not as intertwined as appears to be the case for men. The "mother's problem" is really a female dilemma that was as prevalent in the 1980s as it is today. It arises from women being pushed to achieve in the professional world while they are also expected to be the primary caretaker of a child. College students are acutely aware of this. A twenty-year-old woman admitted, "We talk about it all the time in the dorm. Do we live for the baby or for the career?"

The strength of this cultural belief may be one reason why young college-educated women have more difficulty in finding a good job in a Chinese company as opposed to a multinational corporation. Chinese male CEOs continue to assume that a young woman who is married will soon become pregnant and want to reduce her working hours or even quit her job. This cultural conviction, that women are less reliable than men, has resulted in looser standards applied to male applicants, which makes it easier for a less-qualified male to be hired ahead of a more qualified female (Hewlett 2009). Today, Chinese men who have a white-collar job earn, on average, $2,000 a year more than women. In this way, the 'glass ceiling" is a continuing reality in most mainland (but not Hong Kong) companies. It is a cultural model that favors men who are primarily in elite, white-collar professions. For uneducated men, however, the marketplace is not as discriminatory. Among the uneducated classes, women are preferred over men in unskilled light and service industry employment. These women tend to speak standard Chinese, which makes them excellent hires in a variety of service jobs (e.g., waitress, shop attendant, hotel employee) that involve meeting the public. Shifting dress and language skills enable many migrant female workers to develop marriage strategies to focus on local potential husbands, and are thus enabled to go beyond the confines of their regional or native place identities. In contrast, young uneducated men who do not have a decent job tend to be more marginalized and have a lower mate value in the urban marketplace. Today, many male youth worry whether they will ever be able to attract a mate. Women, on the other hand, seldom talk about this.

In sum, the shift from a command economy to a market economy has transformed China into a risk society that no longer follows a stable, socially prescribed formula for success. There are now many possibilities. Within this new milieu, China's single-child generation has come of age and now confronts many personal issues, ethical dilemmas, and uncertainties absent in their parents' generation. To more fully explore some of the personal consequences embedded in China's social transformation from a collectivist society to a more consumer-oriented, capitalist one, we will probe some off the personal, social, and moral dilemmas manifested in the emergent urban dating culture. This kind of culture typically flourishes where society provides a prolonged youth phase.

THE CULTURE OF COURTSHIP

Courtship cultures are organized around a family's interest more than an individual's interest (Bailey 1988; Collier 1997; Moore and Wei 2011). Based in an ethos of duty and thus social obligation, public performance is the preferred idiom of conversation and social script used for moral evaluation. Within this cultural milieu, an individual's reputation is critical, and thus shame is regarded as more important than private remorse or guilt. Moreover, mate selection criteria are organized around explicit material factors that range for men from political and social position to income; whereas for women they range from sexual inexperience, including virginity, to degree of physical beauty, and a pliable or self-sacrificing personality.

Courtship cultures often rely on chaperones and are organized around a process of negotiation that involves various family members who are concerned with finding an appropriate person who meets as many of the socially prescribed criteria as possible. The primary goal of courtship negotiation is marriage. It differs from dating in its emphasis on normative rules, social judgment, and conventional standards for articulating romantic involvement. It is conducted according to rules that organize dating into a semi-ritualistic sequence of private and semipublic meetings, characterized by incremental increases in the public expression of commitment, usually resulting in marriage.

Throughout the socialist work unit (*danwei*) era (1949–1992), there was a strong cultural consensus concerning what constituted appropriate conduct. In every way, Maoist China, like many villages and small townships around the world, remained grounded in a shared code of public conduct. The totality of public consensus contributed to fostering uniformity in outlook and conduct. The agreement over the meaning of propriety ensured a standardized reaction. The cultural consensus did not mean everyone always followed the rules; many did not. There was always some fudging at the margins. The presence of a courtship culture did mean, however, that when a deviation became public knowledge, everyone, including the deviator, agreed the transgression was inappropriate. This cultural consensus was especially evident in the way an individual searched for a spouse.

Within this setting, courtship was characterized by its semi-ritualistic sequence of private and semipublic meetings and incremental increases in the public expression of commitment that usually resulted in marriage. Although Chinese courtship practices shared similarities with courtship practices in other societies, there were differences too. Unlike Spain in the 1960s where courtship practices were chaperoned and organized around double standard ethics that allowed males greater freedom of behavior (Collier 1997), urban China was somewhat more egalitarian. Chinese women did not have to grant sexual access if they do not want to. Moreover, men were also constrained by courtship norms and wider conceptions of decency. In urban China neither gender had freedom equal to what the men in many patriarchal societies enjoy. For example, if a Chinese man were to obtain a reputation as a philanderer or simply come to be known to have had a previous "girlfriend," his reputation as being a virtuous and steadfast fellow would be damaged. Consequently, men and women both strove to hide their personal involvement through denial. The strength of the ethos of emotional/sexual chastity was a powerful incentive and it resulted in restraining personal behavior and thus personal appetite.

By the mid-1990s China's reform era policies resulted in the abandonment of the work unit as the primary means to organize society. This transformation, along with the retreat of the state from actively monitoring its citizens' daily acts, provided more opportunities for individual experimentation. Individuals, no longer contained in a web of earnest social surveillance, found the market economy provided greater anonymity. Late-night restaurants, entertainment clubs, and dance halls provided a privacy zone in which individuals could engage in personal behaviors that had previously been deemed inappropriate. For example, the singleton generation (i.e., the generation raised with the one-child policy) has adopted a more open attitude and thus increased tolerance toward bodily decoration (e.g., tattoos), career mobility, foreign travel, casual dating, spontaneous sexual trysts, a desire to find one's true love, increased tolerance for divorce, cohabitation, and the distribution of pornography, along with an emphasis on the value of parenthood as the primary means for establishing a proper social identity.

In contrast, a dating culture is organized around individual rights and autonomy with little or no parental involvement. The end goal of dating is not marriage per se but the vigorous pursuit of personal happiness. The date is conducted according to very practical rules and based on shrewd common sense and situational standards. It largely consists of expressions of sympathy and kind regard whereby potential partners try to prove how compassionate they can be (Brooks 2010, 30). Unlike informal, or secret, meetings common to the work unit (*danwei*) socialist era, contemporary dating is conducted publicly. It is flaunted more than denied. For example, a high school student at a Western-style restaurant, when asked if her male companion was her classmate, burst out with, "No! We are lovers." In this way, dating constitutes a profound transformation in generational authority away from the senior generation's striving to control the sexuality of its youth in favor of the junior generations' preference for and ability to ignore parental suggestions and recommendations.

Within this new milieu, lovers fight less with their parents and more among themselves. Moreover, personal reputation or shame becomes more of a secondary consideration in contrast to the weight given to feelings of regret or guilt over actions that contributed to harming another. Mate selection criteria shift away from frankly displayed material factors toward emphasis on idiosyncratic personality attributes. This does not mean material factors, such as a potential mate's social status, income, or (particularly for females) relative physical attractiveness are no longer valued. They clearly continue to be positive attributes. But they are no longer the most important or only factors when deciding who to "go on a date" with or select as a marital partner. The shift from a courtship to a dating culture, however, is not without its dilemmas. The explicit rules readily understood in a courtship culture have given way to a more tacit and thus more vague set of rules that are not readily understood even by the participants themselves, much less by the public. The transformation in the rules of the game has made what was once explicit now subtle or tacit.

China's singletons are the pioneers whose social experimentation is reshaping public and personal behavior. No longer constrained by social convention, China's youth are increasingly pushing the boundaries of social propriety. The shift in China's generational outlook, much as in the case of the American baby boomers, is remaking Chinese society. Courtship rituals stand in direct contrast to dating that is more open-ended and less precise in its meaning and consequences for those involved in this type of arrangement. It was not until the mid-1990s that urbanites started to explicitly "date." Previously, dating was conducted in secret and, thus, was often accompanied by denials of involvement. For example, individuals preferred to characterize their "dating" partners as being nothing more than classmates, workmates, or neighbors. People often knew or expected otherwise, but out of politeness, seldom questioned a couple's characterization of their relationship. By the late 1990s, however, even people in China's more provincial interior cities were willing to admit to boyfriend or girlfriend relationships.

In this, and in many other ways, China's courtship system was transformed away from a formalized system of mutually understood rules of conduct into an informal, decidedly open, and highly expressive dating culture. This does not mean that formal courtship norms and practices are no longer adhered to. For some, courtship norms continue to provide a useful and needed means to find a spouse. For others, especially singletons, the acceptance of a dating culture provides an opportunity to experiment with social relationships and thus delay making a strong commitment to another person. More significantly, China's cultural transformation has made what had been conducted in secrecy (e.g., dating, kissing, touching the opposite sex) become not only readily acknowledged in casual conversation, but also easily observed in a variety of public settings. The sexual maturity of China's singletons (i.e., those born after 1979) did not eliminate courtship as much as render it one of several possible avenues useful to search for and find a partner or spouse. The fact that dating norms that approve of relationships of short duration, casual commitment, and physical intimacy now stand alongside the more staid courtship rituals is remarkable. The shift in the normative order is indicative of a deeper shift in the local meanings of romance, sexual expression, and marriage in contemporary China.

To better illustrate the significance of the cultural shift in meanings we can consider the emerging normative features of a typical date in urban China. The source of our data is a survey given to 132 individuals between the ages of nineteen and twenty-five, with 102 being in their twenties. In 2000 and again in 2006, Jankowiak collected information about Hohhotian men's and women's attitudes and behavior toward a variety of acts that ranged from who kissed whom first, how long they dated before they kissed, the frequency of weekly contact, frequency of sexual intercourse, attitudes toward premarital sex, willingness to inform parents about having a boyfriend or girlfriend, and intentions of marrying their current boyfriend or girlfriend.

THE DATING EXPERIENCE: PATTERNS AND THEMES

At the beginning of a relationship most men tend to talk about, first of all, their futures, including the money they will earn, the type of car they will buy, and the size of the apartment they want; some, who are more modest, might talk about the importance of saving for the security of the family. The other kind of talk amounts to chatting and making funny insights often by providing perpetual commentary on life and people. In this way, young Chinese men have much in common with young American men— both are insecure about not having a good occupation or wealth to purchase expected and desired objects. All young men have is their imagination, dedication, social skills, and bravado, which they hope will lead to a more prosperous future. This is not unique to Chinese males; research on American conversational patterns found that men tend to spend twice as much time talking about themselves as women do (Brooks 2010, 30). For some Chinese and American woman, a man's ability to sell his future prospects can and does attract her and hold her interest. This is especially salient when marriage and parenthood are no longer markers for adulthood. Now, a more vague and subjective criterion that is suggestive of personal maturity has become the standard for assessing the presence or absence of social maturity and adulthood.

Young men, for the most part, talk more than women, who initially prefer to listen and actively encourage their date to present himself in the best possible light. Eibl-Eibesfeld (1989) points out among nonhuman primates, voice tone plays a role in courtship with the males signaling interest through the rising or lowering of voice tone. We did not focus on this dimension per se, but instead focused on who talks to whom the most. We found that young couples, who were not married, and who were at the earliest stage of dating, strove to create an environment in which the man either spoke more often or assumed the posture of an attentive listener ready to respond to a query or support his date's observations.

Personality differences, more than gender expectations, can distort the preceding pattern. More extroverted females talk more than introverted men; but overall, in an early dating setting, men tended to talk more, but not always, than females. In contrast, among couples in their thirties and forties, women overwhelmingly talked more often. In a way, dating men are trying to attract a woman's interest and, thus, commitment, whereas after marriage, men, in a public setting, tend to withdraw from active engagement with their spouses. Chinese women are aware of men's shift in behavior. An insightful twenty-six-year-old, unmarried woman noted that, "men hustle to attract a girl's interest and then, once they have it, lose interest in keeping her interested." Men do, however, continue to engage their spouses in conversation within the home.

The initial stages of dating, much like in the courtship era, is a discovery process, whereby men and women look for signs of commonality, agreement, and trustworthiness. For example, a young man discovered that it is important to agree with your date, at least in the beginning. He offered the following account: "We went to see the film *Poseidon*, and we discussed who should have died, the older man or the younger man. I thought the younger man but she thought the older man. So we quarreled and she got so angry she walked quickly away and turned and said she was taking the bus home alone. I learned from that that it is important to 'just agree with a woman.'"

Dating is also a time to learn about another's life goals and notions of what makes a good marriage. A female college senior, for example, had a first date where, over dinner, she learned that the man thought he should be the leader of the family and she should be obedient. She argued for an egalitarian relationship, but he insisted on becoming the family's patriarch—she never returned his calls.

The earliest phase of dating is a liminal period, a time of uncertainty as to what to do. During this phase neither person should request much from the other. To do so may lead one to be perceived as greedy (this is especially so when dating Japanese or Western men, who are more inclined to think that Chinese women only want a man's wealth). The concern with being seen as considerate and thus not greedy is evident in the following instance where a twenty-three-year-old woman recounted an instance of going on a first date where she incorrectly assumed they would go to dinner before going to a film. She did not, therefore, have anything to eat. When she met the man at an agreed-upon meeting place she discovered he had already eaten and just wanted to go to the movie—wanting to make a favorable impression, she did not say a word, even though she was quite hungry. "I was afraid," she told me, "if I asked for something he might think I was greedy."

Besides requesting favors or gifts too early from your partner, it is considered crude to talk about your former boyfriend(s) or girlfriend(s). A young man recalls, for example, how his date talked about her former boyfriend throughout the dinner. "When she realized," he adds, "I was annoyed, she stopped talking and we finished our meal in silence. I was so annoyed; I did not kiss her goodbye." Another twenty-one-year-old woman admitted with some pride that her current boyfriend had several previous girlfriends and this made for both awkward and somewhat rewarding incidents when they bumped into one of his former girlfriends. She admitted she enjoyed knowing he was now hers and not theirs. She also admitted that she was not ready for marriage and her relationship was just for fun.

Women and men often look for evidence of a potential partner's ability to demonstrate consideration for the other. For example, a twenty-six-year-old man said he was concerned about his girlfriend, who has a crush on him and wants to marry him, but, he adds, "I am not sure. She lost ten pounds for me, but I find she talks too much about everything. I usually talk a lot and then listen. But with her all I do is listen to her comments. This worries me." Other people look for signs of a person's willingness to make a commitment. The ability to make a personal sacrifice in use of time or with resources is seen as proof of a person's willingness to make a long-term commitment. For example, a Hohhotian girl met a boy who lived near the airport whereas she lived in the center of the city. She always met him (only a thirty-minute bus ride) near his home and they had dinner and walked around the nearby park. When she asked him to come to the center of the city he always made excuses. After a year of seeing him, she broke off their relationship. She told me that if he could not make a small concession and compromise over this small matter, what would he do if a major issue faced them? She felt it was not worth pursuing the relationship further.

The appearance of a money economy combined with an expanded emergent youth phase has increased, however, the potential to misunderstand intentions. For example, once a woman feels there is a connection, she may test a man's sincerity through asking for small gifts. It is assumed that if her boyfriend truly likes her, he will obtain them and, if she accepts them, it is understood they are a couple. But this expectation can be manipulated to benefit the woman. In Hohhot there are a number of college students from the Mongolian Republic who often date Hohhotian Mongolian men who share local Han students' dating norms and cultural sensibilities. They assume, therefore, if a gift is accepted, the woman has all but agreed to become a couple. Women from the Mongolian Republic do not share this moral precept, however, and thus readily receive gifts with no intention of becoming a couple. Mongolian Republic women see nothing wrong in taking gifts they did not ask for from local men.

Once a relationship is established, the frequency of interpersonal interaction increases in its intensity. In 2000 it was understood that boys called girls' dorms more than girls called boys' dorms. The popularity of texting (*duanxin*) as the preferred medium of communication altered this sex difference. Young men and women now text their partners on average three to five times a day. The texts vary from a simple "hi" to "Where are you?" to "What are you doing" to more sexually intimate words. For example, a twenty-three-year-old man said his girlfriend sent him the following text: "Last night, I had a beautiful dream, I saw you walk toward me. I felt your hug and your passionate kiss on my face. I saw your smiling eyes look at me." A twenty-nine-year-old woman texted her new boyfriend this romantic message: "I had a beautiful dream. We walked hand and hand to a small café and ordered dinner. The smell of the food makes us hungry and we eat. The candlelight is romantic, we dance, and everyone dances with us. After dancing, we drink rose tea and sleep in a big bed."

There are sex differences in the frequency in which men and women text each other. Once a "dating" relationship is established, females send more than males. A man pointed out, "If you go out with a male friend, who has a girlfriend, he is always answering the phone or sending a reply to a text query." "It seems," he adds, "that girls like to tell their boyfriend about what they are doing right now, but unless the girl asks, a boy seldom tells their girlfriend what they are doing." Young Chinese females assume that a man's response time is evidence of his dedication to her. If he is slow in responding she often assumes he is losing interest in her, which often results in an angry outburst that leads to the man striving to placate or reassure his girlfriend that he is still interested in her and her alone.

A man's reluctance to express his feelings of attachment is a constant source of disappointment. Everyone agreed it would be cool to have a partner who expressed his feelings. But, alas, this is something that most girlfriends and wives seldom receive, or if they do, not to the extent that they would like. A twenty-four-year-old female revealed that the number one complaint among her friends is that their boyfriends do not communicate their desire or love for them enough. She admits, "We all complain that our boyfriends never tell us they like us. We tell them, but they say they show it through their behavior, but not with words. We prefer words."

Chinese women's desire to receive reaffirmation and celebrate their relationship or marriage has contributed to the popularity in which Valentine's Day, Christmas, and International Women's Day have become another opportunity for couples to come together and celebrate their union. Women, but not men, are the primary initiators in seizing upon these days as couple time. Men, for their part, feel obligated but are not always excited about using these days to celebrate their relationship. In America, Valentine's Day is the celebration day men admit to disliking the most. China has yet to conduct a public survey of men's attitude toward these Western celebrations. Many men readily admit to wanting to avoid having to "participate in a silly event." What is significant, however, is that Chinese men, much like their American counterparts, might privately grumble while still participating so as not to upset their lovers.

FEMALES AND THE CONTROL OF SEXUAL INTIMACY

Don Symons (1979) pointed out, in his influential book on human sexuality, that coitus is a service women render to men, but it is seldom perceived as a service that men render to women. The Chinese concur. The following comment by a twenty-seven-year-old woman is representative. She acknowledges, "I am not an easy girl to have sex with a man. I only have sex with a man I love." Another twenty-eight-year-old female nurse said, "I had a boyfriend but never slept with him. He always wanted my body. I refused as I was not sure how sincere he was." A twenty-four-year-old college student seconded her reluctance to immediately sleep with a man. She thought sex without love is not fulfilling. "If there is love, there is sex. Any normal person wants sex. But love should be first, then sex." A forty-two-year-old woman agreed, stressing that "feelings are very important. Deep feelings are best. I think sex is good but only if there is love. Without love, sex has no feeling. It makes no sense." Men, for their part, invoke love thoughts more quickly than women. It is part of a strategy that may involve attachment or just serve to reassure the women that they are interested in them and not just sexual release. Women report that men are forever pleading to have sex more often. To this end, some men argue with their girlfriend that they "are old-fashioned" in wanting to withhold sex. Other men use a different tactic. They argue that their girlfriend is not in touch with contemporary trends as they argue that "Shanghai girls (the symbol of high modernity) have sex quicker, so why don't you?"

Hohhotians' continued valorization of female virginity contributes to a woman's reluctance to become sexually intimate in that city. In the 1980s everyone, especially males, stressed the importance of virginity and told stories from the countryside and in Chinese history of the lengths people went to in order to protect a female's virginity. The strength of this ideal is evident in numerous surveys published on Chinese youths' changing sexual attitudes. A 1990 survey found that 70 percent of students admitted that a woman's virginity is more important than her life (Evans 1997, 108). In 2003, 60 percent of the men admitted they wanted to marry a virgin (McMillan 2006). A 2010 Shanghai undergraduate survey found that around 30 percent of Shanghai college women are virgins (see Farrer's [2002] discussion of Shanghai women's conceptual ambivalence over virginity as a cultural value). This is nearly identical to the percentage reported for American women. Today, virginity remains a salient ideal continuously challenged by the emotional and pragmatic realities inherent in a dating culture.

In the 1980s, engaging in premarital sex could result in imprisonment or being labeled a petty criminal. By the mid-1990s the anti–premarital sex laws were enforced from time to time but for the most part were ignored. A survey found that less than half of students sampled admitted they were in a dating relationship (*tan lian ai*), with only 6 percent of women and 10 percent of men admitting to having had sexual intercourse (McMillan 2006). In contrast, Jankowiak's 2005 Hohhotian undergraduate survey found a higher frequency of young people admitting they were sexually involved. For example, thirty-four out of eighty or 43 percent of the males admitted to sleeping with their girlfriends. As in the 1980s, the majority of men were leaning toward marrying their girlfriends. Only fifteen out of eighty-nine or 19 percent thought they would marry their girlfriend, with another thirty out of eighty-nine or 38 percent admitting to some ambivalence. If we combine the ambivalent "maybes" with the affirmed "yeses" there are forty-five out of eighty or 57 percent of the sample that continue to associate sexual intimacy with a commitment to marry. The association of sexual intimacy with the expectation of marriage was also found within the courtship culture. What is new is that almost half, or 43 percent, of the males interviewed no longer believed that sexual intimacy signals a marital engagement.

Not withstanding the value many Chinese continue to place on the desirability of virginity, Hohhotian youth are becoming sexually involved at an earlier age and at an earlier point in the relationship. The erotic female is celebrated in public media, and it is an image that Chinese women have adopted to attract and hold men's interest. Today, half of all abortions are on unmarried women. This is true in metropolitan Shanghai where health clinics advertise that abortion is easy, painless, quick, and inexpensive. These hospital ads are less obvious in the provincial city of Hohhot. Discussions with local doctors in this city revealed, however, that 50 percent of all abortions at the city's major hospital were conducted on unmarried women. The doctors admitted that they could not determine how many abortions were on single women in a dating situation compared to women who are engaged to marry but whose economic or social conditions make it inconvenient to now have a child. What is clear is the increased frequency in which urbanites in a dating situation are sexuality active. William Parish's national survey found that premarital sex is "one of the most conspicuous markers of the degree of liberalization towards sex" (Parish 2007, 158). His survey found that among China's youngest cohort, those who turned twenty around 1995, more than 40 percent of the men and 25 percent of the females admitted to having had premarital sex.

The image of sexuality as a natural desire and thus a fundamental human need has legitimized emotionalism, or if the body needs something, then it should be allowed to have it, is an accepted idea. The acceptance of this idea carries implications for male–female interaction, whereby men plead and demand sex by justifying their need to satisfy what is for them a natural desire. It would be wrong to infer this rationale as another case of the "sexually pushy male" and the "reluctant prudish female." In China, both sexes are influenced by the naturalism ethos. For example, a twenty-two-year-old female indicated that she is annoyed if her partner has " a condom with him, as it means he was planning to have sex" when she wants the experience to be "more spontaneous". Her opinion is not representative, but many women in a relationship do not insist that their partner wear a condom. This is due to men not enjoying sex as much wearing a condom, a tacit desire to become pregnant, and a feeling that the best sex is natural sex. To use the current jargon women often prefer sex "bareback" style (i.e., wearing no condom or using any birth control devices). When asked if their refusal to use a condom is motivated by what Tiantian Zheng (2009) insists is a political motivation to reject the state's authority to regulate sexuality in the bedroom, everyone burst out laughing at, what was for them, a preposterous explanation.

The ability of young Hohhotian men to manipulate their girlfriends to have sex earlier than they may prefer stems from a deep-seated concern that women readily voice that borders on a paranoid fear that if their man does not have access to sex, he may leave her. It is significant that the two examples (noted earlier) where women were able to deny their boyfriend access to sex were cases where the woman was absolutely sure her boyfriend loved her and would not leave. Hohhotian women, like men, are anxious about becoming involved in a nonreciprocal relationship. They do not want to make an emotional commitment that involves sexual intimacy only to be dropped and abandoned.

Women are caught in something of a bind. They want a boyfriend and they want to please him and not lose him to another girl who will sleep with him. To this end, women often use smart sex as a means to attract, hold on to, and ultimately induce a commitment. In this way, early sexual involvement may result in a greater payoff: it engenders an emotional commitment that might never have been made. It can also have a downside: it can result in a stronger, albeit one-sided, emotional attachment and thus a more painful separation. Women often express their anxiety over a lover's or potential mate's dedication to sexual fidelity by rhetorically asking her partner if he is "a one-woman man." Or, if he thinks it is okay "after marriage to travel with a new girlfriend." The pervasiveness of this concern is readily apparent among college students, who share stories of friends who fell in love with a man and moved into his apartment, only to be abandoned later for another woman. These stories are repeated and over time are transformed into morality fables that serve as warnings of potential disasters for anyone who rushes to act on their love too quickly. Moreover, there is often some truth in these morality tales. Females, more so than males, commonly talk of having been in intimate relationships that ended badly. There is often a subsequent reluctance, outside of a promise to marry, to become sexually involved with another boyfriend. A woman's reluctance to begin a sexual encounter does not mean she does not also want to be sexually desired.

Most Chinese women want to be perceived, especially by their lover or husband, as sexually attractive. When a man they are interested in fails to show sexual interest, women can quickly become annoyed. For example, a twenty-six-year-old admitted that "my boyfriend only put his arm around me for three months but that was all. What is his problem? I simply lost sexual interest to him." Another twenty-six-year-old woman complained that "at first we had hot passionate sex. But lately we have less and less sex. He is younger than me. I wonder why I have to do all the relationship work. It is Chinese tradition that the man should be older and thus make all the plans for the relationship. I wonder why I have to do all the work." Still another young woman was disappointed that her boyfriend showed a lack of excitement with being with her. She told me "I text a lot; my boyfriend does not. In fact, he seldom says, 'I like you.' He told me this once. I tell people I have no boyfriend. I have a distance boyfriend. I notice if I am distant or aloof he wants me, but if I come closer, he does not want me." Another woman acknowledged that her boyfriend is always too busy for her. "He has no time to care of me. He cannot remember my birthday. After a painful year, I said good-bye to him. Although he is indeed a man of potential, he lacks basic responsibility which is an indispensable quality in a good husband."

China's singleton women, much like Western women, prefer an emotionally connected relationship. Hohhotian females, if not most Chinese women, do not view a sexually intimate encounter as a casual undertaking. Moreover, research in America and in China has found that women, compared to men, attach a stronger emotional value to sexual intimacy. This means that sexually active women, compared to men, can potentially lose more not only in terms of their social reputation, but also in their psychological reaction to becoming sexually active with someone not interested in becoming their steady boyfriend.

CONCLUSION

The full impact of China's economic and social reforms was not felt until the late 1990s when China's work-enterprise (*danwei*) system was completely transformed away from an insular command economy toward a more open and vibrant market exchange system. The shift in economic organization has given way to an increasingly unpredictable milieu where social and economic interests compete for China's youth as laborers, consumers, and agents of cultural production. Young people, especially those who have some economic capacity, will be able to transform individualistic modes of expression through their economic decisions into newly created cultural habits. This ongoing and future transformation is a demonstration of the manner in which youth often serve less as agents of cultural reproduction than as catalysts for cultural innovation. Given such historical trends, we can expect that many dramatic developments are in store for the PRC and, ultimately, for China as a whole.

Economic development makes possible the period of independent identity exploration that is at the heart of emerging adulthood (Arnett 2004, 24). Everyone is in solid agreement that full adulthood means much the same thing in urban China that it has come to mean in the U.S.—being able to take responsibility for your actions; make independent decisions about your life; and, lastly, become financially independent (ibid., 209). However, youths continue to define themselves in opposition to adults and do so while engaged in a variety of activities that often enhance cognitive skills and the ability to navigate the challenges of uneasy transitions, fluid careers, and changes in life orientation (Gerson 2009b). The shift in the positive value given to individualism has heightened people's awareness of themselves as special agents, which has, in turn, reinforced the belief in the importance of themselves as unique persons.

There is a gender difference in the speed in which males and females want to emerge out of their youthful stage into adulthood. Females seem more mature earlier than their male counterparts and thus want to begin a family earlier. Males from a similar social class have invested everything in their careers and want to wait for some time to begin a family. The new sexual ethos enables men to delay marriage as their sexual needs can easily be met through prostitution or by just having a series of girlfriends. Women, on the other hand, would rather not engage in anonymous sex with strangers or run through a series of boyfriends. Consequently, women are often more impatient; stressed; and, at times, angry, at the shift in cultural norms. This presents something of a paradox for women. On one hand, they have benefited from the opportunity to explore their inner lives and perhaps achieve a deeper sense of fulfillment. On the other, they may also remain anxious over their inability to find a viable mate who can fulfill their image of creating the "happy family." The search for a life partner who is also a soul mate more than simply a spouse is a strong cultural fantasy constantly articulated in Chinese young women's talk, much more than it is among young men, in both private and public discourse.

Today, twenty-first-century Hohhotian singleton youth are kissing earlier, sleeping together sooner, and having more dating partners than any other generation in Chinese history. The newfound personal freedom, typical of an emergent youth phase, is not without its ambiguities. What is the appropriate time to date, marry, and start a family is less clear-cut. The criteria for assessing maturity has changed and with it the criteria for establishing a responsible sexual self. This is even in the frequency with which young men and women misunderstand one another. An active life within an emergent youth phase is often filled with happiness, joy, and contentment as well as disappointment, regret, and anger over their inability to achieve what is wanted when it is wanted.

ACKNOWLEDGEMENTS

We would like to thank the follow people for their suggestions, encouragement, and editorial insight: Dan Benyskek, Victor DeMunck, Shanshan Du, Vanessa Fong, Peter Gray, Bonnie Hewlett, Sadie Hinson, Deb Martin, William Parish, Alice Schlegel, Pan, Tianshu, and Shen, Yifei.

NOTES

1. A word on methods. In 2000, over one hundred Hohhotian youth were asked to respond to an occupation and gender stereotype survey. Jankowiak conducted his dating survey between 2000 and 2008 using a survey instrument, in-depth interviews with males and females, as well as focused observational studies. The primary sample population is China's youth (aged seventeen to twenty-five). However, we also relied upon a variety of impromptu conversations with men and women concerning their expectations of what to do in a dating setting as well as how to respond once love arises.

REFERENCES

Arnett, J. 2004. Emerging Adulthood: The Winding Road from the Late Teens through the Twenties. New York: Oxford University Press.

Bailey, B. 1988. From Front Porch to Back Seat: Courtship in Twentieth-Century America. Baltimore, MD: Johns Hopkins University Press.

Brooks, D. 2010. "Social Animals: How the New Science of Human Nature Can Help Make Sense of Life," The New Yorker, 1–17, 30.

Collier, J. 1997. From Duty to Desire: Remaking Families in a Spanish Village, Princeton: Princeton University Press.

———. 1999. In the Red. New York: Columbia University Press.

Eibl-Eibesfeldt, I. 1989, Human Ethology. New York: Aldine De Gruyter.

Evans, H. 1997. Women and Sexuality. London: Hurst.

Farrer, J. 2002. Opening Up: Youth Sex Culture and Market Reform in Shanghai. Chicago: University Chicago Press.

Fong, V. 2004. Only Hope. Stanford, CA: Stanford University Press.

Gerson, K. 2009a. "Adulthood Redefined." New York Times, October 30, 2.

———. 2009b. The Unfinished Revolution: How a New Generation Is Reshaping Family, Work and Gender in America. New York: Oxford University Press.

Hewlett, D. "They're Not Going to Take It: China's Women, Facing Pervasive Discrimination, Decide to Fight for Their Rights," Newsweek 8, no. 17 (2009): 19–23.

Jankowiak, W., R. Moore, and Tianshu Pan. 2011. "Growing up in an Emergent Market Economy: China's Young Men" in Young Men around the World, edited by Noel Dyck. Berghahn Publishers, pp. 157–188.

Jankowiak, W. 1993. Sex, Death and Hierarchy in a Chinese City. New York: Columbia University Press.

Louie, K. "Constructing Chinese Masculinity for the Modern World: with Particular Reference to Lao She's The Two Mas," The China Quarterly 164 (2000): 1062–1078.

Mageo, J. "Male Gender Instability and War," Peace Review 17 (2005): 73–80.

McMillan, J. 2006. Sex, Science and Morality in China, New York: Routledge.

Moore, R. "Generation Ku: Individualism and China's Millennial Youth," Ethnology 4 (2005): 357–376.

Moore, R. and Rizor, J. "Confucian and Cool: China's Youth in Transition," Education about Asia (2008): 30–37.

Moore, R. and Wei, L. 2011. Love in Modern China, in The Psychology of Love, vol. 3, Meaning and Culture, edited by M. Paludi. Westport, CT: Praeger.

Parish, W., Ye Luo, R. Stolzenberg, E. Laumann, G. Farrer, and Suiming Pan, "Sexual Practices and Sexual Satisfaction: A Population Based Study of Urban Chinese Adults," Archives of Sexual Behavior 36, 1 (2007): 5–20.

Southwell-Lee, M. 2009. "Women with Money, Women with Minds: Social Status, Gender, and Marriageability in Urban China Today." PhD thesis, Australian National University.

Symons, D. 1979. Human Sexuality. Oxford: Oxford University Press.

Watson, J.L.1997. Golden Arches East: McDonald's in East Asia. Stanford, CA: Stanford University Press.

Zheng, T. 2009. Ethnographies of Prostitution in Contemporary China. New York: Macmillan Books.

Perspectives on Adolescent Identity

Alice Schlegel

The chapters in this book are rich in information that lends itself to extended discussion on a number of topics. However, in this overview I shall restrict myself to the central theme of adolescent identity and follow it through the chapters, commenting on the authors' discussions of identity when such a discussion is present and, when it is not, inferring what we have learned about identity from the authors' data and theoretical positions.

"Identity" is a slippery concept because it has more than one meaning. On the one hand, it means to identify with a person, social group, or social role; on the other, it means to have a concept of oneself as a particular kind of person. In the large literature on identity, these are generally referred to as social identity (identity with) and personal identity (identity as) (see Markstrom, this volume). Although both kinds of identity have cognitive and emotional aspects, social identity is flexible and contingent on circumstances like age or social status and role, whereas personal identity generally implies the sense of what kind of person one believes oneself to be. The two kinds are not entirely separable, for "to identify with" can lead to "to identity as" and vice versa. They may represent two ends of a continuum rather than distinct entities, as when affiliation with a social, religious, or political group becomes a part of one's concept of oneself—the attributes of the social identity becoming deeply held convictions of the personal identity—or personal identity impels an individual to identify with a person, role, or group. Nevertheless, it is useful to keep these kinds of identity analytically separate, as personal identity usually develops over a longer span of time and usually is less amenable to change. For a discussion of identity as a concept comprising both psychological and social processes and a review of the psychological literature on adolescent identity, see Côté (2009).

Erikson (1968) established the study of identity as a task of adolescence, when one integrates earlier identities into a coherent adult one. Marcia (1966) built on Erikson's work to construct a paradigm of identity based on (a) choice, or the conscious deliberation of alternatives, and (b) commitment to these beliefs or courses of action. This paradigm has four cells—low choice-low commitment, low choice-high commitment, high choice-low commitment, and high choice-high commitment. These form a continuum from identity immaturity to identity maturity in that order. Much of the psychological literature on identity has developed, tested, or disputed that paradigm. Marcia calls the low choice-low commitment form "identity diffusion" and the low choice- high commitment form "identity closure." These terms will appear later in this discussion.

One of Erikson's most widely used concepts was that of an identity crisis. This was often interpreted as a severe crisis in adolescence, although that interpretation is no longer accepted. As we shall see, adolescence in some societies can be quite placid, whereas an identity crisis may occur at other points in the life cycle. When personal identity does change suddenly, as in a sincere religious conversion or because of a major life event that shatters existing concepts of oneself, the change may be accompanied by an emotional crisis. This does not seem to be inevitable, however. After a life-threatening illness or accident, it is not uncommon for survivors to reevaluate their beliefs about themselves gradually and realize that they have become more compassionate and responsive in their relations with others. Looking across cultures, we see that the development of identity in childhood and adolescence and the changes that may occur during the process are not necessarily accompanied by an emotional crisis; in fact, they may be very incremental and slow. (Similarly, the changes in personal identity at the other end of life, as one transitions into old age, may also be gradual and devoid of any kind of crisis for those whose personal identity is not dependent on physical strength, dominance, or sexuality.)

If identity change does not necessarily involve self-doubt or confusion, then how do we account for crisis-present vs. crisis-absent? Do differences depend on factors, heritable or epigenetic, that are specific to individuals? Do particular circumstances or cultural conditions, beliefs, and values contribute to the presence or absence of a crisis? In the review that follows, I shall address some of these issues.

BIOLOGICAL AND COGNITIVE BASIS FOR ADOLESCENT IDENTITY

Bogin and Ellis both look at adolescence from an evolutionary point of view. Bogin's approach defines adolescence as a biological developmental stage, which may or may not correspond exactly to adolescence as a culturally defined social stage. Adolescence is treated by all cultures for which we have evidence as a social stage intervening between the social stage of late childhood, which usually begins around age seven and ends around puberty, and some recognition of adulthood such as marriage or the assumption of adult productive and civic roles (Schlegel and Barry 1991). (Bogin's juvenile stage, from adrenarche to puberty, roughly corresponds to the social stage of late childhood.) In human evolution, our hominin ancestors evolved through natural selection into a species with a shorter infancy and a longer period of childhood and adolescence. Human adolescence differs from the short transitional period, between puberty to the beginning of effective reproduction, that our near kin the great apes experience (Walters 1987).

The appearance of these new stages, lengthening the period of high dependence on adults for survival, made it possible for humans to store up reserve capacity and to acquire greater physical and cognitive capacity than is necessary for growth. This has important implications for later life; for as capacity becomes depleted over the life span, capacity stored up in the juvenile and adolescent stages allows life to extend beyond the reproductive years. Thus, post-reproductive life did not evolve per se, nor was it the by-product of better nutrition, control of predation, and social organization that allows for care for the sick and elderly. It was a consequence of the greater reserve capacity accumulated during these juvenile and adolescent years.

This argument gives a biological underpinning to what we know from observation, that "the child is the father of the man." Resources spent on helping individuals develop reserve capacity, what others might call physical, cognitive, and social capital, pay off in the distant as well as the near future. For humans, we might add cultural capital, the knowledge of how to operate in and use one's culture to achieve one's goals, including one's successful reproduction through children and, eventually, grandchildren.

Where does identity fit into such an evolutionary discussion? Chimps, our closest primate relatives, appear to have a physical self-identity. Experiments show that they point to the red dot that has been painted on their foreheads when they look in a mirror. This is of a different order from the dog that barks at its mirror image, seeing another dog but not recognizing itself. Chimps may also have a social identity, derived from the way others treat them as male or female, juvenile or old, a member of the troupe or an enemy. But it is hard to believe that they have personal identities. That would seem to require self-reflection, dependent on the kind of cognitive capacity only humans have. The new stages of juvenile and adolescence comprise the life period in which personal identities can fully develop.

Ellis turns to another aspect of evolutionary theory, the response of the developing individual to environmental cues. He applies life history theory, which deals with reproductive strategies as contingent on cues presented early in life. Life history strategy (LHS) refers to the strategy that will produce the most offspring who themselves survive to reproduce, depending on food security, predation vulnerability, and, in humans and perhaps great apes, the ability to control or at least manage the environment. A slow LHS is one of slow growth to maturity, few offspring, and care of the young to a greater or lesser degree, and it is the LHS of humans and great apes, among other animals. A fast LHS is one of quick growth, many offspring, and little or no care of the young.

Although different species have characteristic LHSs from fast to slow, there can be variation toward one form or another within a species depending on cues to reproductive success. In humans, the contrast is between reproducing as early and as much as possible within the limits of our spe-cies, hoping that some offspring will get adequate care and survive, and reproducing fewer offspring later and providing them with more than ade-quate care—in Bogin's terms, building up their reserve capacity.

Ellis posits that high risk taking in adolescence is a form of (relatively) fast LHS as a response to cues in early life that life is unpredictable and may be short; therefore, it is important to reproduce as early and much as pos-sible. For both sexes, this means early sexual activity and reproduction. For boys, it means leading to activities that have a high immediate payoff even though they may be dangerous, such as gaining material resources through illegal activities and social resources through physical dominance. These resources imply, however falsely, high mate value, and this attracts multiple females. Girls are willing to reproduce if they foresee adequate resources for child survival from a mate or other sources. Humans are cooperative breeders, i.e., we get help from people to whom we are tied through kinship or other social relations. Even just enough help to allow most offspring to survive is sufficient although not optimal. Fast LH strategists, and the chil-dren they produce, are unlikely to be able to store up the reserve capacity (to use Bogin's term) to help them in the near and distant future. High risk taking is a strategy based on the fact that something is better than nothing for those who face early death or disability: get what you can now, as there is no guarantee of getting it in the future.

An earlier view of high-risk takers was based on a moral model: the unde-serving poor—aggressive, often criminal, and promiscuous, who had many children early in life without providing good care—were immoral and had to be controlled. A more recent model is a medical one: such behavior is dys-functional and maladaptive and individuals need to be treated. (The develop-mental psychopathology model that Ellis refers to is a variant of the medical model.) An evolutionary model maintains that such behavior is not maladap-tive but, rather, adaptive to the conditions these people face. This implies that to change the behavior, change the conditions that cue such behavior.

Where does identity fit in? Within their social milieu these high-risk takers, when they succeed, are admired. This may lead to a strong social identification with the group and with those on whom they depend and who depend on them. We have no clues here as to personal identity, and we wonder how they see themselves. Judging by the actions of these high-risk takers, they fit into Marcia's (1966) category of diffused identity: little self-regulation or purposiveness, more self-focus, and risky behavior. We shall return to this question when we consider Kovats-Bernat's chapter, in which he looks into the lives of high-risk takers.

The first sections of Chandler and Dunlop's chapter critique the position that adolescence is a time of identity crisis. They believe that this position is too mechanical and not supported by evidence. Their theoretical position is that with the growth of cognitive competence, older children and adoles-cents begin to have doubt. The term *doubt* has negative connotations and can imply indeterminacy and the avoidance of commitment. A more theoretically neutral way of looking at this is that older children and adolescents begin to see alternatives and then evaluate what they have always taken for granted. Self-reflection and the construction of a personal identity based on choice, made with or without conscious awareness among a greater or smaller range of alternatives, is a function of normal development. Growing awareness of alternatives is probably gradual, unless one is thrown into a radically new environment. Choice of alternatives may be gradual as well, and it may change during late childhood, adolescence, and early adulthood, or later in life when faced with inconsistencies or dilemmas.

Awareness of alternatives in adolescence, in my view, depends not just on growing cognitive competence, but also on shifts in social and emotional orientation, away from almost exclusive dependence on the family and attachment to familiar individuals toward greater involvement with and attachment to peers and to adults outside the family. During late childhood, children form same-sex peer groups, more structured and emotionally salient than the informal play groups of early childhood. This social and emotional development may be triggered by the hormonal changes in adrenarche (Campbell 2008). During adolescence following puberty, interaction and involvement with adults, not necessarily kin or authority figures, is added (Schlegel and Barry 1991), and the emotional dependence on the family is weakened. This distancing prepares adolescents to form a new attachment with a relative stranger who will become a mate, and to have social and emotional ties to adult peers when they themselves are adult. One cannot separate the construction of a personal identity from either cognitive development or from hormonal changes—adrenarche, puberty—and their social and emotional consequences.

CULTURAL CONTEXTS OF IDENTITY DEVELOPMENT

The ethnographic chapters deal, implicitly or explicitly, with identity formation during adolescence or post-adolescence. Two of these chapters, by Hewlett and Hewlett and by Takeuchi, are about the Aka, foragers of Central Africa. Hewlett and Hewlett tell us that Aka adolescents do not have an identity crisis as defined by Erikson. Following Chandler and Dunlop's argument that self-awareness of a personal identity, and an identity crisis, are initiated by doubt, or by confrontation with alternatives, we must take a close look at the absence of an identity crisis in this foraging society. Aka teenagers are aware of several different ways of living, as they encounter foreigners, such as NGO personnel, and know about the capital city to which they could move. Some adolescent boys go to lumber camps as temporary laborers (Takeuchi). The closest and strongest alternative lifeway is that of their farming Bantu neighbors. Aka increasingly are taking up some farming, but for many this is not an alternative they choose (Bonnie Hewlett, personal communication). For most Aka, adolescent social and personal identity as Aka appears to be a continuation of a social and personal identity chosen, or more likely automatically assumed, earlier in childhood.

The Hunter-Gatherer Childhood Model of late weaning, infant indulgence and close physical contact, variable responsibilities in childhood, and multiage play groups (Hewlett and Hewlett) is the basis for close attachment and expression of intimacy. (Some of these features also characterize small-scale farming cultures [cf. Lancy 1996].) The foundational schema of Aka culture (Hewlett and Hewlett), which is transmitted through child socialization, includes egalitarianism, autonomy, flexibility, and trust. When children learn this schema through experience with others, they are likely to become autonomous, flexible, sharing, and trusting and trustworthy people, with a strong sense of self-worth. Why should they choose to become anything other than Aka? Self-identity and cultural identity are closely entwined.

Takeuchi expands on Hewlett and Hewlett's discussion of Aka adolescence to describe the process by which an indulged child becomes a responsible adult. Adolescent initiation rituals, somewhat more elaborate for girls than for boys, ritually move children into a kind of social apprenticeship. Both sexes distance themselves somewhat from their parents and younger siblings by sleeping away from home: boys in a men's house (hut), and girls in small individual huts they build next to their parents' hut. Boys leave the settlement for prolonged periods to visit other settlements in search of girls. They spend much of their time hunting, sometimes with adult men. Girls stay closer to home and work with mothers and other women. Boys become men when they are socially recognized as competent hunters; girls become women when they have given birth.

Considering alternatives is a cognitive process, even though it might be the result of hormonal changes and their social consequences as much as cognitive maturation. However, we should not neglect the emotional factors that color identity formation. As Hewlett and Hewlett tell us, Aka children grow up in an emotional environment of great trust and strong familial attachment, even as independence is stressed and children are socialized for autonomy. Along with this independence of action goes the high degree of social and emotional dependence on kin and neighbors, for foragers' survival depends on maintaining and affirming close bonds with others through physical contact and emotional intimacy. These firm attachments, formed in childhood, persist in adolescence and would modify tendencies to separate emotionally from the family. It may be that for the Aka, the identity that developed in childhood is not in question, and strong emotional intimacy continues from childhood into adolescence, counteracting emotional separation and diminishing it. In Marcia's (1966) terms this would be identity foreclosure, but nothing here indicates emotional immaturity among the Aka. For those who choose to remain in the settlements and identify as traditional Aka, this is a life of social and emotional security, which also allows a great deal of autonomy and freedom of action.

For both sexes, social identity changes when adolescents become recognized as adults. Across cultures, marriage almost always involves a change of residence for at least one spouse. The result can be an identity conflict as the spouse must learn to identify with his or her new mate and possibly other household members. Such a conflict has been widely reported for young wives in patrilocal households. Young husbands in matrilocal households can feel the same way when they come under the authority of parents-in-law, as my own talks with Hopi Indian men and women revealed. For the Aka, residence is relatively flexible, and attachment to the spouse need not conflict with loyalty to one's natal family, as couples can move between households. In this case, the circle of social identity is expanded more than shifted when one marries.

Adolescence seems to be rather placid among the Dominicans, as depicted by Quinlan and Hansen. In the small remote village they studied, the residents, like the foraging Aka, had few attractive local alternatives. Migrants, on whose remittances some local families depended, tended to move permanently or for long terms and thus did not continually bring back goods and ideas from the larger world (Marsha Quinlan, personal communication), as do migrants who make frequent trips home.

Quinlan and Hansen studied how the introduction of television affected this small closed community. The answer seems to be "somewhat" rather than "greatly." Watching television is a social activity of family members and neighbors of all generations, who gather to watch programs together. Adult men go off together in the evening, sometimes to watch television, but the adolescent boys stay home with the women and children (Marsha Quinlan, personal communication), and all chat or comment on what they are seeing.

Dominican boys, like adolescent boys in most traditional societies (Schlegel and Barry 1991), spend most of their leisure hours together away from women and girls (Marsha Quinlan, personal communication). In the evening, however, television provides an incentive for them to be with female family members and neighbors. This may be a first step in breaking down the gender separation that still characterizes Dominica. If so, it could be the beginning of a change in male gender identity, in how one defines oneself as a man.

Rather than replacing interaction with kin and neighbors, television adds another dimension. Watchers comment on the behavior on-screen, so that, as in other forms of fantasy production like folk theater, the television program is a vehicle for social and moral commentary. Parents blame television programs for the cheekiness of younger children, the less modest dress of adolescent girls, and the dress and talk of the adolescent boys when they copy the "gangsta" style they have viewed. Nevertheless, parents see benefits in improved Standard English and more information about the world. Television has been incorporated into long-standing patterns of family and community relations; it has not disrupted them nor has it led to greater social isolation.

What can we infer from this study about adolescent identity in Dominica? With little change in family or neighborly relations, children seem to ease into and through adolescence without much stress. A major decision for both girls and boys is whether to emigrate. Those who do emigrate may find that their major identity conflict occurs in young adulthood, for it is then that they are faced with the "between two worlds" problem, the discrepancy between the one from which they came and the one they are living in.

Jankowiak and Moore consider the lives of post-adolescents, the young adults of China. They face rapid change, from life under Maoist communism to life in a communist society that embraces economic capitalism while at the same time it resists many of the social changes that the globalization of capitalism brings. Rather than a clearly defined youth stage intervening between adolescence and adulthood, modern Chinese post-adolescence is more like Arnett's (2004) "emerging adulthood," where there is no single event like marriage to mark the beginning of full social adulthood. Young adults have much greater independence than they did under either the traditional Chinese or Maoist systems, including greater sexual freedom. This independence and sexual freedom are not without costs, for the result is greater insecurity in the first and greater uncertainty in the second instances.

Young men are the ones who are most affected by insecurity. When one depended on the family and kin group or the Party for one's economic position, one's future prospects might be unsatisfactory but at least they were relatively clear. The future almost always included marriage and fatherhood, without which male social adulthood was incomplete. Today, however, marriage is more problematic, as young men have to earn enough to support a family and to find a wife who meets their expectations.

Young women are most affected by uncertainty. In order to succeed on the job, they have to be competent and businesslike; yet, to attract a suitable husband, they have to be feminine. This was not such a problem in pre-communist China, when young women were expected to be feminine and demure. Under Maoism, outward marks of femininity were discouraged as distracting from social goals. Today's young Chinese women are like the young American women of the 1970s and 1980s, eager to succeed in public life but uncertain about how feminine to appear on the job and whether displays of their competence discouraged desirable men. It took a long time in the U.S. for the feminine half of the "power couple" to replace the corporate wife as the ideal mate. In spite of some spectacularly successful and married female entrepreneurs, China isn't there yet.

China's young women foresee the problem common to modern women everywhere: how to balance career and childcare. Women's greater participation in the workplace has not been accompanied by more household help on the part of husbands. An overriding theme in young women's personal identity, then, revolves around what they see as two competing social identities, the competent career woman and the self-sacrificing wife and mother. How should they balance the traditional wife-mother ideal and the modern career woman ideal? This adds to the uncertainty in young women's lives.

Identity themes for males in both pre-communist and Maoist China were the genteel scholar-official, or *wu*, and its opposite *wen*, the tough aggressive man. Both of these imply competence in controlling the situation: the scholar through wisdom and judgment, and the aggressive man through social dominance. Today these are combined, so that the ideal modern male is in control through both good judgment, which entails some emotional distance, and assertiveness. This is *ku*, the Chinese interpretation of the Western term *cool*. How to be cool in the face of intense competitiveness, job insecurity, finding a girlfriend and meeting her demands while fulfilling others' expectations—all this requires considerable image management and flexibility.

Post-adolescents rather than adolescents are the focus of Jankowiak and Moore's chapter. Future research could examine the trickle-down effect of this shift in social and personal identities on younger girls and boys.

Young people in Kuwait also face competing social and personal identities, but these are less between generations than between more traditional and more modern families. Although almost all native Kuwaitis are urban, economically secure, and Muslim, they are surrounded by thousands of immigrant workers, most of whom are Christian. Wide use of the Internet and other media also exposes adolescents to different ways of behaving and viewing the world than they find in their homogeneous traditional society. Although Arabic lacks a term for *adolescence*, it is informally recognized in the ways that these young people behave and are treated by others.

In their study of adolescent personal identity in Kuwait, Ahmed and Gibbons used both questionnaires and drawings of the ideal woman and ideal man. They drew their sample of adolescents from public schools, which segregate girls and boys and thus would seem to favor a traditional viewpoint. Nevertheless, the drawings reveal that some adolescents see ideal adults as modern in their dress and settings. "Modern" drawings showed modern dress, more isolated figures, and the workplace, whereas "traditional" drawings showed traditional dress and often adults accompanied by children. These features were true for drawings by both sexes of both women and men. Do contrasting and somewhat conflicting social identities as traditional or modern, with their accompanying personal identities as commitment to one or the other set of values, lead to identity conflict in adolescents who have not yet made a clear choice? There are cases where whole cultures, like the Pueblo Indians of New Mexico, hold separate and conflicting sets of religious beliefs without apparent identity conflict. The term applied to this ability to hold conflicting sets of beliefs is *compartmentalization*, in which one set of beliefs applies to some settings or circumstances, and the other set of beliefs applies to other settings and circumstances.

Kuwait adolescents who favor traditional over modern, or vice versa, may eventually compartmentalize, becoming the man, or less likely the woman, who has a job in the modern sector for which he or she dresses in modern style, and then comes home to traditional dress and more traditional sex roles. Such compartmentalization requires a rather strict division between public and private life, especially for women who take on nontraditional roles in public life. For them, this may only be possible under certain social conditions such as access to extended networks of family and kin who provide domestic help and support, or the availability of servants to take over many of women's time-consuming domestic duties. Even so, they may face the same dilemma of personal identity that young Chinese women face (Jankowiak and Moore).

Like the Kuwaitis, Navajos and Apaches of the American Southwest can also select elements from both modern and traditional cultures. (Much of the "traditional" is actually relatively recent, dating back only to the late nineteenth century when the tribes were pacified by the U.S. government and turned to farming and market-oriented herding as their principal economic endeavors. Girls' ceremonies, however, undoubtedly date back well into the past of these groups, when they were foragers.) In the chapter on identity formation in American Indian girls, Markstrom discusses the rituals performed in early adolescence, particularly those for Navajo and Apache girls.

The transition from childhood to adolescence is not ceremonially marked in modern American culture, but for Navajos and Apaches, the girl's ceremony was the turning point to a period of serious preparation for adult responsibility in economic tasks, marriage, and motherhood. The ceremonies emphasize health, strength, and good moral character.

These ceremonies are sponsored by the girls' families and involve the extended family and kin as contributors to the present-day considerable financial cost. Some extended families may not have the means, others may be unstable and unable to organize a ceremony, and members of some of the Christian churches on the reservations may disapprove (Carol Markstrom, personal communication). There are also girls who are more interested in "modern" activities who do not see the ceremony as consonant with their social or personal identity. Even if family members strongly urge their daughter and granddaughter to have a ceremony, the final decision is up to her.

Most of the families that hold a ceremony live on one of the tribal reservations, where they are embedded in kin and community relationships and are constantly reminded of their ethnicity. It is likely that most of their daughters also include ethnicity in their social and personal identities. The ceremony strengthens this and reinforces the values they have learned by including physical activities and ritual objects that symbolize these values and give them a physical presence. The spirit of Changing Woman (Navajo) or White Painted Woman (Apache), the supernatural figures who embody all the female virtues, enters the girl and transforms her. After that it is her responsibility to live up to the standard of female behavior personified in these deities. The ceremony engenders powerful emotions and a commitment to fulfill the expectation of good womanhood. The social and economic participation of family and kin predicts that their support will also be there for her in the future.

The aboriginal peoples of British Columbia, who appear in the latter sections of Chandler and Dunlop's chapter, at first glance all seem to live in dysfunctional communities, as indicated by the high suicide rate among the Indigenous youth of the province. Chandler and Dunlop propose that these youth believe that they have no future, brought on by such severe disruption of their culture that their culture has no future. They ask whether severe cultural disruption leads to despair, which is a motivation to commit suicide.

On closer look, they found that not all Indigenous communities suffer from high suicide rates; in fact, some of them have rates as low as, or lower than, white communities, with more than half of the Indigenous bands in the province suffering no youth suicide during the six-year research period. Ninety percent of the suicides occurred in only 12 percent of the bands. Dunlop and Chandler studied both the high- and low- (or no-) suicide bands, drawing hypotheses from their theoretical position. They identified six variables related to local control: over local government; over delivery of three civic services; over cultural resources; and over future access to traditional tribal lands using the Canadian court system. To this they added a seventh, control over child protection services, and two additional variables, band-level knowledge of the Indigenous language and the proportion of women in band government. They found that every band characterized by all of these features experienced no youth suicide during the research period, whereas those lacking any of these features suffered rates far above the national average. They account for this by considering those communities that had these features as building connections to their traditional past, whereas those without them had lost connection. This loss of cultural connection at the community level, then, translates into despair among youths of those bands.

It is surely true that youths who live in dysfunctional communities, those that offer no hope for the future and do not prepare their youth for successful adult lives, are more likely to feel hopeless than youths who see paths to a fulfilling future. But there may be factors other than, or as well as, cultural continuity or discontinuity involved here. I say this because for the Ijo communities of Nigeria studied by Hollis and Leis (1989), it was the traditional village in which adolescents had little hope for the future and for future fulfillment, and the modern one in which they were more purposeful and better prepared for their futures.

A central feature of the successful communities in Chandler and Dunlop is the fairly high level of control that these bands, and the people in them, have over their own lives and futures. We would like to know more about the successful communities as compared to the high-suicide ones. Did they differ by access to well-paying jobs or other secure sources of income that the bands or individuals within them controlled (i.e., not welfare)? Greater economic opportunities for adults can result in better familial relationships, and these possibly transmit the adaptive value of a slow LHS to the children. What about educational opportunities for youth, both academic and vocational, allowing them to take advantage of economic opportunities and expand their vision of the world? Are there links to the larger society—social and political capital—that communities and individuals can draw on for access to people who can help them and institutions they can utilize? Are low-suicide communities better integrated into broader Canadian life than high-suicide ones?

Reviving cultural traditions does not come automatically. Markstrom points out that Navajo and Apache ceremonies resurged after the tribes began using the national legal system to gain control over ancestral lands and took advantage of policies designed to provide education and other resources to Indigenous peoples. One might say about cultural revivals what has been said about revolutions: they are born of hope, not despair.

Both the U.S. and Canadian governments now have laws and policies that are designed to right some of the grievous wrongs committed against Indigenous peoples in earlier times. The ability to use these laws and policies to gain control over various kinds of resources, both traditional ones like land and modern ones like education, paid jobs, and healthcare, is an important factor in whether a tribe will be successful in providing hope and opportunities to its youth. But as Chandler and Dunlop point out, knowledge of what one came from, and a positive view of that ancestry, also contribute to self-worth and a positive self-identity. Young people so fortified are unlikely to commit suicide.

Van Meijl also considers adolescents in Indigenous societies that came under the control of dominant European-derived societies, this time in the Pacific Islands. He refers especially to Tongans who have migrated to Australia and to the aboriginal Maori of New Zealand. In many of the Indigenous communities, local traditions are alive and strongly held. When adolescents want to venture out from the close circle of their ethnic communities, they are criticized. For them the problem is to negotiate both an ethnic identity and one that encompasses the advantages of modern life. They speak about ethnic confusion. Some go through a period of disaffection; they leave the church, a central institution of many contemporary Pacific Island communities, which has become part of their traditional culture as it was redefined after American and European colonization. They experiment with drugs, alcohol, and alternative lifestyles, not unlike disaffected adolescents in the dominant culture.

Individuals have multiple identities. Van Meijl turns to the concept of the dialogic self, based on Bakhtin's metaphor of the polyphonic novel and William James's distinction between the "I" and the "me," to understand the question of identity formation and change. The dialogic self allows for not only plural but also competing identities (as does compartmentaliza-tion). He states that this dialogic perspective on the self is not intrapsychic but rather relational, drawing forth the identity most appropriate to the situation. And indeed, modern adolescence is a time when there is much experimentation with social and personal identities expressed through slang, style of dress, personal appearance, and various aspects of expres-sive culture like recreational activities and styles of music.

For many Pacific Island adolescents, identity formation is made more dif-ficult by older people in their families and communities who feel threatened by any perceived rejection of traditional ways. They throw up roadblocks by implying that these young people are inauthentic. Most adolescents are resilient and creative enough to weather this period; however, for those who are not, there is no single way to resolve this conflict.

One way these adolescents could possibly manage conflicting ethnic identities is by compartmentalizing and by adopting flexible personal iden-tities. Another is to identify not so much with a particular ethnic group, from which one may or may not distance oneself, as with a broader group, Pacific Islander. (This is similar to the pan-Indian social identity in the U.S. that first arose in the Indian boarding schools during the late nineteenth and early twentieth centuries, when children began to identify as Indian along with their tribal identities.) Such a social identity provides the basis for political and social action by uniting groups that once had few contacts or possibly hostile ones. This process has just begun for Pacific Islanders, so the outcome of this new identity form has yet to be seen.

If the future is unpredictable for Pacific Islander adolescents, it is only too predictable for the street children, many of them adolescents, of the slums of Port-au-Prince. Haiti is one of the poorest nations on earth. The slums in which many of the capital city's inhabitants live are the battlefields of gangs in control of the illicit activities that constitute much of the local economy.

About two-thirds of the street children are boys, and most of them are estimated to be between the ages of nine and sixteen or seventeen (Christo-pher Kovats-Bernat, personal communication). They live as best they can, one way being to work for a gang boss running errands, acting as lookouts, or otherwise being useful. Their payments come in the form of food, small sums of money, alcohol, and glue for sniffing. Their bosses, some of whom are older adolescents who may be as young as fifteen or sixteen years old (Christopher Kovats-Bernat, personal communication), provide them with some protection and provision. This care, such as it is, is a mixed bless-ing, as it involves them in extremely dangerous activities and provides no guarantees for the future, or even that they will have a future. It is the only alternative to homes that provide little or no care, and these children and adolescents believe they are better off on the street than they would be if they returned home.

Things were bad enough before 1995, when the government of Presi-dent Aristede disbanded the army but did not disarm the soldiers. Today, about 90 percent of small arms are in the hands of civilians, and weapons continue to be smuggled in, mainly from Florida. The result of arming desperately poor people in overcrowded, socially disorganized slums is as one might expect—the formation of armed gangs that control narcotics trafficking and dominate neighborhoods through intimidation and protection rackets.

The effects of gun proliferation have exacerbated the dangers the street children face. As they compete with one another for resources, or defend their reputations against perceived insults, violence that once caused injuries but was rarely lethal can now be deadly. And many are killed: assault and homicide are the leading causes of death among adolescents. Killing, once deplored, is now accepted as something that just happens. In Ellis's terms, these adolescents are high-risk takers of the most extreme sort.

What can we infer about identity in this catalogue of misery? It is unlikely that these young people have the luxury to experiment with various social identities. Marcia (1966) might characterize them as having a diffuse personal identity. It seems to be tied to their standing in the eyes of others, for they are willing to fight and kill in response to a perceived insult. This implies that their sense of self is very fragile. The description of the lives of these adolescents suggests a very deep sense of emotional isolation and impermanency of attachments. It must be difficult to form a strong personal identity when life is hand to mouth and random violent death is ever present.

CONCLUSION

We began this review with a look at some central features of research into adolescence. Bogin gave us the evolutionary importance of adolescence as a period for physical and cognitive development during which reserve capacity is built, and Chandler and Dunlop pointed out the cognitive component of identity formation during adolescence. Ellis looked at why risk taking is a normal part of adolescence, and how its extreme form is adaptive to environmental conditions that predict poor reproductive success.

I have already discussed high-risk taking, a component of Marcia's (1966) concept of identity diffusion, as it characterizes the Haitian street children described by Kovats-Bernat. Here we wonder why some children and adolescents in these desperately poor slums become street children and why others do not, even though the larger environment is the same. What are the cues that inform the young child that resources are unpredictable, and what kinds of resources are we talking about? Is high or low parental care, including care by parental surrogates, the link between the environment and the development of a fast or slow LHS? Are the FLH strategists in effect thrown into the street, or into this strategy, by neglectful or indifferent parents? Are cues that a FLH strategy is adaptive transmitted epigenetically, through changes in brain function that result in changes in neural pathways?

Ellis refers to studies that look into the mechanisms by which cues are translated into behavior, and why some individuals are more susceptible than others to cues that a FLH strategy is adaptive. We might also ask about the disaffected Pacific Island youth who turn to drugs and alcohol (van Meijl) and the hopeless youth of some British Columbian tribes who commit suicide (Chandler and Dunlop). Not all young people from these backgrounds choose these paths. Here the medical model of finding and intervening in these mechanisms, which is aimed at individuals, could add to other forms of intervention when the damage has already been done or when individuals can be identified as needing this treatment before they harm themselves or others.

The evolutionary model tells us that risk taking is a normal part of adolescent development in both sexes, and risk taking that is neither destructive nor antisocial should not be discouraged. Indeed, life without risks is a life that is dull and colorless. Meeting challenges is a way of proving competency, and that is an important component of self-esteem and self-worth.

The evolutionary model also tells us that a FLH strategy is adaptive when the calculated advantages outweigh the risks. However, not all adolescents in a dysfunctional environment, even from the same family, follow a FLH strategy; so other factors must also be considered. Heritable dispositions seem to play a part, as Ellis's discussion of differential susceptibility implies: the high-stimulus seeker, who in a different environment might become a commodities trader or test pilot, is drawn to the high-risk and possible high-reward activities of the street. Do peer cultures of high-risk taking develop, so that adolescents who are neutral or even averse to high-risk taking follow the norm established by the successful risk takers to avoid being stigmatized by their peers? Do all of these factors play a part in the development or use of this strategy? If so, how do they interact?

Another concept introduced by Marcia (1966) into the identity literature is that of foreclosure. Persons with foreclosed personal identities are characterized as conformist, obedient, identifying strongly with parental beliefs and values, and rigid in their thinking. This poses problems for cross-cultural perspectives on identity, for small-scale stable cultures with few role or status alternatives themselves are high on conforming to established beliefs and values. In many cultures, children are socialized to be obedient to elders. Does this mean that people in such cultures are rigid in their thinking? Carried to the logical extreme of Marcia's paradigm, are they thus less mature and psychologically complex?

Anthropologists who have lived in such cultures would not characterize the adult members as immature or psychologically simple. Such a characterization seems a better fit for rigid, highly conformist people in modern cultures, who choose not to consider alternatives because of fear of change or emotional fragility. The Aka and the Dominicans who choose to remain within their cultures do not necessarily do so without considering the alternatives (moving closer to a Bantu lifestyle and emigrating, respectively), nor do they necessarily do so because of fear or fragility. For many, the close emotional ties and the satisfactions that life in the home culture brings are of higher value than novelty or possibly greater economic gain.

One aspect of socialization is learning the rules of one's cultures. Another is when and how to break the rules, i.e., how to manage the sometime discrepancy between cultural expectations and individual interests. The competent individual in any culture knows when and how to conform and when and how not to do so. In spite of our emphasis on individual autonomy, Americans are highly conformist and obedient, compared to many other nationals, in paying income taxes and following the rules of the road when driving; people in some other cultures are more obedient and conformist in their private lives but less so in public. Individuals can find autonomy and act with agency in any culture or condition that is not despotic, creatively using their culture rather than being passive followers of it. Adolescence is a time when one begins to learn these cultural strategies.

Can we use the theories and findings in these chapters to advance our thinking about public policy? The high-risk-taking adolescents of Kovats-Bernat's chapter may be adapting in the best possible way to their particular individual environments, but that does not mean that they are pursuing a life course that will give them the greatest satisfaction. The suicidal youth of the Canadian tribal groups that Chandler and Dunlop describe are escaping through death rather than adapting to their conditions, which leads neither to life satisfaction nor to reproductive success. The Aka and the Dominican adolescents, on the other hand, do not exhibit antisocial or personally destructive behavior. The Aka whose personal identity is strongly tied to their home culture express strong emotional attachment to kin, and both they and the Dominican adolescents are embedded in the social networks of kin and neighbors and are in frequent interaction with them.

The medical model of risk taking, which seeks to prevent and change destructive high-risk taking and connected forms of antisocial behavior, is applicable to programs of prevention and change that operate on the individual level. Various interventions designed to promote self-regulation have been tried, some with considerable success. These indicate that it is possible to modify high-risk taking. It may be that only some individuals are amenable to change, those with lesser dispositions to stimulus seeking or those whose early life contained some cues that counteracted other cues that life is unpredictable. Whatever the reasons that interventions work with some individuals and do not with others, interventions are limited in the numbers that can be affected.

The evolutionary model implies that high-risk behavior that is dangerous or antisocial can be prevented by changing the conditions that give those cues in early life. Sociologists, pointing to years of research, might recommend economic and social improvements that make life more predictable and hopeful. Anthropologists and psychologists like Chandler and Dunlop who work with ethnic minority groups might point to changes in political policies that give local groups more control over their lives and resources, as well as the possibility of gaining new resources or regaining traditional ones. Psychologists and family studies researchers might show how teaching young adults how to be responsive parents can help to improve the emotional environment of their young children, and contribute to building that reserve capacity (Bogin) for their near and future development.

The evolutionary model also shows that we are among the mammalian species that are cooperative breeders. In most cultures, children are cared for by a number of persons in addition to parents: siblings, grandparents and other kin, neighbors, paid or unpaid caretakers. Fosterage of older children and adolescents, sending them away into other families to help out or to learn practical or social skills, was common in many cultures and historical periods. Adolescents in most cultures are often in the company of adults. They work alongside adults, and they frequently take their leisure with or near them (Schlegel and Barry 1991). In all of these settings, children and adolescents participate in normal community social life. We see examples of this in the Aka, where adolescent boys may hunt with men (Takeuchi), and Dominica, where all ages gather to watch television (Quinlan and Hansen). The Navajo and Apache girls who go through their adolescent initiation ceremonies (Markstrom) are consciously choosing tribal identity as a component of their personal identity; this reinforces the ethnic identity already developed through years of close interaction with adults in their large social networks based on kinship, clanship, and community membership.

Close participation with adults reinforces other methods of cultural transmission and promotes a sense of cultural identity with the adults, whether this culture is ethnic, religious, occupational, or that of a particular status group. There is plenty of room within cultural identity for the development of highly individual personal identities based on temperament, personal experiences, and reflection on what one has seen and learned. Cultural identity comes into question when the home culture does not provide opportunities for a life that the adolescent foresees as satisfactory, like the Pacific Islanders who want to break away from what they seem to perceive as the chokehold of their traditional communities (van Meijl).

Taken together, these chapters provide a rich source of materials that expand our understanding of social and personal identity. Some researchers on identity may find that the theories and data presented here challenge their models, which are based for the most part on participants in modern Western culture. Others will incorporate these theories into their own conceptual frames and use the ethnographic case studies to balance studies based on Western populations. Whether or not identity is a focus of their interest, all those interested in adolescence will find these chapters illuminating and thought-provoking.

REFERENCES

Arnett, J. 2004. Emerging Adulthood: The Winding Road from the Late Teens through the Twenties. New York: Oxford University Press.

Campbell, B.C. "Adrenarche and the Evolution of Human Life History," American Journal of Human Biology 18 (2008): 559–589.

Côté, J.E. 2009. Identity formation and self-development in adolescence, in *Handbook of Adolescent Psychology*, 3rd ed., vol. 1: *Individual Bases of Adolescent Development*, edited by R.M. Lerner and L. Steinberg. Hoboken, NJ: John Wiley and Sons, pp. 266–304.

Erikson, E.H. 1968. Identity: Youth and Crisis. New York: Norton.

Hollos, M. and Leis, P.E. 1989. Becoming Nigerian in Ijo Society. New Brunswick, NJ: Rutgers University Press.

Lancy, D.F. 1996. Playing on the Mother-Ground: Cultural Routines for Children's Development. New York: Guilford Press.

Marcia, J.E. 1980. Identity in adolescence, in *Handbook of Adolescent Psychology*, edited by J. Adelson. New York: Wiley, pp. 159–187.

———. "Development and Validation of Ego Identity Status," Journal of Personality and Social Psychology 3 (1966): 551–558.

Schlegel, A. and Barry, H. 1991. Adolescence: An Anthropological Inquiry. New York: Free Press.

Walters, J.R. 1987. Transition to Adulthood, in *Primate Societies*, edited by B.B. Smuts, D.L. Cheney, R.M. Seyfarth, R.W. Wrangham, & T.T. Struhsaker. Chicago: University of Chicago Press, pp. 358–369.

Contributors

Ramadan A. Ahmed, Ph.D, is a Professor of Psychology in the College of Social Sciences, Kuwait University, Kuwait. He received MA degree in Psychology from Alexandria University, Egypt, and Ph.D. in cognitive psychology from Leipzig University, Germany in 1981. His research interests cover topics such as the development of moral reasoning, cognitive development (Piaget), attitudes toward family members, risk perception, orientation toward forgiveness, identity statuses, children's and adolescents' perception of parental acceptance-rejection, children's drawings, women issues, and history of psychology, especially in the Arab countries. With U. P. Gielen, he edited the first English volume on "*Psychology in the Arab Countries, 1998*". His publications include more than 60 scientific papers, 40 book chapters, and 3 books. Dr. Ahmed presented his research in several local, regional and international conferences and meetings. He is a member of several local, regional and international scientific associations, among them: APA, ICP, SCCR, and ISIPAR. Dr. Ahmed received the Egypt's State Incentive Award for Social Sciences (Psychology) in 1994, and the Outstanding International Psychologists' Award, APA (for researchers outside the USA) for 2008. Dr. Ahmed is the ISIPAR Regional Representative for the Middle East and North Africa since 2006. In January 2011, Dr. Ahmed became a member of the Editorial Board of the newly published APA journal "*International Perspectives in Psychology: Research, Practice, and Consultation.*"

Barry Bogin is Professor of Biological Anthropology, Centre for Global Health & Human Development, School of Sport, Exercise & Health Sciences, Loughborough University, UK. Prior to joining the Loughborough faculty, Bogin was the William E. Stirton Professor and Professor of Anthropology at the Department of Behavioral Sciences, University of Michigan-Dearborn. His research area is human physical growth and development. Since the 1970s Bogin has been working with Maya families living in Guatemala, Mexico, and the United States. Maya children in the United States are much taller than Maya in Mexico and Guatemala, with most of the increase due to longer legs. This is a sign of improved health. But, the children are also heavier—about 50% are overweight and/or obese. Maya-American children may be at risk for weight problems now, and health problems later in life, due to inter-generational metabolic impairments interacting with United States diets, patterns of physical activity, and work. Another area of Bogin's research is the evolution of the pattern of human growth. Human beings evolved two new stages of development—childhood and adolescence—stages not found in other mammals, even in our closest primate cous-ins. The unusual physical, behavioral, and emotional characteristics of children and adolescents help us to grow into healthy and productive adult, but only if the special needs of children and adolescents are met. Bogin received the University of Michigan-Dearborn Distinguished Fac-ulty Research Award in 1993, and the Distinguished Teaching Award in 1998. In 1999, he received the Michigan Association of Governing Boards Distinguished Faculty Award. In 2004 Bogin was awarded the William E. Stirton Professorship, the highest academic honor of the Uni-versity of Michigan-Dearborn.

Michael J. Chandler is Professor Emeritus, working at UBC's Department of Psychology. His ongoing program of research features an exploration of the role culture plays in constructing the course of identity development, shaping young people's emerging sense of ownership of their personal and cultural past, and their commitment to their own and their communi-ty's future well being. These efforts, along with more than 150 published books, articles and book chapters, have earned Dr. Chandler the Izaak Walton Killam Memorial Senior Research Prize, led to his being awarded the Killam Teaching Prize, and resulted in his twice being named a Peter Wall Institute for Advanced Studies Distinguished Scholar in Residence. His research and scholarly efforts have also resulted in his being appointed as Canada's only Distinguished Investigator of both the Canadian Insti-tutes of Health Research (CIHR) and the Michael Smith Foundation for Health Research (MSFHR). Dr. Chandler's research with children at risk began more than 35 years ago with an article (co-authored with A. Sameroff) that was selected by the Society for Research in Child Develop-ment for inclusion in a book entitled Twenty Studies That Revolutionized Child Psychology. Professor Chandler's program of research dealing with identity development and suicide in Aboriginal youth was singled out for publication as a book and as an invited Monograph of the Society for Research in Child Development (recently translated into French), and is the only program of Canadian research featured in WHO's just released report on the social determinants of health.

William L. Dunlop is a Ph.D. student in developmental psychology at the University of British Columbia. His research interests include the development and nature of identity, social cognition, character, and personality coherence. He examines these topics using variable and person approaches.

Bruce J. Ellis, Ph.D., is Professor of Family Studies and Human Development and the John & Doris Norton Endowed Chair in Fathers, Parenting, and Families at the University of Arizona. Dr. Ellis was originally trained as a canonical evolutionary psychologist in David Buss' laboratory at the University of Michigan, where he studied adult sexual and romantic relationships. Developmental processes were largely taken for granted in this context. Dr. Ellis became dissatisfied with this approach, undertook three years of postdoctoral training in developmental psychopathology at Vanderbilt University, and shifted from studying adult behavior to developmental processes and mechanisms. His theoretical writings and empirical work seek to integrate evolutionary and developmental perspectives on the role of family environments in development of child stress reactivity, puberty, and adolescent sexual behavior. His work has been recognized by major awards from the American Psychological Association, the Human Behavior and Evolution Society, and the John F. Kennedy Center for Research on Human Development. Dr. Ellis leads the Frances McClelland Institute initiative on Fathers, Parenting, and Families at the University of Arizona.

Judith L. Gibbons, Professor of Psychology and International Studies at Saint Louis University, studies the developmental psychology of adolescents in cross-cultural and cross-national perspective, gender and the development of girls, and intercountry adoption. She is a past-president of the Society of Cross-Cultural Research, a Fulbright scholar at the Universidad del Valle Guatemala, the editor of an American Psychological Association journal, *International Perspectives in Psychology: Research, Consultation, Practice,* and the president-elect of the Interamerican Society of Psychology (better known by its acronym in Spanish, SIP). With Deborah Stiles she authored *The Thoughts of Youth: An International Perspective on Adolescents' Ideal Persons* (Information Age Publishing, 2004) and with Karen Smith Rotabi she is the editor of *Intercountry Adoption: Policies, Practices, Outcomes* (Ashgate, 2012).

Jenna R. Hansen earned a B.A. with honors and distinction in Anthropology from Washington State University in 2008. She conducted summer fieldwork in Dominica in 2007 and 2008, collecting interview and direct observational data for her honors thesis and this chapter. She is currently pursuing a career in Nursing.

Barry S. Hewlett is a professor of anthropology at Washington State University, Vancouver. He is the author *Intimate Fathers: The Nature and Context of Aka Paternal Infant Care* and editor (with Michael Lamb) of *Hunter-Gatherer Childhoods, Father-Child Relations: Cultural and Biosocial Contexts,* and several journal articles and book chapters. He has conducted research with central African foragers and farmers for over 40 years and is interested in hunter-gatherers, parent-child relations, social learning, evolutionary approaches to culture, and biocultural approaches to the control of infectious and parasitic diseases.

Bonnie L. Hewlett is a registered nurse and adjunct professor at Washington State University, Vancouver and has published extensively on adolescent development and the cultural contexts of infectious diseases. Recent publications include: Listen, Here is a Story: Ethnographic Life Narratives from Aka and Ngandu Women of the Congo Basin (Oxford University Press); "Contributions of Anthropology to the Study of Adolescence" in Journal of Research on Adolescence, co-authored with Alice Schlegel; "Vulnerable lives: Death, loss and grief among Aka and Ngandu adolescents of the Central African Republic" in *Culture and Ecology of Hunter-Gatherer Children; Ebola, Culture, Politics: The Anthropology of an Emerging Diseases,* co-authored with Barry Hewlett (Wadsworth Publishing Company). Current research projects include social learning and innovation among central African forest forager adolescents; and, adoption, health, and attachment behaviors of Ethiopian orphans. She was a Fulbright scholar in Ethiopia in 2010–2011 and has conducted research in sub-Saharan Africa for over 10 years.

William Jankowiak is a professor of anthropology at the University of Nevada, Las Vegas. He is a relentless field ethnographer who over the last 20 odd years has been "in the field" investigating some facet of the human experience that range from ritual, hierarchical, family life to the sexual and the romantic. . He has conducted field research in New Orleans on African-American street parades, Mardi Gras festival, and 20 years research in Inner Mongolia Autonomous Region, China. Locally he has conducted over 16 years research in Colorado City, a Mormon Polygamous community as well as one year study on how Las Vegas swingers use ritualized sex to sustain their marriage. To date, he is author of eight books, monographs, and edited collections as well as 102 articles, book chapters, and scholarly references. In 2007, he hosted an eight part series on the "Rites of Passion" for the History Channel. When not in the field he writes on romantic love, the phenomenon it is and the phenomenon social scientists would like it to be.

J. Christopher Kovats-Bernat is an Associate Professor of Anthropology at Muhlenberg College and the author of *Sleeping Rough in Port-au-Prince: An Ethnography of Street Children and Violence in Haiti* (University Press of Florida, 2006). Since 1994 he has studied the everyday lives of street children, political violence, and Vodou in Haiti. In 1995, he served as an International Civilian Observer of the presidential elections in Haiti, and in 2004 arrived in Port-au-Prince during a rebel uprising that toppled the president, in order to study the transformation of social life that resulted from that conflict. Kovats-Bernat also studies the impact of small arms proliferation on Haitian civil society, and serves on the Executive Committee of the international Society of Small Arms Scholars. Recently, Kovats-Bernat arrived in Haiti in the wake of the 2010 earthquake to work with a relief team providing food, water, and medical aid throughout the country. In 2012, he traveled to Haiti to research the role of Vodou in safeguarding community security against armed gangs in the Cité Soleil neighborhood of Port-au-Prince. That work is in support of his second book, in progress, entitled *Dangerous Crossroads: Vodou and the Crisis of Childhood in Haiti*, a study of the role of Vodou beliefs in the rearing of children in the Haitian countryside.

Carol A. Markstrom received her Ph.D. in developmental psychology in 1988 from Utah State University. Currently, she is Professor in the Dept. of Technology, Learning, and Culture at West Virginia University and a core member of the Native American Studies Program at that institution. Her research has focused on pubertal rites of passage among American Indians, identity formation within social and cultural contexts, and ego strength and adolescent participation in adult-sponsored structured activities. She is Past President of the Society for Research on Identity Formation, and a member of the American Anthropological Association and the Society for Research on Adolescence.

Toon van Meijl studied cultural and social anthropology as well as philosophy at the University of Nijmegen and at the Australian National University in Canberra, where he completed his PhD in 1991. Since 1982 he has conducted thirty months of ethnographic fieldwork among the Tainui Maori in New Zealand. Currently he is professor of cultural anthropology and head of the Department of Anthropology and Development Studies at Radboud University Nijmegen in the Netherlands. He is also academic secretary of the interdisciplinary Centre for Pacific and Asian Studies at Nijmegen. He is mainly interested in sociopolitical questions emerging from the debate about property rights of indigenous peoples and in issues of cultural identification and the self, in particular of young people growing up in multicultural societies. Major publications include the co-edited volumes *Property Rights and Economic Development; Land and Natural Resources in Southeast Asia and Oceania* (Kegan Paul International, 1999) and *Shifting Images of Identity in the Pacific* (KITLV, 2004). He also contributed a chapter on the anthropology of identity to *The Sage Handbook of Identities* (2010), edited by Margaret Wetherell and Chandra Talpade Mohanty.

Robert L. Moore is a professor of anthropology and the Coordinator of Asian Studies at Rollins College in Winter Park, Florida. In 1993–94 he served as a foreign expert on the faculty of Qingdao University in the People's Republic of China. On the basis of his ethnographic research in China and colonial Hong Kong, he has published a series of articles on China's youth culture, covering such topics as parent-adolescent relations, dating and courtship, Internet slang, the growth of individualism, and the continuing influence of Confucianism.

Marsha B. Quinlan is an ecological and medical anthropologist in the Department of Anthropology at Washington State University. Her research focuses on ethnomedicine, family health behavior, and ethnobotany. She has worked in North and South America and in Dominica, at the site of the present chapter, since 1993.

Alice Schlegel is Professor Emerita of Anthropology at the University of Arizona and currently a Distinguised Research Professor in the Frances McClelland Institute for Children, Youth and Families there. Her major work on adolescence is Schlegel and Barry, 1991, *Adolescence: An Anthropological Inquiry* (New York: Free Press). She has written a number of articles on adolescence, both ethnographic and cross-cultural. She has conducted research on adolescent industrial apprentices in Germany and Wisconsin and adolescent participation in the contrade of Siena, Italy. Her current interest is in adolescence from an evolutionary perspective, and she continues to be interested in the constants and variants in adolescent socialization across cultures.

Kiyoshi Takeuchi is Associate Professor of Cultural Anthropology at Faculty of Humanities, University of Toyama, Japan. He has carried out ecological-anthropological fieldwork among the Aka forest hunter-gatherers in Republic of the Congo since 1988. His main research interests are in inter-ethnic relations between the Aka and neighboring horticulturalists and the current social transformations of the Aka societies.

Index